LIFE IN THE MIDDLE AGES

from the Seventh to the Thirteenth Century

HANS-WERNER GOETZ

Translated by Albert Wimmer
Edited by Steven Rowan

UNIVERSITY OF NOTRE DAME PRESS

Notre Dame   London

Leben im Mittelalter
Hans-Werner Goetz
© C.H. Beck'sche Verlagsbuchhandlung
(Oscar Beck), München 1986

American edition:
Copyright © 1993 by
University of Notre Dame Press
Notre Dame, Indiana 46556
All Rights Reserved

Manufactured in the United States of America

Library of Congress Cataloging-in-Publication Data

Goetz, Hans-Werner.
    [Leben im Mittelalter.   English]
    Life in the Middle Ages : from the seventh to the
thirteenth century / Hans-Werner Goetz.
        p.   cm.
    Includes bibliographical references and index.
    ISBN 0-268-01300-4
    1. Civilization, Medieval.   2. Europe—Social life
and customs.
    I. Title.
    CB361.G6413   1993
    940.1–dc20   92-56868
                                                            CIP

∞ *The paper used in this publication meets the minimum requirements*
of the American National Standard for Information Sciences—Permanence of Paper
for Printed Library Materials, ANSI Z39.48-1984.

CONTENTS

PREFACE

The history of everyday life, an approach to the past recently discovered, or perhaps rediscovered, has attracted such great expectations because it makes important insignificant details of daily life common to the experience of every human being, touching him or her directly, beneath the surface of great "historical" events. It leads us in this way to an increased identification with the past, perhaps even to an active historical consciousness. Everyday life undoubtedly unveils an important aspect of our past. Though still a young discipline, the history of everyday life has already spawned heated discussions and controversies, which remain far from settled despite some rapproachement. The source of this conflict does not so much lie in the subject matter of the discipline itself, since its relevance is widely recognized. Rather, the discipline's own insufficiently analyzed concepts, its new methods still incomplete and too uncritically handled, inherently generate controversy. Some authors also occasionally evince hostility toward all theoretical considerations whatsoever, overestimating the claims which can be made for the history of everyday life. A modern history of everyday life which aims to satisfy scholarly standards must subordinate both its questions and their resolution to the methods and discoveries of current historical science. Only such mutual enrichment will yield a meaningful expansion of our historical vision. These arguments and unresolved issues require us to undertake a more detailed discussion of our subject.

Despite a steadily increasing number of publications on the history of everyday life, it is no accident that there as yet is no adequate, comprehensive portrayal of everyday life in the earlier Middle Ages, that is, from the seventh through the beginning of the thirteenth century—the period covered in this book. This reflects the lack of preliminary research, but especially the nature of the sources. Writing a history of everyday life during the early Middle Ages is not yet possible, and researching it exceeds one person's capabilities. Yet the current state of research and source materials should not lead us to exclude an age that is important and interesting in so many respects. It is important to attempt a beginning, to open paths, to pose problems, thus to render accessible an approach, a first glance, into the various forms and possibilities of everyday life during the early Middle Ages. That (and nothing else) is the purpose of this book, a work that must certainly be understood as a first attempt, albeit as yet an imperfect one. Readers will properly appreciate its results only if they take into consideration the peculiar preconditions of the subject as well as the author's limited goals; these must be mentioned in order to preclude excessive expectations and assumptions.

1. In view of these preliminary remarks, the goal of this book cannot be the most graphic possible description of everyday life; rather, the work will seek to elucidate different spheres of society set out in greater detail in the introduction, each viewed in terms of its specific conditions and background and distinguished in terms of: (a) institutions, (b) the inhabited space, and (c) the men and women who lived within them, with their mutual interrelationships. Thus, this study will attempt to respond to the principal question of comprehending everyday life in terms of its institutional, physical, and social environment and influences; in short, how was everyday life lived under these conditions? This limited agenda views everyday life in very specific terms, incorporating the latest research in the field. Several thorough studies of the spiritual, social, and political climate of medieval life have recently appeared which can be turned to good account. This investigation will also focus on a variety of themes which must be part of any history of everyday life, since everyday life did not evolve in isolation from the political and social order, but rather was embedded in it. Indeed, political, economic, religious, and cultural decisions and conditions constantly bore on the individual. Conversely, society could build only on structures the physical and spiritual life of the masses would permit. Against this background, facts and findings will be assembled reflecting the current state of research.

2. The chronological limitations are justified primarily by the fact that the later Middle Ages, far better documented, have already been covered by several surveys (Introduction, note 21). Moreover, a deep change in structures divided the two epochs which undoubtedly also influenced everyday life. Therefore, late medieval everyday life cannot be projected back into early medieval conditions; they must be investigated separately.

3. Certainly, considering the breadth of the subject, life itself can be viewed only in terms of examples. Insofar as possible, these examples have been chosen in such a way as to testify to typical aspects in keeping with what we presently know about the Middle Ages. Yet, we continue

to depend on examples preserved and known more or less as a result of accidental preservation. Many an issue must be relegated to the scrutiny of future specialized research. In our desire to describe typical forms of life and offer a broad overview, we will have to generalize, neglecting various chronological, social and—above all—regional differences.

4. The idea for this book originally arose from an introductory course for history students. It underwent substantial revisions prior to publication, but its goal, which was to serve as an introduction to the subject at hand, remained constant. The work is intended for a broad audience of readers and for students interested in both history and the Middle Ages, to initiate them in the themes and issues of medieval history. Medieval scholars will find very few new insights; still, the presentation and arrangement, together with the way specific issues have been stated in terms of their effect on everyday life, dare to present new insights.

The bibliographical entries at the end of the book include only the most important and relevant publications used. They consist, above all, of more recent basic works and surveys. Their arrangement follows the outline of the book. It goes without saying that much important literature remains unmentioned because of the bibliography's selective nature. Additionally, research consulted on specific themes is documented in the notes. It is here that one can also find specific references which, for reasons of simplicity, will cite bilingual editions whenever possible. In principle, all quotations will be translations from German. On the other hand, more general statements excerpted from works pertaining to individual subjects, or themes mentioned in the respective sections of the bibliography or references, will remain undocumented in order to keep down the number of citations.

The following is to be viewed as a preliminary sketch, not a final answer. Much remains to be done. If this book stimulates detailed studies of everyday life, one of the author's objectives will have been met.

Everyday Life and Physical Environment—Justifying a History of Medieval Everyday Life

To some, the term "history of everyday life" is a challenge; to others, it represents the discovery of a new, vivid past which draws their interest. The history of everyday life is such a fashionable concept that no one has specifically to justify its existence anymore. It is "modern" not in the sense of something fashionable, but rather in the sense of something timely. It accommodates today's demands for a history not limited to politics, and it incorporates daily human life with all its behavioral variations and expressions, particularly the life of "simple" people, who may not influence world history but are nevertheless an integral part of it. A history of everyday life responds to the growing historical consciousness shared by broad segments of the population, since it considers not only a few politically active individuals to be historically significant and singularly worthy of historical research, but all human beings. The history of everyday life mediates between "large-scale political history" and a structured "material history" with a socio-economic focus, observing individuals who have their being between these two poles. Initially, this emphasis on the human aspects of history was certainly also a reaction to recent structural historiography, which used descriptive rather than narrative methods. Structural history tended to summarize events as if they had been long-lasting processes, even while paying special attention to supra-individual forces and searching for explanations with the aid of theories.[1] A tendency to ideology also renders the history of everyday life quite controversial, so that we will need to clarify the subject at hand, its objectives, its value, and its limitations.

1

Introduction

At one time, during the "joy of discovery" of its first phase, the history of everyday life dealt chiefly with the most recent past, tapping a new type of historical source by questioning living witnesses (oral history); it did without a theoretical foundation, contenting itself with the presentation of concrete examples.[2] Second thoughts were raised by philosophers,[3] sociologists,[4] and only later, historians.[5] This examination proved necessary because the concept and function of everyday life had been conceived and evaluated in various ways, producing even a "socialist" and "Green" historiography in historical workshops which rejected history as it was being pursued on the university level.[6] The first problems arise from the very concept of everyday life, since it is typically ignored by most encyclopedias. The term "everyday life" has commonly been employed as a "counterterm"[7] dealing with the work-day in contrast to holiday, with that which keeps recurring time and again (Elias refers to it as "routine") in contrast to that which occurs only once, with private life in contrast to "public" history, and with a history of the little person in contrast to histories of great personalities and events, to name only a few of the most important parameters.[8] In summary, the history of everyday life is often characterized (not unproblematically) as "history from below"; one could also refer to it as a "history from within," insofar as the perspective of those involved is reflected in terms of their own private experience.

Certainly, such definitions derive from the fact that today the history of everyday life has been pursued mostly as a history of work-ers. That meets a legitimate need to make up for past neglect, yet it must not lead to inappropriately restricting the concept of everyday life itself. Indeed, the definitions cover segments from an everyday life not representing the lower levels of society alone; every human being experiences his or her everyday life, not just a work-a-day life, but also free time, holidays, and vacations. This everyday life encompasses not just recurring activities, but also the highlights of individual life; not just private life, but also the private person in the public arena. Historians only agree that the history of everyday life amounts to more than "material culture." Even though material culture constitutes one aspect and is an important source of everyday life,[9] it must be evaluated primarily in socio-historical terms. Everyday life is human life as embed-ded in its own material culture. However, this life unfolds in a context which has already left its mark. That is why the history of everyday life asks how living conditions were perceived and experienced by those affected by them, and how those conditions were molded in keeping with their needs. The history of everyday life represents an "analysis of a subject-oriented environment,"[10] including those vital conditions which influence people in an unconscious way. If, in summing up, one were to look for a positive definition not derived from paradoxes, then one may perhaps paraphrase "everyday life" as human life itself in its daily passage within the framework of the corresponding conditions of life. Thus, the history of everyday life could be the investigation and description of this life as exemplified by the men and women of times past (up to the present).

In a history of everyday life understood in this fashion, the fate of individual human beings serve only as examples rather than a goal in their own right. The object to be known is the "average human being" (the sum total of all individual fates), "human kind," as Heidegger calls it, or "everyman."[11] To be sure, such an average human being does not exist in real life, but merely as a type, a generalized historical construct understood from the point of view of structural history, which remains close to reality only if the individual is not ignored in the process.[12] In this respect, the history of everyday life is also a form of structural history applied to the life of people and the marginal conditions of their existence, a typifying portrayal placed in the context of historically active forces.[13] First of all, this means selected examples must be as representative of their time as possible; this requires quantitative integration, a prerequisite often impossible to meet in view of the state of sources from the earlier Middle Ages. Secondly, differences must not be leveled out too much; rather, everyday life must be differentiated (depending on the society involved) according to social status and birth, age and sex, education and occupation, nationality, religious and regional affiliation, and mobility. Closely dependent on the study of attitudes, the history of mentality and anthropology, the history of everyday life must rely on the results and methods of social history.[14] Thirdly, evidence from the sources must be carefully examined for what they reveal about everyday life. Such examination applies also to those sources which seem of no value to political historians, for whose benefit the modern methods of source criticism were originally developed. Evidence from sources such as financial ledgers and inventories is now gaining in importance, but it is above all examples from art and literature which are quoted, sources whose fictional nature does not quite reflect reality, since they definitely bespeak a tendency to emphasize representation or ethics.[15] Indeed, medieval literature has been portrayed as a fictional counter-design to reality;[16] its real contents are not found in the text itself, but in the intentions hidden beneath its surface in the form of mentality, ideology, awareness, and emotional lives of its representatives.[17] Therefore, using the analogy of legal sources reporting a legal norm, the reality-content manifested in medieval literature must be examined before a source is used.[18]

A concept of the history of everyday life understood in this way cannot be separated from the issues and methods of traditional historical research, to which it remains tied. In full consciousness of the methods involved, the history of everyday life must pursue its objectives. Basically, the controversy concerning the history of everyday life is more an argument over methodology than over subject matter. It must proceed by critically evaluating evidence and questioning information often handed down from completely different contexts. It also must employ the pioneering methods and insights of modern historical research. Last but not least, it must include those insights gleaned from theory.[19] The history of everyday life possesses no method of its own, but it is indebted to *the* historical method (a fact often overlooked). It must not surrender to subjective partisanship at the outset.[20] Only on this basis is everyday life an important supplement, offering a special perspective (Niethammer), thus distinguishing itself from the cultural history of the nineteenth century.

As with other forms of historiography, the history of everyday life does not have to restrict itself to ages close to the present. Even if such a remote past as the earlier Middle Ages no longer forms part of our own experience, medieval everyday life is as meaningful a notion as is the Middle Ages within the framework of history as a whole. Therefore, it is as important to the historical picture as the everyday life of other eras. Because the period is difficult for us to understand, it will be necessary to elaborate the historical context in more detail than would be the case with more recent eras. During the past several years, a series of collective volumes and summaries about everyday life in the late Middle Ages has appeared,[21] while corresponding efforts concerning the early and high Middle Ages in the German-speaking area still await publication.[22] In France, in contrast, several volumes of the extensive series *La vie quotidienne* deal with this epoch.[23] It is hardly accidental that such studies are more structural histories (including living conditions and mental attitudes) than histories of everyday life due to the state of their sources. It is nearly impossible to write a history of everyday life during the earlier Middle Ages which is sufficiently concrete and securely documented to satisfy our queries, since the people of that age had entirely different aims, never describing everyday life for its own sake. On the contrary, they expressed no interest whatsoever in everyday affairs. As a result, the sources contain at best sporadic and incidental information, not yet systematically collected, critically screened, or evaluated. This leaves much to be done, and the results are bound to remain fragmentary. As mentioned in the preface, the aim of this book will be more modest. It will highlight the concept of everyday life just described, emphasizing the variety of conditions and possibilities of everyday life during this epoch, uncovering the causes of typical aspects of life within specific settings.

As has already been said, there is no such thing as *the* everyday life; rather, as Arno Borst has emphasized, there is only a series of various forms of life, which he defines as modes of conduct practiced by historical societies.[24] Like one's own mentality, everyday life is determined by several factors, two of which predominate: belonging to certain groups and levels within medieval society, and the space these groups inhabit.

The concept "form of life" designates above all a specific caste, estate, class, or social level. The Middle Ages in Western Europe knew no such religiously determined castes or economically based classes. The consciousness of the nobility was not based on the ownership of the means of production; only rather late and in isolated cases did peasant consciousness come to be based on the value of peasant labor. Yet medieval society did distinguish among legally defined estates (clerics—laity; freemen—serfs; knights—peasants). These distinctions came about rather slowly, and levels of society depending on social status are very difficult to trace during the Middle Ages because of a lack of unequivocal criteria.[25] Therefore, although a specific differentiation may remain uncertain, influence on the mode of living and way of thinking that flowed from affiliation with some group is obvious. It has long been known that the earlier Middle Ages, which Gerd Tellenbach described as a "portraitless age," had no sense for the individual.[26] Neither historiography nor art showed any interest in the individual human, rather, individuals were of interest either for a function they performed or as members serving a specific group. It was only as embedded in a community that they were enabled to live (Schmid). There is evidence, in most cases, of many such affiliations into which one was born. As individuals, medieval men and women were members of a family, a tribe, and a kingdom; as Christians they were members of the one Church which manifested itself in the parish; and as legal subjects they either represented their estate as members of the nobility, or were subjects of a manorial lord (if serfs). In addition to affiliations of birth, there were also voluntary affiliations. (These, to be sure, were not entirely individual in nature; rather, they were frequently determined by parents and relatives, or by a commonly practiced norm.) For instance, one could enter a monastery as a monk or belong to a fraternity (a community bound together by an oath) with various forms of affiliation and objectives. Guilds, which only start to emerge in the eleventh century, and even then primarily as mercantile associations, provide a notable example; yet even they were only one of a number of similar "sworn associations" (*coniurationes*) and dinner-clubs (*convivia*), both characteristic forms of early medieval group affiliations closely linked to village and parish.[27] In contrast, late medieval guilds would be compulsory associations.

Such affiliations were also conditioned by the space in which everyday life evolved; everyone was a resident of one's own village or town, for example. If, as Borst demonstrates, there was a variety of forms of life in the Middle Ages, then this was particularly true because individual life unfolded in various distinct places. The horizon of medieval men and women was limited, since hardly anyone except imperial nobles and bishops ever left his or her familiar surroundings, but also since everyone had limited means of communication. While it is obvious that rural life differed from life in the city, and life in a castle or a palace differed from monastic life, distinct forms of living can still be detected within given social groups in a given space; the everyday life of the nobility, for example, differed from that of their servants, though both remained functionally related to one another. If social history tends to stress the differences among these groups, then we will have to focus our attention on affiliations between human beings by incorporating all facets of the relationships involved when we are trying to concentrate on physical space. Thus, everyday life evolved against the background of a sphere of life depending on space and groups,[28] on the environment and the conditions which characterized life, but which was also shaped by people in accordance with their needs. We must pay particular attention to such reciprocal relationships; for this reason, five such exemplary spheres of medieval life shall be presented.

After a brief introduction to the general conditions of medieval life in the first chapter, the second chapter will examine the family as the smallest social unit, its physical space centered in the house. The family is fundamentally important because it was also viewed as an ideal building block for other forms of society. The Middle Ages considered the monastic community together with the community of serfs at a manor house a *familia*. Even a system of political alliances was occasionally interpreted in terms of the "family of the king" in the traditions of late antiquity and the Byzantine Empire. Only general characteristics will need to be discussed here, while the features which typify a given social level and physical space will be dealt with in subsequent chapters.

The third chapter will cover the form of clerical-ecclesiastical life which is monasticism and its physical space, the monastery. The monastery played a prominent role within medieval society, especially during the early and the high Middle Ages, affecting not only religious, but also social, political, economic, and spiritual life. The traditional religious orders lost their importance and influence during the later Middle Ages, making way for new mendicant orders which are to be attributed primarily to the urban sphere.

The fourth chapter will deal with peasant life in the country. Here we shall focus on an example which most strongly typifies the Middle Ages, that is to say, the social and existential forms of the medieval manorial system. The manorial system, including social ties between the lord of the manor and his community of serfs, became a living space transcending any single social level or class during the earlier Middle Ages, while in the later Middle Ages it increasingly assumed a purely economic form.

The fifth chapter will deal with the apparent antipode to the peasantry, the life of the ruling class, particularly in the form of the "courtly life" of the high Middle Ages. In principle, the lords were identical with lords of the manor, yet we will primarily concentrate on the socio-political level of princes and kings, and life at princely courts.

Finally, in the concluding chapter, I will attempt to evoke the life of the burgeoning urban strata in the early medieval and high medieval town, which did not become crucial until the late Middle Ages. It nevertheless represented an alien element in a medieval world determined by agricultural standards during this early era. Later, its importance would grow to the point where the structure of the later Middle Ages would be unthinkable without it.

By highlighting these five vital spheres, I shall have reviewed a major portion of life in the early and high Middle Ages. Five specific physical spaces will be discussed, offering us a good survey of the conditions at this time. Since this proposed division could easily give the impression that these living spaces were strictly separated, I ought to emphasize at the outset that interrelationships between specific forms of community did indeed exist.[29]

Except for the first two chapters, which dictate different structural arrangements, the discussion in the large chapters on individual physical realms will deal initially with the conditions of everyday life in this order:

1. the institution in question
2. the pertinent inhabited space
3. representatives of the sphere of life, that is, the people who lived within this environment
4. the background and course of everyday life.

I

People, Nature, Culture: The Conditions of Everyday Life during the Middle Ages

Population, Areas of Settlement, and Horizon. Independent of any given form of living, there existed typically medieval conditions shared by all. These arose from interaction between the existing natural environment and human encroachment on nature, including the regulation of community life. The available inhabitable space depended on the topography of the land and the number of people living on it. However, there are no reliable population figures for the Middle Ages. During the late Middle Ages, tax rolls and census lists from various individual towns or from France as a whole (*Etats des feux* of 1328) provide us with at least some hints. However, during the early and high Middle Ages we have to rely on projections based on a few lists— kept for entirely different reasons—which merely capture segments from a limited area at a certain point in time. Louis the Pious appears to have ordered census surveys of freemen obligated to serve in his armies,[1] but we know of no results; in fact, we do not even know if the commands were ever carried out. (Considering the conditions of a largely non-literate society, it would be difficult to imagine such an undertaking.) Surveys (*Urbare*, manorial registers indicating ownership and levies) are suitable for demographic calculations only—as in the case of the famous polyptych of the monastery at Saint-Germain-des-Prés near Paris of about 820—if they listed the number of peasants and family members residing on the *mansi*. However, neither male serfs nor peasants not belonging to that manor are listed, which makes the usefulness of such demographic data questionable.[2] Uniquely reliable information to the extent that it has been preserved is provided by the

9

so-called Domesday Book for England around 1086, which records all landowners as well as the value and extent of their holdings. Archaeologists and anthropologists have also contributed through analyzing skeletal remains buried in medieval cemeteries. Their studies indicate the number of men, women, and children, their ages and possible diseases. However, entire cemeteries have only very rarely been dug up. All these figures, in themselves equivocal, can be projected only by considering the (equally estimated) density of settlements. Admittedly, there is no history of the demography for the Middle Ages; there are only isolated estimates which, depending on what they are based on, may vary substantially from one another but reveal common tendencies which merit brief explanation.[3]

Compared to today, Europe during the earlier Middle Ages was sparsely populated, although there were regional differences. The highest concentrations of population within the Christian West could be found in the urban areas of Lombardy and also the Low Countries, together with France and Italy. People preferred to settle along coastal areas, on river shores, and in fertile plains. In Germany, this meant above all the lower Rhineland, lower Saxony, the Rhein-Main Lowlands, and the upper Rhenish plains, but also the valleys in the central Rhine region, along the Moselle, the Lahn, the Neckar, the Tauber, and the Main rivers, and in the lower Weser mountains and Swabian Jura. The sandy heathland and the marshes and moors in the north, along with the mountainous regions in the south, harbored hardly any population to speak of in the early period; the higher lying areas of the Mittelgebirge remained almost entirely unpopulated. Nevertheless, one can recognize development over time: abandoned villages, receding agriculture, and plague epidemics permit us to conclude that the population decreased in the course of the migrations (fourth to sixth century), continuing a decrease of perhaps a third begun in late antiquity. By the ninth century the population recovered, a fact reflected by the ever-increasing size of the churches; indeed, it may have doubled by the year 1000. During the following two centuries, the rate of growth was especially high, possibly doubling the population again by the first half of the fourteenth century. After this, however, and in large measure because of the severe plague epidemics after 1347, a rapid decline occurred, reducing the number of inhabitants by more than fifty percent in certain regions.

The fluctuations in population affected the areas of settlement. Rural areas were frequently devoid of any settlements; since huge, often impassible forests formed natural barriers, villages amounted to more or less isolated settlements.[4] A 1073 report by Lampert of Hersfeld is frequently cited, telling how Henry IV was besieged by the Saxons at

Harzburg castle, itself surrounded on three sides by a vast forest. After their escape, the royal forces traveled for three days on a neglected path through the thicket without food.[5] Two-fifths of even such a densely populated a region as the Ile-de-France consisted of forest in the ninth century. Thus, from the very beginning, areas of settlement were hemmed in by the natural lay of the land. It is interesting to note that miniature initials from this period tend to illustrate people and animals battling plants. Certainly we are able to detect a trend here: as the population increased, it became crucial to create new areas of settlement, particularly at a time when the age of conquests came to an end in the Frankish kingdom toward the end of the eighth century, as it had a century earlier in France. As a result, it became necessary to cultivate moors, dike the coastal lands along the North Sea, develop the higher lying areas of the mountainous regions, and above all clear the woodland. All of these undertakings reached highest intensity during the twelfth and thirteenth centuries. Villages which already existed were enlarged, and new settlements were founded, arranged as appendages around the older places. Countless village names ending in *-hagen, -holz, -wald, -rode, -rath, -ried*, or *-reuth* testify to such origins even today.[6] Clearings frequently were the work of monks, particularly Cistercians, who preferred to retreat to more solitary locations, but clearance was most often done by peasants. Yet the increase in population was not the sole reason for the clearings. Walter Janssen has asserted that abandonment of settlements was not characteristic of the fourteenth and fifteenth centuries alone; rather, they spanned the entire Middle Ages, roughly contemporary with new settlements, with greater concentrations during Carolingian times and during the twelfth and thirteenth centuries. Since many villages merely existed for a limited period of time, one must assume that early medieval settlements might be abandoned for other reasons as yet undiscovered, such as deteriorating soil conditions.[7]

There is no doubt population increase gave rise to the colonization of the east during the twelfth and thirteenth centuries, which not only absorbed part of the surplus population, but also led to the gradual Germanization of Slavic regions beyond the Elbe and Saale rivers as far south as Transylvania. These were for the most part organized ventures in which a *locator* took care of surveying and distributing the land on behalf of a manorial lord. The locator subsequently often stayed on, representing the authorities as chief administrator (*Dorfschulze*) of the village.[8] As a rule, villages in many areas in the high Middle Ages grew closer together, often being only a few kilometers apart, which greatly facilitated social contact. By 1300 the network of settlements had grown denser than had ever been before or ever would be again, since forest began to advance again at the expense of previously cultivated land with the decline of the population during the late Middle Ages.

Whatever the density of settlement, the geographical horizon or living space of people remained rather limited. Apart from the higher nobility and clergy ruling over widely scattered holdings, who frequently gathered at the court of the itinerant king, and the long-distance merchants, traveling remained a rare experience for normal people. It was made even harder by poor road conditions.[9] Richer of Reims, a monk, writes about a trip to Chartres, where he intended to consult some rare manuscripts.[10] The course of the road was so poorly marked that he lost his way on several occasions; his pack-horse was unable to withstand the hardships and soon collapsed. In the dark, the monk hardly dared set foot on the bridge across the Marne leading to Meaux, because of the many holes. On top of all this, he was in constant fear of robbers. (See Illustration 1.) Only after a journey of three days did Richer finally arrive at Chartres. Because of his feeble body, the aging Einhard took seven days to get from Aachen to Seligenstadt.[11] There were no aids for orientation. While medieval world maps adapted the charts of the ancients to their needs, they primarily told the story of salvation instead of providing geographical orientation.[12] During the eleventh and twelfth centuries, a time of mobility and traveling dawned. Patched-up roads were frequented by pilgrims from all walks of life, traveling minstrels, and students. Separate hostels for pilgrims as well as inns appeared, augmenting the lodging provided at monasteries and private homes.[13] However, the majority of the peasants still had a living space confined largely to their immediate village, a milieu that provided only occasional contact with neighboring villages and the next market. Travel (or pilgrimages) to far-away places remained an exception which contrasted dramatically with everyday life. As far as news was concerned, one had to rely on the reports of passing merchants. As a result, the horizon of medieval men and women was generally quite limited.

Sense of Time, Climate, and Anthropological Conditions of Life. Since people depended on the natural environment within their living space, with only limited capacity to alter it artificially, their way of life was still determined significantly by a nature, whose timing, seasonal rhythm, and weather patterns created immutable conditions. Indeed, time exhibits a dual character: physically speaking, it is a phenomenon of nature from which there is no escape (the aging process); it is also something people cannot change but they can utilize in response to their needs, divide and measure according to selected criterior. Thus

Illustration 1: *Dangers of the Road*: A Traveler Is Mugged by Robbers and Robbed of His Possessions (Herrad of Landsberg, *Hortus delicia-rum*, twelfth-century illustration of the parable of the Good Samaritan).

emerges "historical" or "social" time, human time.[14] To what extent and in what way natural cycles such as the rhythm of the sun's activity influence humans unconsciously, through certain diseases or psycho-logical moods, has hardly been researched and was totally unknown to medieval people. The passage of time itself was, of course, consciously experienced. "Natural" time consisted of the year with its seasons (as a result of the earth's orbit around the sun), and the days with their alternation between day and night (as a result of the earth's rotation). Months (as phases of the moon) were less significant, and the seven-day week, as well as the counting of the hours, represented artificial divisions of time created to satisfy human needs. People counted time by inventing ways and systems of measuring it. The Middle Ages in particular, which were rarely satisfied with just one specific reference to time, are accused of being obsessed with dating things. While this practice was limited to the educated in the areas of politics and law, it certainly expressed their uncertainty about chronology. Simple people were not interested in the number of years; in all likelihood, they did not even know when they were born. On the other hand, the rhythm of the seasons and the alternation of night and day were all the more important to rural society. Nights were dark and could be lit up only scantily with tallow or wax candles (in wealthier homes), making them unsuitable for many activities. Everyday life and work were restricted to daylight, which began at sunrise with the cock's crow and ended at sunset. Thus, daily life in Europe lasted much longer during the summer months than during winter. There were no exact ways to measure time. The time of day was determined by the position of the sun or the sound of the bells of a nearby church. In an ecclesiastical and monastic environment, however, exact determination of time was crucial in order to assure the punctuality of hourly prayers (in three-hour rhythm). Thus, there were primitive "clocks" of various kinds: candles of a certain length which burned for a specific period of time; (semi-mobile) sun dials which, however, functioned properly only during the day and in fair weather; and extravagant water clocks, *clepsydrae*, whose hands (marking the gradual flow of water) could tell the progress of time, but ceased to work when temperatures fell below the freezing mark.[15] As early as 807, emissaries of Harun al Rashid presented Charlemagne with an expensive water clock which struck the Frankish Imperial Annalist as nothing short of miraculous.[16] It was not until later that sand clocks came into use. All of these clocks were relatively inaccurate and depended on human operation, since water containers needed constant refilling and sand clocks required periodic turning. Mechanical clocks using gears still lacked indicators to mark the minutes. They remained unknown until the waning thirteenth century and were not widely used until the fourteenth and fifteenth centuries. At that time they assumed the form of tower clocks, since an urban society demanded more precise planning, ushering in a new epoch in our relationship with time. Imprecision was the characteristic mark of the early Middle Ages (Leclercq). To be sure, scientific theory divided the hours very precisely into 4 points (*puncti*), 10 minutes, 15 parts (*partes*), 40 moments (*momenta*), 60 signs (*ostenta*), and 22,560 atoms[17]—making an atom last exactly 0.16 seconds! But in fact no one was in a position to measure even hours with real accuracy. One should not therefore conclude an indifference to time, as has been argued, but merely that medieval life did not proceed in accordance with a definite "time table." Time was important because it limited one's actions; however, it remained a natural phenomenon that one could not influence. Therefore, hours and minutes as such seldom figured in planning one's time.

Similar to time, people depended on another natural phenomenon, climate. Medieval people were completely at its mercy. Here two factors were primary, temperature and moisture.[18] Long-term fluctuations determined vegetation and agricultural cycles. (Based on the prevailing type of forestation, both the Middle Ages and modern times are considered to be the Era of the Copper-Beech.) Worsening climatic conditions, together with enduring droughts, can usher in drastic changes; in this vein, it has been frequently assumed that Germanic migrations were caused in part by climatic changes. Conversely, warm periods might also cause flooding along the North Sea coasts due to the melting of the polar ice cap. Today's German coastal topography was not formed until the Middle Ages; once there had been settlement all the way to the Halligen Islands, but tidal waves later washed away the land. As a result, large areas of Jade Bay formed in 1219, and Dollart Bay in 1277-1287.

Overlooking regional variations and a wetter, cooler interim during the ninth century, a favorable climate prevailed between the eighth and thirteenth centuries, as measured by the annual rings of old trees, certain types of pollen, and other observations. The period from 300–700 A.D. was wet and cool. Optimal conditions then prevailed between 1150 and 1300. Even though the temperatures averaged only 1° C above today's average, the consequences were far-reaching. Beginning with this epoch, which unsurprisingly coincided with an epoch of expansion and population growth, agriculture experienced a tremendous boom. Weather began to deteriorate in the course of the thirteenth century, at least if one can trust contemporary reports about advancing glaciers and an increased number of frozen rivers.

Of course, contemporaries did not recognize such long-term changes; instead, they were all the more dependent on short-term fluctuations, as these were the ones affecting the harvest. The incidence or absence of famines, high prices, and illnesses due to inadequate nutrition were thus directly related to the climate—hence the rather accurate reports on rainfall, frost, natural disasters, and periods of drought in the annals and chronicles of this period. For example, the Frankish Imperial Annals report for the year 820, "This year, persistent rainfall and an inordinate amount of moisture in the air led to great hardships. People and animals alike have both been ravaged everywhere by such violent epidemics that there was hardly a district in all of France which appears to have been spared. Even grain and vegetables were ruined by constant rains and either could not be harvested, or rotted in the granaries. Wine did not fare much better; the harvest was meager, and it was harsh and sour because of a lack of sunshine. In some areas, it was impossible to take care of fall planting because of flooding of the plains by rivers, so that not a single kernel of grain got into the soil prior to spring."[19] There are numerous reports of this sort.[20] Agriculture depended entirely on the weather: if the winter turned out to be too long, leading to a shortage of grazing land, domestic animals died of hunger and cold;[21] if the summer remained dry, grain withered, and if it was too wet, it rotted. Moreover, there was occasional threat of wild animals and grasshoppers which could make quick work of entire fields. Every bad harvest, whether on a regional or on a larger scale, engendered famines, leading in turn to grossly inflated prices and profiteering. There is an anecdote by Notker of St. Gall in which a bishop is accused of withholding his grain from market in expectation of higher prices, even as others suffered from hunger.[22] Hrabanus Maurus, archbishop of Mainz, demonstrated greater social awareness during a famine in 850 when he ordered that more than 300 poor people be fed daily. In the same year, a man on his way to Thuringia even considered sacrificing his own child in order to be able to survive; the boy was saved by a "miracle" when two wolves brought down a doe whose meat could be eaten by the hungry.[23] Such miracles—which naturally did not happen every day—often provided the only chance of reprieve, since people were generally helpless. A royal capitulary from the days of Charlemagne[24] ordered the people not to wait for a royal edict to be issued during dire times, such as famine or epidemics, but immediately to pray for God's grace (which probably did not always help either). Another capitulary went so far as to order a fast during the threat of famine,[25] a measure which was certainly superfluous to the hungry, but which was religiously inspired and directed at the richer people and the monks, since crop failure was considered a form of divine punishment for all. In 873, for example, priests set out to meet a swarm of grasshoppers, carrying holy relics and crucifixes in order to ward off the damage.[26] Famines were fairly common during the entire Middle Ages; they occurred particularly often during the twelfth century, a period of economic upswing. On the whole, there were great numbers of poor people (*pauperes*) in the Middle Ages who depended—in whole or in part—on help from monasteries.[27]

Epidemics and diseases arose from famines. Medical skills were negligible, and the care of the sick was another task for the monks. It was only the influence of Arabic doctors which stimulated medicine to emerge during the high Middle Ages. Hostels specializing in the care of the sick were established in towns in the late Middle Ages. Herbs helped against less serious illnesses, and blood-letting was the popular cure of the day. As a result, people were once again left to hope for miracles, resulting in stories about miraculous cures, since any recovery from serious illness had to be viewed as a miracle. The sick rushed to the relics of saints because those were considered more salutary than doctors. In addition to the books about miracles, findings based on the examination of skeletons inform us of the state of health of medieval people.[28] According to the evidence provided by these sources, diseases caused by inadequate nutrition and epidemics were the most frequent results of the many famines. Leprosy also represented a constant threat, and lepers were sequestered from society and specifically prevented from entering the cities because of a fear of infection. Typhoid fever, smallpox, cholera, malaria (in the Mediterranean countries), tuberculosis, dysentery, and various other illnesses often proved fatal. Furthermore, the lame were numerous, as were people crippled by rheumatism, the blind and partially blind (glasses remained unknown until the fourteenth century), epileptics and the mentally ill (the "possessed" during the Middle Ages). According to the evidence based on skeletal examinations, dental condition was poor, though tooth decay was rare in an age still unfamiliar with sugar. On the other hand, bone fractures often seemed to heal surprisingly well.

Illnesses were frequently also the result of inadequate hygiene. Although baths, heating, and toilets were already known during the Middle Ages, they tended to be more a luxury for only a few. However, even if strict monastic rules limited full baths to twice a year (Christmas and Pentecost) for reasons of asceticism, or if Bishop Udalrich of Augsburg only used to bathe once during Lent for the same reason,[29] bathing was otherwise apparently quite common, and widespread enjoyment of bathing was tied to pleasures of various kinds provided by the late-medieval bathhouses. There have been public baths ever since the twelfth century.

Those people spared by famine and diseases might fall victim to wars, feuds, and widespread robberies, resulting in a correspondingly low life expectancy, averaging between twenty-five and thirty-two years. However, an infant mortality rate of sometimes up to forty per cent was in large measure responsible for these extremely low figures. Anyone who survived childhood and adolescence could count on getting somewhat older, men on the average approximately forty-seven, women forty-four years.[30] (Apparently, the mortality rate of men was less affected by wars than that of women was by the risks of giving birth. Charlemagne outlived three wives, a fact which carries a certain amount of weight, although it is not necessarily typical.) Certainly, social differences played a role as well, but the average age even of kings fell well below fifty years. As a result, old people were both rare and respected, in part because of their experience, although they could also be perceived as a burden to society when famine threatened. Biblical exegesis often painted a dismal picture of old age,[31] and in the *Ruodlieb*, a medieval Latin epic written during the eleventh century, the mother points out the horrors of old age to her son, if only to coax him into getting married: an old woman possesses bleary eyes, a runny nose, loose teeth, droopy breasts, stringy hair, and a halting, pounding gait; an old man depends on help from others and is frequently mocked should he dare to express a desire to dance again.[32] Three generations of a family living under the same roof, therefore, were probably more the exception than the rule.

Based on skeletal analysis, men not only lived longer than women but were also considerably taller (on an average by more than ten centimeters) as well as in the majority (at a ratio of 114-118 : 100). The reasons for this disproportion have yet to be explained, but all these factors necessarily had an effect on the composition of society and on communal life, even though their impacts still await closer scrutiny.

The "Culture" of the Middle Ages. People tried to win the upper hand over perils by intervening in nature, creating a culture[33] and environment which set new conditions for everyday life. They did this by employing technical aids and methods which shaped their actions, especially their work; by creating an institutional framework of government, administration, and legislation; by instituting political organization and regulating the legal sphere; by establishing economic structures and emphasizing the monetary system; and above all by establishing social bonds and conventions essential to people who, as a rule, acted in groups (which will be discussed in greater detail later). Finally, medieval men and women acted out of characteristically "medieval" conceptions of the world, meaning, thought, and behavior peculiar to a class or group that accompanied and determined their way of life, and in which apparently (to judge from the sources) religion (and superstition) predominated. It is not our theme here to describe these conceptions of the world; yet it is impossible to avoid addressing medieval mentalities, since it is only human actions and thoughts which convey knowledge about the past. In this context we must also remember the importance of language and linguistic norms. Linguistic meaning presents a particular problem during the Middle Ages since the traditional language of culture, Latin, merely translated vernacular languages which medieval people spoke and in which they conceived their thoughts.

Finally, customs, the shaping of the external world, and various accomplishments, including those of artists[34] and artisans, all belong to human "culture" and a history of everyday life. Eating habits, for example, are essential to one's survival and even though they may demonstrate differences of social background, they also illustrate common tendencies.[35] The most important sources here are tribute ledgers kept for peasants, as well as the physical remnants of plants, seeds, and pollen. During the seventh century, burial gifts interred with the dead from the upper levels of society are also of interest in this regard. Lastly, valuable information is obtained by examining medieval latrines.[36] The main staple was grain, processed into bread and porridge but also used in brewing beer[37] and as feed for animals. In the early period, spelt barley and, to a lesser degree, oats and wheat were also grown, at least in the northern regions. Later, rye became the favorite grain.[38] Cereals provided needed carbohydrates. In addition, people ate cheese, vegetables (celery, beets, cabbage, pumpkin, squash), berries, fruit (apples, pears, plums, cherries), and nuts, providing necessary protein, salts, and vitamins. Fat was obtained from oil plants (linseed, poppy). Honey was the only sweetener. On the whole, seasonings were very expensive unless they could be grown in one's own herb garden. Utensils as burial gifts (such as roasting spits) and the evidence of animal bones from settlements suggest that meat was an important staple during Merovingian times, at least among the upper classes, though the growing of grain expanded slowly at the expense of husbandry (see Illustration 2). As a result, meat was probably not an everyday food; particularly in simple households, it was served only at special occasions. As a rule it was cured, since the animals had to be slaughtered prior to the onset of winter so that they did not have to be fed all winter. (Thus, in peasant speech, November was referred to as "slaughter month.") One Swabian landowner who had himself cared for in a monastery in exchange for a donation of land received a daily ration of bread, beer, vegetables, and milk, but he received meat only on holidays.[39] Because of the numerous fast-days fish was also important, at least at manorial tables. Generally, meals ought to be imagined as rather paltry; it is therefore no mere coincidence that full stomachs abound in fantasies about a "land of milk and honey." On the other hand, the variety of home-grown produce or imported foods, both at manor houses as well as at urban consumer centers, is impressive, a fact that clearly testifies to the great variety of medieval cuisine. Naturally we must expect great differences among social levels and households. Whenever the occasion arose, people enjoyed imbibing, particularly wine and beer. When a capitulary barred anyone from forcing another to drink, an almost modern style emerges, in which drinking was also a social occasion.[40]

Illustration 2: *"Hic coquitur caro"*—*"Preparing Meat"* (From the Bayeux Tapestry, late eleventh century).

Apart from a few luxurious and exquisite items, dishes and utensils were rather primitive prior to the thirteenth century, with little differences between the nobility and urban households. They consisted mostly of wood (which have rarely been preserved) or were made of ceramic, generally on the potter's wheel and exported from certain pottery centers.[41] There are variations in color and shape, depending on region and time. During the early Middle Ages, the pottery popular in western and northern Germany was chiefly manufactured in the Rhineland, at first at Badorf from the eighth to the tenth centuries (with its characteristic red-painted round pots, jugs, and oval storage vessels made with light yellow clay, as well as egg-shaped storage vessels). Later (ninth to twelfth centuries), much pottery was manufactured at Pingsdorf, with its hard-fired wares, buff, red or reddish-brown in color. Cups, kettles, pans, pots (*Grapen*), jugs and bowls made of metal or bronze were rare and treasured valuables.[42]

People differed above all in the clothes they wore,[43] since these revealed a person's social status. During the early Middle Ages, however, the clothes worn by the various levels of society differed more in terms of quality and adornments than shape. It was not until the thirteenth century that strict dress codes were issued for individual levels of society. Preferred materials were linen, flax, wool, and occasionally silk (imported as a luxury article from the East). During the early Middle Ages people particularly valued "Frisian" cloth (actually from Flanders). The most important and often sole piece of clothing for more impoverished men was the tunic, a knee-length smock; underneath they also wore a shirt of equal length. "Underpants" (*bruech, femoralia*) were known, but generally did not become fashionable until the thirteenth century. The legs were covered with wrapped stockings or pants. Leather shoes were made of one piece and sewn together at the top. The typical "Frankish" dress (see Illustration 3) which Notker has Charlemagne wear in the ninth century, consisting of scarlet-red linen pants with puttees laced at the top, was hardly being worn any longer at that time and probably served as a festive costume.[44] Women wore long undergarments and an outer garment with wide sleeves, first shorter and later longer. Married women wore a scarf or a veil. Anybody who could afford it owned a coat, fastened at the top with a fibula and, if possible, with a belt. Clothes did not tend to emphasize the body. A changing "fashion" did not develop as such until after the high Middle Ages. Previously, fashion was limited to the upper classes' imitation of foreign (Italian or Byzantine) influences.

Everyday life itself consisted mainly of daily work, meals, occasional forms of entertainment and merriment, and social contacts and

Illustration 3: *The Dress of High-ranking Franks: Dedication Picture for Charles the Bald* (excerpt from the Vivian Bible, Tours, c. 845/46).

communication, all depending on one's class, social status, "occupation," and sphere of life, but all carried out within the community and largely shaped by habitual forms of conduct. Life was subject to a definite order, at least according to medieval theory. What would be considered trivial today often carried symbolic meaning.[45] Daily routine was interrupted by life's high points: by weddings, births, local visits of dignitaries, church holidays, and work-related festivities (May celebrations, harvest festivals). Here too, nearly everything was regulated by custom, even though we still know only very little about the concrete shape of these events.[46] Such high or low points (deaths) were social events in which the entire community participated. The many dangers of the period increasingly forced medieval people to seek security in social relationships within their own spheres of life and communities. Everyday life (including workaday life) evolved primarily within the family and will therefore be presented in its general characteristics, regardless of class distinctions. Though no longer viable as a unit unto itself during the earlier Middle Ages, the family was the smallest and most natural sphere of life and was embedded—though still generally considered a distinct labor and legal unit ("family enterprise")—in the extended communities on which we will concentrate in later chapters.

II

The Family

The term *familia* had various meanings in the Middle Ages;[1] it described a household community or association of relatives in the modern sense, but in a derivative sense it could mean the monastic community or a community of serfs within the framework of the manorial system. An especially telling illustration for the Middle Ages is provided by the ecclesiastical sphere, where a sort of spiritual marriage existed between the Church and the priest. That is why priests were prohibited from getting married in the secular sense (a view, however, which began to take shape only gradually, since married clergy were still quite common until the great ecclesiastical reform of the eleventh century).[2] Thereafter, nuns as well as the Church perceived of themselves as *sponsa Christi* (bride of Christ). One of the most frequently explicated books of the Bible in the Middle Ages was the Song of Songs, where the biblical love imagery was interpreted as Christ and his bride, the Church. The term "mystical marriage" was used to describe the entire complex of relations.[3] All of these interpretations shed a meaningful light on the specifically medieval outlook. However, this chapter will discuss the family in a strictly secular sense.

1. House and Clan

The medieval family is in no sense to be defined simply.[4] As already mentioned, it incorporated both an association of relatives as well as the household community, without any strict separation between the two. (Even today we speak of a "royal house" when we really mean a family.) In a narrower sense (the agnatic family), such an association of relatives as a clan (*Sippe*) comprised blood relatives, but in a broader sense (the cognatic family), it included all relatives by marriage. The entire family gathered for large celebrations and holidays.[5] During the Middle Ages, the family was still characterized by closeness and a sense of unity—a fact which certainly did not preclude altercations among family members. The family still formed a unit in public life, but as a rule it no longer represented a geographic settlement or a distinct community; the family as a unit manifested itself mostly within the household. Yet the household community was only partially identical with the family association. On the one hand, it was separate from the large-scale family, consisting merely of the core family based on marriage: the husband, the wife, and children, as well as parents and collateral relatives living under the same roof. Still, as a family in a broader sense, it also included all persons living in the house, such as the domestics who were part of the family, as well guests living in the house on a temporary basis. The deceased are also not to be forgotten, since they continued to live on in the memory of family members.[6] Let us now examine the structure of these two basic units of household and kinship more closely.

During the Middle Ages, according to Germanic tradition, the household was autocratically organized and focused on the man of the house. Physically speaking, the household formed a compact unit which was enclosed by a fence at an early date;[7] the husband exercized his legitimate authority, *Munt*, over his fellow household members. The "state," which was the king with his instruments of government, was unable to curtail the legitimate rights of a husband. The king was only able to interfere when several households and kinships feuded with one another, and even then such assistance had to be requested. Thus, the household constituted an autonomous realm of peace and law where private and public spheres coincided. The lord of the household also assumed tasks we would today consider governmental functions. According to the theory developed by Otto Brunner and Walter Schlesinger, the *Munt* was (with certain restrictions) the source and innermost component of all forms of government during the Middle Ages. Even the lordship of medieval kings still clearly displayed the traits of an extended household government (with court officers), and on the manorial level, the lord of the manor made decisions concerning his *familia*, the community of dependents.[8]

During Germanic and early medieval times, the chair of the man of the house was passed on to his oldest son upon his death, together with all its rights and privileges, while the community of brothers remained intact as heirs in common. (This applies also to the Frankish kingdom; because all the sons needed an inheritance, the rule had to be divided time and again during Frankish times, while the realm as a whole was supposed to remain a single unit.) At the moment of her husband's death, a widow had to surrender to the *Munt* of her eldest son, who was to take care of her. If he was still a minor, the widow was to administer the estate; however, she often also received part of the estate to be held in tenancy for life.[9] Daughters inherited only if no brothers lived.[10] In Alamannic law, sons inherited only if they were married to women of equal social rank. Here too, there was no guarantee that everything proceeded as harmoniously as provided by the legal norm. There were, of course, seditious sons who rebelled against their father's rule, particularly sons of kings seeking to rise to power themselves. In fact, the family as a household community was subject to constant change; younger brothers moved away and established households with families of their own, and sisters were given away in marriage, thus surrendered to the house and authority of their husbands. It was not until well into the Middle Ages that the idea of a community of brothers came to be abandoned and property was divided among the sons—at least in some regions such as Swabia. As a result, the property of the individual continuously shrank unless new sources of property could be tapped—such as a marriage. In other places, property was passed undivided to the oldest son; the younger brothers were "portioned off," receiving a settlement in kind. This was one of the reasons for a form of social mobility. Male offspring of noble families soon presented a problem; often without any possessions, they were forced to offer their services to greater lords. The chivalry of the high Middle Ages, the readiness of knights to seek a new homeland during the Crusades, may be explained by this practice. Another favorite solution was for parents to order a son to enter a monastery at an early age. Thus the household evolved in the course of the Middle Ages. In the beginning, it represented the basic unit, the core of the political order; however, in conjunction with changes in the laws of succession, it eventually dissolved into a smaller unit with more limited rights.

Like the household, the clan (*Sippe*) also formed an institution of public law in accordance with Germanic tribal laws, although its significance is disputed.[11] (*Sippe* was not a contemporary term.) The clan was an association whose goals were stability and the preservation of law and order. It achieved this by providing peace within and protection against the outside. For instance, relatives assisted one another by rendering oaths in court; during disputes, they were the traditional partners who negotiated the penalty for a homicide or injury whenever they declined taking blood revenge. The wergild, later stipulated by tribal laws for such cases, had to be raised by the clan of the perpetrator and paid to the clan of the aggrieved party. The family was also a guardian of morals. Gregory of Tours, the most important historian of the Merovingian age, writes of a woman who had an affair with a priest and was subsequently burned alive by her relatives. The priest was arrested and forced to pay a fine.[12] Gradually government agencies reduced the legal sovereignty of the clan; individual members, however, remained integral components of the family association, which continued to be held liable for damages.

Even though the function of the clan as a legal association is indisputable, its competence remained as vague as its own limits. It is more important in this context to ask what the family of the early Middle Ages looked like. Any attempt to ascertain concrete degrees of consanguinity encounters substantial difficulty, both since sources establish lineage only very rarely, and since by Germanic custom people at this time had only one name.[13] The practice of carrying only one name frequently prevents unequivocal identification of certain persons, not to mention determining genealogical descent—thus a family can only rarely be traced over any period of time during the early Middle Ages. Although this was first perceived merely to be an impediment to genealogical and prosopographical research, it was above all Karl Schmid who brought valuable light to bear on the structure of families during the earlier Middle Ages, primarily those of the nobility, by asking why individuals cannot be clearly identified.[14] A name, which at first conveyed a specific meaning in Germanic-speaking areas,[15] soon became part of a family tradition and of the "inheritance," since families tended to pass certain names to their children.[16] Since Germanic names were usually formed of two parts (Chlodo-vech), there were two possible ways to name descendants: either the entire name was passed on or one part of it (the stem itself or its end part, called the "name variator"). During earlier days, it was the second method which prevailed. Two sons of the Merovingian king *Chlodwig* (Chlodo-vech) were named *Chlod*omer and *Chlot*har. A favorite example is the two (legendary) heroes, Hilde*brand* and Hadu*brand*. However, after the eighth and ninth centuries, the nobility began increasingly to prefer to pass the entire name (of the father, the grandfather, or another family member). As a result, certain thematic names evolved which, since they offer no additional clues, do not suffice for purposes of identification, assignment to a certain family, or determining the exact degree of relationship in the sense of earlier genealogy. There were no definite rules governing the passing of names, yet they constitute an expression of family awareness tied to the name, which frequently resulted in an entire clan being named for an individual (such as Carolingians, Conradians, Ottonians). Karl (Charles), Ludwig (Louis), and Pepin were typical Carolingian names. Thus, a name was not only a first name, but also a clan-name (Schmid), frequently classifying an individual as a member of a certain family association. For instance, the author of the *Vita Bennonis* mentions specifically that this later bishop of Osnabrück received a name common within his family (*ex cognationis denominatione*).[17] There were even cases where a son was simply "re-baptized" following the death of a brother, to preserve the name within the family. For instance, the name of Karlmann, one of Charlemagne's sons, was later changed to Pepin. The name bestowed was not necessarily determined by the family of the husband, but could also (if less frequently) be determined by the wife as well. Consequently, the early Middle Ages were not dominated by a strictly agnatic consciousness, as is the case with modern dynasties, but rather by a cognatic one; in principle, a wife's relatives were as significant as those of the husband. Therefore, Schmid speaks of an early medieval clan structure in contrast to the high medieval and late medieval dynastic structure. (To be sure, "clan" is used here in a broader sense.) Names were taken preferably from the socially more elevated family in order to enhance social ascent. The Carolingians best exemplify this: their name did not derive from the family of Bishop Arnulf of Metz and his son Ansegisel, but that of the family of Pepin the Elder (Ansegisel married Pepin's daughter, Begga) because the Mayor of the Palace held higher office than the Arnulfings. Relationships such as these explain why early medieval families can rarely be traced over more than two or three generations; names and family consciousness were continuously being altered as a result of marrying into another family, changing the "family" from one generation to the next. Entries in memorial books, commending entire families to the prayerful memory of a monastery, offer almost inexhaustible sources for research. Since bishops and abbots were often integrated into the context of their families,[18] spiritual office did not produce a strict separation between clergy and lay people; rather, family relationships were preserved, a fact easily overlooked if we perceive "Church" and "world" as opposites during the Middle Ages.

The self-awareness of noble families was shaped by the position and function of their highest office holders. "Proximity to the king" in the form of holding high government offices, marrying into the royal family (or both) was particularly important, and families close to the king changed from reign to reign (Schmid). We possess good documentation of such an awareness among the nobility in the form of a guide, or "handbook" assembled for her son William in 841-843 by Dhuoda, wife of Count Bernard of Septimania.[19] Dhuoda especially enjoined three things on her son: pure faith in God, loyalty toward the king, and loyalty to family traditions (adding, carefully, a list of relatives). However, family consciousness was oriented nonetheless toward the royal court.

Other families concentrated their interests on bishoprics, trying time and again to secure specific bishoprics for their relatives. Three bishops by the name of Salomon followed each other at Constance during the ninth century. The lives of saints, too, were frequently a result of family traditions written down by relatives.[20] Later on, the use of noble titles predominated. If a family failed repeatedly in its efforts to procure high offices for their members, it went into social decline (Schmid). Thus, we can see how greatly the consciousness of early medieval noble families depended on distinctions and offices.

A change occurred in the structure of noble families in the high Middle Ages. Even before then, sons were considered important to assure legitimate succession, and saints were often implored to grant sons. During the eleventh and twelfth centuries, the nobility acquired a firm point of identity in ancestral castles from which they derived their names. The first group to do so, significantly enough, was the lower nobility, who had not previously been universally recognized.[21] (Hence the prefix *von* (from), indicating noble lineage.) Soon the family was no longer an open clan, but rather a definite dynasty, a "house," where the agnatic principle predominated. The noble families began to record their *genealogiae* in lists or family trees, commissioning the writing of their own dynastic histories.[22] The family had found its central point, which also permitted genealogy to supply more precise information.

Although we have been examining the structure of noble families, it appears that the insufficiently researched conditions of the lower levels of society are fundamentally similar.[23] Serfs, as a rule, were married, in contrast to earlier opinion.[24] In the beginning, the lord probably had the right to choose their spouses,[25] or separate the couple again when they were sold. Imma, the wife of Einhard, intervened with her woman friend on behalf of the woman's male servant, who had married a free woman, but who subsequently fled to Seligenstadt, seeking asylum there out of fear of his lord.[26] Families and family connections thus existed among serfs. The names of children were also patterned after those of both parents.[27] These references may suffice here, since a more detailed discussion of the peasant family will follow in the chapter on the manorial system.

2. Marriage

The Wedding

Marriage represented the founding moment and the foundation of the family. Originally, the wedding was also an event performed under the rules of the clan, leading to a clan-like bond between two families, whose approval for the transaction was naturally required. (Within Western European culture exogamous marriages were common everywhere.) One from the St. Gall formulary dating from the ninth century concerning the dowry of a wife began with the words, "May it be known herewith to all and everybody that, with the approval of my parents, I am taking your niece named X. for my wife."[28] (The uncle played a special role according to Germanic law, particularly if the father was already deceased.) As a result of marriage, the wife was transferred from her parents' *Munt*, that is to say, their protection and rule, to that of her husband (see Illustration 4). It is obvious such marriages often reflected the wishes of the parents—particularly the bride's—rather than those of the newlyweds. Only in the course of time did canon law stipulate the consent of the bride, and eventually marriages were entered into solely between the groom and the bride.[29] Nevertheless, many marriages continued to be arranged by the parents when the children were at an early age. According to canon law, the minimum age came to be fourteen years for the husband and twelve for the wife. The average age at which people did get married ranged between twenty and twenty-four for the husband and fourteen to sixteen for the wife. It is possible that the few known examples of premature marriages have received too much attention.[30] At least among the upper strata of the population, marriage was frequently a means to social ascent as well as a political occasion so that, especially among premature marriages, love was hardly ever a reason for getting married. As is well known, the second marriage of Louis the Pious to the Welf Judith hurled the Frankish Empire into a deep crisis since the late-born Charles (the Bald) had to receive his share, upsetting earlier plans for the division of the realm. Fights among the brothers arose which were not finally settled until the Partition of Verdun (843).[31]

The wedding itself followed pre-established forms: the *petitio* (a request in the sense of proposal) was followed by the betrothal (*desponsatio*) (considered binding), and finally, the wedding itself (*nuptiae*). Prior to that, the bridegroom handed over the bridal gift, the so-called *Wittum* (*dos* = dower). This was originally given to the clan of the bride, later to the bride herself,[32] who owned it, in part, as a kind of widow's insurance benefit. Among well-to-do people, the dower generally consisted of a piece of property with a house, storage buildings, land, animals, and serfs, along with clothes and jewelry. The value of the gift was determined by the wealth of the bridegroom. Louis the German gave his son Charles seventy-six *mansi* in the Breisgau with which the son could "equip" the woman "whom his lord [his father], had given

Illustration 4: *A Medieval Wedding: The Parents Present the Bride* (Herrad of Landsberg, *Hortus deliciarum*, twelfth-century illustration of Luke 14:20).

him in marriage."[33] Extant marriage certificates often include threats of sanctions against relatives; thus, one had to consider the possibility the heirs of the husband would dispute the wife's right to the dower, since the heir to the property acquired at the time of marriage was not the spouse but, in the absence of children, the husband's or the wife's family.[34] The wedding or *traditio*, (a handing over) was a solemn but secular, publicly witnessed act during which the words of consent constituted the decisive element.[35] This was followed by "taking home" the bride to the groom's house and climbing into the nuptial bed before the assembled relatives, who probably volunteered some last-minute advice to the newlyweds. Following the wedding night, the wife received a "reward" in the form of a morning gift (*Morgengabe*), which also became part of the dower. During the Christian era, blessing by a priest was added.

The type of marriage described here (*Muntehe*) prevailed during the early Middle Ages. Originally there were also other forms of marriage besides the one just described. Marriage was not always a contract between clans, but could also be the result of abduction (without the bride's consent) or elopement (with the bride's consent, but against the will of the family). At an early point, tribal laws, capitularies, and council decisions opposed such procedures. The oldest Frankish law, the *Pactus legis Salicae*, threatened with the death penalty those who abetted somebody else's son or daughter in marrying without relatives' consent.[36] Indeed, the frequency of such sanctions stresses the fact that abductions were still widespread among the Franks. The practice continued later, probably restricted to isolated cases. Thietmar of Merseburg, a historian during the early eleventh century, relates the story of Count Liuthar from the Nordmark, who had asked on behalf of his son Werner for the hand of the daughter of Margrave Ekkehard of Meissen in 998; the two clans gathered, and Ekkehard consented at first, but then withdrew his consent for undisclosed reasons. Werner then eloped with his bride. Abbess Mathilde of Quedlinburg, who was administering the Empire's affairs at the time, raised the hue and cry to pursue the outlaw. At a Diet at Magdeburg, the princes decided against the wishes of the bride and had her returned. She subsequently had to wait until her father's death before she could return to her husband.[37] Hence, one should not contend that love played no role whatsoever during the Middle Ages.

Although abduction or elopement merely affected the form of the wedding, there were other forms of marriage which contrasted with or paralleled the traditional *Muntehe*, such as what is called *Friedelehe*. This was based on the consent of both husband and wife and it therefore represents, in contrast to the politically motivated *Muntehe*, a "love match" (Old High German: *friudila* = friend, lover). It was also performed in public, but without the benefit of a wedding ceremony or a dower; it retained a gift for the morning after. Thus, a man could have only one wedded wife, but also, if he could afford it, several *Friedel*-wives. The woman was apparently forbidden to enter into such multiple matches. These various forms of marriage can be observed coexisting among the Merovingian and early Carolingian kings.[38] The *Friedelehe* was soon condemned by the Church, which viewed it increasingly as a form of concubinage; indeed, it could hardly be distinguished from concubinage in practice, though a concubine had no marital rights at all. Thus, the sole recognition of the *Muntehe* also affected the family structures described above, as well as the laws of succession (Mikat). Naturally, concubines continued to exist, especially so-called *Kebsverhältnisse* (concubinages between a freeman or nobleman and a female serf). In the beginning such relationships were neither considered adulterous nor recognized as marriages, since any marriage below one's station in life was forbidden by Germanic law, although offspring enjoyed a specific right to support. Royal sons born out of wedlock were barred from succession to the throne, but they were well endowed and installed in high offices. The fact that a lord would want to enter into a relationship with one of the female servants living under the same roof is easy to imagine; indeed, in the early days, he actually had a right to do so until the Church sought to limit the practice. According to a canonical handbook by Regino of Prüm from the early tenth century, a married man who slept with his maidservant was to do penance for a year, whereas the woman merely needed to do so for forty days, unless she had been a willing party.[39] A free woman who had an affair with a male servant suffered radically harsher punishment, namely death.[40] Provisions such as these reveal the obvious influence of the Church.

The Influence of the Church

Despite the strong influence of the Church, the marriage ceremony remained a secular act throughout the early Middle Ages. The Church had no special provisions for wedding ceremonies, although a priest's blessing at such events is attested beginning in the fourth century. Between the ninth and the twelfth centuries, a more fixed ecclesiastical ritual developed.[41] After the twelfth century, consecration by the Church became the rule. The publication of the banns dates to this time as well, and it eventually became customary for the priest to place a ring on the bride's finger. From the twelfth century on, marriage was considered a sacrament.

Even before there were marriages in the presence of priests, the Church exercised a decisive influence on everyday married life through its marriage theory and the marriage provisions in canon law. At the same time, the Church found itself in a quandary, since marriage was also considered an institution testifying to the sinful state of humanity. There was no need for marriages or procreation in heaven, according to one writer from the tenth century, since the number of the just would be complete there.[42] Particularly in the beginning of Christianity, preserving one's virginity was a high ideal. The lives of saints from late antiquity and the early Middle Ages tended to combine martyrdom—the ideal sainthood—with the ideal of virginity in women, and the Church venerated saintly, Christian virgins who had refused to yield sexually to heathen men and were martyred for it. It also supported married women who wanted to escape from marriage.[43] People frequently cited the parable of the three "estates" depicted in the twelfth century *Speculum virginum*: wives harvested thirtyfold, widows sixtyfold (it was apparently blessed to survive one's husband), and virgins a hundredfold. Chastity, of course, was a self-evident requirement for marriage; by extension, preserving one's virginity within one's marriage was also meritorious. On the occasion of a parentally arranged marriage of a noble senator to a wealthy heiress, Gregory of Tours relates that the wife fell into deep sadness the day of her wedding, finally admitting that she had already betrothed herself to Christ and that now, as a result of this marriage, her chances of paradise were dwindling. Both spouses then pledged to remain chaste as an expression of their true love, ultimately revealing itself in a miracle. After their burial, their previously separate graves miraculously became one.[44] It goes without saying that such a miracle illustrates the exception rather than the rule, and such an ideal hardly reflected everyday reality. People were probably also inclined to interpret childlessness retrospectively as a sign of sacred chastity, as was the case with Emperor Henry II and his wife Kunigunde. However, the ideal had already shifted by that time: now, instead of virgins, married women became the majority of those canonized.

In spite of its initial idealization of celibacy, the Church eventually developed an ambivalent attitude which was, on the whole, positively disposed toward marriage. No longer was marriage merely relatively good, as an institution commensurate with the state of sinfulness; rather, it had been instituted by God at the time of creation. Thus paradise, though still childless, was frequently interpreted in terms of marriage; it was the natural life community of a man and a woman.[45] In many illustrations of married couples, Christ crowns and blesses the partners while they hold each other's right hands; graves also frequently displayed joint epitaphs for husband and wife. The threefold purpose of marriage was also considered good. First, it was primarily intended to fulfil the obligation of procreation; according to some theories, a marriage did not commence with the wedding ceremony, but with first intercourse.[46] Second, in the opinion of theologians, marriage was intended to promote the spreading of love so that it was marriage which led to love and not the other way around.[47] Finally, citing St. Paul, marriage helped prevent fornication, which was any form of extramarital sexuality. That is why marriage was also occasionally characterized as "legitimated fornication." From this point of view, voluntary chastity was by no means a mere ideal: on the contrary, Carolingian capitularies punished anyone who did not sleep with his or her own spouse (which must actually have happened).

Against this background, through its matrimonial laws and in its role as guardian of the legitimacy of marriage and everyday marital life, the Church intervened decisively in the practical aspects of marriage. The synods developed a fairly active marriage legislation, and ecclesiastical penitentials denounced marital trespasses, indicating that such transgressions did occur.[48] Church regulations on marriage, based on the *Muntehe*, demanded fidelity. Adultery was punished severely, particularly a woman's. In most cases, a man had to accept several years' penance, up to seven years, and practice abstinence (sometimes also toward his own wife, who was thus punished along with him); furthermore, it was illegal to marry somebody with whom one had previously committed adultery.[49] On the other hand, we do not know the extent to which such legal regulations were actually applied in practice. Some cases boggle the mind. At the synod at Tribur, deliberations were held concerning the possibility of a husband sleeping with his wife's sister (who lived under the same roof) without noticing the difference, thus becoming "innocently culpable" (a favorite theme in epic literature later).[50] Such an event notwithstanding, deliberate adultery was the rule, occurring despite severe punishment. During an exorcism, the administrator of an estate from Utrecht allegedly possessed by the devil suddenly disclosed adultery and acts of lewdness among many of his fellows, creating understandable uproar in the town.[51]

However, canon law already interfered with the wedding ceremony itself by stipulating to whom one could get married in the first place. According to Germanic law, marrying close relatives, the wife of another, or women from another social class was ruled out. This applied also to kinship through marriage. An edict by Childebert of 596 forbade

royal followers from marrying the wife of their brother, the sister of their
wife, or blood relatives of the parents.[52] Marriage to the (second) wife
of one's father carried the death penalty. According to the Germanic
way of thinking, using the image of a body, relatives were categorized
as a special kind of relationship, referred to as *Magschaft*: the two
parents formed, together with the children and the parents' brothers and
sisters, the head; shoulders symbolized the grandparents, grandchildren,
uncles and aunts, nephews, and nieces; the elbow joints were the great-
grandparents, great-grandchildren, second-degree cousins, etc. Christian theory, however, counted the degrees of relationship patrilineally,
that is to say, according to the descent from the father in a direct
and a collateral line: the married couple with their brothers and sisters
comprised the first degree; children, parents, as well as the children of
brothers and sisters, the second, etc. Family trees, which have survived,
helped to make these relationships understandable. At first canon law
forbade marriages up to the seventh degree, later only to the fourth,
but without ever reaching a uniform rule.[53] Thus, finding a proper
partner became rather difficult for the widely intermarried nobility.
Although the Council of Orléans of 541 still forbade marriage to a *filia
aliena*, a woman of non-Frankish origin,[54] this restriction soon had to
be abandoned. In fact, there were many marriages between relatives—
Pepin I, for instance, was married in the third degree to Bertrada, a
grandniece of his grandmother Plektrud, wife of Pepin the Middle.
These marriages were mildly denounced by the Church, but were,
conversely, also reasons given for divorce. The majority of marriages
probably did comply with the rules and regulations of canon law. This
increased the tendency toward mixed marriages between partners from
various social strata, and it also promoted opportunities for social climbing by means of marriage.[55]

Divorce

While the dissolution of a marriage was originally a relatively
simple matter, starting in the ninth century, it became increasingly
severely restricted due to the Christian theory of marriage's indissolubility. Initially a marriage could be dissolved by mutual agreement or
unilaterally for sufficient cause through the expulsion of the wife by the
husband. Reason for such peremptory expulsion might be because one
partner presumed free was really not free, or had become free later,[56]
or because the wife had committed adultery, or (already the influence of
Christianity) because one of the partners had entered a monastery.[57] In
the ninth century, Jonas of Orléans reluctantly acknowledged that physical handicaps or poverty had once been considered sufficient grounds

for divorce, but he no longer wished to recognize them.[58] Finally, the synod of Tribur of 895 dismissed legal and social inequality as reasons for divorce,[59] and even adultery soon came to be considered only conditionally sufficient grounds. As a rule, the only recognized basis for dissolution was that marriage had been entered into illegally, for instance because of too close a blood-relationship. Getting remarried was already made more difficult by Frankish tribal law, which required payment of "ring money" by the second husband, as well as the consent of the relatives of the first husband. In effect, a woman had to buy her freedom from the clan of her first husband: in the presence of witnesses, she had to supply a bench and chairs, decorate her bed and bedspread, and leave them behind on her departure. Only then was she left in peace by the relatives and allowed to take two-thirds of her dower with her into the new marriage. A husband had to proceed similarly.[60] According to canon law, remarriage was forbidden and severely punished for as long as the first marriage partner remained alive.[61]

In practice, especially in higher circles, the dissolution of a marriage was not merely a legal issue, but also a political matter. Four famous examples will illustrate this:

1. There were hardly any problems in this regard during Merovingian times. According to Gregory of Tours, Charibert, a son of Chlothar

Illustration 5: *A Later Portrayal of Divorce by a Priest Who Separates the Husband from His Wife and Child* (Sachsenspiegel, Heidelberg illustrated manuscript, c. 1330).

I, who was king of the partial kingdom of Paris from 561 to 567, first took Ingoberga for his wife, had subsequent affairs with two of her servants, left Ingoberga, and took one of them, Merofledis, for his second wife. In addition, he married Theudogildis, the daughter of a shepherd, followed by Marcoveifa, sister of Merofledis. He was then excommunicated for this (to little effect), not because he had remarried, but for being related to these women by marriage. Not until the death of Marcoveifa, interpreted as divine judgment, did this situation terminate.[62]

2. By the ninth century, everything had grown more difficult. The divorce of Lothar II achieved a degree of notoriety at a time when the Church had begun to pay more attention to the observation of marital vows.[63] In 855, Lothar married Thietberga, a lady of high nobility and the sister of the lay abbot Hucbert of St. Maurice. However, after 857, he persistently sought a divorce in order to marry his lover (and possible *Friedelfrau*) Waldrada, whom he had known from childhood and who was also of noble birth.[64] The degree to which love was involved, as insinuated by Regino of Prüm's chronicle, can no longer be ascertained. What remains certain, however, is the fact that Thietberga remained childless, whereas Waldrada had borne Lothar a son who, in the event of a marriage, would have succeeded him to an as-yet unsecured realm threatened by his uncles. (As a matter of fact, at this time the successor kingdoms were in the process of formation.) Since Thietberga's infertility was no longer sufficient grounds for divorce—the biblical example of Sarah who had borne Abraham a son at the age of ninety was frequently invoked in cases such as these—Thietberga was accused of incest with her brother. (People had to get rather dramatic in order to come up with sufficient grounds.) Although she managed to have the charges dismissed through an ordeal, she was still forced to make a confession, so the marriage ended in divorce after all. However, since remarriage was still out of the question, Lothar's marriage had to be annulled at the synod of Aachen in 862. Only then was Lothar able to marry Waldrada–or rather, attempts were made to pass her off as his legitimate wife while Thietberga fled to Western Francia and appealed to Pope Nicholas I. Archbishops Thietgaud of Trier and Gunthar of Cologne, who had presided over the divorce proceedings, were deposed by the papal legates despite the prior recognition of Lothar's marriage to Waldrada. By threatening to excommunicate him, the new legate, Bishop Arsenius of Orte, forced Lothar to take Thietberga back (865); still, the king managed to convince his wife to ask the pope to annul the marriage. Nicholas was only prepared to do so if both lived henceforth unmarried. Arsenius excommunicated Waldrada and forbade Lothar to all eternity from marrying her (866). In 867, after Nicholas

I's death, Lothar once again asked the new pope, Hadrian II, for a divorce. He went to Rome and submitted to the eucharistic ordeal to prove his innocence. Unfortunately, Lothar died on his way back, prior to a new synodal investigation. Contemporaries interpreted his death as a form of divine intervention. Lothar had not succeeded despite persistent attempts. In the Treaty of Meersen of 870, his kingdom was divided between his uncles Charles the Bald in the west, and Louis "the German" in the east, representing a step on the way to the emergence of the kingdoms of Germany and France.

3. Another famous example is the case of Otto of Hammerstein's marital problems in the early eleventh century.[65] This time, the marriage was threatened from outside against the will of the partners because they were too closely related; apparently they were related in the fourth degree. It did not seem unimportant that the Emperor, Henry II, disapproved of the marriage of the Conradian to Irmingard for political reasons—Otto and his family were among the emperor's opponents—as well as because of territorial disputes with the archbishop of Mainz. In 1018, a synod at Nijmegen excommunicated the couple because they refused to heed repeated summonses; needless to say, they disregarded the excommunication as well. A synod at Mainz in 1023 reached a less severe verdict because Otto was said to have mended his ways; indeed, at Seligenstadt, an attempt was made to calculate the degrees of relationship differently, while at the same time ruling out appeals to Rome. The fact is, the dispute took place against the background of a test of strength between the German episcopacy and the pope, to whom Irmingard had appealed. No sooner had the pope forbidden the archbishop of Mainz, Aribo, to wear the pallium, than a storm of protest broke loose among the German bishops. Ultimately, the proceedings against Otto of Hammerstein were quashed at the request of the new emperor, Conrad II.

4. A final example (as related by Lampert of Hersfeld) dates from the later eleventh century.[66] King Henry IV sought a divorce from his wife Bertha, but was unable to furnish sufficient grounds. He claimed that he was unable to consummate his marriage with her (*cum ea maritalis copiam habere*). In order to be able to marry again, he swore he had preserved his wife's virginity. Those present felt (according to Lampert) that this could not be reconciled with the king's dignity. However, when the princes and bishops seemed prepared to yield to the king at a synod at Mainz and dissolve the marriage, the papal legate, Peter Damiani, objected on grounds that no king was allowed to set such an un-Christian example. They agreed, and Henry had to keep his wife (who subsequently remained always at his side, even during his

famous pilgrimage to Canossa). Not until her death in 1087 was Henry able to marry again.

These four examples illustrate the development the indissolubility of marriage had undergone over the centuries. Divorces became more and more difficult; however, enforcement depended not only on the increasing influence of the Church, but also to a significant degree on political constellations. We know nothing about the frequency of divorce among lower social strata; yet if Church synods needed to deal with them time and again, they must have caused serious problems.

The fact that marriage and the household community were largely characterized in theory and legal practice by the husband's control has been explained. Consequently, it will be all the more important to examine more closely the role of the wife within the framework of the family.

3. The Wife

So much has been written recently about women in the Middle Ages that, for all the gaps in information, it will be impossible to summarize their position in medieval society briefly.[67] In order to be able to assess accurately the role of women within the family, it will be necessary to offer at least a few preliminary general observations.

It is a fact that, compared to men, medieval women were at a significant disadvantage. Women were excluded from the official Church and prevented from active participation in worship—though not from entering religious life.[68] In most cases they were prevented from holding public offices as well. Two things must be kept in mind here. First, being considered less worthy was not thought by the women themselves to be discrimination, but was accepted as natural; there was as yet no self-consciousness about emancipation. Women were considered different by nature. In his etymological encyclopedia, Isidore of Seville combined *vir* (man) with *virtus* (that is, ability, but also virtue!), but *mulier* (woman) with *mollitia* (that is, weakness, but also tenderness). Liutbirg, a nun living during the ninth century, could have been a master teacher, according to her biographer who admired her masculine strength, had the weakness of her sex not been in the way.[69] In general, handbooks used by the various classes distinguished between social functions (such as king, bishop, judge, peasant, etc.), while women were classified as a separate group with specific characteristics and habits. It is no accident that the "estate" of women tended to be placed near the bottom of the social hierarchy.[70]

On the other hand, the low social position of women did not imply disdain; rather, women were supposed to be honored in a special way and appreciated above all. Outright misogynous statements do not surface until the advent of middle-class literature. Protection and domination were mutually conditioning realities during the Middle Ages. A wife subject to her husband's *Munt* was under his authority, but she was also under his protection. Germanic tribal laws attest to a patriarchal family order, leaving marital life largely untouched. Instead, they sought to protect the wife from other men and their advances. Even the oldest Frankish tribal law, *the Pactus legis Salicae*, threatened high, graduated fines: anyone touching the finger of a free woman had to pay fifteen shillings, her arm drew a fine of thirty shillings, whoever went as far as the elbow was fined thirty-five shillings, anyone who as much as touched her breast to "the extent that blood would spurt forth" was fined forty-five shillings.[71] Alamannic law kept its scale of fines lower and no longer proscribed (painful) touching, but rather the undressing of a woman: he who uncovered the head of a free woman in the road *per raptum* (an act of "rape," that is to say, against her will) was fined three (or six) shillings;[72] lifting a woman's clothes to her knees drew a fine of six shillings; anyone who lifted them up high enough so that her genitals or her posterior (*vel posteria*) became exposed, had to pay twelve shillings; and a man who forced himself on a woman (*fornicaverit*) was assessed forty shillings. The rates doubled if the woman was married.[73] Widows in particular received protection from importunate men, especially during their thirty days of mourning.[74] Finally, pregnant women enjoyed special protection. Regulations such as these led only gradually to an improved legal position for women, and while they assured women of a degree of security before the law, women were still not equal here, since they required an advocate (*Vogt*) to represent their interests in court. Not until the appearance of municipal laws during the high Middle Ages were men and women treated equally before the law.[75]

The Germanic notion of women's need for protection accorded with the Christian doctrine, especially the teachings of Paul:[76] St. Paul taught that wives were to obey their husbands and receive love in return (Ephesians 5:22ff.). The favorite theological reason for the weaker legal position of women championed by the Church Fathers—by no means the Christian position from the beginning—was that Eve had been created from Adam's side and was the first person to be seduced by Satan. That is why medieval artists often portray women (as Eve) as instruments of the devil, especially during the period of the ecclesiastical reforms of the eleventh and twelfth centuries directed against the widespread practice of clerical marriage. In addition, our sources for this period, clerics and monks, understandably viewed women as the greatest obstacle in the way of their salvation, since women were prime instruments of temptation. One must, however, be cautious and avoid any large-scale social generalizations derived from these images and views.

As a matter of fact, the Christian image of women was not at all characterized by negative implications alone, considering that the sinfulness of Eve was contrasted with the purity of the Mother of God, Mary, whose veneration reached dramatic proportions during the later Middle Ages. Thus, artists portray women not only as victims of seduction, but also crushing the head of the serpent. The Church, too, is always portrayed as a woman, a crowned queen. The Christian view, which in turn is merely an expression of the spirit of the times, is therefore as responsible for the low position of women as it is for the high regard of them. During the twelfth century, the creation of woman was interpreted accordingly. According to Hugh of St. Victor, who understood marriage in terms of partnership, followed by Peter Lombard, God created woman not from the head of Adam so as to lord it over him, nor from his foot so that she might be his slave, but from his side so that she would stand beside him as his companion.[77] Moreover, chances for salvation were considered the same for both women and men. (Nevertheless, a count of the lives of saints handed down to us reveals that, with a few variations in dates, only fourteen percent of all saints were women. Most saintly women lived from the eighth to the early tenth century, with the fewest during the sixth and the eleventh centuries.[78]) The fact remains that women constituted an important factor in religious life. During the period of Christianization, women often were the first to accept the faith, subsequently converting their husbands. This was, for instance, the case with the Burgundian Chrodechilde and her husband, Chlodwig, the king of the Franks, an event crucial for the future direction of Western Civilization. Starting in the Carolingian period in particular, many women lived in convents and foundations,[79] where they received a certain degree of education. Several distinguished themselves through their scholarly writings, such as Hrotsvith of Gandersheim, Hildegard of Bingen, and Herrad of Landsberg. As superiors of a monastic *familia*, abbesses exercized political rights. Anyone who wishes to interpret the life of a nun as merely a flight from a male-dominated world[80] overlooks the fact that there were at least as many monks as there were nuns. The principal motivation here was undoubtedly piety. Women were also active participants in religious reform movements which began during the twelfth century,[81] as well as in the heresies to which they flocked in greater numbers when the official Church grew more rigid (Schulenburg). °

The courtly lyric (*Minnesang*) of the high Middle Ages served as another sign of high esteem for women, since it assigned a central position to ladies belonging to courtly society. Through the medium of courtly lyric, a lady, often well educated and well versed in contemporary literature, was able to turn her attention—in purely Platonic terms—to somebody other than her husband and accept a knight's services.

Jurisdiction, theology, and exclusion from ecclesiastical and political office combined to locate the woman's everyday activities not exclusively, but preferably and increasingly, within home and family. It goes without saying that one will have to differentiate between a queen or noble lady, a peasant woman, and a city woman—and again between a patrician woman, the wife of an artisan, or a female servant. (This will be discussed in later chapters.) During the sixth century, Venantius Fortunatus describes in his biography of St. Radegunde[82] how she wiped the floor, carried wood, built a fire, fetched water from the well, cooked, and did the dishes. Naturally, these were uncommon ascetic activities for Queen Radegunde, since noble ladies and wives of wealthy burghers were supposed to supervise such activities, but they must have been quite normal for a common woman, or her maidservants. Nevertheless, being tied to the home still did not make a woman a "housewife." The notion that a woman's primary duty was to look after her husband was not widespread until it was adopted by wealthy burghers during the later Middle Ages. A wife was thus integrated into the family enterprise, where she was responsible for clearly defined chores; these included working with textiles and, in the countryside, caring for animals. In addition, a wife was responsible for rearing children, attending the sick, and supervising anything which had to do with hygiene and bathing. There was indeed a division of labor according to sex. Miniatures depicting the story of creation on the famous Bernward door at Hildesheim (c. 1015) have Adam appearing with hoe in hand and ready to work the soil after the expulsion from Paradise, whereas Eve is portrayed nursing an infant under a canvas canopy in the shape of some sort of tent. (This depiction was in no way meant as a deprecation.) (See Illustration 6.) Later, hoe and distaff became symbols for male and female respectively. Despite the authority of the husband, the home was primarily considered the domain of the wife in an economic sense.

On a limited scale, women also participated in public life. Queens frequently moved around the country with the king and his court, and

Illustration 6: *Distribution of Roles according to Gender in Medieval Thought: Adam and Eve Following the Expulsion from Paradise* (from the Bible of Grandval, Tours c. 840).

they presided over the "chamber," the most "intimate" part of the court, including the entire court administration and royal treasury.[83] Whether in her house or at court, due to her role as her husband's deputy, the activities of the wife could definitely include political functions. Beginning with the late ninth century, the queen even drew up documents in her own name, intervened in the drafting of documents up to the period of the Hohenstaufen, and was frequently referred to as *consors regni*, participating in the king's rule.[84] Gisela, the wife of Conrad II, was particularly active in the government. Since kings were often still minors, the role of regent frequently rested with the king's mother, as was the case with the legendary Brunichild during the time of the Merovingians, Theophanu and Adelheid sharing the regency for Otto III or, finally, Agnes for Henry IV. No one apparently found fault with this practice.[85] (It was no accident that all the queens mentioned had come to Germany as foreigners.) The *Privilegium minus* of 1156 for the first time permitted female succession within the Austrian duchy. As a rule, a wife was able to dispose of her possessions with the assistance of an advocate, and she frequently took part in transfers of ownership,[86] although this tendency was perhaps reversed during Carolingian times.[87] However, she frequently acted on behalf of her husband, and in his absence she took care of all of his affairs. Based on their domestic function, high-ranking women thus managed to secure a place for themselves in public life. Widows, who apparently enjoyed special recognition by society, were able to act most independently, particularly so long as their children remained minors.

Nevertheless, full integration into the labor process did not lead to an emancipation of women during the Middle Ages. It seems characteristic of the times that women—perhaps more so during later centuries— were respected and held in high esteem socially, but the notion that women were weak by nature, needed protection, and were relatively without rights were not abandoned. The differences between the sexes were held to be a natural condition of creation's inviolable order.

4. Love and Sexuality

Love certainly played a role in the relationship between husband and wife, although one can hardly presume everyday marital life was characterized primarily by love. As already mentioned, according to medieval theory marriage was not purported to be the result, but rather a prerequisite for affection. "Love" (*amor, dilectio, caritas*) was a frequently used term during the Middle Ages, although it usually referred only to love of God and neighbor. At first, marital (or extramarital) love was mentioned merely in passing. This changed dramatically during the twelfth century when, as has been shown, love was rediscovered (Dinzelbacher). Its beginnings were once again rooted in the religious sphere. To be sure, "love of God" and human love cannot simply be equated, but a great number of texts with titles such as De diligendo Deo prove a change in mentality: God was no longer perceived only as the distant, impassive Lord of the World; rather, people wished to be close to him. Indeed, mysticism during the high Middle Ages transferred worldly love experiences into their visions, depicting encounters with God as if they were love affairs, including the exchange of deep kisses with God. Rupert of Deutz writes: "I was not satisfied until I touched him [God] with my hands, embraced him, and kissed him . . . I held him, embraced him, kissed him for a long time. I sensed how reluctantly he accepted these caresses—then he opened his lips so that I might kiss him all the more deeply."[88]

Of course, this is to be understood symbolically; yet according to medieval thought, symbols carried a much higher degree of reality than would be the case today. Incidentally, this new attitude was also reflected in art: in portrayals of the Madonna, the infant Jesus nestles close against his mother. In biblical exegesis, which was the most important theological discipline in the Middle Ages, the Song of Songs (*Cantica canticorum*), a collection of love songs (in which the bride impatiently awaited her bridegroom during the wedding night), then ranked among the most widely commented books of the Bible. Of course, this too was interpreted allegorically: Christ was the bridegroom, the Church his bride.

However, the rediscovery of love affected the "profane" realm as well. An increase in the distribution of manuscripts of Ovid during the twelfth century is particularly striking.[89] Above all, love developed into the central theme of high-medieval courtly literature. We will have to think primarily of courtly love poetry (*Minnesang*), which in its typical German form speaks of the rather secretive and unfulfillable, hence chaste love between a man and a married woman in her role as his lady-love. At times the lady was not even aware of his love; sometimes the singer was rewarded, but merely with a friendly glance or a fleeting kiss. The mood expressed in at least early German love poems is one of sadness: *liep âne leit mac niht sîn* (there cannot be love without suffering) was the motto, either because of the infidelity of the suitor, or because society had been too vigilant, preventing lovers from daring to pursue their love. Love (*Minne*) was often merely service for the sake of love, without any appropriate reward; this "knightly" love renounced the forceful conquest of a lady—or so it was idealized in lyric poetry.[90]

The epics of the high Middle Ages favored an equally idealized, though distinct portrayal of love: here a knight's courage is nourished by the love for his lady. Frequently the title-figures are couples, such as Erec and Enîte, or Tristan and Isolde. In contrast to courtly lyric poetry, love in these narratives quickly led to marriage. (That was also the intention behind the tragic love between Tristan and Isolde, except that the wrong partners happened to have drunk the love potion.) The story of Erec and Enîte, originally written by the premier French medieval epic poet Chrétien de Troyes and subsequently rendered into German by Hartmann von Aue, is typical of the genre: in the course of several adventures Erec, a prince, wins over the beautiful Enîte and marries her. Then, however, he became guilty according to the standards of the courtly code of ethics because he was so much in love that he failed in his knightly duties; Enîte even had to remind him of them herself. The two set out on a perilous journey, in the course of which Erec rediscovers his values, while at the same time recognizing the true nature of courtly love, which is love as a social responsibility. Certainly all of this must not be confused with everyday life, but courtly society was definitely groping for an ideal when it adopted such a concept of love. Even class distinctions had to be dropped (in literature) in the face of love, as the French "novel" of *Jehan et Blonde* illustrates. Here Jehan, an impoverished country squire, succeeds at great pains in abducting

Illustration 7: *Courtly Love* (Albrecht of Johannsdorf, The Great Heidelberg Song Manuscript, early fourteenth century).

and marrying his beloved pupil, Blonde, the daughter of a count, against her father's will. It is true, though, that in the story the social order was restored when the King made Jehan a count, thus making him an equal of Blonde: love "ennobles."

The fact that the labors of love were not merely components of unrealistic poetry is illustrated by the example of Duke William of Aquitaine, one of the first troubadours, who had himself banished by his bishop on account of his relationship with the Vicomtesse de Châteaurault, and then subsequently began a feud with him.[91] On the whole, "courtly society" was probably far less dominated by love than courtly literature might have us believe. In reality a man's pre- and extramarital affairs were far more tolerated than those of a woman, but German poetry appears to have consciously held up a love relationship directly at odds with this fact.[92] French literature, on the other hand, was frequently closer to reality. In fact, the lyrics of the troubadours contain allusions to physical love (called "base love," *niedere Minne*, in German literature). The genre of a *romanze* described the yearning of a maiden for her distant lover. The *pastourelle*, or shepherd's song, dealt mostly with a knight seducing a shepherdess, although the motif also occurs in modified forms: in one of the poems by Gavaron Grazelle, the knight is spent after having intercourse with the girl three times, and she subsequently ridicules him. In yet another poem the girl rapes the man, turning literature into parody.[93]

If we follow the poets, the beauty of a woman represented the primary reason for a man to fall in love despite any and all obstacles. (Enîte received several offers of marriage during her journey; Iwein fell in love at first sight with the widowed wife of his mortal enemy.) Certainly the medieval ideal of beauty had its own laws. In the twelfth century, a Cistercian monk described as beautiful, for instance, breasts "which are only slightly pointed and swell moderately."[94] Love even became the subject of didactic prose writings and scientific treatises without anybody being able sufficiently to explain the phenomenon. French teachings about love defined it simply as a "derangement of the mind,"[95] and a French cleric, Andrew the Chaplain, devoted an entire book to love (*De amore*). Here love was depicted with a mixture of scientific teaching and satire, and it was defined in the beginning as "an innate passion [or also an innate suffering: *passio quaedam innata*] which strikes when looking at, or when imagining inordinately, the appearance of the other sex." Accordingly, Andreas believed a blind man to be incapable of love. This passion "resulted in the irrepressible desire to embrace the other person and heed all the commands of love which spring forth from the mutual desire for the embrace."[96] "*Amare*" means to "seize"; he who is in love is imprisoned by the shackles of desire (1, 3). To Andrew, love is a "natural act" only between the two sexes (1, 2). It may evolve for several reasons, among which are figure, character, eloquence, wealth, and credulity (1, 6). The following two hundred pages contain—classified strictly according to social categories—dialogues providing guidelines for a love conversation, an initiative naturally the privilege of the male (though, he says, there are men who lose their speech at the sight of a woman). As for the rest, love follows certain rules, and Andrew enumerates a number of such rules: for instance, one ought to preserve the chastity of one's lover; one should not fall in love with someone else's wife or with a woman from a different social class, but only with one whom one would also want to marry. Andrew also examined the symptoms of love, such as jealousy, becoming pale, and throbbing of the heart at the sight of one's lover, or insomnia, or lack of appetite. Love can only take place between two human beings. Anybody with more than one lover does not truly love. Therefore, any new love will displace an older one. Love is not static; it either grows or vanishes. That is why Andrew describes, in a second book, how one can preserve love, or enhance perfect love even more (even if certain aids, such as dreaming of one's lover, will not necessarily suffice). Love becomes shattered as soon as trust is broken. Once this has happened, love cannot be revived again. Finally, Andrew cites a number of sentences handed down by the typical French "love court": during the high Middle Ages, love had become a subject of general fascination.

Concerning one's "everyday" (but not necessarily marital) love life, sexuality,[97] sources such as these remain peculiarly silent. Medieval poets frequently wear themselves out offering subtle allusions in this regard. "Why should I describe something that is familiar to everybody anyway?" asks the author of the story of "Moritz von Craûn."[98] Frank disclosures such as those in the "Ruodlieb" narrative,[99] in which an elderly husband surprises his wife in the embrace of her youthful lover, were rare:

> One hand was reaching for her breasts,
> while the other had disappeared up her leg
> Though she hid it with her dress,
> making sure it was covered well.

Prior to that, the poet relates the following conversation between two lovers (7, 85f.):

"I am asking for my reward:
yield to me three times today!"
She answered: "If you are able to do it ten times
and if you want to do it more often, go right ahead!"

One of the provisions of the Council of Tribur of 895 offers a rather
explicit description of intercourse: the woman is being "perforated by
the spikes of lust" (*libidinis perforata aculeis*).[100] More information,
but on entirely different authority, is supplied by the penitentials of the
Church:[101] not intended to depict reality, but rather, to lay out penalties
for sexual infractions. Thereby something that was to be hidden made its
appearance and therefore part of reality, even if we know little concerning its details. Every sexual activity depended on two conditions: marital
community and the intention of procreation, since even the sperm was
held to be a creature not to be wasted.[102] Thus, according to the will of
the Church, not only extramarital practices, but masturbation and homo-
sexual activities were proscribed as being "unnatural" (*contra naturam*).
What this meant concretely cannot be easily determined, since such
offences were all subsumed under the rubric of fornication. According
to Regino's handbook, women who masturbated or committed lewd acts
with others were to do penance for three years, for seven years if they
were nuns. Men were similarly punished if they penetrated "from behind" (*a tergo*); they had to do penance for one year if they "committed
lewdness between the thighs" (inter femora fornicantes).[103] Here, like
everywhere else, homosexuality—often referred to as "sodomy"—was
neither punished more severely, nor held in greater disdain than other
"offenses." The question of whether homosexuality was widespread—
especially in clerical circles—during the high Middle Ages, and whether
it was widely tolerated, as has been recently asserted,[104] can hardly
be settled, since the evidence (mostly from poetry) attests at best to
homoerotic inclinations. People considered "unnatural" any number of
abnormal "positions" even during heterosexual intercourse, for instance,
when the man lay on his back (*retro*), since this was apparently viewed
as detrimental to procreation, though it only drew a mild penalty (in
most cases forty days). On the other hand, oral and anal intercourse
(*in tergo*) were severely punished. Regino likened that to "sodomy,"
assessing a penance of three years. Other penitentials demanded the
same amount of penance as for premeditated murder, seven years.

If procreation was to be the purpose of marital intercourse, then
any attempt to prevent conception also had to be forbidden. Penitentials
mention a number of such methods, among them onanism (*coitus
interruptus*, in reference to Onan in Genesis 38:9), and particularly

the use of herbal potions; the latter poured into the vagina prior to or following intercourse, apparently the most common form of birth control. Only abstinence was permitted by the Church. Conversely, aphrodisiacs were also prohibited. Here, too, human imagination knew no limits. Thus, we read that semen was to be mixed in with the food of a woman, or menstrual blood into that of a man.[105] Abortion was known and forbidden, though the methods were anything but modern: again, herbal potions were supposed to accomplish the desired result.[106] The tenth-century decree of Burchard of Worms reduced the amount of punishment if the mother acted because of poverty.[107]

Ironically, while Church regulations had forbidden any form of birth control, they also (unintentionally) restricted the frequency of births through rules demanding abstinence during a number of ecclesiastical holy days (Advent, all of Lent, the week preceding Pentecost, Sundays, partly also on Wednesdays and Fridays, as well as before and after taking communion). Moreover, abstinence was the penance of choice for sexual offences. Finally, intercourse was prohibited during menstruation, during and after pregnancy, and, occasionally, even on the wedding night. Prohibitions such as these stemmed primarily from an imagined uncleanness rather than a desire to protect women, whose sexual needs received hardly any attention. Besides, Liudprand of Cremona, a historian at the Ottonian court during the tenth century, had already related the story of a Greek woman who let Duke Tedbald of Spoleto have a piece of her mind, since he wanted to have enemy prisoners—including her husband—castrated. In doing so, she argued, war was being waged not against the men, but against their wives. In fact, the duke ought to feel free to blind them, cut off their noses, hands, or feet, for these were part of a man's own body, but never their testicles, since these belonged to their wives and served both their gratification and the procreation of children.[108] Liudprand, to be sure, reported this anecdote as an amusing exception (*ludibrium*).

We have already learned in the course of our discussion of the various forms of marriage that extramarital intercourse was, indeed, quite common, particularly in higher circles. Liudprand of Cremona, who had little love for Italian kings, reports that King Hugo of Italy refused to have intercourse with his wife, instead, turning to his numerous concubines, three of whom he found especially delightful: by Pezola, a serf, he had a son whom he later elevated to the bishopric of Piacenza, by Roza he had a daughter, and by Stephanie he had a son who rose to become archbishop of Milan. "And since the king had not been the only one intimate with them [concludes Liudprand], their children were fathered by unknown men."[109] The same Liudprand describes the life of Marozia, who gave birth to a son fathered by a pope (Sergius). She later had the son elected pope[110] after allying herself with Margrave Wido of Spoleto, who happened to rule the city of Rome. Yet this is hardly typical of normal everyday life. All the same, practice hardly comported fully to canon law regulations, or there surely would not have been any need for threatening such punishments described if the respective "offenses" had not existed.

5. The Children

Despite the periods of abstinence that had been imposed on people (but certainly not always heeded), and in spite of various efforts at birth control, most marriages were fertile. Sufficient scientific explanations for birth were almost non-existent. It was believed that both the male and female ejaculated sperm during orgasm. The excess female sperm was thought to be gathered up and excreted during menstruation; it was up to this point that a woman's sexual appetite was supposed to keep increasing. During the twelfth century, William of Conches explains the infertility of women as the result of a specific composition of their bodily fluids.[111] If the sperm ended up in the right half of the uterus, the result was thought to be a boy, and if it lodged in the left half of the uterus, a girl. Whenever the sperm was lodged close to the center, the boy was thought to possess female and the girl masculine traits.[112] Yet according to Hildegard of Bingen, the gender and character of offspring depended on the intensity of love and the strength of the sperm; only if the sperm was strong and love was mutual would a strong, smart, and virtuous boy be born.[113]

Although hardly the rule, there certainly were families with many children. Charlemagne had eighteen children—by eight different women, to be sure—nine of them by his second wife, Hildegard, though only six survived. Charles's successors had considerably fewer children, and, as is well known, the male line of the Carolingians eventually died out. Frederick I Barbarossa had eleven or twelve children (by two wives), of whom only nine survived; his grandson, Frederick II, had ten children by four wives, yet two generations later, the male line of the Hohenstaufen died out. Thus, even a relatively large number of children in itself could not assure the continuation of a family. Besides, such a large number of children was only possible because upper-level males frequently married several times, especially since, as mentioned earlier, women tended to die at an early age. Consequently, husbands were frequently older than their wives. Frederick I Barbarossa's second wife, Beatrix, was between twelve and fourteen years of age when the forty-four-year-old emperor married her. According to measurements taken on the pubic bones of female skeletal remains—providing that it will be in order to list the statistical results in fractions—an individual woman gave birth to 4.2 children, though this was merely an average. Many women died during childbirth before they reached this average, while others bore a significantly higher number of children. Because of miscarriages and a high infant mortality, the actual number of children in a family was lower. More than 50 percent of those buried in certain cemeteries were children under the age of seven, and it is doubtful that infants who died before they were baptized were even buried properly prior to the tenth century. Later, the non-baptized were not buried facing east, since they could not participate in eternal life, according to the views of the Church. Recently three cemeteries in Zürich from the seventh to the eleventh century were examined for infant mortality.[114] No infants had been buried in the two older cemeteries. At the Münster cemetery, there were twenty-four stillbirths and neonates (children who died on the day of their birth) (= 14.4 percent), eight infants (up to one year of age) (= 4.8 percent), and forty-five children and youths (up to the age of 18) (= 27 percent). Thus, 19 percent of the children died before they reached the age of two, and an additional 27 percent died up to the age of eighteen. Only 54 percent survived and grew up to be adults (in our sense of the word).[115] In summary we may conclude that the families could not have been all that large. On an average, they probably consisted of the parents and two or three surviving children. Indeed, this corresponds accurately to the much-discussed, generally complete numbers provided by the polyptych of Saint-Germain-des-Prés near Paris of c. 820: these peasant families had—if one only counts the couples and parents with children—an average of merely 2.5 children at home at any given moment.[116] Rarely did they have nine or more children.

It is striking that there was an unnaturally large surplus of sons at Saint-Germain (144:100), a ratio which could not have occurred naturally. The traditional explanation for this fact, namely that girls were more likely to be killed at birth if one could no longer feed them—the number of girls, moreover, increased at larger farmsteads with a larger nutritional base[117]—has been received with much skepticism.[118] There is no doubt that infanticide existed; in fact, some Germanic tribal laws even permitted the practice, usually for girls. As late as the ninth century in his *Vita Liudgeri*, Altfrid reports [119] an early pagan practice among the Frisians permitting the killing of infants before they had begun nursing. At the request of his great-grandmother, Liudger's mother was supposed to have been drowned by a servant, but she was miraculously kept alive. We already mentioned a father who wanted to slay his child during a famine. Reports such as these are rare, however, and we certainly ought not to overestimate the number of infanticides, nor should we allow ourselves to explain the absence of children from early medieval cemeteries by the fact that a large number of babies had been murdered.[120] On the other hand, synods dealt with mothers who had accidentally squeezed their children to death in their sleep.[121] With increasing frequency, infants who could no longer be fed were abandoned, typically at church entrances, according to the synodal reports. Thus, there was a sizeable number of orphans, and not just as a result of the death of their parents.

Nevertheless, the previously held view that children were generally perceived to be a burden and little loved has been refuted. Burial with tombstones and the preserved letters of consolation written to parents whose children had died[122] contradict such a theory. By the tenth century at the latest, small children were considered full-fledged members of society. Indeed, art historians have long held that children were not treated like children, but rather, were viewed and treated as "little adults."[123] If, in the twelfth century, Christ is increasingly portrayed as a child, this undoubtedly points to a change in mentality. However, the adult facial expressions of Christ and the childlike portrayals in saint's lives can in any case also be explained by the fact that early maturity was consciously emphasized here as exceptional. On the whole, there can be little doubt that children were treated lovingly and were permitted to engage in children's games. It is also true, however, that childhood ended much earlier than nowadays, since the idea was to raise children to be adults as quickly as possible. Thus, raising children to be adults was an important task that began at a very tender age. Small children were completely committed to the care of their mothers or a nurse. Childhood ended by age six or seven at the latest, and education took over. Einhard tells us about the education of Charlemagne's children.[124] Initially, they were all instructed in liberal studies to provide a basic education. Then the sons learned how to ride, use weapons, and hunt, while the daughters learned to spin. One may assume that this was typical of the way children of noble families were educated, since they needed to master weapons as quickly as possible.[125] To be sure, lay education remained a privilege of the uppermost families prior to the twelfth century, while the children of peasants had to pitch in very early. Because majority was to begin at twelve (according to Salic law), children were considered adults at this age; by the high Middle Ages, sons of noble families were eligible for knighthood at age twelve, and princes could begin their ruling. Only clerics required a longer education, since, as a rule, nobody could be ordained a priest prior to the age of thirty. The spiritual form of life experienced by monks will occupy us during the ensuing chapter. A monk could not establish a family in the sense described here; still, the monastic community as a whole reveals features of a family structure and family life.

Monasteries and Monastic Life

Monastic life represents the most important form of religious life during the Middle Ages. Considering the constant influence it exerted on the rest of society, its significance is almost impossible to overestimate. Originating as a form of lay life, it purposely separated itself from the hierarchial Church, yet monasticism soon became a component of a Church which played a much more significant role during the Middle Ages than it does today. Monks formed, in a sense, a third estate located between clergy and laity, yet their form of life became a model for both clerical and lay communities. The great number alone of monks and monasteries in itself testifies to this significance. Unlike today, monasticism was by no means a peripheral phenomenon. Monks were not considered social outsiders; rather, they constituted a normal, necessary institution fully integrated into society. It may be surprising to realize that an age experiencing such massive food shortages could afford to support so many monks who produced little themselves, so that they had to be sustained in addition to everybody else. On the other hand, this fact in itself actually corroborates the relevance of monasticism. The Christian Middle Ages supported monasticism so monks could pray for the others. As far as social status was concerned, monks enjoyed great respect; indeed, monasticism was widely held to be the most perfect of form of life. In keeping with this status, the influence of monasteries and their abbots on religious, cultural, social, political, and even economic life was great, while the monastery itself remained for the most part an almost independent entity. In addition, monasteries for a long time were the most important centers of education. Education, which after Carolingian days and throughout the high Middle Ages was largely reserved for members of the clergy and monks, took place mainly at monasteries. During the earlier Middle Ages, schools attached to bishoprics and collegial churches existed side by side with them. It was not until the later Middle Ages that universities emerged which would only gradually manage to rid themselves of Church supervision. The role of monasteries necessarily extended beyond the religious realm, since religion was a much more integral part of everyday life than is the case today. The monasticism of the Middle Ages was not only a mere component of the Church, but also of the "world," above all the world of the ruling classes. Joachim Wollasch entitled his book on medieval monasticism *Monasticism of the Middle Ages Between the Church and the World*. Despite their original intent, not even monasteries were able to escape the mingling of secular and clerical affairs so typical of the Middle Ages. In a manner of speaking, medieval monasticism was a lordly life in grand style, albeit in religious form. Therein lay a significant portion of its success, as well its historical significance. Nevertheless, this secular aspect contradicted the originally religious goals and led to perennial conflicts. Before we can discuss monastic life as such, it will be useful to offer an overview of the eventful history and the functions of this institution.

1. The Institution:
Benedictine Monasticism in the West

The History of Medieval Monasticism

Beginnings and Benedictine Monasticism. Monasticism arose from a desire for asceticism (ασκειυ = to exercise; *exercitium* is the term used in Latin sources). Monasticism represents "exercise" in the battle against sin and the world. It arose out of the desire for a genuinely religious life through the imitation of Christ and poverty, and indeed monks referred to themselves as *pauperes Christi*. Therefore, ever since the third century, monasticism's essential characteristic has been its separation from the remainder of the Christian community. Monasticism evolved in two forms in the East (Palestine, Syria, Asia Minor and Egypt): either as the life of a hermit, a solitary life marked by self-denial and seclusion; or as the life of *cenobitism* first propagated by Pachomius (†346) in Egypt, a form of religious communal life which is the dominant form of Western monasticism. The main characteristic of cenobitism was the *vita communis* (life in a community), and eremitic life frequently led to such a monastic life. This community perceived itself as a "family." However, community life demanded strict control under an abbot (*abba*), the "father" of the family, and under a discipline which soon became obligatory in the form of a series of monastic rules. Life in keeping with a common rule led to unification of forms of life, and soon monastic orders emerged. While the rule of Basil of Caesarea (c. 330-379) became an early guideline for Byzantine monastic orders, the West experienced a proliferation of private monasteries during the second half of the fourth century. Still, from the very beginning these were embedded in the organization of the Church. Among the many rules of the fifth century, we must especially mention the Rule of St. Augustine, the *Rule of the Master*, and the Rule of St. Benedict of Nursia (c. 480-c. 560), which derived, probably somewhat later, from the *Rule of the Master* and was destined to point the way for Western, or rather "Benedictine," monasticism. The Rule arose out of the great rush to communities founded by Benedict, first at Subiaco in the Anio Valley and then at Monte Cassino, and a subsequent need for strict regulation; of course, centuries were to pass before it would become the sole valid monastic rule of the West.

In the beginning, medieval monasticism entered western Europe via Southern Gaul. There, in particular, two forms of monastic life gained in popularity. The first was Martinian monasticism, which relied on Bishop Martin of Tours (†397), patron saint of the Frankish kingdom. This form sought active involvement in the world; it had neither a geographic center, nor a definite rule, yet, originating in Aquitaine, it exercised great influence on all of France.[1] Even more important was the so-called Rhûne monasticism, with principle centers at Marseille (St. Victor) and on the island of Lérins. Lérins was a monastery founded in 410 by refugee aristocrats from Northern Gaul who had been expelled by the Franks, and it was instrumental in developing Western monasteries into institutions occupied by the nobility. It exerted an equally strong influence on the remaining Frankish kingdom in the course of the sixth century due to its literary activities. Initially, education was considered detrimental to Christian life; thus, it took some time for the Church to embrace at least that part of the education of antiquity indispensable for faith and theological studies. The Church subsequently became the prime vehicle for passing the culture of antiquity into Western Civilization; in doing this, monasticism played a decisive role. During the fifth and sixth centuries, education had become a significant aspect in Church and religion. Many bishops, even popes (such as Pope Gregory the Great), came from the ranks of monks, and close ties between monastery and diocese promoted a continual expansion of monasticism. Some monks received ordination and could be called on to serve parishes. Yet, as important as their incorporation into the official Church may have been, patronage from kings and nobility was equally significant, since monasteries would not have succeeded without their support. During the seventh century, Northern Gaul all the way to the Rhine came to be densely populated with monasteries, especially in the Moselle and Meuse regions. After 690, new monasteries were established beyond the Rhine.

The monasticism of Gaul underwent renewal as a result of the activities of the Irish and Anglo-Saxon missionaries. Irish missionaries, referred to as "Scoti" by medieval sources, had developed their own form of ecclesiastical life, with the monastery as its center. The abbot also served as bishop or was superior to the bishop. Irish missions were inspired by the ideal of *peregrinatio*, experiencing an "ascetic homelessness"[2] which entailed cutting all ties to family, homeland, even one's own monastery, thus encouraging continuous travel. The first and most important representative on the continent was Colomba, who (after c. 590), driven by his disapproval of the Frankish kings, founded several monasteries in succession: Annegray, Luxeuil, and Fontaine in France, then Bregenz in Alamannia and finally Bobbio in the Lombard kingdom in Italy. These monasteries—especially Luxeuil—extended their influence further by founding a number of affiliated monasteries of their own. The strict monastic rule of Columban the Younger had further impact, although its full effect was not felt until the "second generation," no longer composed solely of Irishmen but also of Franks driven by Irish missionary fervor (called Iro-Franks).[3]

The second wave of missionaries came from Anglo-Saxons affiliated with Rome, whose most famous representative, Boniface, founder of the monastery at Fulda, was commissioned to organize the Frankish Church in Germany, an act of great importance for posterity. The intimate joining of monastery and bishopric in one place was also typical of the Anglo-Saxons.[4] The bishop was also abbot, but this time it was the bishopric which was the decisive institution. Monasticism owes its expansion east of the Rhine all the way to Bavaria to Anglo-Saxon missionaries. Under their influence, there was a movement toward simplification. Although monasteries had hitherto adhered to a mixed rule, since the seventh century Gallic synods had demanded that everyone follow the Benedictine Rule alone. The Rule of St. Benedict was known as the "Roman rule," probably finding its way into the Frankish kingdom through the efforts of Pope Gregory the Great and Columban the Younger himself.[5] This development culminated under Louis the Pious as a result of the reforms of Benedict of Aniane. This abbot of Aquitaine, born Witiza, who specifically tried to draw attention to Benedict of Nursia by adopting his name, succeeded in enforcing the exclusive acceptance of the Benedictine Rule in the entire realm at three synods at Aachen between 816 and 819. It is only now that we may speak of Benedictine monasticism, although the process of adoption took the entire ninth century to complete in some areas. The Benedictine Rule was augmented by what were called *consuetudines*, administrative regulations to clarify whatever Benedict had omitted or failed to express with sufficient clarity; these regulations, however, were far less unified, and on certain specific issues they were hotly disputed.[6]

Monastic Reforms and New Religious Orders. Benedict of Aniane stood at the beginning of a series of monastic reforms. These reforms arose from a concern about the discrepancy between the religious goals of monasticism and its social function. Despite the typically medieval symbiosis of religion and society, monasticism periodically needed to take stock of its traditional goals.[7] Wherever a monastery neglected its religious obligations, it no longer served its purpose and had to be reformed. The history of monasticism is therefore also a history of monastic reforms which, far from being directed against secular rulers, were often carried out by them, even against the will of the monks. Ultimately, Benedict's reform spirit did not last very long; monastic discipline soon began to slacken in many places, giving rise to a new wave of reforms as early as the beginning of the tenth century from two centers: one center was in Burgundy, where the influential monastery of Cluny was established in 909/910, and the other was in Lorraine (at Brogne near Namur, Dijon, and above all at Gorze near Metz, which exercised substantial influence far into the German realm). While these different movements were subsumed under the rubric of the "Cluniac reform movement,"[8] Kassius Hallinger has made us aware of the autonomy of the individual reform efforts, which sometimes expressed completely opposed ideas, differing also in the attire worn by their proponents. It was at Cluny that the "black monks" arose, with the ample, wide, long-sleeved cowled frock (*froccus*) which became the general standard for monastic garb. These reforms owed their effectiveness to the active support of secular lords: Brogne belonged to its lord Gerard, who was also abbot at the monastery, and Cluny was founded by Duke William I (the Pious) of Aquitaine who, by relinguishing the honor of becoming the abbot, retained his rights as advocate, thus creating a model for the future. The nobleman no longer became a lay abbot, a spiritual father, as had frequently been the case in late-Carolingian times;[9] rather, befitting his social status, he was advocate and hence secular protector of the monastery. This function was connected with further rights and additional incomes, leaving the religious-spiritual sphere of the monastery untouched. In this fashion, a nobleman gained a share in the religious process without having to relinquish his own rights. Monasteries, in turn, were integrated even more strongly into the life of the nobility: the nobility made extensive donations and, in exchange for them, accommodated members of their families as *conversi* (literally "converts") in the monasteries, supplying monks who entered the religious life at an advanced age rather than in their youth.[10] Generally speaking, monks came increasingly from the ranks of the nobility, until monasteries came to accept only noblemen. This class-bound aspect of the reform, the aristocratization of monasticism, ran parallel to its spiritual aspect, which was the Christianization of the nobility and their reception of religious movements.[11]

In terms of content, these reforms constituted a revival of order and stricter observance of the rule, which everywhere had been augmented by customs, *consuetudines*, resulting in diverse interpretations and adaptation to changing needs. Most of the time, enforcement and propagation of reform took place through the appointment of a new, more respected abbot to a monastery needing reform, and by assuring that at least some monks came from a monastery which had already been reformed, whose consuetudines were also adopted. This practice did not always succeed without resistance from the old monks, who were naturally disinclined to relinquish their more pleasant lives. Often they actually had to be expelled.[12] At the beginning of the eleventh century, Thietmar of Merseburg polemicized against the investiture of a reform abbot at the monastery of Berge in conjunction with a monastic reform championed by King Henry II, saying, "As a matter of fact, people praised for novel appearance in both attire and manner are often not what they pretend to be."[13] Nevertheless, the triumphant advance of the reform could not be stopped. Branching out from monasteries already reformed, affiliated monasteries emerged; Gorze alone initiated ten such affiliated groups, although this is a rather simplistic description of the actual situation, since most monasteries had several "fathers" and assembled their own "monastic customs." Cluny alone gradually developed a special form, because all monasteries reformed by it remained under the rule of the abbot of Cluny, not subject to the authority of their own abbots; rather, these monasteries were headed by a prior.[14] In this fashion, a closely knit association of Cluniac monasteries emerged, consisting of sixty-four monasteries at the time of Odilo (first half of the eleventh century). At their peak, there were far more than a thousand monasteries, almost nine hundred in France alone. In the German Empire, Cluny had little success for years, in contrast to the reform that spread from Gorze and its filial foundation of St. Maximin in Trier; both Gorze and St. Maximin kept a rather open mind toward the

Ottonian system of a national church and did not violate any sovereign rights. Here, too, Cluny had taken a separate course when William of Aquitaine placed his monastery directly under the pope's authority. (Admittedly, the process of its actual extrication from episcopal rule lasted over a hundred years.) Cluny did not oppose the concepts of either a proprietary church or feudalism; nor did it prepare the way for the struggle over investiture, as once held. However, the new, ascetic religiousness in which the Cluniacs played a substantial role ultimately merged with the great eleventh-century ecclesiastical reform, which was in essence a struggle over investiture. Characteristically, it was at this particular point in time that Cluny gained its first foothold in the Empire when the Swabian monastery of Hirsau was reformed about 1080 via the Italian monastery of Fruttuaria.[15] Once again, reformed monasteries fulfilled a political purpose as well: they were mostly dynastic monasteries of rising princes who joined forces against the system of the imperial Church as well as against the king.[16] Again, different approaches ensued. According to Lampert of Hersfeld, Siegburg, a monastery established by the archbishop of Cologne, Anno II,[17] influenced Lorraine and all of France, the original centers of the reform.[18] It seems there were some monasteries already in need of reform in that area. At the same time, the individual reform parties vied with one another, and Lampert polemicized against the monks at Siegburg, against whom he had been unable to prevail with his own ideas at Saalfeld.[19]

Although such reforms were inspired by old ideals, a truly novel, decisive wave of reforms (based on the revived ideal of eremetism and poverty) emerged in reaction to the wealthy monastic communities toward the end of the eleventh and into the twelfth centuries. These monks recalled the old ideal of solitude, desiring to lead an "evangelical" or "apostolic" life. The success of individual attempts rendered regulation necessary (mostly during the second generation of monks), and the promulgation of rules led to the creation of new religious orders. The Camaldolensians, established by Romuald of Ravenna at Camaldoli near Arezzo (1023/26), and the Carthusians, founded by Canon Bruno of Cologne at Chartreuse near Grenoble (1084), both combined the ideas of an eremitic life with that of cloistered cenobitism. Each monk occupied a house of his own, but it was connected to the church and community rooms. The most important of these new orders was undoubtedly the Cistercians,[20] whose artless, uniform churches lacking an extensive narthex bore external witness to the ideal of poverty. In 1070, Robert established a monastery at Molesme (near Cluny), then a monastery at Cîteaux in 1098 (south of Dijon) which he appropriately named *Novum monasterium*. No firm rule emerged until the third abbot, the Englishman Stephen Harding (1108-1133) wrote one in form of his Charta caritatis, which emerged in stages. Frequently there were twin houses, one for monks and one for nuns. Excluded from full admission were the so-called converts, lay brothers with various social backgrounds who initially outnumbered the monks; these led a communal life without fully qualifying as monks. They had their own living quarters, worshiped in assigned areas in the church, and functioned essentially as servants and workers for the monks, providing the monks with contact to the outside world, especially in the areas of agriculture, crafts, nursing, business, or administration.[21] Still, at least in the beginning, the monks themselves professed the old work ethic, for the oldest statutes at Cîteaux stipulated, "Members of our order must work for a living, till the land, and raise animals."[22] Many a book miniature shows a Cistercian monk clearing or working the land. (See Illustration 8.) The vow of poverty forbade all income from outside sources so that monasteries had to rely on highly self-sufficient farms managed by converts. In contrast to the general development of the manorial system, these individual granges pursued autonomy and developed into model farms because of their surpluses and a properly designed policy for land acquisition, testifying to the Cistercians' substantial participation in agricultural innovation during the high Middle Ages.[23] By establishing branches which, in turn, founded additional Cistercian communities, or by adding established monasteries by reforming them, the order quickly spread all over Europe from its original center between the rivers Seine, Saône, and Meuse. By 1153 there were 344 Cistercian communities in existence (Clairvaux alone founded 66 of them), while the formerly important imperial monasteries were now populated by only a few monks. Because of that most important of Cistercian monks, Bernard of Clairvaux, the twelfth century is properly referred to as the "Cistercian age." Individual Cistercian communities deliberately appointed abbots of their own, in conscious contrast to the "old" monasticism of earlier-reformed orders such as the Cluniacs. They also formed an association of monasteries remaining closely linked to Cîteaux, where the annual general chapter of all Cistercian abbots convened as its highest authoritative body. The distinction between these communities and older monasteries was also reflected in the simple, undyed attire which made Cistercians "white" monks, in contrast to the "black" Cluniacs.

Contrary to practices under Benedict of Aniane, even more than the reforms of the tenth century, this reform did not result in uniformity, but, in further splintering monasticism. Since the Cluniacs did not surrender easily, a bitter doctrinal struggle ensued over the better way to salvation, the true *vita religiosa*. In his *Apologia ad Guillelmum*

Illustration 8: *Reformed Monks: A Cistercian Harvesting Grain* (Manuscript of Augustine, Citeaux, twelfth century: initial for the letter Q).

abbatem, Bernard of Clairvaux accused Cluniacs of disregarding the monastic rule and of eating and drinking too much. He alleged that healthy monks preferred to rest in sickbeds, since they received meat to eat there. He faulted their rich attire (their habits were supposedly fashioned from the same cloth as knights' raiments), their ornate architecture and expensively appointed churches and monasteries, brimming with gold and silver utensils, as well as the princely retinue of up to sixty horsemen which followed their abbots. He chided the abbots for acting like lords of castles (*domini castellorum*) rather than fathers to their monasteries (*patres monasteriorum*), territorial princes (*principes provinciarum*) rather than shepherds of souls (*rectores animarum*). Peter the Venerable, abbot of Cluny, responded by saying that the proper concern of monks was the kind of love (*caritas*) which could only be found in traditional monasticism, and he accused the Cistercians of inhumane rigidity.[24] Canon law had to decide whether it was permitted to change from one order to another, usually only permitting transfers to a stricter order. The struggle for the proper way, as well as the diversity of forms of life within monasticism, were typical of the twelfth century, which learned to accept heterogeneity. Bishop Anselm of Havelberg expressly justified the various forms of religiosity as equal paths to salvation, and the Cistercian bishop Otto of Freising concluded his chronicle with a praise of monasticism regardless of direction; it was only because of monasticism, he contended, that God had postponed the overdue end of the world.[25] Monastic reforms found a response among the clergy; new religious orders of canons regular such as the Praemonstratensians, or the Augustinian canons, revived the traditional ideal of the *vita communis*.

It was, ironically, their material success which was soon to enrich the Cistercians in ways they had previously denounced. By the end of the twelfth century, western monasticism once again demanded new reforms, in ways which would create still further differentiation. The point of departure was once again the ideal of poverty. Poverty was now to be implemented in an entirely different direction by the mendicant friars, who demanded poverty not only for individual monks, but for the monastery as well. They made the sermon the center of their mission, and they purposely relocated their ministry in towns, which had been intentionally avoided by traditional monasticism. Mendicants thus symbolically illustrated the change from dynastic monasticism to a monasticism serving the bourgeoisie. During the late Middle Ages, mendicants became champions of pastoral care, scholarship, and the struggle against heretics (inquisition); however, that subject goes well beyond the chronological parameters of this study. This survey of the history of monasticism clearly demonstrates that we must not imagine it as an appeal to a single rule. Beyond diversity of expression, monastic life was also shaped by the various functions of the monastery within early medieval and high medieval German society, which now deserve attention.

The Function of Monasteries

Founding a Monastery. According to the stereotyped narrative of lives of saints, early monks and abbots located their cells at places in the wilderness as inaccessible as possible, utterly removed from civilization; indeed, monasticism symbolized a renunciation of the "civilized" world. Columbanus the Younger founded his monastery Luxeuil in a desolate region where he had discovered the ruins of an ancient Roman fortification, inhabited only by wild animals.[26] Even if they only made a symbolic statement, such "solitudes" were typical only in the beginning. Important monasteries such as Luxeuil soon evolved into much-frequented centers. In Gaul, for example, when not located inside the towns themselves, they were often just outside the town walls. The early history of the monastery of St. Gall is typical in many respects: in 612, after seeking a secluded spot, the Iro-Frankish monk Gallus (a pupil of Columbanus the Younger) established near the Steinach river a cell which was subsequently named after him. His biography tells of miraculously victorious struggles with bears, symbolizing the remote nature of the place; it also tells of "inner" struggles against the temptations of Satan, in the guise of naked water-nymphs he drove away.[27] The second phase began over one hundred years later and, as was the case with many other monasteries, was influenced by secular considerations from the very beginning. About 724, Walram, a nobleman and tribune of Arbongau on Lake Constance, established a monastery on his property at the site of St. Gall's old cell; it was soon to become a center for the Alamanni. By the time the Franks had established themselves in Alamannia, Abbot Otmar (from Chur-Rhaetia, as was typical) had handed the monastery over to Pepin, the first Carolingian king. Disputes ensued with the Frankish counts, Warin and Ruthard, who had been duly installed, and they subsequently arrested the abbot. The abbot died in exile (a reason to canonize him later, particularly since his body was found still intact ten years after his death). In addition, the monastery had to brace itself for disputes with the diocese of Constance, which also registered its claims. Soon after, when Abbot John (759-781) became bishop of Constance, St. Gall claimed the status of a tributary monastery belonging to the bishop. Not until 854 was the tribute suspended with the treaty of Ulm, done in the presence of the king. By then, the monastery had become a royal monastery under the supreme lordship of the king.

The history of St. Gall vividly illustrates the phases of a monastery's development as well as the influence the secular world exerted on it: monasteries without lords were only conceivable during the early days of medieval monasticism. Irish and Anglo-Saxon missionaries in particular sought ties with the royal house and the high nobility from the very beginning, and their monasteries were fully integrated into Frankish imperial culture.[28] Later foundings developed differently from the pattern of Luxeuil or St. Gall. When Bishop Luidger of Münster, for example, wanted to found a monastery, he first traveled to Rome and Monte Cassino, returning with the Benedictine Rule and relics. After searching for a suitable site, he finally decided on Werden on the river Ruhr and after 799 began acquiring the property through purchase, barter, and donations to begin constructing the monastery and church. Until the buildings' completion, monks lived in tents.[29] Although the forest had yet to be cleared at Werden, soon one could no longer call it a genuine place of solitude. For instance, during the Carolingian period Saxon nunneries were all ideally situated along trade routes, in the vicinity of a castle. This characterized their relationship to the family of the donor and their incorporation into the politico-territorial complex of the nobility.[30] Bavarian monasteries were also well situated, with links to their individual properties, primarily along rivers and lakes and (in their role as outposts) near borders.[31] Seclusion and proximity to civilization were not mutually exclusive either, since the countryside was still sparsely populated. The larger monasteries in turn assumed a central role, providing cores for artisans and merchants to settle in their immediate vicinity. Some cities (St. Gall, for instance) owe their origins to the prior foundation of a monastery.

This centrality necessarily arose from the act of foundation, which set certain goals from its very inception. Founders of monasteries were primarily the Frankish Merovingian and Carolingian kings, who established numerous monasteries on royal properties. These were located between the Loire and Meuse rivers, especially in the Paris basin, followed by the Meuse-Moselle region under the Carolingians,[32] who incorporated them into their political system as royal monasteries. Additional founders included churches, particularly bishoprics, which retained control over monasteries under their authority; nobles, who established monasteries on their properties; and "dynastic monasteries" themselves, which often could not survive and were subsequently handed over to bishops or kings. As a result, the number of episcopal monasteries and, even more, royal monasteries, immensely increased. Not until after 1045 did this vogue end, at which point the monasteries were more commonly presented to the pope.[33]

The reasons for the interest of kings and nobility in the monasteries may be seen in the rulers' traditional self-perception as protectors of religion, as well as in their religious beliefs. Noble interest also evolved from the function of the monastery as an instrument of power totally integrated into the political structures. Let us first observe the religious and, in their turn, secular functions and relationships of early medieval monasteries.

The Monastery as a Component of the Church—Pastoral Care, Education, Welfare. Because of its original, specific mission, the monastery was naturally a place for religious communal life in accordance with certain rules intended to foster the salvation of each individual monk; there will be more about this later.[34] In a certain sense, all of society— especially the founder and his family—laid claim to this monastic life "in the service of the Lord" by engaging monks to pray not only for themselves, but also for others. The monks remembered the deceased and living members of the founding family in their masses, praying for their salvation. Furthermore, under Anglo-Saxon influence, they also prayed for the salvation of fellow human beings who had fraternized with the monks, or who had secured their prayerful services in exchange for special acts such as donations, and whose names were entered in the fraternity-lists and memorial books.[35] (Medieval people could not do enough for their eternal salvation; while people sinned no more than today, they did much more to make amends for these sins.) The prayer service followed strict rules: for example, the monks of the monastery at Aadorf in the Thurgau, the dynastic monastery of Count Udalrich of Linzgau during the late ninth century, were enjoined to celebrate three masses daily and three psalms for the deceased every week, as well as one mass for the salvation of the living members of the family.[36] Initially an individual commemoration was made for each of those listed in the memorial book; however, as their numbers increased, one eventually had to be satisfied with a summary commemoration.

Since the monastery was integrated into the organization of the Church, it was, in a spiritual sense, subject to the jurisdictional and consecrational powers of a bishop. Pirmin's attempt to exempt his monasteries from episcopal oversight could not prevail against Boniface's strict ecclesiastical organization.[37] Consequently, the monasteries had no autonomy of consecration; anytime an altar, a church, or an abbot were to be consecrated, the ceremony had to be performed by the local bishop, to whom the monasteries in Merovingian times were obligated to provide hospitality and tribute. Not until the period of reforms, especially during the twelfth century, did the monasteries rebel against the sovereignty of bishops.

As a part of the official Church, abbeys did take over ecclesiastical tasks. Monks were increasingly called on to provide pastoral care; as such, the monastery church frequently became a parish church. Although, for the purpose of simply safeguarding monastic worship, only a few monks were ordained in the beginning (as subdeacons, deacons, and priests), their numbers increased substantially, especially in the course of the ninth century, until the overwhelming majority of monks were also members of the clergy. At Saint-Germain-des-Prés near Paris, ordained monks were still in the minority during the eighth century, but in the course of the ninth century, almost every monk achieved at least one level of ordination.[38] At St.-Denis in 838, 65 percent of the monks were ordained, and at St. Gall in 895, 42 of the 101 monks were ordained.[39] During the period of the realm's formation, missionary tasks were assigned to the monasteries by preference. Fulda, for instance, was specifically established as a missionary monastery to serve Thuringia. Such monasteries could easily face a crisis after Christianization was completed in the ninth century, since they then had to invest in new tasks. In spreading the Gospel, monasteries occupied by Frankish monks and expressly supported by the kings simultaneously propagated Frankish political culture. In the same vein, Charlemagne endowed Italian monasteries following his conquest of the Lombard kingdom in order to enlist their aid in integrating Italy into his realm.

Monasteries fulfilled these tasks because they became centers of training and education, generally responsible for salvaging classical antiquity for Western Christianity, a role which could scarcely have been envisioned by their founding fathers. In his *admonitio generalis* of 789, Charlemagne decreed that every monastery was to have a school and schoolbooks of its own ("schoolbooks" were manuals for the teacher then).[40] Future monks at larger monasteries were educated in what was called an internal school, particularly after it had become customary to commend children to the care of monasteries as *pueri oblati*. An external school educated future members of the clergy, who then went on to serve churches as secular priests. The collective knowledge of the age was assembled in monastic libraries. Next to the schoolbooks dealing with the liberal arts (*artes liberales*)—grammar, rhetoric, dialectic; arithmetic, astronomy, geometry, and music, the "general education" of the day[41] —these libraries primarily housed the Bible and liturgical books for daily worship (sacramentals, antiphonals, missals), Bible commentaries, homilies, lives of saints, monastic regulations, and lastly the writings of the Church Fathers, whose authority predominated throughout the Middle Ages. These libraries harbored scientific treatises and encyclopedias, particularly the *Etymologiae* of Bishop Isidore of Seville, of which more than a thousand manuscripts have survived to the present. They also housed historiographic works, poems, legal texts, classical authors of antiquity—in short, they contained nearly everything available in writing. Libraries naturally varied in size, and it is no accident that the library was frequently called the *armarium* (a closet, or chest), simply because it often consisted merely of a wooden chest in which valuable books were stored. However, important monasteries had greater holdings; we know of them because of numerous library catalogs handed down to us.[42] The ninth-century catalog of St. Gall, for example, contains more than four hundred entries.

Writing and copying were important occupations for many monks, copying in those days being indeed laborious, and the writing monk was the most frequent subject of miniatures painted by artistically gifted monks. (See Illustration 9.) Even more typical of the monastery than the library was the *scriptorium*, the writing room or school. The Carolingian age in particular was the zenith of copying activity, when the cultural traditions of antiquity were preserved in such rooms. The invaluable

Illustration 9: *Typical Work of a Monk: the Monk as Scribe* (Notker of St. Gall) (from a lost Notker manuscript, photograph taken from von den Steinen, Homo Caelestis).

parchment codices contained a number of writings, sometimes gathered together haphazardly, but often by design. The "Carolingian Renaissance" was essentially the work of monasteries, and monks responsible for the creation of the prime script of the Middle Ages, the "Carolingian minuscule." Writing was deemed meritorious; a canon at the monastery of Klosterneuburg, for example, intended not only to further his own salvation, but also that of all his brethren, predecessors, successors, and friends. In his *History of the Church* of the early twelfth century, Ordericus Vitalis reports that a sinful monk saved his soul because God cancelled a sin for every letter written; fortunately for the monk, in his specific case just one letter remained to his credit.[43] People went to great lengths to obtain the monks' rare manuscripts, as illustrated by the journey of the monk Richer of Reims to Chartres already mentioned.

To be sure, monks did not just copy books in the monastery; learned monks, frequently the monastery's teachers themselves, composed new works, often imitating traditional works and usually at the request of a superior.[44] Historiography, too, originated largely in monasteries. The annals of monasteries recorded most important events of the day; later, entire histories of monasteries or of the acts of abbots were collected. Around the eleventh century, the practice of recording one's own historical tradition arose: the act of foundation was first recorded in charters, then in independent reports on the founding of a monastery (*fundationes*), and finally in histories of individual monasteries.[45] Last but not least, there were the lives and the miracles of saints venerated at a specific monastery. These were revised time and again in order to adapt to the prevalent taste of a given period, and they certainly constituted the favorite devotional readings for monastic life. The more famous the miracles of a locally venerated saint, the greater the respect enjoyed by the monastery. Monasteries became centers for the veneration of saints and miraculous activities—mostly in the form of healings—and they sometimes became fully fledged goals of pilgrimage.

Monks were also active in another cultural area, the realm of art. Not only did the monks create precious covers for exquisite codices and adorn their pages with miniatures, but they also frequently crafted the liturgical vessels and other valuables, or they worked as architects.

At a time when the "government" had no social policy whatsoever, monks became responsible for a third great task in the service of society, working not just in pastoral care and education but also social welfare. The care of the aged, the sick, and the weak was primarily the responsibility of families, some of whom became impoverished to a degree that they depended on assistance from churches and monasteries. Monks were obligated "by profession" to perform acts of neighborly love and welfare: "There is always a pious, God-fearing friar sitting [at the gate] receiving all arriving guests, pilgrims and poor people, as friendly and kind-hearted as Christ himself, accompanying them first to the oratory and then to the guestroom, after having washed their feet and administered to them all the humble services of neighborly love," writes Otto of Freising in his "praise" of monasticism.[46] The poor were fed by the monastery on certain designated days; they were cared for, bathed, shaved and, if necessary, clothed. Larger monasteries had true poor houses (*xenodochia*) attached.[47] Feeding the poor was considered part of the memorial for the dead and, as such, was rooted in a religious purpose; the monks remembered certain departed people in their masses whose daily rations were then handed to the poor. Marxist research tends to interpret this function of social welfare as a conscious attempt on the part of the Church to lessen tensions between poor and rich.[48] The fact, however, is that the poorest posed the least threat. The Frenchman Georges Duby makes much more sense by stating that in this way a large part of the contributions made by the serfs exploited (but also cared for) by the higher classes flowed right back to them.[49] This cycle was part of the natural sociological picture of the Middle Ages, and it still afforded the lords a style of life befitting their position in society. On the other hand, feeding the poor could assume proportions monasteries were no longer able to handle, resulting in the impoverishment of some monastic communities. The dead, says Wollasch, consumed the living in the guise of the poor.[50]

Accommodating, entertaining and feeding pilgrims and travelers (particularly since there was only a rather limited number of "inns" prior to the twelfth and thirteenth centuries) was also part of social welfare.[51] Larger monasteries, therefore, had an attached guesthouse. The Benedictine Rule prescribed, "All who arrive as guests are to be welcomed like Christ . . . proper respect is to be shown to all, particularly to those of one family with us in the faith (*domestici fidei*) and to pilgrims."[52] Even though Benedict permitted no differentiation, by Carolingian times guests were received in keeping with their status, and a strict distinction was made between the house for the poor and the guest house. There were also likely to be some permanent guests (with full room and board). In 873, for example, a Swabian landowner donated arable land to the monastery of St. Gall to benefit the *domus perigrinorum* so that he could live, be fed, and clothed there until the end of his days, specifically with one linen and one woolen outfit per year, and a coat and shoes every three years.[53]

Finally, the monks were also responsible for caring for the sick. To the extent that medical care and knowledge were available at all, they could be found in monasteries, where herb gardens provided necessary remedies and where the sick could be cared for in an attached hospital. The house for the poor and the hospital were often one and the same building.

The Monastery as a Component of the World—Private Monasteries. Although religious tasks were foremost among the functions discussed thus far, several additional tasks arose from the "secular" nature of the monastery when a private monastery was located on the property of the founder and his family who wished to participate in religious life in this way. At first, the nobility and bishops took advantage of the piety of the monks in the form of prayerful assistance already described. Also, admission into the monastery was naturally available to those members of the founder's family who wished to become monks. As a result, private monasteries were thought of as homes for sons born after the eldest (in order to prevent further division of the estate) and especially for daughters (whom one either could not or did not want to marry off); their foundation was frequently inspired by this intention. The upshot was that the nobility preferred establishing nunneries, whose abbesses were frequently their own daughters. The monastery at Gandersheim, founded by the Liudolfing dukes of Saxony, was ruled by three daughters of Duke Liudolf and his wife Oda in succession, the first of whom, Hathumod, was merely twelve years old when she took the office of abbess, followed in office by her sisters Gerberga, and Christina. The fourth abbess, Liutgard, was probably also a relative.[54] Even in cases where monasteries were turned over to the king, the person doing so would reserve the abbot's see for himself and his descendants (until the Cluniac reform), though the practice of "lay abbots" was probably more widespread in the ninth century (Felten). Moreover, the founder or his spouse liked to be able to enter their monastery at an advanced age, as soon as they had turned their affairs over to their sons; religious dedication at the culmination of their lives once again enhanced their chance of salvation. In the case of husbands, it was frequently a sign of impending death; widows, on the other hand, frequently entered a convent after their husbands' death. Oda, for example, became a nun at Gandersheim after the death of Liudolf. These endowed monasteries frequently also served as burial places for the family of the founder, Liudolf and Oda, Hathumod and Gerberga all being interred at Gandersheim. Others assured themselves of a place to retire at an early point (since there were no other provisions for the aged outside the family). In all, religious and utilitarian motives went hand-in-hand. When Karlmann, Frankish king and brother of Pepin I, renounced his throne in 747 and joined the Benedictine monastery at Monte Cassino, he passed himself off as a murderer and had himself severely punished in order to avoid detection. Not until the cook kept beating him repeatedly did a companion reveal his true identity, so that both the monks and the abbot threw themselves at the feet of Karlmann, their true lord.[55] The story of this "drop-out" illustrates Karlmann's desire to gain salvation by living the life of a simple monk, but also the difficulty a king had escaping his role.

As a "dynastic monastery," a private monastery also served a symbolic function, representing the religious as well as the cultural center of a noble family. It integrated the various estates of layman, monk, and cleric, while preserving the family's continuity.[56] Monasteries became a symbol of the unity of Church and nobility during the Middle Ages. We must consider this fact the norm, not an incipient secularization deviating from the original task. The establishment of a monastery raised the esteem of the nobility and thereby exceeded its primarily religious purpose. The founding of a monastery was, according to contemporary opinion, tantamount to an act of "self-sanctification" on the part of the founder and his family (Prinz), who thus regained some of the sacral position they had at first relinquished in Christianity without themselves actually becoming saints.

Still, the Middle Ages would not be the Middle Ages if religious purposes had not engendered material advantages; private monasteries were simultaneously spiritual institutions and exponents of the rule of the nobility (Prinz). It was a home away from home any time a lord needed it, a place he could count on for accommodations and food. The lord of the monastery disposed of monastic holdings, which soon increased well beyond the original endowment as a result of numerous donations by others. According to a provision in one charter, the holdings of the monastery of Aadorf were expressly to benefit Count Udalrich and his family, as well as the livelihood of the monks.[57] The monks could be enlisted to perform all sorts of services, particularly as writers of letters or messengers, and like the abbot, vassals of the monastery had to perform military service.[58] The landed property just mentioned, a prerequisite for maintaining monks and their fulfilling various functions as well as artistic and building activities, contributed a great deal to the secular character of monasteries. Donations were intended as contributions to one's own salvation, removing legal disputes once and for all, and of assuring one's children would be admitted to a monastery. Donations also safeguarded the proper management of one's property during long periods of absence. Most donations were in the form of *precaria*, which guaranteed to the donor lifetime use in exchange for an annual rent to the monastery. Donations of property from all sources created such a mass of landed property that the most important monasteries were also among the biggest landowners and most progressively managed enterprises in the country; they afforded their residents a comparatively comfortable life from the tributes of serfs. In 900, the monastery of St. Gall controlled almost two thousand dues-paying peasants. Because of the many individual donations, monastic estates were widely scattered; individual monks were commissioned as provosts to visit properties. Around 1030, St. Emmeram at Regensburg owned thirty-three manors, each administered by a monk for a specific term. Produce and tributes also had to be hauled to the monastery, all transactions resulting in continuous contact with the outside world, interfering with a solitary life.

Both landed property and contact to the outside world demanded written and legal documents, so that abbeys became self-reliant legal institutions entitled to carry a seal. Since the high Middle Ages they had devised collections of canon law in order to support and defend their rights.[59] In the course of monastic history, frequent disagreements arose between the monasteries and their lords, advocates, and bishops; disputes jeopardizing manorial authority and autonomy, arguments over the proper way of monastic life, and contests over the rights and self-government of the brethren, were frequent between individual abbots and monasteries.

The Monastery as a Component of National Politics—Royal Monasteries. The royal monasteries,[60] either founded by the kings themselves or handed over to them, were the most deeply integrated into the major undertakings of medieval society and politics; they enjoyed royal support, but in exchange had to serve the realm, a development which began during later Merovingian times and only grew with time. Beginning in the first half of the eighth century, abbots were increasingly present alongside the bishops at council meetings. Soon, becoming an abbot or a bishop was considered equally desirable in terms of a clerical career. The Carolingians pursued a regular, well-reasoned monastic policy[61] with concrete goals in mind. Thus, in the years between 775 and 782 (at the time of the Saxon conquest), Charlemagne supported the Thuringian monasteries of Hersfeld and Fulda, apparently selected to spread the Gospel among the Saxons and mold them in the Frankish spirit.[62]

The means at the disposal of kings will be examined by revisiting the monastery of St. Gall, which shows itself typical in this respect. First of all, in addition to extensive land donations, the bestowal of rights needs to be mentioned. St. Gall, which supposedly commended itself to Pepin, was granted immunity by Louis the Pious in 818. As a result, the monastery came under the direct jurisdiction of the king and was no longer subject to the authority of the count. Royal officials were no longer permitted to enter the area of immunity for purposes of discharging official duties, such as sitting in judgment or collect taxes. In this way, monasteries gained administrative autonomy and were permitted to sit in judgment over those living within their immunity. Discharging these rights, which had previously been the privilege of counts, was now the task of the advocate of the monastery, a layman who ended up competing increasingly with the monastery during the high Middle Ages, after the office of advocate had become hereditary in major noble families. Ever since Louis the Pious, immunity was closely connected to royal protection (thus to royal rule), a fact linking the monastery even more closely to the king.

The second important privilege granted to St. Gall in 818 was the right freely to elect its abbot. This too reveals royal rule, for it was the king's prerogative to appoint the abbot, and it was specifically in this way that the kings sought to assure themselves of their influence over the monasteries. They distributed abbeys in the manner they assigned other offices to loyal followers, as if monasteries were fiefs, and through Carolingian times the abbots they appointed could also be laymen. Magnates also sought such abbeys for the purpose of rounding off their power: the monastery had developed into an attractive instrument of control, one which was used with increasing frequency in the West after conquests ended and large land donations were only possible at the expense of the royal domain (Felten). Many a nobleman acquired several abbeys, so that the abbot often no longer personally resided at the monastery. At abbeys where the counts did not become abbots themselves—as mentioned, lay abbots began disappearing in the ninth century—they made at least an attempt to secure the abbotship to relatives among the monks. The privilege freely to choose an abbot provided a certain degree of relief here, but it still amounted simply to the monks' permission to choose and propose an abbot from their own ranks; the election itself was always subject to royal consent and did not become final until after the investiture by the king. Thus, controversies surrounding an election simultaneously rebounded to the monastery along with the right to choose the abbot.

In order to keep from jeopardizing the brethren's support, a distinction began to be made in the ninth century between a *mensa fratrum* and a *mensa abbatis*; so that possessions and profits were divided between the abbot and the monastery, since some abbots had appropriated assets to an extent that the monasteries themselves approached financial and economic ruin. This is why the *Gesta abbatum Fontanellensium* referred to the leadership of abbot Teutsind (who had misappropriated one third of his monastery's possessions, sharing it with his relatives and royal vassals) as "tyranny," rather than as "government."[63] Still, as late as the eleventh century, the monks at Fulda complained about their abbot, Widerad, because he had "illegally awarded possessions belonging to the Church to vassals and because he had reduced the brothers' allotment of food that had been granted by generous earlier abbots"; however, the king protected the abbot.[64]

Despite all undoubtedly important religious motives, the support of a monastery was not an end in itself; privileges did not curtail royal sovereignty but were supposed to enable monasteries to meet their obligations. Foremost among these was the prayer-service already discussed, prayer for the kings and their families as well as for their predecessors. Conrad I, though not a Carolingian himself, decreed for his endowed monastery at Weilburg that prayerful petitions be made for his father as well as for all the Carolingian kings.[65] Moreover, as subjects of royal sovereignty, the monasteries were obligated to pay *dona regia*, annual taxes to the king. For instance, according to a charter of 854, St. Gall had to deliver two horses, two shields, and spears every year.[66] We may assume similar tributes by other monasteries.[67] Finally, like bishoprics, imperial monasteries were obligated to serve the king (*servitium regis*). This primarily entailed accommodating, feeding, and entertaining the traveling king and his entourage. Generally speaking, the ruler was above criticism; despite the burden, a royal visit was considered an honor which one would recall with fondness, and sometimes a king was even accepted into the community of brothers.[68] The abbot and monks met him, and together they entered the monastery church in solemn procession in keeping with an established ritual.[69] Ekkehard of St. Gall proudly reports a visit by Conrad I at Christmastime.[70] The king was even permitted to dine with the monks in the refectory and participate in their assemblies, an honor strictly forbidden to others—even to Bishop Salomon of Constance. Conrad paid special attention to pupils permitted to take turns reading to him; the fact that he gave them a three-day vacation for playing games was certainly quite improper and unmonastic, and it was intended to illustrate the king's generosity. If

Ekkehard emphasizes that Conrad put up with the simple fare of the monks—not even bread and hulled beans had been promised by the provost for the next day—he certainly wished to underscore the king's exemplary modesty. The king did, however, conclude the third day with a feast after making a gift of some estates to the monastery's saint with the proviso "that our enlisted brothers should eat more sumptuously as a reward for yesterday's meal during the week preceding the feast of St. Otmar . . . and in commemoration of him." Ekkehard continues, "The meal commenced early; the dining room filled up; the lector could hardly utter a single sentence: love which can do no wrong was permitted to dispense with etiquette. No one spoke up, insisting that this or that was not permitted, although it had neither been seen or heard in earlier days. The monks had never smelled the spicy odor of game and meat. Jugglers danced and jumped about; musicians played and sang. Never before had the hall of St. Gall been filled with so much jubilation." Ekkehard did not seem to be bothered by the fact that one monastic rule after another was being broken. Only the concluding sentence contains a slight innuendo: "Listening to the singing, the king looked at the more staid brothers, laughing about some of them, for, since everything was completely new to them, they made wry faces." The king had the right to relax the rules (by way of exception and certainly to the delight of many a monk) so that the above description by Ekkehard would appear more suited to our chapter on courtly society rather than monastic life. Whether everything happened in the manner described by Ekkehard is a matter of conjecture, since Ekkehard wrote well over two hundred years later. As a result, the anecdote offers us less information about reality than how we should picture a good king at a monastery, and what one could expect of him during his visit. On the whole, kings called on the services of their monasteries much less than on those of the palaces and bishoprics. Kings hardly ever conducted political affairs there, but rather used the time for prayer.

The second duty within the framework of *servitium regis* was military service. During royal campaigns, or at the king's request, the abbots themselves led a contingent of monastic vassals into battle; indeed, important imperial monasteries were often obliged to muster as many armored horsemen as the bishops.[71] In general it was the abbots the king called to duty, representing a liaison between monastery and royal court. They were deployed on diplomatic missions or as royal messengers, and according to the interventions in the royal charters were frequently present at court. Abbot Grimald of St. Gall (841-872) also served as the abbot of Wissembourg in Alsace (another important royal monastery), and as archchancellor of Louis the Pious he headed the royal chancery and royal chapel, assuming responsibility both for worship at court as well as for the entire royal correspondence. It is understandable that the abbot was hardly ever present at the monastery.

In passing, one should mention a final purpose of monasteries which was never originally intended, that of guardhouse. Since there were no prisons, "political prisoners" (rebels)—including the sons of kings, such as Karlmann, a son of Charles the Bald who required permanent care after his blinding, or Hugh, son of Lothar II—were more frequently sentenced to forceful service in a monastery.[72] As a rule, making them monks was tantamount to a pardon or stay of execution. Of course, this presented the monasteries with new problems. Therefore, demanding stricter adherence to monastic rule, twelve monks at Fulda complained in 812 in a petition to Charlemagne about these and other abuses after a cleric who had murdered a monk was forcibly committed to their monastery; certain duties (such as working in the kitchen) should, they felt, be reserved for monks.[73]

On the whole, the imperial monasteries constituted an important element of royal government during Carolingian times as well as under the "Ottonian-Salian imperial church system." Their various functions necessarily had an effect on the lives of individual monks and the entire monastery, yet they also determined monastic structures and shaped the space of monastic life into a single functional system.

2. The Space:
The Monastery as Residence for Monks

In his *Casus sancti Galli*,[74] Ekkehard describes how Salomon, chancellor of the king and later bishop of Constance, attempted time and again to make his way "barefoot but with a cowl" (so that nobody would recognize him) into the innermost chambers of the monastery of St. Gall, where he had been educated. "We never were . . . and still are entirely unaccustomed to anybody entering our innermost rooms without wearing our habit. Since it was customary to have two brothers stand guard over our cloister, it was decided that these two watchmen, who alone were permitted to speak, would approach him with a candle on his arrival and softly ask him who he was." When Salomon was discovered in the churchyard by an elderly monk, he begged, "'Venerable Father, please, let me at least go next door into the chapel of St. Peter! As soon as I have finished my prayers there, I will never again enter the cloister in this garb except when accompanied by one of your superiors, in accordance with the statutes of the monastery. However, with your help and that of brothers suitable for this task, I will ask the abbot tomorrow to permit me to enter the cloister dressed as a monk; I will live there with you like a monk and then will leave again, but permit me to walk outside before my knights and all the others dressed like a secular priest.' The other one replied, 'Pray to St. Gall that you never take off the habit for the rest of your life once you have donned it, except at times customary for monks.'" Whether true or not, the story typifies monasticism in many respects. We find out something about the vow of silence and monastic attire, as well as the predicament into which the powerful Salomon—who later became the monastery's abbot—placed the monks. That is why the abbot granted his wish, hoping that he would really become a monk, which Salomon rewarded with generous donations. Yet this obliging behavior was clearly justified only as an exception; because of its purpose, the cloister (*claustrum*), the living space of monks in a narrower sense, remained strictly off limits to others. As the core-area of the greater expanse of the monastery, it gave the monastery its German name, *Kloster*. Monks were themselves subject to *stabilitas loci*; they were only allowed to leave their monastery very briefly and with the specific permission of the abbot, but even that was considered dangerous. Benedict directed, "When brethren return from a journey, at all the canonical hours of the day on which they return, they should lie prostrate on the floor of the oratory, as the Work of God comes to an end, and ask for the prayers of all, for any faults that may have overtaken them on their journey, such as the sight or hearing of an evil thing or idle chatter. No one should venture to tell another anything he may have seen or heard while outside the monastery, for that does much harm."[75] (One can easily imagine the curiosity of the other monks and how they would besiege any returnee.) The reform synods of Aachen of 816/17 tried once again to reduce the number of journeys by the residents of monasteries. However, toward the end of the tenth century, Abbot Rodulf of St. Remi complained at one of the synods that monks frequently slipped out of the monastery alone and unwitnessed.[76] This is evidence that the rule was frequently disregarded.

Benedict only expressed vague ideas about the architecture of a monastery.[77] If at all possible, the monastery was to be organized so that all its needs, such as water, a mill, a garden, and various crafts, could be met within its premises. Various types of rooms are mentioned only in passing. Aside from the churches themselves, early medieval monastic structures have not been preserved; however, we can get an idea of a complete lay-out by studying a unique, remarkable document from the early ninth century: the so-called Plan of St. Gall.[78] (See Illustration 10.) This schematic does not present a faithful reproduction of the monastery

1 = Herb Garden; 2 = Doctor's Home; 3 = Hospital; 4 = Cloister and Archway;
5 = Chapel; 6 = Novitiate; 7 = Cemetery; 8 = Orchard; 9 = Vegetable Garden;
10 = Gardener's Quarters; 11 = Poultry (Geese); 12 = Poulterer's Quarters; 13
= Chickens; 14 = Leeching House; 15 = «Paradise»; 16 = Business Office; 17
= Baths; 18 = Kitchen for the Sick; 19 = Kitchen; 20 = Novitiate Bath; 21 =
Host Bakery; 22 = Latrine; 23 = Barn; 24 = Threshing-Floor; 25 = Scriptorium
and Library; 26 = Sacristy; 27 = Vestry; 28 = Heating; 29 =Abbot's House; 30 =
Choir; 31 = Sitting Room; 32 = Dormitory; 33 = Bathhouse; 34 = Workshops; 35
= Saddlery; 36 = Shieldmaker; 37 = Tannery; 38 = Swordmaker; 39 = Shoemaker;
40 = Chamberlain; 41 = Turner; 42 = Goldsmith; 43 = Forge; 44 = Fuller; 45
= Apartments; 46 = External School [a] Gatekeeper, b] Principal, c] Guestrooms
for Clergy; 47 = Reading Stand; 48 = Pulpit; 49 = Chapter Hall; 50 = Monastery
Church; 51 = Baptismal Font; 52 = Towers; 53 = Guardian of the Poor; 54 =
Visitors' Room; 55 = Cellar; 56 = Pantry; 57 = Refectory; 58 = Clothes Room;
59 = Pilgrims' Accommodations; 60 = Monks' Kitchen; 61 = Breweries (Monks &
General); 62 = Bakeries (Monks & General); 63 = Wine Press; 64 = Mortars; 65 =
Mill; 66 = Guesthouse for Distinguished Guests with Great Hall, Horse Barn and
Servants' Quarters; 67 = Coopery; 68 = Storage; 69 = Malt-Kiln; 70 = Bunkhouse
for Shepherds; 71 = Mares; 72 = Cattle; 73 = Altars; 74 = Confessional (Tomb
of a Saint under the Main Altar); 75 = Passageway to the Holy Sepulchre; 76 =
Entrance Way; 77 = Livestock-Sheep; 78 = Goats; 79 = Dairy Cows; 80 = Servants'
Quarters; 81 = Pigs; 82 = Horses

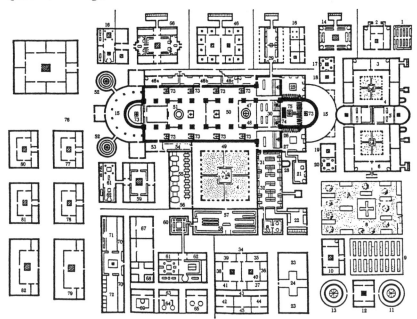

Illustration 10: *The Monastery as Living Space: The Plan of St. Gall*
(first quarter of the ninth century), from *Handbuch der deutschen
Wirtschafts- und Sozialgeschichte* I, p. 100.

of St. Gall, but rather represents a master plan probably drawn up in the southern part of the Empire by a person close to the reform of Benedict of Aniane and the Aachen synods of 816/17,[79] a fact which makes it particularly informative. The entire grounds measured 154 x 205m. The various tracts reflected their monastic functions; the religious tract (including the church and the cloister) was naturally located at the center and was almost exclusively reserved for the monks. The monastery church (measuring 116m in length, 39m in width, and 19m in height) was 360 feet long, 120 feet wide, and 60 feet high in the original measurement. Understood symbolically, these figures formed multiples of 60. The church possessed two round towers, dedicated to the archangels Michael and Gabriel, with a crypt for keeping relics underneath. The north outside front included cells for the gate-keeper and the school principal, and guest quarters for visiting monks. In the northeast corner were located the scriptorium (downstairs) and library (upstairs); to the northwest were the sacristy (upstairs) and a chamber for liturgical vestments (upstairs). The southern section of the church was bordered by the cloister, with a quadrangularly shaped gallery along its inside walls, and the secluded living area of the *vita communis* of the monks. Within, there was a plot used for a cemetery in some monasteries. Toward the outside were the two-story buildings, the chapter room for meetings of the monks, with the "reading hallway" downstairs, equipped with benches. To the east was the communal dormitory over the only heated room of the monastery; to the south was the clothes room over the communal refectory; to the west were the cellar and the storage rooms. The kitchen was located between the refectory and the cellar. In addition, there were areas provided for bathing and a latrine.

The eastern section of the compound was made up of buildings still serving a religious purpose, but which had to remain outside the cloister. First, there were quarters for novices and pupils of the monastic school (that is, future monks) who were still not permitted to set foot in the actual monastery. Second, there was the hospital, kept outside because of the danger of infection. Both were included in the plan of St. Gall, but following the lay-out of smaller monasteries, this section had its own gallery, in the center of which was its own chapel. Adjacent to the hospital was a leeching house, a house for physicians, and an herb garden.

The buildings in the northern section supported contact to the outside world: there was a house for distinguished guests with stables and a special bakery, the external school, and—owing to the superior position of the often-absent abbot—a separate house for him (the abbey) with a business office. Pilgrims, on the other hand, were housed in a building equipped with its own bakery and brewery, nestled next to the cloister, near where the guardian of the poor had his accommodations. This proximity to the cloister attests to the fact that the most essential tasks of monks were still considered to lie outside the narrower definition of monastic life.

The entire southern and western sections consisted of agricultural buildings and workshops serving to support the monks, dovetailing surprisingly with the regulations of statutes from other monasteries.[80] Here were the orchard and the vegetable garden, houses for chickens and geese, a small granary and a building housing workshops of artisans such as shoemaker, saddler, shieldmaker, turner, tanner, and blacksmith. Other statutes mention the parchmentmaker, mason, and carpenter. Also located in these outer buildings was the mill, the wine press, and the malt-kiln. The brewery and the bakery were connected to the kitchen. The western section housed stables for livestock (horses, cattle, pigs, goats, and sheep) with lodgings for shepherds and farmhands. Despite the many outlying properties, the main business areas in the immediate vicinity of the monastery guaranteed that the necessities could be produced under the monastery's own eyes while monks made themselves useful, especially in bakeries, breweries, and kitchens, all in close proximity to the cloister for that reason. Woodworking and metalworking shops were run by more specialized craftsmen who certainly did not manufacture goods for their own needs alone (Schwind). As has recently been written, the monastic community was a "religious organization based on standards of efficiency."[81]

Even though the plan of St. Gall represents an ideal monastery, its principle of a monastic compound is coherent and frequently confirmed by history (though not this perfectly). Thus, the *Gesta Aldrici episcopi Cenomannensis*[82] report that Bishop Aldrich established a convent with a main church and *claustrum* with *refectorium, dormitorium, celarium et cetera officina*, a well providing water at the center; again, all the characteristics of the *vita communis* are present. The monastery of Cluny (II) at the time of Odilo (c. 1000) was very similar to the layout of St. Gall.[83] As always, church and gallery made up the center. In the eastern wing were the chapter hall, parlor, reading room and work rooms, and the dormitory. In the southern wing were located the heated sitting room and the refectory; in the western wing, kitchen, pantry, and library. Therefore, the distribution of Cluny differed only slightly from the plan of St. Gall, preserving its principles. Again, to the east of the church were enclosures for the sick and the hospital, and in the northern section were a guesthouse with sections for men and women as well as accommodations for the poor. Typical of Cluny, to the west were stables below the living quarters of the lay brothers (converts). To the south there were workshops and the bakery, and between them the novitiate.

Cluny already possessed a separated system for supplying fresh water and draining waste.

Generally speaking, the medieval monastery was a functional building complex which took into account the various tasks of the monks while affording them a monastic life. The third determining factor for this monastic life are the monks themselves, who are to be considered above all else as a community.

3. The Inhabitants:
The Monastic Community

Admission

The reasons for becoming a monk could vary widely. In the first book of his thirteenth-century *Dialogus miraculorum*, Caesarius of Heisterbach describes a variety of motives in individual stories: one future monk had been eyewitness to a miracle performed by an abbot and was so impressed by it that he decided to enter a monastery; another had run away from home as a child because he sensed his calling to the monastic life (apparently not all parents were pleased by this); yet a third became a monk in order to avoid an impending death penalty (trading death for life-long penance for his crime). In many cases, concern about one's salvation was the driving force. Caesarius himself had heard of a vision about eternal life according to which the Virgin Mary personally wiped the sweat off monks' foreheads. Since he did not want to miss this treatment, he entered the monastery.[84] However, the majority probably did not become monks voluntarily, but were presented to a monastery by their parents while still young; there they were raised and disciplined as *pueri oblati* under the supervision of a custodian, in accordance with the Benedictine Rule [c. 63, 18] so that they could become monks. Actual admission to the order occurred, normally, at the age of fifteen. Others did not enter a monastery until they were of an advanced age, in order to perform rapid but timely penance for their sins.

The monastic community formed a self-contained family which one could not easily join. Acceptance into a medieval monastery depended on two conditions. First, an initially voluntary but later increasingly mandatory donation was required in support of admission. Since relinquishing one's personal possessions was a prerequisite of monastic life according to the Benedictine Rule [c. 58, 24], at least part of one's possessions was deeded to the monastery. Benedict had stated, "However, if they . . . want to have the merit of giving something as alms, they should make a donation to the monastery of whatever they want to give [RB c. 59, 4]." In time, those "alms" became substantial land donations. We have a great number of charters detailing such donations which were supposed to open the doors to a monastery (immediately, or in case of need) for the donor or one of his children. Therefore, before one could become a monk one had to be a landowner, so that many monasteries eventually became monasteries for the nobility alone.

Second, a prospective monk had to demonstrate personal aptitude for monastic life. For purposes of accustoming the petitioner, the Benedictine Rule [c. 58, 1ff.] stipulated an examination lasting four to five days, along with several days in the guesthouse. Thereafter the candidate lived as a novice in the *cella noviciorum* separate from the cloister under the watchful eye of an older monk. After two months, the Rule was read to the candidate for a first time, after an additional six months for a second time and then again, after another four months for a third time. Only then (after one year), was a candidate accepted into the monastic community, henceforth no longer to leave the monastery. The future monks took their final vows, professing to remain in the monastery from then on (*stabilitas loci*), to conduct themselves properly (*conversatio morum*), and to be obedient (*oboedientia*) [RB c. 58, 17]. They were subsequently dressed in monastic attire, indicating that they had been accepted as the newest members of the community.

The Community

The age at which monks took their final vows played a significant role in the order of precedence inside the convent, for the monks were certainly not of equal rank. Indeed, there was a definite order of precedence which was strictly observed in the choir, during communion, and on other occasions. Each monk had his assigned place in the choir, determined according to the day he entered the monastery [RB c. 2, 19; 60-62], although the order could be changed [already at the time of Benedict, RB c. 62, 6] in keeping with a monk's general reputation and conduct. Benedict had ordered that clerical degrees of ordination be left out of account. Nevertheless, lists of monks were occasionally also drawn up in keeping with clerical degrees of ordination, though these were more frequently based on the age at which final vows had been taken.

The Benedictine Rule generally distinguished between two groups of "senior" (*seniores*, also *priores*, "the earlier ones") and "junior" (*iuniores*) monks. Seniors commanded proportionate respect, for according to the Rule, "Juniors must show respect for seniors, the seniors must love their juniors." There were also set forms of address: a senior addressed a junior by calling him frater (brother), a junior addressed a senior with *nonnus* (grandfather), and the abbot was both *dominus* (lord) and *abbas* (father) [RB c. 63, 10ff.]. A junior was always to offer his seat to a senior and was not to sit down until the senior had given him his permission. Still, there were also tensions between those monks who had been trained at the monastery and those who had entered it later. Occasionally, we even witness "generational conflicts" in the convent. Abbot Widerad of Fulda, who had lost his claim to the bishop of Hildesheim for the right of being seated next to the archbishop (in an armed conflict), had squandered monastery assets and damaged its reputation; he thus met with fierce opposition by the monks upon his return to Fulda, especially since he also reduced their food allotment. When the abbot tried to mend his ways, the "older and more mature monks" were inclined to forgive him while the "juniors" remained unforgiving. Finally, sixteen monks left the monastery in order to beseech the king to depose the abbot. Officials at the royal palace were horrified at such a breach of the Rule, which was seen as more egregious than the abbot's mismanagement. The king had the ringleaders arrested, the rest dragged into court, and some were even flogged and expelled, or shunted to other monasteries; once again, monastic order had been restored. Yet, as Lampert writes, Fulda was to suffer for years to come from the memory of this infamous deed.[85]

Next to this "internal" organization of the monastic community, it will be of particular interest to look at its composition in terms of the number and the origin of individual members, which has been intensively researched for some time with the help of existing monastery rosters. A five-volume study of the monastery at Fulda finished some years ago has been pioneering; in it, a complete roster of monks has been made available and a preliminary attempt made to evaluate it.[86] By comparing different monastic rosters, death annals (unique to Fulda), and the rest of the tradition, one can discover the development of the houses and the monastery's external relations. The actual number of monks varied from monastery to monastery, but it also vacillated within individual houses over time. The number was not unlimited, since it depended on the wealth of the monastery. In principle, entering a monastery required the death of a previous monk, though in practice there was a substantial amount of leeway here. There were mini-monasteries (from two to five monks), alongside medium and gigantic ones. Montier-en-Der in Champagne, one of the oldest monasteries in Northern France, comprised 35 monks in 1050.[87] At Remiremont, at least 80 nuns resided during Frankish times;[88] St. Gall had a population of 101 monks in 895;[89] a monastic roster from St. Germain near Paris listed 213 names (which were probably not all members of the convent) at the time of Irmino (at the beginning of the ninth century). Under Ebroin (during the reign of Louis the Pious), St. Gall numbered 123 names. At the same time, 132 monks lived at St. Denis, and at St. Martin near Tours the numbers at the time of Charlemagne (808/11) ran as high as 218 names.[90] The rosters of the most important monasteries all range within similar numbers. Again, however, our most reliable information comes from Fulda. The list of Hrabanus Maurus dating from the ninth century contains 602 names, though not all of these were members of the mother house; rather, they were living in large part at branch monasteries dependent on Fulda. Approximately 134 monks resided at the main monastery in 822. The development at Fulda during the tenth century is typical. Around 928, a high point had been reached with 142 monks; by 935 (a mere seven years later), there were still 116, but in 952, only 79 were left, a definite sign of the decreasing importance and diminishing wealth of this once pre-eminent cloister among the royal monasteries east of the Rhine. The varying figures also reflect changes in the general importance of monasteries. During the period of reforms, formerly prominent royal monasteries such as St. Gall or Reichenau contained a relatively small number of monks, while the new religious orders, first the Cluniacs and later the Cistercians, became very popular and can be compared favorably with the numbers listed for the houses already mentioned.

Investigations concerning age structure within the monastery at Fulda (gained by comparing successive rosters) prove that the majority of monks entered the monastery very young and that a good number of them reached advanced age. Although there are no exact figures, the life expectancy of monks was undoubtedly above average; roughly one-fourth of the former pupils of the Fulda school no longer appears in later rosters, indicating they either died or (more commonly) did not remain in the monastery.[91]

Concerning the origin of the monks, evidence is very fragmentary. In the beginning, monasteries were probably open to people from all walks of life, including serfs, but the trend over the years was in the direction of social exclusiveness. Important monasteries of the Middle Ages in particular were primarily, if not exclusively, occupied by members of the nobility. Regional origins of monks reveal the shifting constituency of monasteries, essentially congruous with the expanse of possessions. At St. Gall, for instance, Rhaeto-Romanic names prevailed in the early days, but these gradually gave way to Germanic, Alamannic names, hinting at a new orientation within the monastery. It goes without saying that many monks came from the immediate vicinity

of the monastery, but the constituency of important monasteries also
extended to distant regions. Thus, the monks of Fulda originally came
not only from Thuringia, but also from Saxony and even from as far
away as Bavaria and other regions. Here, too, the inventory of names
for the ninth century reveals a change, for while many monks had
previously come from the central and upper Rhenish regions, now
Grabfeld (on the Main) prevailed, where the monastery's possessions
were concentrated.[92]

Using names, strong evidence is also given on the family origins
of monks. One frequently encounters the same names for monks over
several generations. This could be an indication that a single family
continued to send members to the same monastery over several generations, which is supported by the fact that the name of monk and
donor were frequently identical. Almost 82 per cent of the names of
donors reappeared as names for monks at Fulda.[93] In order to arrive
at more precise conclusions, many individual studies would have to
be undertaken.

A convent with such heterogeneous composition required strict
leadership. Similarly, monastic life itself and the various functions undertaken by the monastery, required an administration expressed in
various monastic offices.

Administration and Monastic Offices

The Abbot. Abbas is the Hebrew word for father. According to
the intention of St. Benedict, the abbot[94] was to be a father to the
monastic family, a position which encompassed a variety of functions.
He represented Christ in the monastery (just as the bishop represented
Christ in his diocese), he was the spiritual father of the monks (*pa-
ter spiritualis*), the teacher (*magister*), and *paterfamilias* (analogous
to the Roman tradition with its comprehensive, sovereign domestic
rights). The Benedictine Rule gave the abbot a great deal of power,
admonishing him to act responsibly: an abbot was responsible for his
"disciples" [c. 2, 6-7.], he was "to show forth all good and holy things
by his words and even more by his deeds," [RB c. 2, 12.] and he was
to minister to the souls of his monks [c. 2, 33-34.]. In doing so, he
was advised to combine firmness with generosity and to be "of profit
to his brethren rather than just preside over them" (*prodesse magis
quam praeesse*) [c. 64, 8], a phrase which would be widely quoted
throughout the Middle Ages. On the whole, Benedict created an image
elevating the superior far above his monks, laying the foundation for the
quasi-princely status of the medieval abbot. This role far transcended
the function of a mere superior, particularly if he ruled over several

monasteries (Wollasch refers to such abbots as *Oberäbte*, arch-abbots). Frequently during Frankish times, abbots were simultaneously bishops; occasionally they were laymen, but in either case they were members of the nobility. The abbot, who resided in a house of his own, stood apart from his monastery and assumed a political position. He became the instrument, or at least the link, by means of which the monastery participated in politics and in the secular world.

The abbot's three-step installation of election, investiture and consecration reflected his special role.[95] Though the Rule of the Master had provided for designation by the predecessor, Benedict sought his ideal in as unequivocal an election by the monastic community as possible, an election of the abbot from among the community's own ranks. Exemplary conduct and education were prerequisites. If there was no agreement on any one candidate, then, according to a provision which was to have severe consequences, the *pars sanior* (the more prudent portion among the voters), was to decide the issue with the assistance of the bishop and neighboring abbots (whose influence as a result increased). Investiture (and probably also consecration, which Benedict overlooked) was also performed by the bishop.

Secular influences were strongly felt during the Middle Ages, so that the right to institute an abbot passed to the lord of the private monastery, while in the case of royal monasteries the privilege rested with the king. Only the privilege of freely choosing an abbot continued to preserve the form prescribed by the Benedictine Rule. Investiture with pontificals, cross, miter, and crosier was still performed by the secular lord, who could refuse a candidate if he so desired. In the case of royal monasteries, a legation went to the royal court together with the newly elected abbot, petitioning for his confirmation. (Ekkehard[96] relates the difficulties experienced by a legation from St. Gall until Otto I finally confirmed young Notker, "the physician," as the new abbot.) As the third party involved, the bishop continued to perform the consecration.

Two examples from the monastery at Fulda may serve to illustrate the point that, under these circumstances, an abbacy would turn into a favorite, yet fervently contested office. After the deposing of Ratger, the election of a new abbot was declared in 818. According to the story reported in the *Vita Eigilis*,[97] two parties fought over it, their position representing two opposed principles. One party wanted a nobleman for an abbot, since only he would have the power to protect the monastery from counts and the powerful, and since he would be able to secure the required favor of the ruler due to his dignity and connection to the royal court. The other party argued that the weak were worth more in the presence of God, and that not being born into a noble family would mean humility and would thus be a merit. A second bone of contention dealt with education, for while one party wished to have a scholarly man for an abbot, the other desired an abbot less educated, who was less likely to twist words. Lastly, they could not even agree on his age, either, arguing over whether he should be an old man or a man in his middle years. Selfish arguments also played a role: "There was no lack of those either," wrote Bruun, ". . . who would whisper secretly: 'if we make you or you our superior, will you do us some favors?'" They ultimately elected Eigil because of his reputation and because he was a nobleman, educated, and (a fact which may have been less significant) already advanced in age.

Two-and-a-half centuries later, in 1075, when the struggle against simony (the buying of ecclesiastical offices) was already in full swing, an intense struggle broke out once more over the election of abbots in the presence of the king, a dispute in which bribery and election promises were the order of the day. "As if engaged in solemnly announced competition, every individual vied for the prize with all his might: one would promise mountains of gold, another immense fiefs carved from Fulda's estates, a third offered extraordinary services to the realm, and one and all disregarded moderation and limits in their offers," wrote Lampert of Hersfeld,[98] who was not favorably disposed to the king, but who possibly agreed with him in this case. Henry IV suddenly appointed as the new abbot of Fulda an extremely reluctant monk from Hersfeld, Lampert's own monastery, acting contrary to the Rule as well as to the privilege of free election of abbots. Such struggles over investiture made everyone aware of the problem, but hardly changed the practice. At any rate, one genuinely good abbot united in his person (as if by chance) many good qualities: Ansegis, the exemplary early ninth-century abbot of Fontanelle, was a nobleman (*ex nobili Francorum prosapia*), but was even more noble (*nobilior*) on account of his exemplary life (a commonly used epithet). He was educated, and he knew not only how to live well himself (*bene vivere*) but also how to guide the monks properly (*recte docere*). He restored the buildings, enlarged the monastery's assets and was (in the prevailing language of the sources) a "father unto the monks." Owing to his care of the poor, he was also a "benefactor of the poor" and a "helper of widows and orphans."[99]

Monastic Offices. No single abbot could take care of the monastery's numerous tasks by himself, especially since he was frequently away. In addition, his decisions were restricted by the Rule and the non-binding advice (*consilium*) of the older friars (*seniores*), or in important issues the entire congregation [RB, c. 3]. Benedict also provided for a number of other monastic offices to share various tasks; the abbot made those and, later, additional appointments. The dean was deputy of the abbot, but he represented the interests of the monks as well. Over a period of time he became primarily responsible for spiritual affairs. On the other hand, the provost (*praepositus*) was in charge of business affairs; he was overseer of properties and assets belonging to the monastery. In the event that the monastery owned large tracts of land, several provosts shared these tasks. The cellarer was in charge of all implements, clothing, and provisions, all elements of the "household" including the kitchen. According to the Benedictine Rule, which describes this office in great detail, he was to be sober, not a great eater, neither self-important nor stingy, nor wasteful [RB c. 31, 1]. In the beginning, he was to oversee all the tasks inside the monastery, but during the Middle Ages a division of offices took place. A number of his duties (such as overseeing clothing and the kitchen) were taken over by the chamberlain (*camerarius*), a *hospitarius* was responsible for guests, and an *alomoniarius* often took care of feeding the poor (as at Cluny). Occasionally a *refectarius* was also in charge of the kitchen, and an *infirmarius* was responsible for the sick. Naturally, whether all these offices were actually filled or not depended on the size of the monastery. The Benedictine Rule mentions a gatekeeper (*ostiarius*, later *portarius*) who had his own cell near the entrance to the monastery in order to be available at all times; as a rule this monk was to be a wise, older monk who knew how to respond to different queries. The sacristan also held an important office; he was responsible for liturgical vessels and vestments, as well as candles, the church's treasury, and the ringing of the bells. Later on he was joined by the *custos*, who was responsible for the church including its holy relics. During the ninth century the office of the librarian was added, often also serving as teacher as well as scholar. Furthermore, there were a number of less significant offices or sub-offices (Benedict had made provisions for "assistants"). Among those mentioned by name we encounter transcribers of documents, mostly young monks. They frequently reappear in higher offices, so that one may speak of the beginning of a monastic career and the possibility for "advancement" (strictly by rank) during the course of a monk's life, even though Benedict stated that age was not to be a criterion in assigning offices. In addition to established monastic offices, monks were also charged with various other functions,[100] serving as witnesses in documents pertaining to the monastery (for which purpose mostly older monks were chosen); as envoys sent to kings, popes, bishops, and other monasteries; or as priests in dependent churches.

Relations among Monasteries and with the Outside World

In spite of their desire for seclusion and independence, not all monasteries were isolated. Not only were there ties to their lords, but there were also many different relations among the monasteries themselves, as well as with the laity. This fact can easily be determined by studying the monastery's donations, especially entries in the memorial tradition reflected in fraternity registers and memorial books.

Fraternities (*fraternitates*) were established among individual monasteries whose monks subsequently included one another in their prayers. In 762 there was a death fraternity of Attigny, in which twenty-two bishops, five abbot bishops and seventeen abbots promised each other to each sing a hundred psalms and say a hundred masses (thirty of them by themselves) upon the death of one of their brethren.[101] The original statutes of the fraternity book of Reichenau[102] pursued such fraternities with a total of fifty-two other monasteries and four endowed institutions, and this was subsequently increased to one hundred fraternities.[103] Some communities, such as Fulda, for a while regularly reported additions, so that they could be subsequently recorded in the Reichenau register. The memorial itself was subject to precise rules. Following fraternization between St. Gall and Reichenau (c. 800), the priests were to say three masses each and the remaining friars were to sing a psalm and hold a vigil after the death of a monk from the other monastery. On the seventh day, an additional thirty psalms were to be sung, and finally, on the thirtieth day, another mass was to be said or fifty psalms sung.[104] In addition to this specific purpose, such fraternities permit us a glance into the vast monastic commonwealth which, in the case of Reichenau, extended as far as the Paris basin in the west, to Bavaria in the east, and to Italy in the south, although Alamannic monasteries were in the majority. In this respect, the fraternity book proves itself to be a "document of Carolingian imperial monasticism"(Schmid).

In contrast, memorial book entries recorded the names of benefactors. The entries were regularly recorded in groups which, in most cases, prove to be groups of relatives. (Groups entered by the same hand and with the same ink represent such associations of relatives.) Thus, alongside the liturgical practices (memorial services) and family connections, memorial books also reveal the special relationships specific monasteries maintained with certain families and persons. Necrologies listing the dates on which individual persons died—also for the purpose of a memorial for the dead—are equally informative. Here, too, inclusion in the register suggests a closer relationship with the monastery. One frequently encounters a vast amount of material. Cluny's death rolls alone comprise over 85,000 names, although so high a number may be a singular exception. Death rolls[105] and documents detailing the monastery's external relations are also highly helpful for understanding Fulda. Kings and the archbishops of Mainz were regularly entered on the monastery's death rolls, and from earliest days Fulda and Mainz maintained close relations. At least seven archbishops came from Fulda (prior to 850 and after 960), in addition to other bishops (resulting from the imperial ecclesiastical system) and certain abbots (for example, Hersfeld, Lorsch, and Corvey). At first, the geographic distribution of monastery members was limited to Thuringia, Franconia, and eastern Saxony, but it expanded significantly after the tenth century, when Fulda became an "Ottonian imperial monastery." Much research remains to be done before we will be able to make generalizations on these issues, but the reader has at least been alerted to the ways in which we can obtain data concerning monastic communities and their external affairs. What has been said indicates that the monks themselves, who wished to withdraw from the world for the sake of a religious life, still remained linked to the outside world in many different ways.

4. Monastic Life

Monastic life[106] depended on the factors described and, in fact, has been often touched on in passing. In the form of cenobitic monasticism, it was intended as a strictly organized community life with primarily religious goals. These were in accordance with a definite rule at a place especially designed for this purpose (the monastery), into which were integrated the community's manifold relationships and functions. Last but not least, the typical monastery was subject to its lord. While this may sound seamless, repeated interruptions did occur in everyday monastic life, as will be shown in detail below.

Pursuant to its religious purpose, the ascetic monastic way of life was understood to be an imitation of Christ. "We propose to establish a school of the Lord's service" (*scola dominici servitii*) Benedict of Nursia wrote in the prologue [45] to his Rule. In book miniatures, monks frequently gather at the feet of the crucified Christ. Though clearly anachronistic, even the four evangelists and, indeed, the angels are portrayed as writing monks (complete with tonsure). (See Illustration 11.) In 1065, Hirsau was settled by twelve monks in analogy to the twelve apostles.[107] Monasticism tended to be idealized in this way. In his *Collationes*, Odo of Cluny (c. 924-942) interpreted monasticism as the realization of the church of Pentecost (the ideal Christian community). It transcended the confines of the physical world (because the life of the monks already pointed toward the beyond), returning to man's original state in paradise, anticipating and realizing eternal peace symbolized by monastic silence, an angelic life.[108] Accordingly, the loosely flowing habit was interpreted as angels' attire: the cowl corresponded to the wings of the cherubim when they hid their faces, and the wide sleeves symbolized the wings.[109] Otto of Freising thus eulogized monasticism:

> Already here on earth they lead a life characterized by celestial, angelic purity and holiness of conscience. They live in community . . . they retire at the same time, rise jointly for prayer, take all their meals in one room and occupy themselves day and night with prayer, reading, and work with such indefatigable diligence that they consider it a gross offence if they pass only a minute fraction of an hour without occupying themselves with the divine, except during that short time when they permit their tired limbs some rest on a sparse bed of straw or a coarse blanket; even during meals, they listen to Holy Scripture and prefer to satisfy their spirit rather than their body.[110]

Granted, Otto of Freising is visualizing a recently reformed version of monasticism, the kind of monastic life a monk would like to lead, an ideal derived from the rules of stereotypical descriptions of the lives of holy monks, but one that cannot be generalized in the way stated in a dissertation from 1870:

> The solemn deathlike silence in the monastery is only interrupted by the sounds of the prayer bell and the singing of pious monks; the monks appear to open their lips merely to speak to their God or to talk about him. Here and then, an involuntary cry of pain rises from a monk's chest whenever the scourge tears into his flesh too severely, but those are at the same time moments of greatest bliss. Overwrought nerves project to the abnormally excited brain all those figures to which the world of thoughts strives to adhere. Direct communication with the world of the spirits compensates amply for fasting and scourging. . . . These are monks whose bodies are kept erect merely by their unbending will, ravished by the mortification of their flesh and by fasting, but with eyes filled with celestial fire, for they have just caught a glimpse of the *gloria in excelsis*.[111]

Such an idealized portrayal equates the Rule with reality. To do justice to the Rule is not exactly easy. Benedict [RB c. 4] lists an infinite number of duties as "instruments of good works," a mere sample of which shall be offered in following:

Illustration 11: *Self-evaluation of Monasticism: the Evangelist (Matthew) and Angels Portrayed as Monks*, Codex aureus of Canterbury, after 750.

In the first place, to love the Lord God with all one's heart, with all one's soul, and with all one's strength. Then to love one's neighbor as oneself. . . . Not to do to another what one would not wish to have done to

oneself. To deny oneself in order to follow Christ. To punish one's body.
Not to seek pleasures. To love fasting. To relieve the poor. To clothe the
naked. To visit the sick. . . . To console the sorrowful. To avoid worldly
behavior. . . . Not to return evil for evil. Not to inflict any injury, but to
suffer injuries patiently. To love one's enemies. . . . Not to be arrogant.
Not given to drinking. Not a heavy eater. Not given to much sleeping.
Not lazy. . . [apparently where danger lurked!] Whenever one perceives
any good in oneself to attribute it to God, not to one's self [the perfect
monk was apparently wont to forget a proper sense of humility] but to
recognize that whatever is evil is one's own doing, and to blame one's
self. . . . Not to love much talking. Not to utter words that are foolish and
provoke laughter. . . . In our daily prayer to God to confess with tears and
groans the wrong-doing in our past life. To amend these wrong ways in
the future. To reject carnal desires. To hate one's own will. To obey the
Abbot's commands in everything, even though he himself (which God
forbid) acts otherwise. . . .

Thus one may guess that the number of perfect monks could not
have been particularly great, and people were certainly aware of the
impossibility of living up to these demands. The holiest and most widely
admired monks were those who scolded themselves for even minute
offenses, fearing for their salvation and doing continuous penance. A
"normal" monk probably required firmer discipline, which the Rule also
provided. Ideal and reality were thus separated in medieval monasticism. One may assume medieval monks were more human than angelic
and that they had their weaknesses, which tended to be ridiculed in
monastic anecdotes. For instance, when Duke Frederick of Swabia's
siege of Limburg caused a famine, one knight suggested his preference
for eating fat monks from the monastery to abandoning the castle due
to a lack of food, whereupon the frightened monks handed over their
cache of food to the defenders. Monasteries did not produce "emaciated
bodies," particularly since they were among the wealthiest landowners.
(By the way, it is the very Otto of Freising who praised monasticism as
a savior rescuing the world from doom who relates this story.)[112] The
fact that monks did not permit themselves to sleep during the day was
the rule and may have applied in many cases; still, many a story features
as its central character a monk who nodded off as the inevitable result
of his tiredness. (In one anecdote narrated by Notker of St. Gall[113] the
friar in question experienced a prophetic dream during the course of
his infraction, which somewhat justified the offense.) Also, Otto's report
that monks listened to Holy Scripture during meals is correct in principle, yet Ekkehard's anecdote concerning the visit of Conrad to St. Gall
also illustrates that the fact that monks did not always pay attention to

the reader, but rather focused on food and on forbidden conversation at table. No doubt, the call to celibacy which Otto mentions a little bit later troubled many a monk; at any rate, in numerous narratives women are portrayed in the eyes of monks simply as temptations of the devil, and resisting them becomes a sign of uncommon holiness. Sometimes an external stimulus was necessary to foster an ascetic life style, as when the monks of Hersfeld prayed and fasted in 1064 because a count purloined a farm from them; the count supposedly bragged jokingly about the fact that he had helped the monks to a better life because they had slackened in their responsibilities toward God.[114]

In other words, the everyday life of a monk was less a life in accordance with the Rule than a more-or-less conscious struggle to achieve a life in keeping with the Rule. At times it was also a departure from the Rule without anyone's ever taking any offense. Therefore, the "norm" of monastic life which one has to presuppose must be checked against stories dealing with the reality of everyday life in the monastic annals (*Gesta*). While these were often anecdotal in their depiction of the weaknesses of the monks, frequently exaggerating them, they nevertheless counterbalance a picture which is too highly idealized. We will have to be mindful of that when we deal with the daily routine in a monk's life.

The monastic day was passed in prayer, spiritual readings, and manual labor; as underscored by Otto of Freising, praying, sleeping, and eating in unison were the principal activities of monastic life. Central to this life was choral prayer, which rigorously divided the monastic day. (See Illustration 12.) The rigid schedule forced the monks to pay attention to time, which is why monasteries functioned as centers for measuring time (albeit by primitive means). When Pepin took the monastery of St. Gall under his protection, he donated a copy of the Rule of Benedict and a bell, which was supposed to announce the schedule at specific times of the day. The day commenced between midnight and two in the morning with matins (also called vigils, or nocturnes), the morning prayers [RB, c. 12ff.] including three readings of psalms with responses and alleluia, lauds, an epistle reading, responses, a hymn, a verse from the Bible, the Gospel and a petitionary prayer–all of this lasted longer on Sundays. Both cantor and reader were selected by the abbot [RB, c. 47]. At the break of dawn the monks once again sang songs of praise (*laudes*). This was followed in the course of the day by the so-called little canonical hours (*horae* consisting of one verse each, three psalms, readings, hymn, and a final prayer): prime (about 6 a.m.), tierce (about 9 a.m.), sext (about noon), and nones (about 3 p.m.). The times varied slightly according to the season of the year and geographical location. Vespers (about 5 p.m.) lasted somewhat longer, with the reading of four psalms and antiphone, readings, response, hymn, verse, song of praise, Gospel, petitionary prayer, the Lord's Prayer, and the concluding prayer. Compline (between 6 and 8 p.m.) brought the day to a close.

The monks retired early, although their rest was not always sufficient, as the stories of the perpetually tired monk illustrate. To sleep outside of designated hours—Benedict permitted some rest at noon—was considered a serious offense. The Cluniacs introduced a custom according to which a lantern was placed in front of a sleeping monk, which he then had to carry with him until he found another monk who had dozed off.[115] Naturally, falling asleep during choral prayers was especially reprehensible. (Caesarius of Heisterbach[116] tells of a monk who fell asleep so frequently during choral prayers—"a most horrible occurrence"—that Christ himself finally descended from the cross and

Illustration 12: *Prayer as Central Task: A Monastic Mass* (The Drogo Sacramentary, Metz, tenth century; D-initial).

gave him such a slap on the ear that he died within three days.) At night the monks slept in their own beds in communal dormitories, in full attire in accordance with the Rule [RB c. 22, 4-5]; one monk probably was in charge of making certain that his brethren really slept.

The time between choral prayers was filled with work. Although the well-known Benedictine motto of *ora et labora* (pray and work) is not found in the Benedictine Rule in exactly these words, Benedict did demand [c. 48] that his monks perform from between three to eight hours of daily manual labor. In the summer this occurred after prime and after nones; during the winter months between tierce and nones; during Lent the hours were somewhat longer. With few exceptions, especially during the founding years of reform monasteries, such as early Cistercian monasteries, this work meant hard labor in the fields. Benedict had written [c. 48, 7] "If however local necessity or their own poverty compels them to work personally at gathering the harvest, they should not be upset about this. For then truly are they monks, if they live by the work of their hands, as did our Fathers and the Apostles." Monks (mostly members of the nobility throughout the Middle Ages) soon frowned on hard work, and during the twelfth century, it was common practice (according to Ordericus Vitalis) for manual labor to be performed by peasants, while monks served God in spiritual and clerical ways.[117] (Monks on horseback were held to be acting in keeping with their station in life.) Monastic labor also consisted of light garden work; according to an anecdote by Notker the Stammerer, some royal envoys observed older monks of St. Gall busying themselves removing nettles and weeding the monastery garden.[118] The work frequently required a craft or skill, often in the form of clerical work or special assignments. Benedict [RB c. 57] even permitted the sale of produce if somewhat cheaper than that produced by lay people. The remainder of the day was passed with reading (primarily Psalms). The Benedictine Rule [c. 48] provided for readings before sext; during the winter months reading took place before tierce and after meals. This hardly suited all monks, since Benedict had to add [c. 48, 17 f.] "It is important that one or two seniors should be appointed to go round the monastery during the hours when the brethren are engaged in reading, to see whether perchance they come upon some lazy brother who is engaged in doing nothing or in chatter, and is not intent upon his book," for "idleness is the enemy of the soul" [c. 48, 1]. During Lent every monk was supposed to obtain one book from the library in order to read it "through from the beginning" [RB c. 48, 15]. Later on, such reservations hardly existed any longer; reading and writing had become the principal activities for monks.

Some brothers were assigned to specific tasks, be it as "controllers" or nurses (c. 36, 10), as hosts during the arrival of guests [c. 53, 16 ff.], as caretakers of the poor, or as fulfillers of one of the monastic offices. Alternating weekly, monks were also assigned to kitchen duty. On Saturdays they cleaned and did laundry, as "he who is ending his week's service together with him who is about to start should wash the feet of all" [RB c. 35]. It has also been argued that increased liturgical service in some of the reform monasteries, such as Cluny, might have left little time for both work and education, as evidenced by the fact that monks could be dispensed from choir duty only with special permission.[119]

Mentioning the kitchen leads us to the subject of meals, which were also taken communally in the refectory. Benedict was rather terse concerning meals; he merely provided for one main meal, to be taken in the summer (except on days of fasting) during sext (noon), in the winter during nones (3 p.m.), and during Lent not until evening (after vespers) [RB c. 41]. This could be augmented by a cold snack in the evening as a second meal, but only so long as it was still daylight. However, later customs show that even more than two meals a day were customary in many monasteries. (There were, however, also numerous days of fasting.) Concerning meals, Benedict wrote [c. 39] "We consider it to be enough for the daily meal . . . that there should always be served two cooked dishes . . . so that if someone cannot eat of the one dish he may still make a meal from the other. . . . And if fruit or tender vegetables are to be had, a third dish may be added. A full pound of bread should be enough for a day, whether there is one meal or those of dinner and supper." Bread was the main staple, though for variety's sake there were different kinds. Bread varied in quality, and on days of fasting, bread of lesser quality was distributed. Legumes were also important, then eggs (prepared in many different ways), cheese, and fish. Meat was forbidden according to Benedict, being reserved for very special occasions. This rule, which was repeatedly mentioned by the *consuetudines*, remained officially in effect, but was broken with regular frequency in spite of what Otto of Freising wrote: "Furthermore, they refrain from eating meat in any form. Some do not eat anything but simple food and drink no wine, at times living only on vegetables, or bread and water."[120] An episode in Ekkehard's *Casus sancti Galli* [121] demonstrates that this regulation was not observed with particular strictness at St. Gall (as was also the case at many other monasteries) during the tenth century. One of the royal inspectors who was to check up on the monks there offered, "Even though horses are not allowed to be consumed, I would much prefer monks obediently eating my nag to their breaking other commands of the Rule. I therefore pronounce with conviction on behalf of Benedict: monks may eat and drink what the abbot freely permits." A bishop added (remembering the former lack of fish in the lake), "Still, at the time, the large majority of brothers did not eat any meat either, though their frugality indeed seemed excessive. Still, there were those who solely ate poultry, and rightfully so, since fish and poultry are one and the same creature. On the other hand, only a few ate meat of four-legged animals in rooms provided by the abbot within the monastery. Surely, I will never encounter a more splendid monk than the one among them who sometimes ate meat." (At the time of Benedict of Aniane, there was still uncertainty concerning the issue of whether poultry belonged to the "four-legged animals," or if it was permissible as a Lenten food.[122]) During the twelfth century, a Sunday meal at the Bamberg cathedral chapter consisted of eight courses, including mutton, pork, chicken, and roasted meat.[123] Other monasteries probably followed similar practices. Thus, even concerning meals, Rule and reality could be far apart. In fact, "feast days," for which Benedict had permitted more sumptuous meals, were sometimes fairly frequent. Because of his frequent duty to host guests, the abbot's table was subject to different rules. Besides, many a monk may not have had his fill by merely eating the amount of food apportioned to him. Ekkehard reports how a monk of Trier by the name of Sandrat had his watchman bring him meat every night until he was caught. (What was so embarrassing about this incident was the fact that Sandrat had come to St. Gall as an envoy of the king in order to watch over the monastery's compliance with the Rule.[124])

Wine was served during meals. Here, too, Benedict, permitted no more than one-fourth liter, and even that was considered a concession, "For although we read that wine is not at all a drink for monks, yet, since in our days it is impossible to persuade monks of this, let us agree at least about this that we should not drink our fill, but more sparingly . . ."[c. 40, 6]. Since Benedict used Roman measurements which later become obsolete, there soon evolved a controversy over the specific amounts of wine or beer,[125] and many a monastic "customary practice" officially increased the daily ration. Some drank the current favorite, wines spiced with herbs. Many a monastic history tells of monks who were too much given to wine (a sin which was small by comparison). Among the "cultural achievements" of monasticism belong both the distillation of alcohol and the introduction of table etiquette—for instance, the custom of jointly raising goblets followed by bowing.[126] As mentioned earlier, the monks listened to readings during meals. The reader, chosen for his aptitude, was assigned weekly by Benedict [c. 38,

1 ff.]. Otherwise, strictest silence prevailed during meals, and in the dormitory and oratory as well; at St. Gall at the time of Ekkehard, total silence was preserved. Some *consuetudines* permitted speaking only during certain hours. If one needed to communicate—indeed, at least some items had to be passed around during the course of a meal—this was accomplished through gestures. Benedict permitted the use of such signs. From that developed a regular sign language during the Middle Ages, on which a number of manuscripts elaborate and which often became even a part of the *consuetudines*.[127] The oldest codification from Cluny, probably incomplete, dates from the late eleventh century and contained 118 signs; the contemporary list of Wilhelm of Hirsau contained 359 such signs. During the twelfth century, an entire series of lists such as these existed. A number of signs had been designed for use in the refectory, including signs for food and drink. For instance, pressing together the palms of one's hands meant asking for cheese, making swimming motions indicated fish, and reaching for one's throat symbolized vinegar. We also learn about meal plans from lists of these signs when, for instance, different recipes for cooking eggs or making different types of bread are listed along with the gestures. A second group of signs concerned itself with the dormitory and contained signs for pieces of clothing, bedding, and sleeping or personal hygiene. A third group was reserved for church and worship services, including signs for liturgical books, for saints, and for feast days. Finally, a fourth group detailed sundry matters, such as offices and activities. This area was subsequently enlarged, so that extensive conversations could be engaged in (surely no longer in keeping with the spirit of the Benedictine vow of silence).

Monasteries placed great emphasis on hygiene and cleanliness, which Zimmermann examined in the light of the monastic rules. He succeeded in pointing out that the image of the ascetic monk completely neglecting personal hygiene was pure fiction. While there were indeed true masters of self-denial, they were exceptions rather than the rule. Strict monastic rules—such as that of Wilhelm of Hirsau—permitted only two baths a year, at Christmas and Easter, but this rule applied only to full baths. Most *consuetudines* prescribed repeated daily washing, and, in the plan of St. Gall, there was a bathhouse within the cloister. Saturday was the day reserved for complete cleaning, including washing the feet. Most of the time, *consuetudines* contain rather detailed instructions regarding hygiene (including specific times for relieving oneself).[128] In a manner of speaking, Cistercians invented "flushing toilets," as they tended to design their monasteries in such a way that a brook would flow through those parts of a building where waste (of any kind) accumulated. The shaving of beards and tonsure also took place at pre-arranged times. The *consuetudines* prescribed who was to prepare hot water and when, where, and how. The monks sat down on facing rows of benches and shaved each other while singing psalms. (At some monasteries such as Cluny the singing of psalms was common throughout the day. The entire routine—as with all its everyday events specified by the Rule—was performed like a ritual).

Monks were not allowed to own personal property. "Everything should be common to all," directed Benedict [RB c. 33, 6]. Violators were punished, and the beds of monks were searched by the abbot for evidence of private possessions. Ekkehard reports at the occasion of his previously mentioned visit to the monastery of St. Gall that King Conrad I had the monastery's pupils read individually, rewarding them by placing a gold piece in each one's mouth. When one of the children cried out violently and spat out the coin, the king commented by saying: "He will become a good monk if he lives long enough."[129] According to the intentions of Benedict, anything monks required they were to receive from the abbot, each according to his needs. Each monk received his own bedding [RB c. 22, 2], consisting of a mattress, a bed sheet, a blanket, and a pillow [RB c. 55, 15], as well as his clothes. Monastic attire consisted basically of the clothes worn by simple Romans during late antiquity,[130] a style which was adapted during the Middle Ages and only received a special appearance then. Benedict had not prescribed certain kinds of clothes because it should conform with local conditions. It was only in the Middle Ages, as a result of the reforms of Benedict of Aniane, that monastic garb became uniform, only to differentiate later in terms of style and color for purposes of distinguishing between orders. A monk's attire consisted of a tunic, the Roman undergarment, and the hooded habit (*Kukulle*) which was worn over it, a cloak whose thickness varied with the seasons. According to Benedict, when monks were to travel the abbot issued them better clothes and pants (*femoralia*) which were regularly worn underneath the habit in colder, northern regions. In addition, monks received the scapular to work in, a garb that later changed its appearance: the medieval scapular (since Benedict of Aniane in the form of the scapulary habit), a knee-length shoulder frock with a sewn-in cowl became the normal house attire of monks who received scapulars. An ankle-length frock with wide sleeves was worn as a coat for going out, but it was also essential in identifying members of various orders. Cluniac monks wore an additional long-sleeved ankle-length frock (*froccus*) over the scapulary habit, rich in material and pleats. Stockings, shoes, sandals and a belt were also part of a monk's attire. Additionally, according to Benedict, every monk was to receive a knife, a pen, writing tablets, a needle, and a handkerchief [RB c. 55, 19]. Any time a monk received new clothes he had to return old ones, which were often distributed among the poor. Dressing correctly was taken very seriously. This is not only reflected in controversies among the orders, but also in a story related by Caesarius of Heisterbach to the monks, about a dying Cistercian who took off his cowl (he was hot, and the abbot had permitted him to do so). However, after his death he appeared to his friars and reported that St. Benedict himself had stopped him at the gates of paradise and refused him entrance, since he was not dressed in accordance with the place of rest. Thereupon the abbot returned his cowl so that he could once again head for his (this time, final) destination in paradise.[131] On the other hand, there were times when customary attire was abandoned. Abbot Rodulf complained toward the end of the tenth century that many monks wore hats reaching down to their ears, as well as expensive and colorful clothes; that they tied their habits too tightly; that they wore wide pants made of delicate fabric which barely covered their privates, as well as pointed shoes with flaps on the sides.[132] During bad times allotments were curtailed, and the cellarer had trouble justifying his austerity policy. Ekkehard reports of a monk by the name of Heribald (known for his erratic ways) who refused to flee with the rest during an impending raid by the Hungarians unless he was to receive his annual allotment of shoe leather. His request was not honored, and he alone remained behind at the monastery. He unexpectedly survived the Hungarian raid and afterwards said, when asked how he was, "Very well! Believe me, I cannot remember ever having seen people having a better time in our monastery; they distributed food and drink with open hands. Before, I could never once get our niggardly cellarer to hand me a drink to quench my thirst; they, however, gave me plenty whenever I asked."[133] Of course, the story was to impress on the monks the proper (that is, frugal) way of life.

Monks probably broke petty rules all the time. That is why the Benedictine Rule provides for punishments [c. 23]. A monk who committed an offense first received two warnings, then he was publicly reprimanded; he was no longer permitted to participate in communal meals and choir services, and if necessary he was also punished corporally. If that still did not prompt him to mend his ways, he was expelled from the community. When he was accepted back into the community he was assigned the lowest position. Punctuality at meals and choir services were especially important to Benedict. He wrote, "If at the night office anyone arrives after the *Glory be* of Psalm 94, which for this reason we wish to be said altogether slowly and deliberately, he must not stand in his place in the choir, but last of all, or in a place set apart by the Abbot for such careless persons, so that they may be seen by the Abbot and by everyone else, until at the end of the Work of God he does penance by public satisfaction"[c. 43, 4ff.]. Anyone late for meals was barred from the communal table—after being reprimanded twice—and did not receive any wine, either.

As these punishments illustrate, the reality of everyday monastic life did not always live up to the rules. Benedict therefore conceded, "Although the monk's life ought at all seasons to bear a Lenten character, such strength is found in only the few. Therefore we urge the brethren to keep the days of Lent with a special purity of life and also at this holy season to make reparation for the failings of other times" [RB c. 49, 1ff.]. Each monk was to make a sacrifice by depriving himself of food and drink, sleep, talking, or something else. The most important virtue for a monk was humility, to which Benedict dedicated his longest chapter [c. 7]; obedience was the primary obligation: all orders were to be executed without delay [c. 5, 4] even if they exceeded one's abilities [c. 68]. If one perceives [says Benedict in c. 71, 6ff.] that one's superior was angry, one should "at once and without delay prostrate" oneself at his feet and offer satisfaction until the anger has been healed with a blessing.

Similar to the lofty spiritual goals, community life at close quarters also demanded discipline and order. For this reason the abbot had to be invested with far-reaching authority, and daily life had to be regulated in minute detail. The daily routine of individual monks remained a constant struggle with obedience to the Rule, varying according to time, place, and the order to which one belonged. It alternated between requiring humility and encouraging one's awareness of belonging to a special class. Being a monk in the Middle Ages did not constitute being an outsider in society, despite the isolation it entailed; rather, it constituted a rise in one's public standing. That is why monasteries retained their attraction to the nobility; indeed, noble families needed relatives in monasteries to remember them in their prayers. Thus, medieval monasticism turned into an "aristocratic monasticism." Monks perceived themselves as *milites Christi*, as "soldiers" or—in accordance with the change in meaning during the high Middle Ages—as "knights" of Christ. In their own way, monks accomplished with prayer what the lay nobility accomplished with the sword: a monk fought for faith, for his own salvation and as a service to society. Monastic life during the Middle Ages constituted a life for society. Monasteries entertained far-reaching relations. They were engaged in politics, and the functions of the "State" would have been unthinkable without them. As a result, the rules necessarily became relaxed, since aristocratic monks wished to live in a style befitting their class; heavy work was out of the question, and the rich attire of the Cluniac monks was not really necessitated by the climate but merely served to impress others.[134] If they exceeded the limits of religious purposes in this process, the resulting countermovements and reforms were themselves in the interest of the aristocracy; for the reputation of monasticism had to be maintained. The regimentation of life in the new religious orders was ever increasing, although the fragmentation of religious orders also stratified ways of life to an even greater degree. Monastic life depended on many factors, above all on ascetic and monastic functions; it changed from time to time, continuing to set itself apart from other forms of life because of these common goals.

Certainly such a religious life in the service of society was only possible because others assumed the responsibility for feeding the monks, who produced nothing themselves. Monasticism, like the rest of medieval society, relied on a sufficient surplus produced by the peasant population (although within the Middle Ages these tributes were considered the peasants' obvious obligation in return for services actually provided). By highlighting the manorial system, in which monasteries ranked among the most important manorial lords, our next chapter will illustrate the way of life and world of the peasants, including relationships with their lords.

IV

Peasant Life and the Manorial System

During the Middle Ages, land constituted both a source of food and the very basis for existence; this was true for the peasants who cultivated it as well as the lords who owned it. (This already implies ownership and cultivation could be in different hands.) Peasants had to produce surpluses in order to support not only themselves, but also the nobility and the clergy and—via markets—increasingly the urban population as well. Thus, in contrast to the urban cultures of antiquity and modern industrial society, medieval culture was agrarian in nature.[1] A process of "reagrarization" had already set in during late antiquity, causing the cities to shrink continually and moving the economic initiative to the land. During the earlier Middle Ages, ninety percent or more of the entire population lived in the country, and the majority of cities were still farming communities in their own right. Consequently, country life during the Middle Ages—quite in contrast to its reflection in the sources—constituted the normal, typical form of life. Agrarian thought patterns were shared by all levels of society.[2] In general, peasant life formed the basis for everyday life; monthly calendar pictures dealt primarily with the work of peasants,[3] and when Charlemagne decided to introduce Germanic names for the months, some were named after agricultural seasons. The month of May was called *Winnemonat* (the "meadow month" during which the animals were turned out to pasture), June was referred to as *Brachmonat* (for the breaking up of fallow soil), July was called *Hewimonat* (hay month), August was *Aranmonat* (harvest month), September was *Witumonat* (wood month, or wood-cutting month), and October was *Windumemonat* (month of the wine harvest).[4] With the exception of Italy, the lords also originally lived in the country. Landed property constituted the economic base, and rule over peasants was the means to utilize these properties. Life in the country was primarily characterized by the life of the peasants, but embedded in an authoritarian structure. We are therefore justified in considering not just general peasant life by itself as an example of the most common form of medieval life but, more specifically, life within the manorial system. The manorial system was by no means the sole form of agricultural life; rather, the Middle Ages also had a substantial number of free peasants. The manorial system, with its relationships between lords and serfs, permits us much better insights into the social structure of the age, and it appears more to typify the Middle Ages than the life of independent peasants, particularly since we are dealing here with a Europe-wide development. Because of the evidence from various sources, life within the manorial system is known much more extensively than other areas of country life. In addition to legal sources and pictorial impressions, records documenting land donations (deeds), and ownership records, and land registers from large manor houses offer us excellent insights. Let us first examine the institutional confines of peasant life, namely the manorial system.

I. The Institution:
The Medieval Manorial System

The Concept of the Manorial System

The term "manorial system"[5] (*Grundherrschaft*) is not contemporary; instead, it is a modern term which reflects a system of rural conditions.[6] In reality, the manorial system encompasses a complex social entity on which were superimposed economic, political, and social factors. The term's two components provide us with an initial insight into these factors. (See Illustration 13.) The manorial system is tied to the soil (*Grund*), or landed property; the power to dispose of the land was the inalienable foundation of manorial authority (*Herrschaft*). Technically speaking, the term implies a certain form of organization, administration, and utilization; together these three comprise the economic aspect of the manorial system. In addition, "manorial authority" or "lordship" entails privileges deriving from land ownership and tied to it. Yet one cannot rule land, only its inhabitants, and this represents the social aspect of the manorial system. "Manorial authority" exists wherever land ownership entitles an owner to exercise lordly rights over other human beings.

The origins and the legal foundations of the manorial system are disputed. Undoubtedly the economy of late antiquity, with its huge landed properties, provided a model, particularly since this *dominium*—hence "domain"—provided the link to protective authority (*patrocinium*) by the lord over his dependent and soil-bound peasants (*colones*). The specifically medieval manorial system, whose classical form incorporated both demesne (*Salland*) and manse-land (*Hufenland*), with services performed by peasants on granted land, was apparently created on the royal domains of Merovingians in Northern France.[7] At any rate, it was first documented for this region. Elements of a dual form of the manorial rule are recognizable as early as 600.[8] The origins of large lay estate holdings can be explained through the original Germanic settlement and the seizure of the Roman manorial system by both kings and nobility. On the other hand, clerical manorial authority accrued primarily from donations; not until the appearance of monastic manorial authority were monks in a position to discharge the tasks described in the previous chapter.[9] Furthermore, there is considerable controversy over whether sovereign rights over landed property and people are governmental in nature (bestowed by the king), whether they were usurped, whether they emanated from land ownership itself (Seeliger), or grew from the noble position of the lord of the manor (Dopsch).[10] According to Otto Brunner, all authority ultimately derived from household authority, a fact corroborated by substantial evidence. However, in a discussion of the origins of these rights, we will have to differentiate as follows: serfs at the manor were controlled by the lord on account of their serfdom; on the other hand, ever more freemen slipped into dependency to a manorial lord either because they voluntarily rendered service to and sought protection of the lord, or as a result of forcible suppression.[11] Ever so slowly, both peasant groups merged to form one stratum of serfs. According to Lütge,[12] the manorial system originated as a result of two processes: on the one hand, the change just described which was experienced by freemen, and on the other hand, the process of serfs becoming peasants after being settled on tenements. The time at which this development was completed is difficult to ascertain, since it was a gradual process which did not occur in various places simultaneously. However, it is possible to gather that the beginnings of the manorial system from the sixth to the ninth centuries were followed by a period of consolidation and expansion between the ninth and the twelfth centuries.[13]

In this context, it will be less important to review and criticize the various theories than to discuss the conditions of peasant life, which depended largely on the organization and the administration provided by the manorial system as a viable economic form. The manorial "system" included a number of varying social ties linking the serfs to the lord, which certainly did not all emanate from the latter's sovereign rights over landed property.

Function and Organization of the Manorial System
as an Economic Form

Upholding the manorial system were the king, the Church, and the nobility, who exploited their often extensive estates by means of that system. The system was characterized by the separation of ownership from labor. The lord of the manor did not cultivate the estate himself; rather, he did so with the assistance of dependent peasants by permitting them the use of land in exchange for rent and services (*Frondienste*).[14] The most important function of the manorial system was the maintenance of the lord and his court. Thus, the peasants had to produce a sufficient amount of surplus to feed not only their own families, but also (and primarily) the lord of the manor, whose lavish style of life will be discussed in the next chapter.

Above all, gradual increase in the Church's land holdings led to various degrees of density in the distribution of the land; often the Church's estates were scattered over great distances, resulting in several different lords in a single region, or even in a single village, which might consist of various lay and clerical estates all mixed together. Though the largest part of the estates was originally cultivated by serfs tilling the land for themselves, the subsequent dispersion of property and bestowals on free peasants who held on to their tenements soon gave rise to the "classical" or dual form of the manorial system. This division resulted in two different economic spheres. (See Illustration 13.) The first was the lord's land (*Salland* or demesne; also called *terra salica* and *terra indominicata*), which was found near the manor house, cultivated by the lord with the assistance of the serfs of the manor (*servi, mancipia*) and manse peasants, who were obligated to render certain services (*Frondienste*). The tenant land or manse land (so called because of the way it was partitioned) was turned over to dependent peasants and cultivated by them in exchange for certain specified services. In general, manse land predominated, with the share of the manorial land in the total area varying greatly. Yet manors did exist which had no manorial land, and there were others without any tenant land. Additionally, a part of the estate—indeed, frequently even entire groups of manors—might be bestowed on nobles or *ministeriales* as fiefs.

The center of such an association was formed by the *curtis*, the manor (*Herrenhof, Salhof,* or *Fronhof*). The inventory of the royal court at Annappes (near Lille), perhaps drawn up on the occasion of

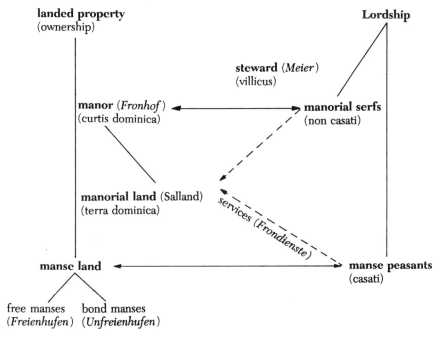

Illustration 13: *Schematic Overview of the Dual Structure of the Manorial System.*

Charlemagne's visit in 800, is most informative.[15] At the center was a royal house built of stone—still the exception at this time—with a "royal hall" and three rooms, eleven chambers, a cellar, and two entrance-halls. Inside the fenced curtis there were seventeen additional, single-room wooden houses, a stable, a kitchen, a bakery, two barns, and three poultry houses. A gate made of stone formed the entrance, together with a platform (*Söller*) from which commands were proclaimed. In the royal quarters on another manor there was also a wooden chapel. Domestic equipment and linens (as a rule one bedsheet each, one table cloth, and one towel), utensils (two bronze bowls, two drinking cups, two bronze and one cast iron kettle, one pan, one pothook, one trivet, one basket with kindling), and tools (hatchets, broadaxe, drills, knives, axe, planes, scythes, sickles, and a sufficient amount of woodworking tools) were listed in detail.[16] Thus, the manor houses were prepared to receive the king and perform chores in conjunction with his visit. The inventory also included livestock. A comparison of similar lists from Annappes and Staffelsee indicates that one has to be prepared to expect differences. Next to poultry, pigs, sheep, cattle, and goats were most important; at Annappes, horses were also important, while at Staffelsee we encounter only one horse.

Manor, demesne, and manses together formed a single economic unit typically concentrated in one location, but which could also extend into the surrounding countryside. At the Werden manor house of Friemersheim on the Rhine, manorial land was scattered over five communities, and the 122.5 manses over twenty-five communities; these were, however, clearly centered around the area between Moers and Friemersheim. The monastery owned only very few manses in more remote villages.

Demesne, often in the form of several fields surrounding the manor house or dotted over several villages and individual manses, shared fields varying in size from manor to manor. They included farmland, pastures for livestock, sometimes vineyards, and last but not least, wooded areas completely integrated into the manorial enterprise. Woods sustained the pigs—the size of woodlands was often gauged according to the number of pigs they could support—and they provided timber for the construction of houses, wood for furniture and tools, and fuel. In addition, the woods were the hunting grounds for the nobility, who reserved the right to hunt big game. Important princes and kings often owned a contiguous, exclusive hunting preserve, called a *Forst* (forest). Furthermore, kitchens, bakeries, breweries, wine presses, gardens, fish ponds, and mills were frequently attached to the manor house. There were fifty mills in the approximately forty domains of the Prüm manor at the end of the ninth century, and the monastery of Saint-Germain-des-Prés near Paris disposed of a total of fifty-seven mills in twelve of its twenty-three domains. Here one must assume a certain degree of centralization, since the number of mills accumulated quite noticeably in certain locations. Large manor houses also utilized *geniciae*, "workhouses for women," where cloth was manufactured.

At smaller estates, the manor (*Salhof*) served as a residence for the lord; larger estates, on the other hand, had a number of manor house groups, each managed by an official, called the steward (*Meier*) or *villicus* (hence the term *Villikationsverfassung*). If properties were located far away, operation by the owner was not worth the effort. Instead, collection offices were established for the purpose of collecting levies. On the other hand, large and concentrated estates necessitated a stratification of administration into major and minor manors. Toward the end of the ninth century, the manorial system of the monastery of Prüm consisted of three major manor houses (those of Prüm, Münstereifel, and St. Goar), to which were attached a total of forty-two manorial estates with well over 4,000 acres of farmland and 2,118 manses. Around 800, the monastery of Saint-Germain-des-Prés owned nine manors with 1,507 manses, of which 1,427 were occupied. A council at Aachen in 816 defined large estates as those with more than 3,000 manses, while an estate of 200 to 300 manses was considered small.[17]

In his famous *Capitulare de villis*,[18] which probably originated in 792/93, Charlemagne gave instructions concerning the administration of the royal estates in his entire kingdom in order to assure sustenance and obviate abuses. Subsequently, the royal estates were divided into administrative districts (*ministeria*), each comprising several manors (*villae*) and each under the jurisdiction of a judge (*iudex*). The judge was responsible for deciding in the name of the king cases involving serfs, as well as for supervising work in the fields and the remaining production; he was also responsible for the yield, and he was in charge of keeping records of the levies, services, income, expenditures, and surpluses. The instructions and prohibitions indicate that there was danger of alienation of imperial estates at the hands of these administrators. The judges themselves commanded a high social position and took care of imperial estates only occasionally, if only part-time. Charlemagne expected them to inspect his estates three to four times a year; so that they were not always available. The actual supervision remained in the hands of their deputies, especially the *maiores* (*Meier* = steward), or *villici* (later, especially in the north, referred to as *Schulte/Schulze*, and *Schultheiss* in the south), whose district (*ministeria*) was to be no larger than what could be supervised on a given day. The steward supervised the work of both peasants and serfs on the manorial land, and he was also responsible for collecting and delivering levies and tithes. There is no evidence of any further authority, such as jurisdiction over the serfs, during Frankish times; however, the steward later assumed judicial responsibility at the manor house.

This manorial organization (= the *Villikationsverfassung*) underwent crucial change during the Middle Ages. In the twelfth and especially since the thirteenth century, the first signs of dissolution of the system appeared. This was because the income of the lords decreased, so that new methods of cultivation had to be found at the same time that peasants had begun to migrate to the rising towns. In many places (though not everywhere, as once believed), either the office of steward was abandoned and demesne divided into manse-land or (more frequently) entire manors were handed over in the form of fiefs or tenancies. Though operation by the lord himself remained an important source of income, it paled when compared to other factors (such as tax income and *regalia*, prerogatives of sovereignty).[19] Land tenure developed, in three stages, into the determining element of the manorial system. At the beginning of the development there was often share-cropping, according to which the possessions and the livestock remained the property of the landlord to whom the tenant owed half of his yield. This was followed (in approximately the thirteenth century) by short-term tenure at specified rates of rent, initially in the form of a contract lasting three, six, or nine years; later, the contract consisted of longer periods of between twelve and twenty-four years. It was not until the fifteenth century that hereditary tenancy finally prevailed.[20] The lord of the manor did not have all necessities produced on the premises any longer; rather, he purchased them at the town market. One can therefore state that the system based on administration by stewards of the early and high Middle Ages corresponded to an economy based on self-production and barter. The tenancy system of the late Middle Ages, however, was more like the monetary system which began gradually to manifest itself, even though one must consider many particular differences here.[21] As a result of discontinuing services, peasants now won time to concentrate on their own private production; still, they were also forced to take their surplus to market and sell it themselves in order to acquire money for rent, so that they became dependent on economic cycles. As a result, the "classical" system of *Villikation* gradually disappeared, although not the manorial system itself. In fact, the term "lord of the manor" (*dominus fundi*) did not even originate until this later time, when one had to differentiate among the rights exercised by various lords. Only a landowner entitled to demand rent was a "lord of the manor," the term no longer related to personal dependency, once so important.[22] These manorial privileges formed the very core of what is considered the manorial system of the early and high Middle Ages.

Manorial Privileges

The manorial system was essentially a relationship between a lord and his dependents, the serfs. The term *Herrschaft*, lordship, had a very specific meaning during the Middle Ages. According to studies by Brunner and Schlesinger, it constituted the very essence of political and public order. The medieval state amounted to "lordship," to matters pertaining to a lord; lordship and association (*Genossenschaft*) formed the two pillars of medieval public order. Consequently, the lord exercised a kind of public authority over his serfs with which the king could generally not interfere. As far as bond peasants were concerned, the lord represented order (coercive and public authority). This is one reason why representatives of the manorial system needed to belong to the upper strata of society, the nobility. "The peasants were largely serfs, villeins (*Hintersassen*), *Holde*, subjects with their lord as 'mediator' over against the state,"[23] and the lord of the manor ranked between the king and the serf. Thus, to the peasants, the lord of the manor constituted the normal reference point, often the only one. The highest judicial authority over freemen was reserved for government authorities, but as far as serfs were concerned, the lord of the manor ruled without any restrictions. According to his biographer, Bishop Benno of Osnabrück was strict when collecting taxes, not hesitating to have a sound thrashing administered in order to make the peasants pay; "but," the biographer adds, "everybody is likely to forgive him for that."[24] Apparently coercive measures such as these were commonly practiced and considered part of a lord's privileges.

The lord held various privileges. As a result of domestic authority, manorial rule consisted of authority (*Munt*, which also included the duty to protect) over members of the household community, in addition to the right to dispose of their possessions (*Gewere*). Typically, serfs who were bound to the manor were referred to as members of the *familia* of the lord of the manor.[25] They formed a closely knit association, with the lord at the center. Rights emanating from any other source were integrated into the assocation. For example, the much-discussed issue of how manorial authority extended to freemen is most easily resolved within the manorial system: free peasants transferred themselves and their possessions to a lord in order to secure his protection. Protection created authority, to the extent that the latter was in fact referred to as protective authority. (It goes without saying that this was not always a voluntary process; the *Acta Murensia* from the first half of the eleventh century tell of a powerful layman at Wohlen to whom others had assigned their possessions, but who subsequently proceeded to suppress the other peasants and to raise demands "as if they had been his serfs [*mansionarii*]."[26]) On the other hand, as is the case with feudal arrangements, those who benefited from the protection offered their services and, in return, received assistance and counsel; furthermore, both parties were obligated to mutual fidelity.

Of course, manorial authority manifested itself primarily in economic rights to services and tributes from the serfs; these amounted to a substantial portion of the income of the lord of the manor and were most important to him. While we possess only sporadic evidence concerning residual rights, medieval land registers frequently recorded such income. The income consisted largely of a fixed rent in return for the permission to utilize manorial land; in the early Middle Ages payments were mostly made in kind. This was augmented by a number of additional forms of income derived from the utilization of manorial shops and installations. According to the *Capitulare de villis*:

> Every official is to report annually on our total yield: how much profit he made with the oxen in the service of our cowherds, how much he made off the manses to provide plowing, how much from pig tax and other (property) taxes he collected, how much he has received in fines and how much for keeping the peace (*Friedensgeld*, court fees), how much for game caught without our permission in our forests, how much from fines, (fees) from mills, forests, pastures, how much toll from bridges or ships, how much rent from freemen and tithing areas on cultivated lands belonging to the crown, the income from markets, vineyards and from the wine tax, how much hay was harvested, how much wood and how many torches, shingles and various other lumber, how much was harvested from abandoned fields, the amount of vegetables (legumes), millet, wool, flax and hemp, fruit, and nuts, how much was harvested from grafted trees and gardens, in beet fields and in fish ponds, how many skins, pelts, horns were collected and how much honey, wax, fat, tallow and soap, how much profit was made from blackberry wine, spiced wine, mead, vinegar, beer, cider and old wine, old and new harvest, chickens, eggs, geese, how much was taken in by fishermen, smiths, shieldmakers and shoemakers, how much money was made with kneading-troughs, chests or shrines, how much turners and saddlers took in, how much profit was made by ore and lead mines, how much was collected from other people who had tax obligations, how many stallions and breeding mares they had; all this is to be presented to us by Christmas in the form of a detailed, exact and clear list, so that we will know what and how much of each we own.[27]

We certainly do not know if any officials complied with the above instructions, and it is true that the list was concerned not with the operation of a specific manor but the total income one could expect from a royal estate. However, the list does illustrate the variety of sources of income from that manor. Capitation and property taxes and fees in return for the use of manorial property were joined by court fees and penalties (fines), tolls and market fees. Moreover, if the lord of the manor happened to be an ecclesiastical lord, he also profited from tithing. Funds from these sources enabled a life befitting lords, often exceeding basic needs. Calculations reveal that beer taxes at Friemersheim would have sufficed to keep the people at the manor houses constantly inebriated, and the 2800 loaves of rye-bread which had to be supplied could hardly have been consumed.[28] The fact is (and the same has been documented for Northern France[29]), a market existed for these surpluses which was also organized according to manorial principles and which provided additional profits for the lords.

However, not all these earnings accrued as a result of the right to dispose of the land. A lord of the manor also exercised authority over his bondmen and held partial jurisdiction (including police authority) over all serfs, while at the same time assuming liability for damages caused by them[30] as well as by seditious peasants.[31] He led the freemen of his manor into battle, and he possessed within the confines of his immunity the right to proscription (that is, the right to order or forbid certain acts under penalty of punishment). The prevailing theory presumes that manor houses of the nobility in fact enjoyed general immunity and were not subject to the administrative authority of the king. In ecclesiastical areas of immunity, this authority was exercised as early as the ninth century by an advocate. In many places, the lord of the manor was identical with village authorities and, in the case of the lords of proprietary churches, with ecclesiastical authority.

On the whole, the manorial system encroached on many aspects of the lives of serfs who were both subject to and dependent on it. The manorial system tended to concentrate various rights in the hands of the lord. It formed an economic, judicial, social and (at times) ecclesiastical unit which simultaneously provided a basis for political, religious, and cultural life; a basis for political and social order; and a basis for orderly living (Bosl). The relationship between service, protection, and authority developed into an association which determined the serf's daily life, often in accordance with customary law rules and regulations.[32] By uniting the most diverse of social groups, the manorial *familia* developed into the most powerful collectivity of the earlier Middle Ages.[33]

During the course of the eleventh century, an attempt was made to lay down the rights and duties of serfs in so-called manor statutes (*Hofrechte*) in order to regulate their lives. Practice reveals, however, that not everything proceeded as peacefully as the ideal of a *familia* would suggest. In the oldest extant manor house statute of Bishop Burchard of Worms (c. 1024/25)[34] we read (sect. 30): "Murders occurred almost daily at the household of St. Peter in the manner of wild animals, because someone became madly enraged at somebody else over some triviality, or was in a state of drunkenness, or was simply arrogant, so that 35 farm-hands from St. Peter were killed without cause by the male servants of this church; the murderers even bragged and raved about it instead of showing remorse." The bishop then issued more stringent laws: murderers were to be flayed and their hair torn out; they were to be branded on their cheeks with a red-hot iron, and they were to pay compensation. Fields, vineyards, domestics, and money were frequent reasons for quarrels (paragraph 31). Various regulations dealt with succession by inheritance among serfs (a son was to get the land, a daughter the clothes of the mother and the money [paragraph 10]), court cases and fines, and also marriages of serfs to partners who were not from their manor. The lord always made certain that his rights were acknowledged or that he was compensated. Whenever a serf died, two-thirds of his property fell to the bishop.

Though the lord represented the dominating element in these rules and regulations, the interests of the *familia* became more and more noticeable in later manor statutes. Thus, many places regulated via statutes the relationships between a lord and his serfs. Rarely was there any genuine opposition to them, and, viewed from the outside, the ideal of the *familia* probably promoted closer ties between serfs and their lord. Still, the heavy burdens must also have led to social tensions.[35]

Manorial authority was not typically questioned during the Middle Ages; at best, there was opposition to specific, unjust lords. Social tensions did not become class struggles because there were still no "classes" in the modern sense. Wherever there are reports of peasant revolts during the early Middle Ages, uprisings are always locally restricted. It was not the accustomed services as such which spurred opposition but rather additional burdens felt to be unjust and contradicting traditional customs were the cause. Following the much-quoted edict of Pîtres of 864, both secular and ecclesiastical lords complained to the king, not because their serfs performed accustomed statutory services of labor and hauling, but because they would not haul marl, which had never been required before.[36] (The king, of course, sided with the lords.) Such "refusals of service" did occur, though their extent is very difficult to measure. The frequently documented *coniurationes* (associations bound by oath) can rarely be interpreted as peasant revolts directed against lords. The only significant uprising of the early Middle Ages, the so-called Stellinga revolt of Saxon freemen and semi-free tenants (*Liten*) during the years 841-42, was undoubtedly directed against the nobility, but it also represented a pagan reaction against Frankish rule and Christianity. These had been established in the region only a few decades earlier. Furthermore the rebellion was linked to the political power struggle among the sons of Louis the Pious (Lothar supported the Stellinga in order to gain influence in Saxony).[37] There are hardly any grounds for assuming that the sources attempted to conceal a substantially larger number of incidents of unrest;[38] indeed, it would have been commensurate with medieval mentality to publicize such revolts as being against divine order, to deter other such movements. Therefore, one must presume that hardly any other extensive uprisings by serfs (or none at all) occurred during the earlier Middle Ages. Also, later ones did not originate among the most downtrodden, but always started among the upper echelon of peasantry. Much more widespread, however, was "passive resistance" in the form of negligent fulfillment of duties, stemming from the understandable desire to keep as much of the harvest for oneself as possible. The fixing of duties expected doubtless arose as well from the desires of the lords of the manor to obtain clarity in these matters. As late as the *Sachsenspiegel*,[39] refusal to pay rent was punished severely, by doubling the rent for each missed day, illustrating the danger facing the lords in this area; laws were not definite and had to be enforced anew. It was also quite common (according to Epperlein) for peasants to flee to other (ecclesiastical) lords, where they hoped to find a better life. Capitularies demanded that new lords return fugitive serfs, and even princes of the Church condemned this flight. Hrabanus Maurus, archbishop of Mainz, insisted in fact on the divinely ordained state of servanthood. (Still, he did distinguish between arrogance and need, the flight from a cruel lord from sheer arbitrary departure.[40]) Rural exodus to the towns amounted to a serious problem for the manorial lords, who sought to preserve their rights by emphasizing their *ius vocandi* (their right to reclaim a serf within a year). In most of these cases, the reason for flight was not resentment against the lord, but the desire for a better life. It was not until the later Middle Ages, when conditions for peasants had remarkably deteriorated as a result of the agrarian crisis and a more pronounced emphasis on the exploitation of serfdom, that the great peasant revolts ensued. These movements allied themselves with religious causes, first in western Europe (the "Jacquerie" in France in 1358 and the revolt of Wat Tyler and John Ball in southern England in 1381-82), and later also within the Empire. To be sure, these were not exclusively carried out by peasants; they were directed more against provincial rather than manorial lords with the goal of gaining, as a class, political influence.

The peasants' contacts with the lord of their manor, whose authority was constantly felt, must not be overestimated by any means. Only at smaller manors was there frequent contact with the lord. At large manors which disposed of many estates, an administrator (the *maior, villicus* or steward), represented the lord's authority. Initially, he assumed a double role. On the one hand, he was a peasant who, at best, owned the distinction of possessing a somewhat larger manse, or two manses, but who took care of his administrative duties in addition to rendering reduced rent and services and performing the chores on his own tenement. The *Capitulare de villis* (chapter 60) had expressly stipulated that the administrators at royal households were not to be recruited from among the wealthier (*potentiores*), but from among the less wealthy (*mediocres*) serfs. On the other hand, he was the lord's local representative and mediated between the lord and his serfs. This dual role was soon exploited for purposes of personal advancement, so that the office itself developed gradually into a hereditary, authoritarian institution. Ekkehard of St. Gall criticized administrators of monastic estates for bearing shields and weapons and being preoccupied with hunting rather than with the care of their farms,[41] in short, for leading lives befitting those of lords. Rarely did the lords succeed in checking this development, as for instance at Gembloux in the twelfth century, where they were still in a position to prevent the office of steward from becoming hereditary but had to recognize its feudal character and were forced to lift some aspects of the bondage of stewards.[42] Over the long term, the steward became the village authority in charge of manorial jurisdiction, leading the village's detail into battle and assessing rent against the serfs. The steward also collected the rent owed the lord of the manor. Later, even lords had a difficult time asserting their rights against administrators. The visitation report of 1290[43] by Abbess Irmgard of Herford concerning her Westphalian estates testifies to difficulties in securing the right of hospitality. At Stockum a legal opinion was required before it could be determined how many of the abbess's horses had to be fed. At Rheine, the steward paid a sum of money to get out of his duty to host the abbess. At Aldrup, the steward was not even present and nothing had been prepared in advance; he was ordered into court and sentenced to pay a fine for his failure to provide the required hospitality. In addition to the stewards who had already risen to be rather willful administrators, the advocates on ecclesiastical estates placed additional burdens on peasants and also began to compete with the lord of the manor. The relationship between the lord of the manor and his administrator was not always so ideal as Hartmann von Aue describes it—by way of exception — in his *Der arme Heinrich* (*Henry the Hapless*), where a free peasant who worked a clearing in the forest was never oppressed unjustly by his lord, and steadily performed his duties out of his own free will (ll. 267ff.). The fact remains that the burdens were rarely light or willingly borne. Bond peasants remained nominally under the sole authority of their lord, but they frequently had to serve two or three lords, since both steward and advocate placed additional burdens upon them (in the name of the lord). This practice ultimately impaired the rights of the lord, whose authority was no longer self-evident; it had to be constantly reenforced. Any rights left unclaimed for a while could easily be forgotten and might simply lapse. Thus, the manorial system became a flexible system subject to constant change.

2. The Space:
Peasant's House, Manse, Manor and Village

Peasant's House

The environment of peasants was partly determined by the demands placed upon them by the manorial system, partly by farm labor, and partly by the need to function as a local community. Because of widely scattered holdings, the manor did not form a physical unit embracing all serfs. While one portion of serfs lived on the manor, others resided on their own tenements. The closest and most intimate sphere for those peasant families was constituted by the peasant's house, which has not been satisfactorily researched to date, since the oldest existing structures date only from the fifteenth century.[44] Descriptions found in tribal codes and excavations of abandoned early medieval villages reveal complex agricultural enterprises with stables and storage buildings, with the house at the center. Living quarters typically consisted of a single room, serving both as a work area and bedroom, with an open hearth. The most common construction was that of the post-house (*Pfostenhaus*), which rested on wooden posts which usually did not last for more than a generation. Not until the high Middle Ages did structures using framing beams prevail, structures permitting a much more durable two-story construction. The walls of the post-house consisted of mud-sealed wicker, the roof thatched with straw or rushes, the floor consisted of tamped-down mud and the "windows" mere openings covered by shutters. In addition there were rectangular dugout houses (square in Slavic regions)—mostly outbuildings—and log cabins. In northern Germany, particularly in marshy areas, the elongated hall predominated, usually three-bayed, combining living quarters and stables in a single large room (*Wohnstallhalle*). At Feddersen Wierde northeast of Bremerhaven, for example, houses of various sizes contained between two and fifteen stalls on each side. Post-barn granaries and structures hollowed out of the ground served as farm buildings. During the eighth century, post-structures are also found in the north, often with an elongated shape. During the twelfth century, the so-called "Low-German hall" prevailed, a wide *Wohnstallhalle* with vast entry gate and storage area for the harvest. Little research has been done on peasant houses in the Rhineland, in southern Germany, or in Alpine regions. Tribal codes of the early Middle Ages attest to fenced multi-structure farms with separate living quarters and out-buildings (stables, granaries, barns, bake houses, and kitchens). Alpine areas and the Slavic East are known to have had log buildings replacing dugouts beginning in the ninth century. In the Mittelgebirge, single-room dwellings prevailed.

The domestic life of peasants took place under rather primitive conditions in a dwelling that was rarely sectioned-off. The hearth was not separate from the remainder of the room, and ventilation was poor due to a single opening in the roof; it was not until the late Middle Ages that hearth and living areas tended to be separate, and there were no enclosed stoves until the fifteenth century. Frequently the animals lived under the same roof. The room itself was probably divided into hearth, living, and sleeping areas. Furniture was limited to a table, benches, and chests, occasionally a bed (if one was not sleeping on a bench on straw mattresses). The land surrounding the house was divided into small cultivated areas (gardens). The true work area, however, was the yard.

Manse

The tenement, referred to in the manorial system as the manse (*hoba, mansus*), constituted the peasant's economic unit. The land belonged to the lord of the manor, but peasants were permitted to use and occupy it, and they could not easily be dispossessed. The origin and the significance of the manse are obscure.[45] According to medieval theory, the manse was often considered adequate to support one peasant family; in practice, however, it was more a generic term with various meanings.[46] It is not clear whether it predates the manorial system in terms of a place peasants settled or was a manorial institution. Within the framework of the manor, the manse constituted the normative tenement, the material basis of a peasant's economic existence, as well as a unit of rent owed the lord of the manor, since services and levies rested on the manse and not on the peasant personally. Otherwise, manses were anything but uniform. At their center there was generally a fenced yard with a garden; the actual plowlands, the *sors*, did not have to be arranged around the house, but could be intermingled with other tenements and distributed across various fields. The greater part of a manse was taken up by arable land (smaller units attested to in the tribal codes suggest there were small areas as well). Pasture was also part of a manse, and in many areas a small section was reserved for vineyards, while the forest either belonged to the lord or was part of the village commons (*Allmende*). The proportion between arable land and pasture varied between 5:1 (at Lobbes) and 20:1 (at Saint-Germain).[47] Raising grain, then, constituted the most important part of the manse economy; it was only in coastal and in higher lying mountainous areas that the proportional share of pastures was considerably higher. The size of individual manses also varied. For instance, at Morsang, one of the territories of Saint-Germain-des-Prés near Paris, arable land varied between 1 and 17 *bunuaria*.[48] At Palaiseau, the average agricultural area of a manse measured 4.2 *bunuaria* and at Esmans 16.2. Thus there were often substantial variations in size among the estates of a manor, as well as among manses within given estates; apparently manses "grew" organically rather than being created by organizing and dividing the land. In addition to variations in size, one must also consider differences in the quality of soil and yield, neither of which is easily measured. In the process of providing for as many peasants as possible, and their sons, manses were often divided; there were manses of merely half, a third, and a quarter of the original size (although under certain circumstances half a manse could be larger than many a full manse due to variations in size just noted).

Many manors distinguished between types of manses which were subject to distinct obligations: there were free manses (*mansi ingenuiles*), bond manses (*Unfreienhufen, mansi serviles*), and semi-bond manses (*mansi lidiles*). This legal classification suggests that granting a manse was originally tied to the legal status of the peasant who worked it, though such legal ties increasingly dissipated so that serfs might easily be working free manses and colonates, or free tenants might even work bond manses. Ever since the ninth century, the legal status of peasants had grown increasingly less important for the economy of the manor. The relationship between bond manses and free manses varied from region to region as well, and from manor to manor. There were only *mansi ingenuiles* at some places and only *mansi serviles* at others, but most of the time both types coexisted side by side. At Saint-Germain, there were 831 free manses and merely 153 bond manses, while the bishopric of Augsburg had 1041 free manses to 466 bond manses, and in the Lorsch imperial land register the proportion was almost even. In terms of size, bond manses were often somewhat smaller in size than free manses.

Manses, therefore, were not uniform in terms of workable land, type, or size. Not even the occupants could be considered uniform. Certainly the most common situation was one in which one dependent peasant worked a manse together with wife and family; this is considered the rule in many land registers, which simply record the occupant and his wife. However, a significant number of manses—the proportion at Saint-Germain was approximately forty percent—departed from this rule.[49] Parts of these manses were worked by individuals, mostly men but occasionally by women. Since some of these women were recorded as having children, such residents were probably widowers or widows, so that one may presume the former existence of a married couple. Various family members—such as the mother, brothers, or sisters of the husband—also lived on the manse. The manse was subsequently no longer a one-couple unit but an (agnatic) family, probably handed down from father to son, which then could keep relatives together. The husband was considered the head of the manse even if he had a lower legal status than his wife, who would always move in with her husband following marriage.[50] Occasionally, although not all that often, married couples took in family members. This fact shows that the right to use the manse became hereditary at an early date. The edict of Pîtres from 869[51] mentions the *mansus hereditarius*.[52] In a series of cases, surprisingly frequently on some estates, several proprietors or several families shared a manse regardless of its size. There was apparently no longer any other way to absorb overpopulation in some areas (such as Palaiseau, in the jurisdiction of the manor of Saint-Germain, at Villance in the Ardennes, or on the lordship of Prüm). Since the polyptych of Saint-Germain sometimes differentiates between the number of manses and the number of hearths (*foci*) on those manses, each of these families had to be living in houses of their own. Most of the time two, three, at times up to five families occupied one manse, while in other cases one or two families were joined by several additional individuals. It is impossible to discern how or whether they were related to each other; in some cases their names suggest family ties,[53] even occupants on neighboring manses (with names following sequentially in the land register) were often related to one another, based on the evidence of their names.

Therefore, if some manses had several occupants, some individual families, on the other hand, owned one-and-a-half, two, or in exceptional cases even three manses. In some areas many manses remained vacant (*mansi absi*).[54] Thus, manses can only be referred to as peasant family units with due caution. Since the performance of duties depended on the manse, the number of persons living on it was indeed very significant for working the land. If there were several males on the manse, it was possible to divide work between one's own and manorial land, though the harvest then had to be shared. In this context, one additional aspect looms important: in addition to the peasant families and their children, male and female serfs (*mancipia*) frequently (but by no means everywhere) occupied the manse. This was also the case on the manor itself. Some manses had up to ten male servants, while they were totally absent from others;[55] these servants belonged with the peasant family and were given away together with it. At Prüm, servants were occasionally drafted into service on the lord's lands (*Salland*). If we take into account that some manses were occupied by several families, that single women were present with varying numbers of children[56] (some of whom were already adults),[57] and finally, that there was a number of male and female serfs (*mancipia*), the result will be that there were substantial differences between the labor forces on any manse, leading to very different basic conditions and social differences in one and the same village. These differences compounded those that came with variations in size, quality of the soil, and differences in services.

Village

As a rule a manse did not stand alone as a single tenement but was incorporated into a group of more or less loosely connected tenements or a village.[58] (By "village" we understand a rural, long-term group settlement with a primarily agrarian structure, regardless of size.[59] The old distinction between village [*Dorf*] and hamlet [*Weiler*], as a step between village and individual settlement, has been largely abandoned today.) It appears there was a smooth transition from the individual farmstead to the village. The concept of *Dorf* itself (from Gothic *thaurp*, Frankish *thorp*) originally referred to an enclosure and did not yet have today's meaning; rather, it is significant that the German as well as the Latin terms (*villa, vicus*) do not distinguish substantially between a village and a manor. Group settlements originated at a rather early stage, while individual farms (*villae rusticae*) prevailed in old Roman provinces (*vici* were settlements of artisans and merchants[60]). Germanic people already lived in villages of various sizes, as a rule.[61] If these settlements had once been associations of relatives, this was no longer the case in Germanic times.

Early medieval villages could have various origins; they could be founded by a lord in the vicinity of his estate, or they could result from the association of free farmers. Many place names ending in *-seli* (*sal*), *-heim*, *-hausen*, *-hofen*, *-dorf*, *-stat*, or *-wilare*, in German-speaking areas, in *-ville* (*from villa*), or *-court* (*from curtis*) in French-speaking areas, carry the name of a person in the first half of their names. These are referred to as patronymic place names, and they attest to foundation by a lord.[62] Indeed, there were villages entirely ruled by lords, and in such cases the manor and village formed a single unit. However, at other settlements we encounter several lords and free peasants.[63] At Dienheim, for example, Schwind could detect more than 200 landowners in the course of the Carolingian period, a period of approximately 150 years. At other places, such as Nauborn in the Lahngau, the donors likely formed an association of relatives. Village and manorial *villa* could thus be identical, but that was not always the case. On the one hand, the *familia* was more comprehensive and scattered over many villages, while members from different families could indeed live in a specific village. Thus, the village did not grow out of the manorial system, and peasants were frequently linked in associations of neighboring villages beyond their ties with the lord of the manor.

From a topographical point of view, the physical layout of a village was not fixed, resulting in great diversity.[64] Most villages were irregular clusters (*Haufendörfer* [Donat]) which had gradually grown together. In addition, planned communities existed even during Germanic times, for instance in the form of a circular settlement or a row of tenements. Typical of planned village forms was that called *Rundling* (especially in the Elb-Saale region), characterized by a circular arrangement of farms around an open center. Further examples are the "road village" (*Strassendorf*), running parallel to a road; the so-called *Angerdorf* (from Anger, meaning "village green"), where the street forked and wound around a pond or a square; and (especially in the colonized areas of eastern Germany) the *Waldhufendorf*, "forest-manse village," whose fields extended directly from the farm into the hinterland. Villages were surrounded (often in concentric circles) by gardens, fields, less intensively worked fields, pastures, cultivated forests, and virgin forest.

Since the high Middle Ages, the arable land (*Flur*)[65] often consisted of one or several contiguous, elongated strips (*Langstreifenflur*) or square pieces of land (*Blockflur*). These were normally predicated on an agreement among villagers for the purpose of collective cultivation, especially when three-field rotation expanded and set entire fields aside for summer crops, winter crops, and fallow land. Each individual peasant held strips of this land. Somewhat more recent (probably as a result of the manorial system) were the shots (*Gewann*), elongated strips of open field allocated to peasants of the village. These were in turn divided into narrow strips and distributed among the peasants of a village, who frequently built their homes there. Personal parcels of land mingled together were combined into open fields. Names for these parcels, which are not found until much later, often provide us with information about their progressive expansion. Such tracts no longer derived their names from a lord and are often named after those who worked them; however, they also typically carry names which refer to the terrain (such as "in front of or near the (stone) bridge," the "loam pit," etc.) or to the four corners of the earth ("north, south, west, east field"), age ("old field"), or specific characteristics ("rape farms").[66] One section of the usable land of the village, the commons (*Allmende*), could be worked by any villager. Normally this included the woods, which provided firewood, wild fruits, feed for pigs, a location for wild beehives, and common pasturage. Later, several villages formed regional associations (*Markgenossenschaften*) for the joint use of woods and pastures situated between them. Such associations are not older than the villages, as once assumed, but more recent, formed in response to an increasing density of population; they are not to be found in the tribal codes. Preferred soils for plowing were light and somewhat acidic, possessing a high nitrogen content and located in moderately wet areas.[67] Evidence from excavations reveals constantly shifting locations for both farms and land, so that some villages existed for only a few centuries. Even during periods when the land was being cleared, places were being abandoned all the time.[68] Deteriorating soil conditions most likely forced peasants to relocate their settlements time and again.

Villages varied in size. Initially, small settlements with three to five homesteads probably prevailed, although there were also larger villages with up to forty tenements. For instance, the Saxon settlement of Warendorf comprised between forty and fifty houses. At the Carolingian village of Menzingen in the Kraichgau, there were over thirty tenements with approximately 200 inhabitants in the years 770-850, and the villages of the lordships of Saint-Germain-des-Prés or Saint-Remi were substantially larger still. The monastery of Saint-Germain held roughly 100 manses at such central locations as Palaiseau, Jouy, or Verrières. At Viel-Saint-Remi a total of 288 men were in the service of the monastery. Large rural settlements are also in evidence in the literature of the Middle Ages.[69] Such villages had a population of several hundred inhabitants. The average size of villages was certainly smaller, however; according to Abel, during the high Middle Ages it typically amounted to ten to twelve tenements with approximately 70 inhabitants.

On the whole, villages were less topographical units than they were places of settlement for the peasants, even though medieval terminology neglected this aspect. Early medieval tribal codes were more preoccupied with individual farmsteads than with village communities.[70] Above all, the village represented an association of neighbors which required regulation of community life and economy, but which also provided mutual assistance in times of need and participated in family events. Such communal life required a certain degree of order. As early as the Frankish *Lex Salica*,[71] moving to a village was permitted only with the consent of all residents; if nobody protested (in an established, symbolic form) in the course of the next twelve months, the newcomer was received by the "neighbors" (*vicini*) and became a member of the village association. It goes without saying that residents of a village belonged to various social groups. Variations in the sizes of houses and the number of outbuildings already suggest substantial differences in the size of properties. In addition to peasants, the villages also contained individual, specialized artisans, occasionally in high concentration.[72]

During the high Middle Ages the village underwent an additional, important change in a long process in which manorial, judicial, and neighborly elements joined forces. From a mere association of neighbors in which manorial ties superseded those of neighborliness, the village developed into a legal association with organs of its own. (These associations, however, were not in evidence until the end of the period discussed in this book.) In short, the village developed into a rural commune (*Landgemeinde*, a term not coined by contemporaries, to be sure).[73] This by no means obliterated ties with the manorial lord, but the manor's functions were restricted more directly to the types of services to be rendered, while personal relationships tended to remain concentrated within the village's realm. There were village authorities who were frequently named by the lord, or one of the lords, or (more frequently) their representative, the steward of the manor. This "village elder" was variously referred to as (depending on the region) as *Schulte, Schulze* (in the north), or *Schultheiss* (in the south), and also *burmester* (*Bauernmeister* in modern German, "master of peasants"). A community meeting of those economically better situated (that is, select villagers only), annually chose local administrative bodies. A village court at a specially fenced place, often under the village linden tree, oversaw the legal and communal life of the village. The village often formed its own protected district of public peace and law. While in the beginning only tenements were fenced in, now a fence surrounded the entire village, making its external limit visible. At an early point, the manor may have transcended the village, since the labor and legal identity of peasants had been more strongly concentrated on manorial land than within the association of neighbors. As a result of the rise of the village as a commune, the manor gradually lost its importance as organizer and administrator of peasant life.

Parish and Market

In addition to the village community and the manorial association, the ecclesiastical organization also defined peasant life. Indeed, ever since Frankish times peasants had been forced to tithe to the Church in addition to meeting manorial obligations. During the early Middle Ages, the church in question was, as a rule, the lord's proprietary church located in the vicinity of the manor. This resulted in a coincidence of manor and ecclesiastical association, particularly if the two further coincided with the village. Not every village had its own church, and conversely there could be two or even three churches in a village. For example, in the case of the twenty-five estates of Saint-Germain-des-Prés, the thirty-one churches of the monastery were scattered over eighteen villages, while there were only thirty-four such churches in the villages of the widely-scattered estates of Prüm. During the course of the early Middle Ages there was a tendency to comprehend the rural area ecclesiastically with a centrally organized network of churches, namely the parish system. In parts of the Rhineland the formation of such a parish system was largely complete by the eighth century, whereas in the Austrian regions this development did not take effect until considerably later. Parish church and manorial church were not identical in all places, nor was there a parish church in every village, so that the parish formed a broader association. (In a legal document of 873[74] drawn up by Louis the German, peasants of the district of Neckarau complained they could not reach the church at Altrip.) Thus, the ties of peasants became further compartmentalized. Wherever there was a village church, it soon became the center of the entire life of the village; the area in front of the church became a marketplace, where festivities were staged: it was a natural gathering-spot for peasants.

While the horizon of medieval peasants ended essentially at the manse, village, manor, and parish church, the sale of any surplus sometimes led them to the nearest marketplace. Local markets had already developed in some areas such as the Île de France as early as Carolingian times. During the course of the high Middle Ages the network of marketplaces became more concentrated and the need to sell goods intensified due to the fact that manorial services could now be replaced by cash payments. Some manse peasants were also obligated to provide transportation services to the monastery or to higher-ranking manors, so that they occasionally had to undertake long journeys. The living space of the peasant, however, extended no further than this.

Let us now turn to the members of the manorial *familia* living within these confines.

3. The People:
Peasantry and Serfdom

Peasants in the Middle Ages

Although medieval society was undoubtedly a peasant culture, discussions about medieval peasantry inevitably encounter problems.[75] Above all, "peasant" is a concept that extends beyond the manorial system. The peasant performs a certain economic function. He tills the land and raises livestock;[76] he manages his own tenement, in distinction to servants or cottagers; he uses a plow, thus setting himself apart from the gardener; and he cultivates the soil with his own hands, thus distinguishing himself from a manorial lord. "Peasant" is therefore primarily an economic term which wins sociological significance when the peasantry is distinguished from other groups. Peasants represent a clearly definable group within society's division of labor.

Even if we proceed from this modern definition, peasants are hardly acknowledged at all by the early medieval sources, despite the fact that the majority of the population was active in agriculture. The concrete nature of the sources followed different criteria. For instance, the *leodes* of the Frankish tribal codes were, contextually speaking, peasants with properties of their own, cultivating their own fields and owning herds of livestock,[77] and the term emphasized their special legal status as free Franks in relationship to the king. Other sources distinguished between *coloni* and *servi*, or the aforementioned *mancipia*, underscoring the relationship to the manorial lord. There was no specific term for "peasant," as we know it, either in German or Latin.[78] At first, the German term *gebur(e)* denoted the resident of a house (*bur*) or a village associate, but not a peasant. The Latin terms vanished for a time from the sources, and *agricola* did not reappear until the eleventh century, while *rusticus* became the disparaging *topos* for a sinful, pagan, stupid person. In Old High German glosses, these terms were paraphrased clumsily and irregularly (with *ackarbigengo*, *lantbûant*, *ackerman*).[79] The earlier Middle Ages were familiar with the function of the peasant, but they had no need for a uniform term; they considered peasants neither as a social group nor a legal entity. (That is why Franz's definition of the peasants as a stratum which sustained the clerical as well as the noble upper levels of society solely by its labor without participating in their culture agrees completely with contemporary thought.[80]) Apparently free and bond peasants had little in common, since they lacked any overarching consciousness of togetherness; thus the peasants did not yet form a class united by a sense of identity. What mattered was their affiliation with the manor or village.

It was not until the high Middle Ages that a gradual change took place. Beginning with the eleventh century, people began to divide society into knights (*milites*) and peasants (*rustici*). According to medieval social theory, peasants—more generally, the workers (*laboratores*)— rose to the level of a functional class together with (but ranking below) the warriors (*pugnatores*) and those who prayed (*oratores*).[81] Only then were peasants understood as a social group, even though there was still no strict closure of the knights as a group until the middle of the thirteenth century.[82] Nevertheless, *rusticus* was not identical with a "peasant class" in occupational and economic terms; rather, it encompassed the broader category of all those persons not belonging to the nobility, deriving its names from *rustici* by virtue of its representing the numerically most significant group. This new articulation of society attests to a far-reaching change in contemporary mentality, for it replaced the ancient grouping into freemen (*liberi*) and serfs (*servi*) at a time when the manorial system had just achieved a levelling of its lower strata into a legally uniform peasantry. In the course of the high Middle Ages, the "peasants" increasingly coalesced into a legal estate. While *milites* (knights) constituted the warrior class of lords, the *rustici* were increasingly deprived of their military role and the ability to carry arms. This development set in as early as Carolingian times, when armies formed of vassals no longer saw any need for peasants. Peasants had become indispensable for an intensified cultivation of the land, but they continued to pay a military tax, replacing compulsory military service. Public Peace laws of the high Middle Ages even contained provisions forbidding peasants to bear arms. In 1152 they were forbidden to carry either lances or swords,[83] and in the Rhenish-Franconian Peace of 1179 peasants were completely forbidden to bear arms inside their villages, while away from their villages they were only permitted to carry a sword.[84] The Bavarian Public Peace of 1244 gave peasants permission only to carry a short knife and an iron rod for the plow.[85] It was impossible to disarm peasants completely, because weapons were still needed for local law enforcement. A series of Public Peace edicts permitted peasants to keep arms inside their homes so that they could intervene against criminals (in compliance with an order by a judge) and against persons who broke the public peace.

However, there is a clear tendency to distinguish a peasant's weapons from those of a knight. Peasant implements, such as hoes, rods, knives, or sickles became symbols of their class whenever they were portrayed in art. Dress codes instituted in this period also ensured separation from lords. As early as the *Imperial Chronicle* of the mid-twelfth century, we encounter descriptions of how peasants ought to dress (vv. 14791ff.):

> Peasants are not allowed to wear any colors other than black or gray. Trim commensurate with this life and cow-hide shoes are sufficient; seven yards of linen for shirts and pants are adequate.... Should a peasant be found in possession of a sword he shall be bound and led to the church fence, where he should be detained and thoroughly beaten. If he has to defend himself against an enemy, let him use a staff.[86]

The Bavarian Public Peace of 1244 also prescribed gray, simple clothing and shoes made from cow-hide, as well as closely cropped hair. (To wear long hair became a privilege of lords.) The peace permitted only one exception, for a peasant who administered an office on behalf of his lord.[87]

Since peasants were described only by non-peasants in the sources, we must not be surprised if some of the characteristics are negative. As early as Merovingian times, some descriptions portray the peasant as wicked, dangerous, and uneducated, likening him more to an animal than a human being.[88] *Rusticus* in fact became a term of abuse. Still, directly disparaging remarks were rare. On the contrary, it appears the work of the peasant was indeed appreciated during the earlier Middle Ages. According to Epperlein,[89] portrayals of peasants at work in book miniatures attest to a positive attitude. One can point out that, in contrast to classical antiquity, peasants were judged worthy of portrayal. While peasant labor was seen as a result of sin—Cain was considered the first peasant—it was also a necessary activity eventually considered appropriate for paradise.[90] Not until class lines solidified during the high Middle Ages would the verdict turn harsher. In a famous sermon at the beginning of the twelfth century addressing the issue of class, Honorius of Autun likened individual classes to parts of a church building which together form the congregation. He compared peasants to the floor upon which one treads, but which also represents the foundation supporting and feeding the remaining classes.[91] Honorius admonished them to obey the priests and tithe on time. Thus the peasants constituted the lowest social class. According to the *Old High German Genesis* from the second half of the eleventh century, *skalche* (male servants) descended from Noah's son Ham (Noah condemned Ham and his descendants to servitude because he had ridiculed the nakedness of his sleeping father).[92] Gradually, biased views of the dull, indolent, gluttonous, envious, and stingy peasant emerged.[93] People became more familiar with specific aspects of peasant life[94] and associated a certain type of mentality with the term. Peasants were reputedly conservative and advocated popular piety, but they were also sedentary and peaceable.[95] The rural population was also accused of superstition and devotion to heathen customs. Regino's penitential handbook from the early tenth century charged peasants with practicing cults involving trees, springs, rocks, crossroads, and grave sites instead of churches; these rites were allegedly conducted by magicians, soothsayers, or women instead of priests, employing incantations and songs instead of the Our Father and the Creed.[96] Funeral rites with wakes and obsequies had assumed peculiar forms, and the Church attempted either to redefine these customs in Christian terms or to abolish them. In 939, the abbess of Schildesche in Westphalia issued a pertinent procession order:

> We order you every year on Pentecost Monday with the help of the Holy Spirit, to carry the patron saint in a long procession in your parishes, cleanse your homes, mourn and collect alms for the restoration of the poor, instead of parading like pagans through the fields. You shall spend the night in the monastery's courtyard, keeping solemn vigil over the holy relics, so that you will end your planned parade early in the morning with a pious procession and return [the patron saint and the holy relics] to the monastery with due reverence.[97]

(In return, they expected a plentiful harvest and better weather.) Old pagan customs such as parading through the fields to entreat the gods to grant a good harvest had merely been replaced by Christian symbols; in place of pagan images, people carried with them holy relics, and they entreated the Christian God instead of the pagan gods. This way of thinking was by no means restricted to the peasant population, though they perhaps resisted such reinterpretations with greater determination than other social groups.

In the literature of the high and late Middle Ages, peasants were recognized by the way they looked. In the story of Garin de Loherain, in the twelfth century, the young peasant Rigaut is described as "A huge fellow with massive arms, broad hips and shoulders; his eyes set apart as far as a hand is wide . . . his hair bristly, his cheeks dirty and leathery; he had not washed them in half a year, and the only water with which they had ever come in contact was the rain from the sky."[98] That same story tells of another peasant, who "had a big head, pitch-black hair, his eyes set apart by more than a hand's width, broad cheeks, a huge, flattened nose with flared nostrils, his fat lips were redder than roast beef, his teeth yellow and ugly." Such descriptions indicate that class distinctions were not to be violated, so they were projected onto external characteristics. In the second half of the thirteenth century, a satirical rhymed epic entitled *Helmbreht* by Wernher der Gartenære describes the downfall of a young peasant who, fed up with working the soil, decided he wanted to drink wine instead of water, eat meat instead of gruel, white bread instead of oatmeal bread. He bore shoulder-length hair (which only noblemen were allowed to wear), bound by a cap elaborately decorated with images showing the conquest of Troy and Charlemagne's battles against the Saracens; he also wore a silver-buttoned coat and a sword. Finally, he rode a horse bought with the proceeds from the sale of four cows and four bushels of grain. He refused to heed his father's warning that rebellion against one's station in life rarely led to success. Helmbreht's destiny had been the plow (here the father expressed considerable self-awareness as a peasant), but the young man left his tenement. He did not become a knight as he expected, but instead the leader of a band of robbers who fleeced peasants. They were finally caught and brought to justice. Nine of the band were executed, but the tenth, Helmbreht, was spared; instead, both his eyes were poked out and he had a hand and a foot cut off. Spurned by his father, the blind Helmbreht was finally hanged by the very peasants he had once victimized. The story is pure fiction, but it signifies the kind of status-awareness which had to defend itself against attempts at social climbing in real life. (After all, Helmbreht was the son of a steward, a *Meier*.) In the songs of Neidhart von Reuenthal, mothers advise their daughters against longing for knights when they were being courted by the son of the steward, to which one daughter retorts: "What should I do with a peasant for a husband; he won't know how to make love to me according to my wishes"[99] (for which she ultimately gets a beating from her mother).

While some peasants would have preferred to imitate knightly life, the words of the senior Helmbreht attest to an increased self-awareness of peasants, their pride in being peasants, and their growing awareness of the necessity of peasant labor.[100] In *Der arme Heinrich*, Hartmann von Aue portrays paradise as a large peasant tenement (II, 775ff.). In opposition to increasing prejudice, peasant cunning was celebrated for triumphing over the arrogance of lords. This is exemplified by an early literary example, the fairy tale epic of the poor peasant Unibos, composed in Lower Lorraine during the tenth or at latest eleventh century. Unibos owned only one ox (hence his name); when he lost this ox and had no choice but to sell its hide at the market, he did not get more than eight pence for it despite bargaining. On his way home, however, he was forced to "relieve himself"; when he reached for grass to wipe himself, he discovered a treasure of silver. His son went to the advocate to get proper scales, but the advocate became suspicious and accused Unibos of theft. When Unibos claimed the money to be the proceeds from the sale of his oxhide, the advocate, steward, and parish priest—by no accident all the village dignitaries—desired to get rich, too. They slaughtered all their cows, skinned them, and took the hides to the city market, with the result that they were unable to get rid of the hides because of the outrageous amounts they demanded. Instead of getting rich, they were dragged into court, fined, and had to pay their fines with the hides. When they decided to avenge themselves and kill him, Unibos resorted to another ruse. He daubed pig's blood all over his wife as if he had killed her, subsequently "reviving" her in front of the dignitaries by playing his flute. All present thought her to be younger and much more beautiful than she had been before. They then purchased the flute from Unibos at an outrageous price and proceeded to kill their wives, led by the priest, determined to be the first murderer on account of his higher dignity. Yet none of them succeeded in reviving their wives by playing the flute. When they once again came to kill Unibos, he performed his next "miracle" by hiding silver in the rear of his breeding mare and called on the three dignitaries to witness that the horse, once petted, defecated coins instead of ordinary dung. They straightaway bought his mare for fifteen pounds. The priest took the mare home and fed her well, but all he harvested was dung, which he examined diligently. He found a solitary penny that had stuck in an old wound, but the advocate and the steward found nothing at all. When they finally resolved to kill him, Unibos begged to be allowed to choose the manner of his death. He had himself placed in a barrel which was to be dropped into the sea. He turned the rest of the money over to the lords so that they could drink their fill. He told a passing swineherd that he was hiding in the barrel because people wished to force him to become advocate. Thereupon the swineherd gladly traded places with the peasant, and when the drunks returned, his protestations that he was indeed willing to become advocate were in vain, and he was dropped into the sea. Unibos eventually returned to the village with the large herd of pigs, and when he was asked the source of his wealth, he responded that the pigs had come directly from paradise on the bottom of the sea, where pigs were plentiful. Thereupon the priest, the advocate, and the steward threw themselves immediately into the sea.

Literary examples do not reflect everyday life, but they do permit us a glimpse of mentality, parodying tensions and differences among social classes through their caricatures. (All of *Helmbreht* is devoted to this subject, and *Unibos* marks an early reaction to the common disdain for peasants.)

Although what has been said applies to all peasants, there were some special conditions within the manorial system which went beyond it, since peasants as well as lords shared a widespread "peasant" mentality, at least in the early days.

The Association of Serfs

Although the serfs on a manor were members of the *familia*, there were substantial social differences among individual groups. This diversification was marked by various criteria, of which four factors were especially significant: legal status, function, property holdings, and available yield.

During Frankish times, it was the legal distinction between freemen (*liberi, ingenui*) and serfs (*servi*) which was emphasized most strongly. Originally freemen had been independent peasants who had surrendered to a manorial lord without foregoing their legal status; legally they continued to be subjects to the king and the count, enjoying certain privileges. Admission to the manor frequently occurred in the form of a leasehold (*precaria*). A freeman surrendered himself and his possessions to the authority and protection of a manorial lord, receiving in return the property just surrendered (*precaria oblata*). Less frequently, he merely received manorial property (*precaria data*), but he was more likely to receive manorial land along with the return of his own property (*precaria remuneratoria*). The relationship between the manorial lord and free serfs was founded on tradition and a tenement; it may therefore be likened to the feudal obligation issuing from a fief. Even members of the nobility or wealthy freemen entered into a leasehold relationship with a church or a monastery by assigning a small portion of their property. Serfs, in contrast, belonged from the very beginning to the bondsmen of the manor. Judging from their position, they were no longer to be equated with the slaves of antiquity, although they were largely dependent on the will of their lord.[101] Between these two classes ranged semi-free persons, including freed serfs (*liberti, epistolarii*), who were former serfs who had been released but not into full legal freedom. In western regions of the Frankish empire, there were great numbers of *coloni* who had once been free but were tied to the land, including the *Liten* (semi-free tenants scattered over northern

Germany). Finally, there were groups elevated to special legal status, owing nothing but dues (*censuales*), especially those who had to pay a levy in the form of wax to the churches (*cerocensuales*). Certainly their numerical distribution varied among individual regions. If we look only at the well-documented manse peasants, the overwhelming majority at the manor house of Saint-Germain-des-Prés near Paris discussed earlier included *coloni*; on several estates they represented over ninety percent of the residents, and women constituted an even higher percentage. In contrast, a much smaller number were unfree, rarely comprising ten percent or more among women. Semi-free tenants appear somewhat more frequently on a small number of estates. Free persons—most of them women—were decidedly rare;[102] although in some regions, such as Westphalia, their proportion was more significant. There was apparently no hesitation to intermarry between individual social groups, in contradiction to statutory prohibitions against such marriages. The great number of *coloni* necessarily led to marriages between members of the same class, but there were still numerous "mixed marriages." This indicates that class identity within the lower strata was no longer all that important. Legal status was directly linked to the person and predated the manorial system. Serfs brought their class with them into the manorial system, and class affiliation was recorded because it served to distinguish persons, but it soon had no bearing on the distribution of functions within the manorial economy. Besides, free persons were at best free before public law; as for the other facets of their lives, they depended on the lord of the manor and were thus also in perpetual danger of social decline. Therefore, it was merely a matter of time before the distinction between free persons and serfs grew less significant. The distinction declined in post-Carolingian times and was subsequently supplanted by functional distinctions. Legally speaking, a uniform stratum of serfs (those dependent on a lord) gradually developed from those serfs who had been free and those who were not. The legal terminology employed during the seventh and eighth centuries disappeared from the pertinent formulae of legal documents during the ninth century, replaced by the terms *servi* and *mancipia*.[103] The contrast between lords and serfs (*domini* and *servi*) now became central, so that *servus* no longer denoted a slave, as in earlier times, but rather a serf *per se*. Those surrendering their properties still emphasized their legal status during the ninth century, and statutory determination of services grew much more important during the tenth century.[104] Such legal status was not a fixed concept; rather, it depended on the kinds of services required. Using the transfer records of St. Gall, Ganahl demonstrated that *servus* was a person to whose services (*servitium*) the monastery was entitled. There were definitely cases during the ninth century when the legal status of a serf could change as a result. During this transitional period, legal and functional stratification assimilated to each other.

This stratification according to function emerged directly from the manorial system and was, therefore, infinitely more important to it than legal status. In conjunction with the distribution of the manorial land, we can discern two large groups. Manse peasants (*servi casati*, serfs with "houses of their own," also *manentes, mansionarii, and hubarii*) worked their manses independently, and they were also obligated to render labor services on manorial land. "Homeless" serfs (*servi non casati*, also in *domo manentes, quotidiani, prebendarii, and stipendiarii*) resided on the manor, and they had to render unmeasured services (therefore, *quotidiani*) and were in turn cared for by the lord (therefore: *prebendarii*). (Among manse peasants, the manse took the place of the lord's obligation for support.) These homeless serfs, who were therefore not peasants in the true sense of the word, were frequently referred to as *mancipia*, a neuter term indicating that they were at least not originally considered persons but chattel belonging to the estate of the lord.[105] A lord could deploy them at will: on the manorial land, in the kitchen, in workshops, in the house, or in certain other capacities. Concerning manor houses, Emperor Conrad II's Code of Limburg of 1035 established that an abbot was to assign the unmarried children of serfs to the kitchen or bakery, that he was to have them do laundry or tend horses, or that he could deploy them in any other fashion; married children were to serve as cellarers, tollkeeper, or foresters.[106] By no means did the *mancipia* have to be "homeless"; rather, some owned a small cottage with some land in the vicinity of the manor house. Hence at the lordship of Prüm they were referred to as *Haistalden*; at Saint-Germain as *hospites*. Between manse peasants and actual manor personnel, there were other intermediate groups. Moreover, *mancipia* did not reside, as mentioned, merely at the manor, but also as hands on individual manses. On the whole, therefore, one may distinguish between a peasant and a sub-peasant stratum (with flexible borderlines) in rural areas. Some of the manorial serfs were also placed on manses as they became available, or which had been recently acquired, thus changing the serfs' functional status.

Statistical relations are hard to establish, since the manorial serfs not expected to generate income were seldom listed by name in land registers. On the whole, manse peasants formed the largest group. At Mehring, the monastery of Prüm owned manses and vineyards (*picturae*) with a total of 53 residents; at the two manorial estates (both upper and lower), there resided 29 married couples each, so that the proportionate relationship appears rather even here, though one must beware of any generalization based on these numbers. At any rate, in one of the Prüm donations[107] the number of manorial serfs was considerably smaller. At Lauterbach in Bavaria[108] there were twenty-three manses with a total of 42 peasants (and at least an additional 35 children and relatives, as well as 3 male servants), as opposed to only 10 manorial serfs (*bervendarii*). All told, this donation by Abbot Siegfried from the monastery at Ilm consisted of seven manors with 55 serfs and fifty-eight manses, with 224 peasants and their dependents. We may assume that the number of manorial serfs outweighed that of the other residents, but that their number continued to dwindle throughout the earlier Middle Ages. Ever since the high Middle Ages, manorial land was increasingly worked by day laborers (*Tagelöhner*), who were paid wages but no longer had to be provided for.

In addition to manse peasants and manorial serfs, there was a third group, the *ministri* or *ministeriales*. They were entrusted with administrative tasks and consisted primarily of the steward and his assistants,[109] who supervised work on the manor and on manorial land. At large manors, supervisors and artisans in the manorial workshops were also recruited from their ranks, people such as millers, bakers, brewers, blacksmiths, breeders, foresters, hunters, or herdsmen. In certain areas others were also recruited, such as miners in iron or lead mines, dependent merchants, and priests at proprietary churches (who, to be sure, had to be emancipated before they could assume office and their stipulated duties[110]). All these *ministri* came from the ranks of serfs, not only from among the manorial serfs—as customarily claimed—but also from among the manse peasants who performed official duties on a part-time basis. As mentioned in conjunction with the duties of the steward, other functions also provided opportunities for long-term advancement, so that the *ministri* soon rose above the rest of the serfs as a higher social rank.

The functional stratification into *ministri*, manse peasants, and manorial serfs does not by any means suggest that one may expect relative uniformity within any of these individual groups. There were substantial differences, especially among manse peasants. Peasants committed to render manorial services were distinguished from *censuales*, who merely had to pay dues. They had far more time at their disposal for work on their own tenements.[111] The chronicle of Ebersheimmünster (c. 1160) divided the *familia* into three groups: the *ministri* (*nobilis et billicosa*), those who merely paid rent (*censualis et obediens*), and those who paid rent but also had to render labor services (*servilis et censualis*).[112] Others (such as the Prüm fighting men, the *Scharmannen*) were mentioned because of special services they rendered (transportation, messenger services, etc.). The nature and amount of services and fees, as well as the sizes of manses and quality of land, generated further gradations, so that over a period of time substantial economic and, therefore, social differences evolved. Preservation of these differences ultimately depended on practices of inheritance. It is possible that some individual peasants also owned land of their own in addition to property leased to them.[113] Like the village community, the *familia* appeared to be uniform from the outside; its composition, however, varied in individual regions, even if no specific proportions are available for the earlier Middle Ages.

In many areas, the vast majority of peasants probably lived close to minimum subsistence level. However, we must consider a variety of differences if we wish to analyze the life of manse peasants, whom Brunner designates as nothing less than the typical European peasant.[114]

4. The Life of Manse Peasants

Labor

There can be no doubt that labor constituted the bulk of the everyday life of medieval peasants.[115] Of course, the attitude toward work was ambivalent. On the one hand, work was considered a curse, the consequence of original sin; on the other hand, it was also understood as penance during life on earth, and as such it was pleasing to God. In miniatures, Adam and Eve are often portrayed with their sons as a peasant family (Illustration 6). Adam is frequently preoccupied with farm chores, while Eve is portrayed busily at work spinning or holding a child to her breast. Since portrayals of peasant labor grace even churches, the work of peasants was apparently not disdained.[116] Work during the Middle Ages served more to produce food than profit, the explanation for which may be found in the fact that any thought of profit was out of the question in all but a few cases. However, hard work was above all a prerequisite for survival. We learn about peasant labor from the service regulations recorded in land registers, from archaeological finds, and finally from book miniatures, especially month-pictures which frequently depict farm chores (Illustration 14).

Peasant work was above all agricultural in nature, encompassing an entire range of activities. In the Werden land register for Friemersheim from the late ninth century, the services performed on the manorial land

Illustration 14: *Farm Labor: Plowing with the Scratch-Plow* (Stuttgarter Bilderpsalter, Saint-Germain-des-Prés, c. 820/30).

are described in precise detail: "During autumn [a serf] is to 'break up' (*gibrakon*) one yoke of arable land, plow it, get the seeds from the manor, and then tamp it down, that is, 'harrow' it . . . each yoke is to be tilled in such a way that it will be clean of shrubs and weeds, and it is to be cultivated in such a way that the harvest will reach the granary intact."[117] First the soil was plowed, sometimes several times. At Friemersheim, some soil even required spading,[118] since some of the plows were still rather primitive. The *aratrum*, which had been used as early as the Romans and sufficed for light soils in the Mediterranean, was a wooden scratch-plow (called *Ard*, or *Arl*) with a coulter and an iron plowshare which merely crumbled the soil (Illustration 14). On the other hand, the *carruca*, in evidence since the eighth century, was a wheeled plow with front wheels, coulter, a moldboard, and plowshare; it deepened furrows, cut the earth, and turned over the sod. The coulter parted the soil vertically, the plowshare parted it horizontally, and the moldboard flung the slice of turf aside, thus recovering the furrows which had been cut during previous sweeps. Since there are no archaeological remains of plows, descriptions are unreliable. While Lynn White[119] insists that agriculture was truly revolutionized by the introduction of the wheeled plow, Georges Duby believes that most peasants were inadequately equipped for a very long time, particularly since our information only stems from the large manors.[120] The fact is that wheeled plows were probably rather rare until the eleventh century. As a rule, this plow was pulled by one or several teams of oxen hitched to the plow by means of a yoke resting on the horns and forehead of the animals, so that the force could be transferred to their backs. Such a team required at least two people: the plowman, who kept pushing the plow into the soil, and a driver, who led the draft animals. (One illustration from the twelfth century symbolizes divine assistance graphically: out of a cloud, Christ touches the arm of the driver, "lending him a hand" [Illustration 15].) According to some illustrations, horses were occasionally used as draft animals. The Salian Code also acknowledged plow horses, and in the inventory from Annappes the reference to *iumenta*—the term used for draft animals— suggests the use of mares. On the whole, however, horses were seldom used in agriculture to this point. This was partly due to their value, but it may also be attributed to the lack of proper technology, since a horse's head stood high compared to that of an ox, and straps attached to the neck made breathing difficult (which is why horses were frequently portrayed with erect necks in illustrations). This led to most of a horse's pulling power being lost. Not until the invention of the horse collar could this problem be solved; a wooden yoke, resting on the whithers of the horse, was connected to the plow by means of a chest strap. First evidence of this device dates from the ninth century, but its use spread only gradually. Despite this invention, horses, with their greater strength and endurance, did not replace oxen even during the high Middle Ages, perhaps also because they required too much feed and were not fit to be eaten.

Illustration 15: *Religious Interpretation of Peasant Labor: Christ Assists during Plowing* (Herrad von Landsberg, *Hortus deliciarum*, twelfth century, in reference to Matthew 24:40ff).

Plowing was followed by sowing, which was done by hand, often by women. Seeds were carried in a basket or in a fold of the outer garment and spread by hand (Illustration 16). Afterwards, cultivation of the soil was advanced by dragging brushwood over the soil, a process of evening and smoothing the soil later completed by means of a wooden harrow. During the months that followed, fields also had to be kept free of weeds.

The next (second) "main season" began with harvest, which was also performed manually by using a short sickle to cut the stalks in half (Illustration 8). This was indeed laborious, but little went to waste; the straw was left for livestock to feed on. Not until the high Middle Ages do we encounter iconographic evidence of the scythe, which permitted harvesting a complete stalk. Cutting was followed by bundling and carting sheafs into the barn. In the land register of Friemersheim the services of the manse peasants were described: "As to the required day's labor, the wife is to bundle the sheafs in five heaps and then, after collecting them, she is to set them up straight. . . . The husband is then to cart two of these heaps to the lord's barn." Wives participated in the harvest. In addition to the grain harvest in the fields, hay had to be harvested in the meadows. Again we read in the records of Friemersheim: "Also, each manse peasant is to mow grass until noon . . . then he is to rake the hay into heaps and take a wagonload to the barn." Following harvest, grain was threshed with flails (which had quickly replaced mere wooden sticks), cleaned, and finally milled. That was often done (for a fee) by the manorial mills. In addition to the old hand-operated mills, water-mills were known as early as the early Middle Ages.[121] Windmills, on the other hand, first appeared during the twelfth and thirteenth centuries

Illustration 16: *Peasant Agriculture: Sowing and Harvesting* (Stuttgarter Bilderpsalter, Saint-Germain-des-Prés, c. 820/30).

in Flanders. The frequency of hand-grinding by peasants on their own tenements must not be underestimated. In the absence of manorial mills, peasants had to grind the lord's grain as well. At Friemersheim, peasants received an annual allotment of two bushels of rye to grind and bake into bread; they were permitted to keep every twenty-fourth loaf. Moreover, they were to grind and sift two bushels of wheat, process two bushels of barley into dogfeed, and render five bushels of acorns into feed for pigs. Flour, bread, and beer were also largely produced on the manses; at Friemersheim, every manse peasant received twelve bushels of grain a year to malt himself and boil in his own vat with his own wood. At other manor houses, such as Prüm, there is early evidence for manorial bakeries and breweries (*cambae*), although according to the land register of Prüm peasants were frequently commanded to make bread and brew beer (*facit panem et cervisiam*).

In addition to the undisputed primacy of the growing of grain, the cultivation of produce (turnips), legumes (beans, peas, and, less frequently, lentils), flax or (more rarely) hemp and oil plants (linseed, rape, poppy) played some role. Peasants also regularly grew garden vegetables (radishes, celery, pumpkins, carrots, cabbage, onions, cucumbers in the east, later also lettuce and spinach), herbs, and fruit or nut trees (especially apple, pear, sweet cherry, plum, nut, and chestnut).[122]

Despite their diversity, it was the seasonal nature of chores which stood out. The introduction of three-field rotation provided for a more continuous distribution of chores over the course of an entire year. Originally the soil was cultivated so long as it yielded crops, and then it was left fallow (*Feldgraswirtschaft*); soon, however, this was replaced in many places by two-field rotation (*Fruchtwechselwirtschaft*). A field was divided into two sections, one planted and the other left fallow, so that the soil would have a chance to recover. During the following year, the two sections were rotated. This system was perfected by three-field rotation. The earliest evidence of this system is a private document from St. Gall, dating from 763, in which a donor to the monastery promised to plow manorial land three times: one day's worth during spring and one fallow field in July, which he would again plow and seed during autumn.[123] The polyptych of St. Amand (chapter 3) also provides a telling illustration:[124] of the thirty *bunuaria* of manorial plowland, ten were planted with winter grain and ten with summer grain, while the remaining ten were left fallow. Thus, the land was divided into three parts. The first third yielded winter grain during the first year (wheat, rye, spelt, barley), planted during fall and harvested early in the following summer, before being left for a stubble-pasture. During the following year, it yielded summer grain (oats, barley) or legumes;

that is, people plowed in spring and harvested during the height of summer. Subsequently, the field was once again turned into a stubble pasture and left fallow during winter. The following (third) spring, the field was plowed in June and once again left fallow until being plowed one more time during late fall, when winter grain was planted and the original cycle was resumed. The cultivation of each of the other two fields was postponed by one year. Thus, the fields, left fallow twenty out of thirty-six months, had sufficient time to recover, while the labor of the peasants was distributed much more advantageously over an entire season. For instance, the summer field was worked during April, and the fallow field plowed in June; at the end of June one could already harvest the winter field, and the summer field during the following month. This could be followed by baking and brewing. About the middle of September, the new winter field was cultivated. Only during the winter months (November through March) was there no work to be done in the fields. Still, three-field rotation provided additional advantages: the danger of poor harvests decreased if the weather was somewhat favorable, and destroyed winter plantings could be offset by a good summer planting. Long periods of fallow, and the fact that harvested fields served as pastures for livestock, improved fertilization. Indeed, fertilization was a basic problem during the Middle Ages, since there was never enough natural fertilizer. Manure from the stables was occasionally hauled to the fields, but lime, marl, peat, and seaweed were also used. Manse peasants were also partly responsible for fertilizing the manorial land.

While three-field rotation, with its improved possibilities and labor conditions, created higher yields and improved quality, it required a redistribution of land. No individual peasant was in a position to divide his small parcels of land into three even smaller segments; rather, village land had to be divided in its entirety into at least three fields, part of which was allotted to each individual peasant. This required a master plan for crop rotation, a prescriptive decree on land-use (*Flurzwang*) by the lord of the manor, with the result that three-field rotation probably prevailed first on large manors. Although historians are cognizant of the existence of three-field rotation, they are chiefly concerned with determining its actual use, which Duby felt was rather limited. Historians are only able to draw conclusions based on indirect evidence, such as pictures of plowing during May and June on the month-pictures, or labor services recorded in the land registers; we do not know anything about how quickly three-field rotation may have become established. The amounts of grain turned over to the lords in the many land registers merely prove that the planting of winter as well as summer grain was already widespread among the Franks (barley serving both as a summer as well as a winter crop).[125]

In addition to farming, peasants also cultivated grapes in regions where this was possible (Illustration 17). Wine-growing originally did not constitute a specialized activity; rather, manses in the polyptych of Saint-Germain comprised a fairly large portion of vineyards as well as plowland and meadows, so that vineyard chores had to be performed along with farm chores despite the somewhat different seasonal rhythm involved. On the Prüm estates, specialization appears to have been more advanced. Here, levies were paid either in the form of wine or grain. The preferred wine regions in France were those along the lower and central Loire, the Paris basin and the lower Seine, and the vicinity of Laon, Soissons, Champagne, and Belgium. In Germany it was the areas along the Rhine and Moselle which were preferred.

During the early days, the chores of plowmen and wine-peasants alike were at least split in two, for livestock always played a significant role in agriculture. Livestock provided not only meat, but also fertilizer. In spite of its importance, however, calculations have shown

Illustration 17: *Farm Chores: Wine-Growing* (Hrabanus Maurus Manuscript, Montecassino, early eleventh century).

that livestock never sufficed as the sole source of food; only livestock and agriculture together could provide the necessary basis for the food supply;[126] it was only in the north and in the mountains of the south that raising livestock was more important than cultivating the land.

The fundamental significance of livestock farming can already be seen in the high fines levied by the Frankish tribal codes against rustlers, for the unit on which these fines were based was not the individual animal but the entire herd (for example, ten horses, twenty head of cattle, twenty-five to thirty sheep or pigs). The fact that peasants were expert at raising livestock is illustrated by the great number of differentiating terms for animals within certain species. For instance, the *Lex Salica* distinguished between suckling pigs from a first, second, or third pen; pigs in sties, paddocks, or out in the field; fattening pigs; hogs; breeding and leader sows; borrowed pigs; and boars. All this prompted Abel to speak of a veritable "pig vocabulary."[127] As for horses, Carolingian land registers differentiated between stallions, breeding mares, and one-, two-, or three-year-old colts and fillies. As for beef cattle, there were oxen, cows, calves, steers, and bulls. Beef cattle were especially important; so that they were occasionally referred to simply as *animalia*, enjoying special protection in tribal laws. They were used as draft animals for plowing and pulling wagons; they yielded meat, butter, cheese, and milk (though hardly one-sixth of the yield of today's dairy cows); and they also rendered hides for furs, leather, and parchment (the most important type of stationery). With the exception of parchment, for which peasants had no use, everything was manufactured on the farm. Oxen, cattle, and cows were frequently part of the regular stock of a manse peasant, although many peasants did not own a team of draft animals of their own. Horses were not necessarily part of a farm's livestock; however, parafredus services by some peasants who resided on free manses, a form of military or messenger service on horseback (hence the German word for horse, *Pferd*), indicate that horses were by no means a rarity on a farm. Numerically more significant than horses and often beef cattle as well, were the small animals (pigs, sheep, and goats). Sheep provided wool, hides (for leather and parchment-making), and meat. Pigs, which may be likened to today's wild pigs with their pointed snouts and ears, were the most important source of meat. They required little care, although they depended on the forest for food; in order to fatten them, especially during fall, pigs were herded into beech and oak forests. Even more common than sheep and pigs was poultry; chickens and eggs were among the most common types of a manse peasant's regular rent payments. Also, there were geese and, less frequently, pigeons and ducks. Some peasants also kept bees which provided wax and honey, the only sweetener of the Middle Ages. In the east in particular, people also raided the hives of wild bees in the forests. Finally, based on archaeological evidence from bones, dogs and cats also frequented the farms. During the summer, livestock remained on the pastures, spending winters in the barn.

There is little information about the number of animals on an individual farm, but there were generally fewer than today. Based on the sparse records kept in Burgundy, we may suppose an average number of one horse on every second manse, as well as between two and four head of cattle and ten pigs and sheep.[128] Considering these low figures, any casualty endangered a peasant's existence. Indications of the value of the animals may be gleaned from catalogs of fines listed in tribal codes. Thus, a horse was worth twice as much as one head of cattle and four times as much as a pig. The later changeover from livestock payments to payments made in cash somewhat corroborates these figures. In the Rhine region, a young pig was worth between four and six pence, a grown pig two shillings. Those were substantial sums in the eyes of contemporaries.

There was more to farm labor than cultivating the land, raising livestock, and growing wine. Agricultural products also had to be processed into bread, beer, wine, butter and cheese, and animals had to be slaughtered and their meat cured and made into sausages. Although hunting, which was a privilege of lords, played no great role in the food supply of peasants, hunting wild animals in order to protect one's livestock and fields was important. Wolves in particular were a constant scourge for a long time. In the *Capitulare de villis*, Charlemagne ordered an annual wolf hunt every spring.[129] An even more important food source was probably fishing in places where nature and manorial laws permitted it. The forest, too, represented an important source of food. Here, fruits and berries were gathered, lumber was harvested, and fuel was collected. Wood was processed and made into farm implements, barrels, furniture, battens for improvements and additions to houses and barns, as well as fence posts for surrounding the tenement and fields.[130] Winter days in particular were passed taking care of these chores, patching and mending were frequently necessary. Again, at Friemersheim, fence mending was considered one of the direct services to be rendered to the manor; each manse peasant had to supply the manor with thirty posts (which he fashioned himself) and replace the fence at regular intervals. (He was permitted to keep old posts and wicker.) Similar chores involved the fences surrounding the plowland, which was supposed to protect the crops from the livestock. Finally, the property, livestock, and harvest had to be guarded against wild animals, strangers, and robbers. Once again, guard duty during harvest time or near herds was counted among the services a peasant had to render to his lord. The villagers probably shared these chores, which were augmented by hauling and messenger services, hosting of guests, and possible military service until well into the ninth century in the case of freemen. Military service, however, could be avoided by paying a sum of money, and it was increasingly performed by noble vassals in their capacity as the warrior class of the day.

A peasant's work was spread over the entire year in such a way that its rhythm divided the year, and the scenes in the month-pictures (a form of medieval calendar) contained themes dealing mostly with peasant life. According to a typical example in a Salzburg manuscript dating from the beginning of the ninth century (Illustration 18), January was characterized by deep winter; the climate and the "lack of physical labor" permitted the peasants to freeze. (Wandalbert of Prüm on the other hand, mentions woodcutting in his poems highlighting the months.[131]) The picture for February shows a hunting scene (whereas Wandalbert mentions cleaning the fields, and other cycles show peasants spading). March and April were spent trimming grapevines and cutting posts[132] or, according to yet another picture, driving livestock out to pasture. The picture for the month of May shows a peasant holding flowers, probably symbolizing the first signs of growth. In June, the peasants plowed. (More southern cycles already show them mowing.) According to the *Salzburger Kalendarium*, hay was not harvested until the beginning of July. During August grain was harvested, in September one could once again begin to plant seeds, the month of October was reserved for the wine harvest, and during November and December peasants slaughtered their livestock. (According to Wandalbert, pigs were still being driven into the forests to fatten them on acorns.) People slaughtered their livestock in order to save feed during the winter days ahead, then pickled the meat. (The high proportion of young pigs at Staffelsee argues against a long life expectancy.) Depending on geographical location and tradition, the seasonal rhythm of these chores shifted somewhat in other calendars, but one fact remains: the everyday life of peasants was determined by the year's cycle.

We have already noted that women at Friemersheim[133] were certainly being assigned a number of farm tasks at an early date, and not only starting in the twelfth century as some scholars are inclined to assert. In addition to the daily chores around the house and the farmyard, women helped out during "high season," which required the cooperation of all the peasants with planting and harvesting, especially until the introduction of the scythe. Women sometimes assisted as oxen

Illustration 18: *Peasant Chores during the Course of a Year* (Salzburg, beginning of the ninth century).

drivers during plowing, and they may even have been in charge of cultivating vineyards.[134] However, heavy farm labor remained the exception for them. When Gerald of Aurillac noticed a woman plowing because her husband was sick, for example, he gave her money so that she could pay other peasants to do it for her and so that she would no longer have to perform "male labor." "For," he said, "God detests everything which is against nature."[135] No doubt, raising livestock and poultry were among women's tasks. This included milking cows, sheep, and goats, as well as shearing the sheep. They also took responsibility for making textiles, from shearing sheep and harvesting fibrous plants (flax and hemp) to finishing clothing, for in this respect peasant families were also largely self-sufficient. Soon the distaff became a symbol for female labor. In conjunction with its prohibition of work on Sunday, Charlemagne's *Admonitio generalis* of 789 distinguished between typically male and female chores:

> We also order that . . . no servants' chores (*opera servilia*) be performed on Sundays . . . that men not perform farm chores, that they refrain from cultivating the vineyards, from plowing the fields, from mowing, from cutting hay or building fences, constructing houses, or working in the garden. [The only permissible chores were carting services during times of war for the purpose of supplying vital goods or, occasionally, for a funeral] By the same token, women are not to manufacture cloth on Sundays, make patterns for clothes, sew, or embroider, card wool, scutch flax, wash clothes in public, or shear sheep.[136]

Thus, with some reservations and restrictions, one may already speak of a division of labor within the family.[137]

This survey illustrates how a peasant and his wife, depending on the size of their household, had little cause for complaining about a lack of employment, so that—with the exception of the short days of winter—there hardly remained time to do anything else. Considering the bulk of a peasant's work, subject to frequent deadlines and vicissitudes of the weather, it stands to reason that peasants rarely adhered to the ban against work on Sunday, which had to be reiterated time and again.[138] Monastic circles also denounced peasants for this. When the peasants living in the vicinity of the monastery of Werden plowed despite a proclaimed holiday, according to a biographer of St. Liudger, the coulters of some peasants broke and the oxen of others bolted.[139] This miracle story illustrates that the only day left for many a peasant's own chores was Sunday. What was so crucial for the bond peasant family's burden was the fact that listed tasks were not only to be performed on a peasant's own manse but also on part of the manorial land, or else appropriate cash payments had to be made. Excerpts from the land register at Friemersheim permit us a fairly detailed initial glimpse at the situation.

Let us now examine in greater detail the extent of these services.

Services and Yield

As already mentioned, bond peasants were obligated to render services and payments. The polyptych of Saint-Germain-des-Prés provides us with a good idea of these tasks, since the demands were relatively uniform. There were six different recurring types of work to be performed on manorial land. First, peasants were to cultivate a certain piece of manorial land (*Salland*) during fall and spring. Partly together with, partly in addition to their other chores, peasants were obligated to cultivate a section of the manorial vineyard, an area exceeding by far the manse's share in the vineyard, as a rule. Labor in vineyards was particularly burdensome on the properties of manse peasants. In addition to scheduled chores, there were non-scheduled services which manse owners were obligated to perform as often as (*quantum*) and wherever (*ubi*) they were told to do so. The *corvadae*, for example, were labor services in the strict sense of the word, consisting of days spent working on manorial land, mostly during plowing season. Peasants had to contribute their own equipment, team of oxen, and plow for this duty. At some manors, these services were scheduled, as at Prüm, where many peasants rendered from one to six *corvadae*. One of Charlemagne's capitularies presupposed specified services whose duration depended on the equipment a peasant happened to have at his disposal.[140] At Saint-Germain, these statutory labor services were joined by the *carropera*, providing transportation services to the manor house or monastery and others which were also unscheduled and did not require the use of a team of oxen (called *manopera*, or *Handdienste*). Occasionally, long-distance hauling was also demanded; this, however, was scheduled (referred to at Prüm as *angaria*). Finally, various services are mentioned which involve cutting wood and felling trees in the lord's forest (*caplim*).

At Saint-Germain, two special types of chores which played a much greater role in other land registers (especially east of the Rhine) were rarely required. The first of these was the obligation of the manse tenant to volunteer services weekly on the manorial land for a specified number of days (*dies*). Three-day services were the kind of encumbrance typical for the manse of a bond peasant. These services were substantially more demanding than those already mentioned, which were distributed over shorter periods of time during the course of a year. Weekly services were considered particularly burdensome, since they had to be rendered during high season, when peasants needed to be working on their own land. Services such as these presented peasants with a serious dilemma at times when bad weather shortened the time available for work in the fields. A second type of service rather typical in many regions was the so-called *noctes*, manorial services which lasted two weeks each (resulting in an absence from home "lasting many nights"). Such services were required one to three times during the course of a year. Peasants were also responsible for the upkeep of the manor house and the fences, and they had to perform sentry duty (after the grain had been hauled into the barn, for example). Using the lord's grain, they also had to bake bread and brew beer, or they had to tend his livestock and feed it throughout the winter. The manse peasants at Friemersheim worked for their lord an estimated total of ten weeks a year (not counting three-day services).[141]

In addition to these services, there were dues which originally consisted merely of payment in kind, whether agricultural produce (grain and wine, or flour, bread, and beer if already processed), livestock or animal products. Regular payments had to be made in the form of chickens and eggs. Often a pig or a hog, a head of cattle, or a sheep was demanded instead, sometimes on alternating years. Less frequently meat products (such as ham), or dairy products, such as butter and cheese, were provided. Moreover, some peasants had to supply wood, especially fence posts, and their wives often had to produce linen cloth or shirts. In addition to levies in kind, cash often had to be paid, though it is possible references to money merely represent the value of the produce they were permitted to pay in kind. Cash payments were the levy of choice in remote areas where the cultivation of manorial land was not profitable, or it was demanded of better-to-do, often personally free tributary farmers (*Zinsbauern*). On the whole, in the course of the high Middle Ages, dues in kind, ultimately services as well in the form of labor, came increasingly to be replaced by monetary payments, which induced some manors to change over to purely money-based economies. Peasants were then forced to sell their produce at the local market first in order to raise money for their rent.

In addition to the constant fees charged for the use of the manse, peasants often also paid rent for the permission to use manorial facilities, for example, for the purpose of fattening pigs (*pastio*) or felling trees (*ligneritia*) in the manorial forest, or for the use of the mill or the bakery. Occasionally the manorial boar could also be borrowed for a fee by pig farmers. Freemen frequently paid a military tax (*hostilitium*) in lieu of military service and provided a horse (*parafredus*) for military and messenger services. Some peasants also paid a poll tax (in most cases, four pence). Finally, there were special fees, for instance on the wedding or the death of a serf; in the latter case the lord received the peasant's best animal (*Besthaupt*). During times of crises, the lord of the manor was entitled to collect a special levy, the *Bede*. In addition to these manorial taxes, the peasant also had to tithe to the Church and, later, pay advocacy fees (*Vogteiabgaben*) to the owner of the local court. Of course, not all of these dues and fees were required of every manse, but they illustrate fairly clearly how extensive and varied the actual burden could be.

Several examples will illustrate how varied the dues were in actuality. The twenty-four free manses at Gernsheim listed in the land register of Lorsch were to supply the following every year: one hog, one chicken, ten eggs, a load of roof shingles, five wagon loads of wood, a shilling for women's work, and the services of one horse. They were also to assist with plowing, harvesting, and transporting the harvest into the barns. The thirty local bond manses also supplied one pig, one chicken, and ten eggs; however; instead of annual manorial services they worked three days a week, in addition to several non-scheduled services, and they paid fifteen pence for women's work.[142] The twelve bond manses at Wallersheim within the jurisdiction of Prüm[143] also provided services three days a week, and also twice rendered fifteen *noctes* and six *corvadae* a year. In addition, they plowed three yokes of manorial land; maintained part of the fence; provided guard services; hauled fifteen bushels of grain and one cord of wood to the manor, paid two oxen and fifteen pence in military tax; and paid dues of one liter linseed oil, three chickens and fifteen eggs, one pig (valued at an ounce of gold), and one hundred wooden slats. All in all, it is likely little time or yield was left. By comparison, more remote manses of the oldest Werden land register district were much less encumbered,[144] paying mostly fees in the amount of twelve to sixteen bushels of barley, a military tax of eight pence, rent between three and twenty pence, and occasionally also some honey and a piece of cloth. Although these levies were high by contemporary standards, they were remitted in place of all services.

The reasons for difference in services rendered and levies paid were manifold. First, they did not depend on the size of the manse. Second, free and bond manses were encumbered in different ways. Third, the distance to the manor house or monastery, as well as the manorial organization, played a role. Finally, regional customs developed, so that manses belonging to different lords within one and the same village often came to be similarly encumbered, which is why some scholars speak of them as veritable "rent regions."[145] Yet this observation will not provide us with a sufficiently satisfactory final explanation, for even within a given manorial association or village the services of peasants often varied so much that they ultimately allow us to presuppose individualized rules and regulations.

Individual levies fell due at predetermined dates. The *Sachsen-spiegel* from the early thirteenth century, for example recognizes a regular calendar of dues illustrated in the Heidelberger Manuscript (Illustration 19). On July 13, the feast of St. Margaret, a tithe of grain was due; on June 24, the feast of St. John, a tithe of meat; on May 1, the feast of St. Walpurgis, a tithe of lambs; on May 25, the feast of St. Urban, a tithe of all fruit and wine; on August 15, the feast of St. Mary's Assumption, a tithe of geese; and on August 24, the feast of St. Bartholomew (symbolized by the skin torn from the saint's body),[146] a tax in pence on eggs and grain. Land registers often stipulated the exact due dates in which the patron saint of the monastery played a special role.

In conjunction with variations in the size of manses and the number of workers, various burdens attributed to social and economic differentiation among peasants, so that a uniform peasant class could not even develop within the association of serfs on a given manor. Therefore, opportunities for peasants varied greatly for one case to the next. One may presume that the majority of bond peasants was severely burdened; however, individual peasants at least had the opportunity for prosperity and gradual social advancement.

It is difficult to say what peasants had left after all these payments, and not only because of the differences mentioned. The actual yield depended on many factors: on the soil, whose productivity was poor most of the time; on the climate; on a favorable location relative to trade; and, naturally, on peasant labor itself. The figures for Annappes (c. 800), for example, are almost frightening.[147] Royal commissioners discovered that of 1320 bushels of spelt, 720 (54 percent) had to to be reused for planting; 60 of the 100 bushels of wheat (60 percent) had to be replanted, and 1,100 bushels of the 1,800 bushels of barley (62 percent). As to rye, everything had to be replanted. Thus, in the case of spelt, the soil had merely produced 1.8 times the amount of seed, in the case of wheat 1.7 times, and in the case of barley 1.6 times. As it happened, these figures applied to a random year in a certain region, so that one must assume it was a particularly poor harvest.[148] Since Annappes was found to have some grain left from the previous year, the harvest must have been better the year before. However, this certainly illustrates how much the yields varied and how much fixed levies must have burdened peasants, especially during years of poor harvest. It is possible that the yield on a privately owned manse may have been somewhat higher than on manorial land, since peasants went to greater pains with their own land, although this conjecture may be too tainted by modern ideas about entrepreneurship. On the whole,

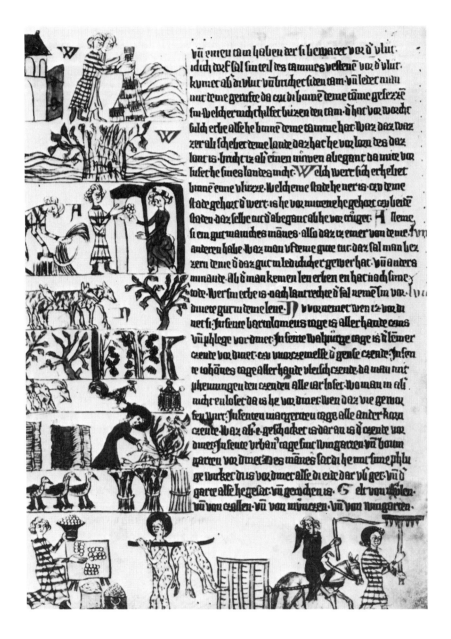

Illustration 19: *Due Dates for Various Manorial Levies* (Sachsenspiegel, Heidelberger Bilderhandschrift, c. 1330).

one may assume an average yield of three times the amount of seed planted, so that the yield was approximately double after deducting what had to be used for the next planting. This amounts to roughly a tenth of today's yield, so that an area which today feeds ten people then barely sustained one person. That is why great numbers of peasants were needed in order to feed a relatively small number of masters.

Now, these yields had to be used to cover the rent owed to the lord estimated at one-third or perhaps even one-half of the total yield. The amount subsequently left for the peasant's family depended on the size of the manse and the number of household members. There were sizable differences, which perennially increased through successive generations. There were peasants who lived extremely well. According to a careful estimate, a manse had to be between nine and sixteen hectares in size in order to produce a sufficient yield. Since manses were substantially smaller than this in many areas, without exact figures or exaggeration we may assume that the majority of rural families barely managed to eke out an existence, and that they depended on sources of income in addition to agriculture to meet their nutritional needs. Nevertheless, as a group, peasants fed themselves as well as the rest of the population through their surpluses. According to estimates provided by Wisplinghoff for Friemersheim,[149] a peasant managed to achieve 22.5 *Malter* (about seven hectoliters) of grain, of which 7.5 were replanted, 4 sent to the lord and 2.25 tithed. This left 8.75 *Malter*, sufficient for baking approximately 300 seven-pound loaves of bread. (Had a peasant used up the entire yield himself, that would have provided approximately 420 pounds of bread per capita and year for a family of five, augmented by pork, chicken, and produce from the garden.) In a more recent land register from Werden (c. 1050), the burdens encountered by the peasants at Friemersheim had grown significantly less. Thus, their lot had improved during the high Middle Ages, especially since technical advances increased yield in many cases. Similar observations can be made in other areas, too, and may be connected to improvements in climate and, above all, the replacement of services by cash payments. On the other hand, land became scarcer as a result of population growth, forcing peasants to clear and colonize new land. Not until the late Middle Ages did agriculture experience decline as a result of falling grain prices, precipitating peasant revolts.

Peasant Life Outside Work Time

While the working life of the manse peasant is reflected rather clearly in the sources, we have almost no information about the rest of everyday life, domestic life. Evidence for the amounts of food consumed by a peasant family may be deduced from the types of crops planted and the stipulations found in land registers for meals given during periods of obligatory labor. Meals consisted mostly of bread, beer or wine, along with the *companaticum* (food accompanying bread, such as sausages, cold cuts, or cheese). The principal staples were undoubtedly grain products, primarily bread, porridge and beer, but also consisting of turnips and cabbage, cheese, and fruit. Meat, usually in cured form, was rather rare and reserved for holidays, although we must take into consideration enormous differences in wealth. Peasant attire, the simplicity of which has already been mentioned, was made by the women on the premises from coarse linen cloth, made of flax, or from sheep's wool. It consisted of a short smock, a tunic with ample sleeves, sometimes leggings, footwear made of cowhide, a straw hat and, on rare occasions, a coat.

Since a peasant's workday began at sunrise and ended, especially during the main season, at sunset, and since the services on the manorial land could be compensated for only by additional work on his own manse, any peasant who did not have a sufficient number of male servants at his disposal could count on having free time only during winter months. The question of how peasant families spent their time after work was therefore only conditionally justified. Sociable get-togethers within the family or among village peasants were probably rather common. In order to compensate for the harsh realities of peasant labor, the few festive occasions during the course of a year were celebrated all the more fervently: church festivities (such as on the occasion of the feasts of St. Nicholas and St. Silvester, before and after Lent, and above all the anniversary of the village church's consecration, called *Kirchweih* or *kermis*), were especially important to rural life, as were the celebration of May 1, the bringing in of the harvest, and the beginning of each season. People celebrated by singing, dancing, and drinking, sometimes while masked; many a pagan custom was preserved in rural life, although individual events (erecting a May pole, processions, harvest dances, solstice bonfires) are only known from late medieval court rulings (*Weistümer*). Of course, social events were also celebrated, foremost among them being weddings and baptisms, in which the entire village participated. But people did not celebrate birthdays, which were largely not known, because they were considered unimportant and were thus typically not recorded. Sumptuous feasts at such occasions made up for many a frugal meal. Neidhart von Reuenthal vividly describes in his songs how the young people in the village enjoyed dancing and dressing festively in headdress and garlands.

There is, however, considerable doubt concerning the degree to which poetry of this kind reflects the reality of exceptional festive occasions in everyday life, especially since Neidhart's songs often turn satirical. For example, a mother and a daughter argue over a dancing dress, only subsequently to compete against each other on the dancefloor; the stupid peasant lads (*dörper, getelinge*) dream of seducing the girls and don their Sunday's best in vain, but "dressed to the nines" and bearing arms, all they do is compete with knights. More likely, the poems indicate the secret desire of peasants to imitate knights, at least at occasions such as these. Apparently the strict social discrimination prescribed by later laws did not always prevail. Leisure and free time, however, were rare and uncharacteristic of the hard-working peasants; they were more typical of the lords who lived off the labor of their serfs, whose position as manorial rulers has been repeatedly touched on in the course of this chapter. In the following chapter, we shall focus on the life of the upper class at the princely courts.

V

Knighthood and Courtly Life

Within the framework of the manorial system, the "seignorial life" which nobles pursued without engaging in any productive labor presupposed peasant life and peasant labor. The seignorial lifestyle was foreshadowed by monastic life as already described, but its most spectacular manifestation was as courtly life. We must remember that the manorial system constituted the most important, if no longer the sole, basis for seignorial life well into the high Middle Ages, even if nobles will no longer be discussed as manorial lords here. Neither can "courtly life" be identified directly with the life of the nobility as a whole, since courtly life concentrated at the courts of princes, the uppermost stratum of nobility. Remaining levels of nobility were integrated into these courts, since they assembled there periodically and attempted to imitate the life of princes as closely as circumstances permitted; such "courts" existed throughout the Middle Ages. Yet the term "courtly life" as we use it specifically combines the way of life practiced by chivalric society with the "courtly culture" of the high Middle Ages which reached its peak during the twelfth and thirteenth centuries. (At that time, "courtly" or "courteous" demeanor typified a specific level of society.) For the first time, thanks to courtly poetry, a lay culture developed in which knights determined their own image, developing an ideal difficult to reconcile with contemporary reality. Herein lies the major difficulty confronting our evaluation of medieval poetry, although it undoubtedly broadens our horizon as a new source of information.

Let us first focus on the institutional background, the princely court.

1. The Institution:
Principality, Princely Courts, and Courtly Culture

A clearly defined courtly culture could only emerge at established courts. For a long time during the Middle Ages, however, "courts" did not constitute something fixed. The royal court convened wherever the king and his retinue happened to be staying. It is well known that there were no established royal residences during the earlier Middle Ages; these first developed in western Europe at London and Paris during the twelfth century, while kings continued to travel from palace to palace throughout the country. In fact, the term "court" signified something local and personal. As a place, it designated where the king happened to be residing at a particular point in time. As such, it was commonly referred to as *Pfalz* (palace),[1] consisting of a series of houses built on imperial land for the purpose of housing a traveling king and an entourage which could reach a size of more than a thousand men and women.[2] It constituted the place where the king's entourage stayed for shorter as well as longer periods of time (such as during the winter months), where government business was transacted, guests were received and entertained, and festivities were staged. A chapel was attached for the benefit of religious life, and one or several nearby estates provided food. Most early palaces were enlarged manorial estates, heavily fortified only during times of external danger. During the Ottonian age a new type combining palace and castle appeared. This castle-like structure characterized Hohenstaufen palaces, which for the most part were located in towns. "Court," however, also included persons, since palaces required personnel for their upkeep. These included administrators, a castle garrison (*Burgmannen*), and servants, in particular the household officials. In a broader sense, then, the royal court comprised all the people surrounding the king, including the personnel and the royal family, clerical and secular officials, and those called magnates who happened to be in attendance. Consequently, the composition of a court was in constant flux, even though each individual king had his preferred circle of retainers.

The kings became the most important, although not the only sustainers of courtly life; there were also bishops with their permanent quarters (*Residenz*) in episcopal palaces, which during this time were frequently next to cathedrals.[3] But it was secular princes who ultimately became the most prominent carriers of courtly life, especially once they began to prefer permanent residences in the twelfth century, each noble with his own ancestral castle (*Stammburg*). Initially only moderate proponents of the courtly style, great secular lords became capable of surpassing even the king in the splendor of their courtly life. This development culminated in the formation of a uniform class of princes and the establishment of vast sovereign territories.

From this perspective, the emergence of courtly life was no accident; rather, it was the result of a political and social development which essentially began in the era of conflict over lay investiture. That was when, as a result of the confrontation between emperor and pope, secular influence over the institutional Church suffered a serious setback, even while the major secular and ecclesiastical lords grew into a third power in their own right.[4] In the course of the twelfth century, against the background of the structural crisis of the old nobility, this highest-ranking social group established itself as a separate power while its position was anchored, at least in a feudal sense, in a strict military hierarchy (*Heeresschildordnung*). The term prince (*Fürst, princeps*)[5] had once described a loosely defined group of secular and ecclesiastical lords who distinguished themselves through their participation in the "Empire," in government. Now princes were defined as direct vassals of the king. Following the ecclesiastics, who held the second rank (after the king), the secular imperial princes of the realm formed a crucial third rank. They were the only ones allowed to receive fiefs from ecclesiastical lords (not vice versa). The fourth rank was claimed by counts and barons. Though imperial princes became more tangible as a group as a result, their direct relationship with the king depended more strongly than ever on the individual lord's situation. First and foremost among imperial princes were dukes and territorial princes, who soon developed a concomitant sense of identity; then came margraves, counts palatine (such as the Count Palatine of the Rhine) and landgraves (such as the Landgrave of Thuringia). A miniature from the Gospel of Duke Henry the Lion portrays the duke together with his wife in the company of their most distinguished relatives, including Emperor Lothar III and his wife Richenza (grandparents); their daughter Gertrud and her husband Duke Henry the Proud of Saxony and Bavaria (Henry's parents); King Henry II of England (his father-in-law); Henry II's mother, Matilda (wife of Henry V). The ducal couple is even being crowned by Christ (Illustration 20)!

Princely status and courtly life were intimately connected with the formation of the territorial states by both secular and ecclesiastical lords. These lords, searching for new ways of government, ushered in a radical transformation of political system from a traditional government based on personal association (*Personenverbandsstaat*) to the territorial state (*Flächenstaat*).[6] Personal ties no longer prevailed; instead, rule

Illustration 20: *Self-awareness of an Imperial Prince: Henry the Lion in the Company of His Family* (Gospel of Henry the Lion, c. 1188).

now had to be as comprehensive as possible and cover a precisely defined territory. One also sought to arrogate as many privileges as possible: manorial rights, already expanding as a result of colonization and clearance, the establishment of towns, privileges allowing nobles to fortify residences, build castles, and exercise advocacy or judicial rights.

New privileges also included convoy privileges, the rights of coinage, and revenue and fiscal sovereignty. We must be wary of picturing early territorial states of the twelfth and thirteenth centuries as completely separate regions ruled by a sovereign, but such a tendency did in fact exist. Territorial states required a class of officials who could assume responsibility in the name of their lord. Imperial advocates and lower *ministeriales* gradually rose from serfdom to the levels of the lower nobility due to their elevated functions, discharging a decisive role in courtly life. Further, permanent administrative centers were needed, primarily politically motivated princely courts which came to develop into social and cultural centers of courtly life. In early France, the dukes of Aquitaine (at Poitiers) and Burgundy emerged as significant proponents of courtly life, followed in the north by the counts of Anjou, Blois, Champagne, Flanders, and Normandy. In the Empire—in addition to the imperial court—proponents of courtly culture included the Landgraves of Thuringia at Wartburg Castle (especially Hermann I at the end of the twelfth century),[7] the Welfs, especially Henry the Lion in Brunswick, the Babenbergers in Vienna, the Margraves of Meissen, the Wittelsbach Dukes of Bavaria in Munich, the Zähringer dukes, and the ecclesiastical princes (such as Bishop Kuno I of Regensburg).

As a result, princely courts developed into cultural centers. Since there were still no stipends for professional artists, poets and artists depended directly on the patronage of these princes. In return, artists assumed responsibility for educating young noblemen and maintaining official correspondence.[8] The great courts of the day witnessed the emergence of special artistic and literary circles composed of well-known artists. An early, outstanding example was the court of Charlemagne, which attracted scholars from all over western Europe (such as the Anglo-Saxon Alcuin and Paul the Deacon from Lombardy). During the Ottonian era, the imperial court remained the most important cultural center. "Here [says Ruotger in his *Vita Brunonis*[9] about the court of Otto the Great] people who imagined themselves to be of some stature congregated from the four corners of the earth.... Here great examples of wisdom, piety, and justice blossomed in a way that had not been experienced since times immemorial. Many a scholar who had thought of himself as exceedingly learned returned humbled and began his studies anew." The exaggeration contained in Ruotger's praise is obvious, since the cultural revival only concerned the liberal arts, what we would call "higher general education," which had "fallen into oblivion."

The courtly culture of the high Middle Ages displayed its own unique characteristics. Patrons were often cited by poets in their works, and the patronage system itself was an expression of courtly display.[10]

It had a definite influence on the types of works commissioned, reflecting the needs and the self-awareness of the princes. Chivalric poetry, written for entertainment as well as for didactic purposes, and courtly love lyric (*Minnesang*) were paralleled by works describing the history of territories and dynasties beginning in the late eleventh and early twelfth centuries. In Germany, for example, there were the *Chronicon Ebersheimense* and the *Historia Welforum*.[11] Courtly writings displayed three characteristics: they were meant to be entertaining, and they were educational, but they were also panegyric in praising the benefactors. Jean de Marmoutier began his chronicle of the counts of Anjou with the following dedication:

> Brother Jean de Marmoutier, the most insignificant of monks and lowliest of clerics, wishes Lord Henry, King of England, Duke of Normandy, Count of Anjou, Tours and Le Mans, Prince of Aquitaine, Duke of the Gascogne and the Auvergne, and also Duke of Brittany, peace, happiness, long life, well-being and health through Him who bestows his blessings on kings. I gathered the history and the deeds of your ancestors, the counts of Anjou, from various learned texts and compiled them in a single volume. . . . Nowadays people imitate the ancients and, like them, though our lives may be brief, we also ought to keep the memory of those whose virtues appear praiseworthy and eternal. We therefore intend to make known the life, customs, and deeds of your ancestors, the counts of Anjou, so that they shall be like a mirror to you. . . . Whenever the chronicle reports the deeds of good men, any attentive listener will be encouraged to imitate them. When it recalls the foul deeds of evil men, a pious and virtuous listener or reader will nevertheless be led to avoid bad and inhuman acts. Listeners will be all the more encouraged to do good deeds and act in accordance with that which is worthy of God.[12]

In the allegorical *Song-Contest on the Wartburg*, the most famous Minnesingers vied for a prize, the favor of the landgravine of Thuringia. Although this was a fictitious gathering, it nevertheless typifies the "courtly" orientation of poets.

In the beginning most poets were clerics affiliated with private chapels, since only the clergy could read and write during the early Middle Ages. Later, they were joined by members of the *ministeriales*, appointed to serve at court for a while and assume various other duties there. The Minnesinger Friedrich von Hausen, for instance, served from 1186-1190 as *secretarius* at the court of Frederick I Barbarossa and took part in government activities. Itinerant scholars and minstrels traveled from court to court, singing of "wine, women, and the game of dice." Courtly poetry proper was undoubtedly directed at a knightly audience and, like knighthood itself, originated in southern France, spreading into the German Empire via Burgundy, peaking between 1170 and 1230.[13] Courtly poetry propagated a knightly ideal which exaggerated everything in terms of splendor.[14] Castles were likened to lavishly appointed palaces, the arms of knights were gilded and studded with precious stones, and the knights without exception were either extraordinary heroes or utter villains. Hence stories about this unreal world of knights were placed preferably in the indefinite past, "the good old days." At the beginnings of German poetry, which imitated French examples more or less slavishly, stand the *Imperial Chronicle*, Lamprecht the Priest's Alexander romance, and *König Rother* (all about 1150) then Konrad the Priest's *Song of Roland* (from c. 1170, composed at the court of Henry the Lion) and Heinrich von Veldeke's *Eneit* (1174). The themes revolved around the cycles of ancient Troy (*Eneit*), Alexander the Great, or Charlemagne, and they paralleled a type of epic poetry indebted to the legendary "histories" of Geoffrey of Monmouth about the kings of Britain, which idealized the timeless and spaceless world of King Arthur's court. These heroic epics—literary scholars distinguish between the heroic epic proper, the *chanson des gestes*, and the courtly epic, such as the Arthurian romances—dealt with two themes, adventure (*aventiure*) and love. Both had to be in balance. As a result, the true theme of poetry came to be testing of a hero whose *mâze* (sense of measure) had been disturbed. As a rule, the hero failed during his first adventurous journey (that is, by the norms of courtly etiquette, not those of a genuine hero); later he would prove himself during his second attempt by making good his mistakes.[15] Iwein, for instance, succeeds in marrying Laudine, whose husband he had slain and with whom he had fallen hopelessly in love. However, he subsequently takes leave for a year to seek adventure, of course forgetting almost immediately about a timely return. As a result, he loses Laudine and goes mad. Not until his second adventurous journey does he have a chance to vindicate himself. After liberating Lunete, the daughter of a castellan, from the clutches of a giant, saving her from certain death in a trial by combat, defeating two giants, freeing noble virgins from servitude, and fighting for a lady whose inheritance had been disputed by an older sister, he is able to win back Laudine, but not before promising never to fail her again.

Although chivalric society as portrayed in literature appears primarily male-dominated, "ladies" (*frouwen*) played an important role in poetry and at court as addressees of love poems, protagonists in epics, and patronesses. (Quite typical for the times is the fact that the "queen" constitutes the central figure in the game of chess; she is not to be conquered violently, but yields gradually to "entreaties.")

In addition to patrons, courtly poetry needed an equally courtly audience which not only expressed interest, but also contributed a certain degree of education. By the twelfth century at the latest, at least in western Europe, the sons of princes were educated at monastic or cathedral schools, or by private tutors, although Germany did not follow this practice until almost a century later. Most private chapels contained a library. Administrative matters were increasingly recorded, requiring a staff which knew how to write. Next to courage and piety, a literary and historical education became increasingly the aspiration of an ideal prince. The saying that an uneducated king was like a crowned ass was attributed to Fulco II (c. 950), at least according to the twelfth-century chronicle of the counts of Anjou.[16] Such an extensive education was limited to a select few, and most knights were almost certainly illiterate.[17] Nonetheless, works were recited before courtly audiences by poets and minstrels, by people who knew how to read, as soon as the texts were available in written form. In *Iwein* (ll. 6455ff.), the owner of a castle as well as his wife had their daughter read to them from a French book. This episode, although mentioned only in passing, seems to typify a common practice of making literary education available to daughters. Moreover, the many allusions to earlier works and songs hidden in the poetry, especially in France, presuppose a general, excellent knowledge of literature. Courtly literature and culture had become a significant component of courtly life.

This patronage system naturally extended also to architects, whose task it was to beautify the living space of this society.

2. The Space:
The Medieval Castle

In the heroic epics, knights roamed the countryside, but their proper living space was castles[18] and the large courts they frequented. Of course, we must not liken the "residences" of territorial princes to grand palaces. Castles were confining and crowded, and the palaces of princes merely differed from them in quality and size, not structure. Our modern concept of medieval castles is distorted, since as a rule no preserved castles date from before the late Middle Ages. Moreover, they were frequently remodeled during the nineteenth century (and not always in proper style), with the result that there are precious few recognizable traces left of knights' castles from the age of chivalry. Even the complex terminology used to describe a castle varies according to author, such as *castellum, castrum, oppidum, civitas*, and *urbs*.[19] Indeed, even a town was considered a *burc* until the end of the twelfth century.

In the west, castles had already undergone a long period of development by this time, and fortifications had existed since the stone age. Later, the large *oppida* of the Latène and Celtic Hallstatt periods (through c. 500 B.C.) existed in the southern regions of central Europe, and traces of fortifications from Germanic times are found all over northern and northeastern Europe. Serving for the most part as refuges (*Fluchtburgen*), they constituted, along with Roman forts and Frankish manor houses, the forerunners of the medieval castle. The construction of early medieval castles developed primarily in conjunction with the defense of the country against Normans, Hungarians, and Slavs during the ninth and tenth centuries.[20] Complete fortification systems were erected in border areas. The primary function of castles was therefore protection. However, Carolingian imperial castles had already developed into regional centers of administration, since the right to build a castle was originally a royal privilege which only devolved gradually and at various times to ecclesiastical and secular institutions in different regions. In Flanders and Franconia we encounter castles belonging to the more powerful dynasties as early as the ninth century, while in Swabia there is no evidence of castles of this type prior to the eleventh century. Toward the end of this period, castles were being erected everywhere by lower *ministeriales*, particularly during the thirteenth century. Early castles were still rather small, moderately fortified, and frequently constructed in the shape of an enclosure with an inner courtyard. However, beginning in the tenth century, people began to build residential castles (*Wohnburgen*), and the politics of castle-building soon became one of the pillars of authority. Watched by the lower *ministeriales*, the castle itself became an instrument of power in the hands of the warrior class. In late tenth-century France, for example, castellanies ushered in an entirely novel political structure when so-called castellans arrogated sovereign rights at the expense of the crown and the counts. During the high Middle Ages, Germany also experienced a boom in castle construction. It was said of Duke Frederick II of Swabia, a contemporary of Henry V, that "continuously moving down the Rhine, he would soon establish a castle at a suitable site and subjugate the countryside, only leaving it behind to build a new one, leading people to muse, 'Duke Frederick always has a castle in tow, attached to the tail of his horse.'"[21] Despite exaggeration, this account suits the situation. The era of the Hohenstaufen was particularly important for castles and the communities they harbored (Maurer).

Castles soon took on a series of different functions. Their originally defensive purpose remained decisive throughout the entire Middle Ages; medieval wars always involved a struggle over castles, and after each victory enemy castles were usually razed. Legally speaking, however, castles served the preservation of peace. A special peace prevailed within a castle (*Burgfrieden*), disallowing any sort of altercation among its occupants. They were often chosen to serve as prisons, and also took on economic functions for the purpose of collecting tolls from roads, rivers, and bridges. In colonized areas especially, castles became general economic centers within the manorial system, and they were even centers of craft production for the market.[22] During the late Middle Ages, castles became economic assets which might be pawned at need. They were thus administrative and political centers for the purpose of establishing a secular authority which soon could only be secured by means of castles and which emerged as the focal points for growing territorial powers, each attempting to incorporate all possible castles, or at least to secure a right to entry. In addition, the political function of castles was closely paralleled by their social significance. They were symbols of the elevated position of their inhabitants, epitomizing their owners' noble status. In effect, building castles became the duty of a nobility who had created for the first time a definite center for itself and linked a new sense of identity to these residences by naming itself after its ancestral castles. Finally, castles were also religious centers. From the eighth century on, castles normally had an attached chapel, or at least a sacred room endowed with special privileges or its own manorial income.[23] Whenever a castle was abandoned, the chapel was frequently converted into an endowed chapter or monastery.[24] On the whole, castles came to assume many different functions; they were a symbol of authority and a center of power, as well as a preferred living space of nobles, who displayed their splendor and passed their days within them.

If we wish fully to comprehend this "space," we must focus on the castle as a structure.[25] Although early castles were still built of wood and earth, the evidence from ninth-century castles corroborates the fact that some were already built of stone. Originally, a castle belonged to some extent to a village (as in the name for a privately owned castle in the plains, *Niederungsburg*), although it often already stood separately by virtue of its peripheral location. After the eleventh century, however, castles slowly came to relocate to mountain tops and hills (elevated castles, or *Höhenburgen*); by the end of the twelfth century, they were completely separated from the community. Numerous names ending in *-berg*, *-stein*, *-fels*, and *-eck* testify to this. During the eleventh century,

castles built on the tops of mountains were preferred (Gipfelburg).
During the thirteenth century, bluffs became the favorite location for
castles, since they permitted easy access from one side (*Spornburg*);
such a castle's elevated location increased its defensive function, but it
also symbolized a distancing of the nobility from their subjects. It goes
without saying that the construction of such mountain castles required
tremendous effort. Construction time for a castle of average size could
easily take from three to seven years (Antonow).

Castles could be designed very differently without ever reflecting a
definite trend; in fact, one could always encounter many different types
of castles in close proximity. Central structures (such as castles built on
tower-like hills), or so-called *Motten* (which were erected on top of an
often man-made mound), were scattered all over central and western
Europe and were favored particularly in eleventh-century France, in
the Rhineland, and in England. Square and rectangular tower castles
(*Turmburgen*) prevailed in France and Italy. Castles that were surrounded by walls (*Ringburgen*) were capable of defending themselves
from all sides. The most common type were axial structures that could
be designed rectangularly, polygonally, in oval, or wedge shape.

A typical castle contained certain construction elements. Since it
was conceived as a defensive structure, it was fortified in such a way
that it could be comfortably defended by as few people as possible. It
was surrounded by a moat and a strong—sometimes double-strength—
curtain wall (*Ringmauer*) which had a bastion (*Wehrgang*) with parapets. The battlements which originally were pierced with parapets were
replaced by embrasures during the thirteenth century. Walls were massive, often measuring two meters deep and more than ten meters high;
however, their circumference was rather modest, resulting in crowded

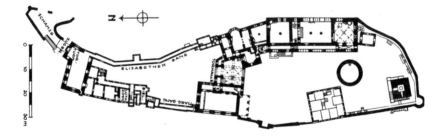

Illustration 21: *Wartburg, the Ancestral Castle of the Landgraves of
Thuringia: Layout* (from Hotz, *Pfalzen und Burgen der Stauferzeit*,
p. 240).

conditions inside. Endangered sides were protected by an additional, even higher inner wall (*Schildmauer*). The most sensitive area within a castle was the permanently guarded gate, secured by a drawbridge or portcullis, and by vaulted gateways which were frequently expanded into veritable fortified towers (*Torburgen*) with advance and side turrets. Machicolations (called *Pechnasen*, gate tower galleries with openings in the floor) served as perches for dowsing intruders with hot water, oil, or pitch. The keep or belfry (*Bergfried*) which constituted both the center of a castle and its main tower was also part of the fortification. Its walls were frequently from three to four meters thick with only a few openings. With a height of twenty to forty meters, the central tower came to symbolize the special status of the castle's inhabitants. This narrow tower served for the most part merely as a refuge of last resort, but was occasionally also furnished with apartments on several levels used as living quarters. Particularly in France, such tower castles (*donjons*) provided living quarters for noble families after the turn of the millennium. The lord's palace (*Palas*) was part of the living quarters and was used for display purposes; at large castles, the walls were decorated with murals and tapestries, but it tended to be a rather sparsely furnished hall. There were also the lady's apartments (*Kemenate*), with the only heated rooms of the castle. (Tiled stoves had become widespread by the middle of the thirteenth century.[26]) Torches, candles, and candelabra provided sufficient lighting. A separate chapel was connected to the palace, except where it had already been incorporated into the structure. Following the example of episcopal palaces, castles during the Hohenstaufen period frequently accommodated chapels on two levels: one for the lord and his family, one for the servants. Finally, there were also a number of offices and service rooms housing the kitchen, the stables and barns, as well as the dog kennels and personnel quarters which were frequently appended to the inside castle wall. The frequently rather narrow inner courtyard (surrounded by the belfry, the palace, and the remaining living quarters and buildings) was more generously designed only at important castles belonging to princes. At these castles the inner courtyard became a center for social life, and the grounds were used for staging tournaments, festivities, and gatherings. As a result, it was splendidly appointed with open staircases, arcades, galleries, balconies (*Söller*), and windows (Illustration 22). Water was supplied by a well that had to be drilled through rock to a depth of as much as 150 meters at elevated castles; in addition, rainwater was collected in a cistern. During times of peace, castles frequently had additional facilities outside the castle walls. According to Rahewin,[27] the Lutra Palace at Kaiserslautern was surrounded by "a lake-like fishpond that was not only pleasant to

Illustration 22: *Wartburg: the Palace Wall, a View from the Inner Courtyard* (Photograph: Hotz, *Pfalzen und Burgen der Stauferzeit*, pl. 141).

look at, but also delighted the palate with its fish and fowl. It was also bordered by a park that held plenty of red deer and roebuck for food." Only important palaces and castles were of a respectable size; the Hohenstaufen castle of Wimpfen had Germany's largest royal palace, measuring 215 x 88 meters, and Wartburg Castle, which belonged to the counts palatinate of Thuringia, was 180 meters long (Illustration 21). However, most castles belonging to knights scarcely exceeded 40 meters in length.

These castles were maintained by lower *ministeriales*, namely the burgraves and castle garrison, although we must not imagine their number to be too large. Burgau Castle in Swabia was manned by five troops, eight sentries, two gatekeepers and one towermaster.[28]

The true representatives of courtly life were the members of the nobility with their families, and the knight who frequented large courts as a guest.

3. The People:
Knighthood during the High Middle Ages

The institution of knighthood was a European phenomenon.[29] Originating in southern France, it spread northward before fanning out via Flanders and Burgundy into the western regions of the German Empire, flourishing between 1100 and 1250. While our overall historical picture of knighthood is for the most part quite clear, it nevertheless remains a constant source of discussion among scholars. Let us therefore present the institution of knighthood as the primary representative of courtly life in light of the current state of research.

The origins of knighthood go back to a military system. Knights (*Ritter*, horsemen) were armed warriors on horseback. Two terms were commonly used in Latin to express the same idea: *caballarius* (which gave rise to French *chevalier*, Spanish *caballero*, and Italian *cavaliere*), and the more commonly used Latin term *miles* (which referred in its basic meaning to simply a warrior, but was increasingly restricted to mean only "knight"). The narrowing of this concept stems from changes in the military structure during the eighth and ninth centuries. While an army consisting of foot soldiers had been recruited from the ranks of free men during Carolingian times, elite military units were now formed with heavily armed horsemen on battle steeds which they had bred and trained themselves. This required constant training, so that one may speak—perhaps not entirely correctly—of a "professional warrior." However, the professional dimension of knighthood was considerably more complicated. It was, for example, certainly expensive to be a mounted warrior; by the eighth century, the value of both horse and equipment approximated that of forty-five cows or fifteen breeding mares, and by the eleventh century it already approached the value of five to ten oxen.[30] Since a certain degree of wealth was a prerequisite for knighthood, knights were largely identical with landowners or—since they did not cultivate any land themselves—with secular manorial lords. Land-ownership existed in different forms, and private ownership (next to the Crown and Church) was primarily in the hands of the nobility. But the economic basis for land ownership was also in the form of a fief bestowed by the king, an ecclesiastical lord, a higher-ranking secular nobleman or officeholder. Thus, in addition to the nobility, knighthood consisted of the royal vassals, ecclesiastical vassals and vassals of the high nobility who were pledged to serve (*servitium*), primarily in the military.[31] The military structure of the high Middle Ages was built entirely on a tiered feudal system with vassals and subvassals. As a result, various functions were discharged by knights who, as a group, were also manorial lords, warriors, and vassals, exhibiting a life-style commensurate with their position in society.

Here we encounter a problem in conjunction with the socio-political position of the nobility, a problem which has been scrutinized by recent terminological studies:[32] the terms describing the knightly class underwent changes. *Caballarius* changed from "groom" to "owner of a horse" who went into battle on horseback. (The English term knight, originally connected to German *Knecht*, underwent a similar change in meaning.) Likewise, according to Duby's research on the Mâconnais region in southern France at the end of the tenth century, *miles* retained its military significance, but by the turn of the century it had also assumed sociological proportions by including the nobility and replacing the term *nobilis*; it was thus rendered into a class-specific epithet for a nobility which began to perceive itself in terms of a new, specifically military aspect.[33] As a result, the dualistic division of society into *milites* and *rustici* prevailed. Almost simultaneously, the *milites* contrasted themselves to the *clerici*, engendering a theoretical threefold division of society into clerics, knights, and peasants. According to research by some German scholars, who view these matters more from the point of view of constitutional history, the issue presents itself somewhat differently. According to Johrendt, for example, *miles* signified a vassal during the tenth century, not the lower levels of nobility (in a class-specific sense) joined later by members of the high nobility (the French view); rather, *miles* described a function with no overtones of class, comprising all warriors from the king down to the *Knappen* or pages (*armiger*). Therefore, the criterion must not be seen as socially rooted, but in terms of feudal relationships; no sociological distinction between nobility and knighthood may be derived from the concept of knighthood. Nevertheless, German scholars in general tend to view knighthood in terms of the lower nobility, similar to previous efforts pointing out differences between France and Germany.[34] Indeed, the emergence of the nobility as a politically and economically separate class represents the final stage in a prolonged development,[35] while social boundaries manifested themselves at a relatively early stage. Therefore, the self-image shared by knights as a privileged warrior class commenced much earlier than any legal standardization or class formation, since that was impossible to implement prior to the Hohenstaufen period. In the Public Peace of 1152, for instance, trial by combat was permitted only to knights from knightly families, and by 1186 sons of priests, deacons, and peasants were excluded from knighthood. However, it was not until the thirteenth century that a legal, if still penetrable segregation had been achieved.[36] Knighthood absorbed the nobility from the bottom up, forcing nobles to set themselves apart, creating the typically late medieval legal distinction between a higher and a lower nobility. This level was finally attained by *ministeriales*, who had previously been bondsmen in the *familia* of a lord and who managed to improve their position by advancing in administration, in the military, and as guardians of castles; they secured these positions by invoking "service rights" (*Dienstrechte*) as early as the eleventh century. As a result, the two groups of lower vassals and the *ministeriales* merged to form the lower service nobility.

The social boundaries of knighthood were also visibly formalized, making knighthood in effect a "career." Sons of vassals were sent to be taught the art of knighthood at about the age of ten to twelve, or to serve as weapons-bearers at the court of a lord. At approximately the age of fourteen, they were referred to as *Junker* (= *Jungherr*, squires), serving as attendants to a knight. They could become knights by the age of twenty, although not everybody reached this level. By the eleventh century, official recognition as a knight required special induction (first attested for kings and sons of kings), the ceremony of knighting by which a knight became a *miles factus*.[37]

Dubbing (*dubbatio*), a blow by hand or sword on the nape or with the flat of a blade on the left shoulder, was an act with which we connect knighting today; it also represented the final stage in a long development. It is found in France by the twelfth century, although it did not become customary in Germany until the fourteenth century. Handing over arms had originally been central to a ceremony performed by solemnly girding the sword (*cingere aliquem cingulo militaris*), the *Schwertleite*, a ritual in turn embedded in a series of ceremonial acts largely borrowed from the royal anointing ceremony. The chronicle of the counts of Anjou reports that on the occasion of the engagement of Matilda, the daughter of Henry I of England, to Godfrey, the son of the Count of Anjou—the source of the Angevine territories under their son Henry II Plantagenêt—the day began for Godfrey with a bath (a symbolic form of cleansing) after which he was dressed in a linen undergarment, a gold-brocaded tunic, a crimson cloak, silken stockings, and embellished shoes. Godfrey then received from the assembled crowd a double-stitched shirt of linked mail, shoes made of iron ringlets and stirrups, a shield emblazoned with the lion coat of arms of the counts of Anjou, a helmet studded with precious stones, a lance, and a very old, valuable sword.[38] During the twelfth century, the blessing of the sword by the Church was added to this ceremony, as shown in John of Salisbury's statement in 1159 that, upon entering the church, the knight placed his sword on the altar and professed his services to God.[39] Toward the end of the age of chivalry, the knighting ceremony was preceded by a day of fasting; the future knight was dressed in white, a mass with communion was celebrated, the sword was blessed, and the knight donned his armor and submitted to dubbing. The knighting ceremony was an expensive affair, since it was frequently the occasion for festivities lasting days, involving many guests, expensive gifts, and tournaments. For this reason, people attempted to combine several knighting ceremonies on the same date.

According to the characterization already made, wars and battles became the principle activities for knights (though not their only one) (Illustration 23). The armored war horses (*dextrarius*) which knights took into battle (and mounted only during actual battles), together with their marching horse (*palefridus*) and one pack-horse, became an object of affectionate description, particularly in German literature. Hartmann von Aue's Erec received a horse from Duke Imein (ll. 1426-53):

> it was neither too strong nor too weak, / its coat was white as ermine, / its mane thick and curly, / its chest was powerful and broad, / its bones neither too heavy nor too light. / It kept its head erect, / was gentle and good-natured, / with huge flanks; / it was easy to ride; / both its back and legs looked impeccable, / oh, how gently it carried its rider./ Quickly it traversed the field / pacing splendidly as if a ship, / always walking smoothly / without ever stumbling./ The saddle was fashioned / perfectly to suit the horse: / all metal parts were fittingly / made of red gold.

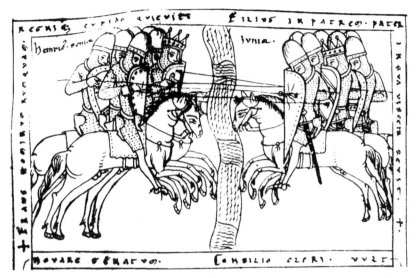

Illustration 23: *Knightly Combat: The Fight between Henry IV and His Son, Henry* (Chronicle of Otto von Freising, twelfth century).

Such a war horse was armored and later often decorated with a colorful or embroidered caparison. Originally, a knight protected himself in battle with a knee-length, shortsleeve (later footlength and long-sleeved) chain mail shirt equipped even with gloves and a cowl. This outfit was made of interwoven, riveted metal links. Underneath it he wore a fabric shirt (a *Wams* or doublet that originally protruded) to protect his skin. Sometimes—in France since the middle of the twelfth century— following eastern custom, knights also donned a tunic (*Waffenrock*) over their coat of mail. Seignorial ostentatiousness displaced functional clothing. By the thirteenth century there was a tendency to cloak both rider and horse completely. The helmet consisted of a skullcap (*Glocke*), and the facial plate was replaced by a casque (*Topfhelm*) with slits (called "windows"). For purposes of easy identification by either friend or foe, distinctive external markings became necessary in the form of a crest and a coat of arms.[40] (The earliest evidence is the *planta genista* branch on Godfrey of Anjou's tomb at Le Mans from 1149.) Pennants attached to lances were also helpful. Among the protective weapons were shields, which tended to become smaller as time went on, as a result of complete armament. Also, stirrups were most important both as a prerequisite for heavy armament and for a new form of doing battle by raising oneself up. (According to a thesis advanced by Lynn White, Jr., the stirrup is the single most important prerequisite of feudalism.) Sword and spear were traditional attack weapons, as well as a tilting lance which measured at least three meters and weighed from two to five kilograms. While riding, the knight carried it vertically, supported by a bracket, and aimed it horizontally at an enemy during an attack. Considering the weight of these armaments, a knight required one or even several attendants (a page and possibly some squires), constituting the basic military unit.

The ideal of such a battle-ready knight was a favorite subject in art and literature. In *Ruodlieb*,[41] the departure of a knight for the royal court is described as follows:

> Only one person was allowed to accompany him—/ his shieldbearer. / He was to carry his travel bag / packed with various things; / since childhood / he had taught him the pains and / toils of being his servant. / He carried the bag over his right shoulder, / and over the left one his lord's shield was slung in piggy-back fashion. / He clutched the quiver with his right hand, / and held the spear under the shield. /For his saddle he used an adequate feedbag. / His lord, however, was clad in armor / covered by a doublet—/ on his head he wore a helmet / made of steel and shimmering like gold. / He had his sword strapped to his waist, / its hilt covered with gold. / He wore a necklace with a griffin's talon / around his white neck / though it was not a complete talon, / it still measured the length of an arm; / at its thicker end there was a bell / and where it tapered toward the tip, / the claw was decorated with pure gold / and held in place with ties of deerskin. / Although not as pure as snow / it was translucent like a precious stone. / When he blew on it, it sounded / better than all the echoes of the world. / He said *"vale"* to his mother and his entire household / and left. / His horse was waiting—black as a raven / as if it had been bathed / with soap; it was dotted all over with white dots. / The horse's mane was thick and / parted down the left side of its neck. / Its headgear was splendidly decorated / to please its lofty lord; / yet nothing was attached to the saddle, / clearly nothing but / a cup / sewn to the leather, smooth / and polished with fragrant resins so that / whatever was poured into it / would taste sweet; then there was a pillow / made of delicate, crimson cloth. / Hardly had he mounted the horse / when it reared with joy / as if it had been happy and delighted / that its master was riding it. / His dog came running—behind and then in front—/ it was a tracker dog—none better / could be found on earth. / No game could hide from it / no matter how big or how small, / it would soon and quickly track it down.

Even though not everything in these lines reflects everyday life, a self-image is revealed that was experienced early on by the knights who made fighting battles, hunting, the seignorial lifestyle the center of their lives. Hartmann von Aue's Iwein, forced to explain to an untutored man what knighthood was all about (ll. 530-37), said, "I am a knight, setting out on horseback to find a man similarly armed who will be willing to do battle with me. If he beats me, his fame will be enhanced; however, if I remain victorious, then I will be judged a hero and my fame will be greater than ever before." Fighting was indeed the most important activity. But one must not overlook the fact that actual warfare was far removed from the heroic battles fought by the epic heroes; rather, war consisted far more frequently of laying siege to castles and burning an opponent's crops than it did individual combat.

The socio-military-feudal element of knighthood which we have discussed here constituted only one of three components which seemed to differ so vastly that scholars have advanced three different concepts of knighthood. Alongside the pronounced feudal type (Painter) of "noble warrior-knight" (Bumke), one also encounters the religious type (Painter) of the "graduate knight" (Bumke's *promovierter Ritter*), who was assigned to perform a religious function; and the "romantic type of knight" (Painter) we encounter in literature. Christian knights fought in the service of the Church,[42] thus becoming—again, for the first time in southern France during the second half of the eleventh century—*milites christiani*. The ideal was patterned after the idea that monks were perceived as *milites Christi*, despite the fact that a knight fought with his own, secular weapons.[43] This religious function ultimately became so self-evident that it combined with the simple *miles*-concept, rendering the addition of *christianus* superfluous. When Urban II called for a crusade at Clermont in 1095, he uttered the now famous words, *Nunc fiant [Christi] milites, qui dudum exstiterunt raptores* ("Now let those become knights [of Christ] who had previously been but robbers").[44] Therefore, religious tasks became part of a knight's life. Such a knight was first shown the path of salvation (that is, the possibility of becoming a saint) in Abbot Odo of Cluny's (927-942) *Vita Geraldi*, the first life of a lay saint since the days of the martyrs. During the twelfth century, John of Salisbury asked: "What is the justification of knighthood's existence? To protect the Church, to fight infidels, to honor priesthood, to protect the poor from iniquity, to pacify the land, to shed one's own blood and, if necessary, to give one's life for his brethren."[45] The oath knights swore obligated them to protect the defenseless and those in need of protection. A concrete application of this duty is found in the so-called Peace-of-God movement which surfaced in southern France toward the end of the tenth century and soon spread to the north, centering on a pledge to take care of law and order under the leadership of the Church. In order to ensure compliance, knights had to promise to preserve peace for the benefit of the Church and the defenseless (clerics, peasants, and women) and to punish peace-breakers—a personal obligation which was naturally also directed against peace-breaking fellow knights. During the crusades, the activities of *milites christiani* were directed outward, against the infidels, first against the Muslims in an effort to liberate the holy sepulchre in Jerusalem, subsequently against all heathens, such as the Slavs in the eastern provinces. Ultimately they were also directed against heretics at home (Illustration 24). The orders of knights which evolved in these activities sought to combine the sword with the ideals of monastic life. If we may judge from the sources, this Christian knighthood in the service of the Faith was at first a "misassignment" on the part of the Church (Althoff). However, one certainly must assume that it coincided with a simultaneous introspection by a nobility espousing monastic ideals under the guise of contemporary

Illustration 24: *Knights on the Way to Doing Battle* (Hrabanus Maurus Manuscript, Montecassino, eleventh century).

reform ideas—especially since a number of knights later entered monasteries. Also primary to the ethics of this movement were the ethics of lordship. In Middle High German literature (especially *Parzival*), Christianization was expressed as divine grace bestowed on a knight (symbolized by the secret of the Holy Grail); however, the fact that the ideal of the *miles christianus* was rarely realized is as indisputable as the fact that the Christianization of knighthood had its own social ramifications. External expansion was necessary, since internal resources had become exhausted, and since some knightly families were in danger of impoverishment.

Since both the social and ethical element had become intermingled, it is very difficult to comprehend knighthood in terms of a distinct social group,[46] a pattern which applies even more accurately to the third, "romantic type of knight." Looking at courtly love, Bumke refers to him as the *Frauenritter* or lady's knight. The ideal of the "courtly knight" (as I prefer calling him) was probably the furthest removed from reality; however, because of its ethical tendency, it contributed to the fact that knights were committed to adhere to a certain code of honor. A scene from Hartmann von Aue's *Erec* (ll. 6507ff.) is typical of this disparity: the fact that a count would beat his young wife (Enîte) enraged all his fellow knights, although he was legally entitled to do it. Central to courtly knighthood was a system of virtues as an expression of new knightly ethics.[47] Knights were constantly forced to prove their knightliness (their *werdekeit*, worthiness) by demonstrating through bravery as well as conduct the qualities of *ere* (honor), *triuwe* (loyalty), *reht* (justice), *milde* (generosity), and especially *mâze* (a sense of balance). Interesting and even seemingly realistic (because they stem from the early period of knighthood) are the king's exhortations given to Ruodlieb upon the latter's return home (ll. 5, 457ff.); when he says, "Even if your road is covered with mud / extending broadly throughout the village / you must not let your horse leave the path / and ride through planted fields." (This warning is reminiscent of the protection granted to peasants in conjunction with the various peace agreements, although the king hardly finishes on a flattering note when he says, "lest the peasant maltreat you and take away your horse.") In matters of love, according to the king, class distinctions were to be observed (ll. 476ff.):

Never treat your own maidservant, / no matter how beautiful, / as your equal, / as if she were a marriageable woman! / [The reason being:] she will rebel / against you / and refuse to show you respect; / for she will certainly believe / that she must now appear as lady of the house; / once she becomes your sweetheart / and sits down at your table / after lying next to you in bed / and eating at your table, / she will always want to lord it over / everything. / All this will bring a good man / dishonor.

Thus the king's advice is rather practical, clearly influenced by contemporary views. Concerning marriage the following is said (ll. 484ff.):

Should you wish someday / to court a truly fine woman / in order to raise children with her, / one that you will want to embrace gladly, / then look for a wife / in a respectable house / and only if your mother / will have no objections against her! / Once you have chosen her in this fashion, / be sure to afford her every bit of honor. / Be gentle and treat her well, / but always remain her lord / so that she may never become contrary / and start arguing with you! / For there is no greater shame / for a husband / than being obedient to the one / whose rightful lord he is supposed to be.

Thus, the highly touted "courtly love" had its practical limitations, and knightly society remained male-dominated. The preceding quotation is followed by sentences such as "do not yield to sudden anger" (l. 498), or "Avoid any kind of argument / with your lord and master" (ll. 502f.). Naturally, religious elements are also present (ll. 511ff.):

And wherever you may be when you travel, / never be in such a hurry / as to not have the time to pause / whenever you see a church / and pray to its patron saint! / Should you ever hear the sound of a bell / and the sacred songs of mass, / then get off your horse immediately, / and walk quickly into the church / so that you may participate in the blessings and the salvation / of Christ's peace.

These rather practical admonitions offered by the king to Ruodlieb illustrate that ethical conduct could easily be tantamount to personal well-being; at the same time, they warn against equating the highly stylized ideal of knighthood found in the later courtly epics with reality. However, this ethical bond provided knighthood with a new, basically timeless sense of worthiness. In an elaborate description, for example, the narrative *Moritz von Craûn*,[48] dating from the end of the twelfth century, transported the origins of knighthood into ancient Greece. Knightly spirit, according to the story, had already existed during the Trojan war and migrated to Rome. (Caesar a knight!) However, it could not gain a foothold there because of the cruelties of Nero. It subsequently continued on to France. (Charlemagne a knight!) Moritz von Craûn, the hero of the story, is portrayed as an ideal knight. "His body was built exquisitely, he was well-educated, intelligent, blessed with an active mind and courtly disposition." Education and manners were all-important, but Moritz was also undefeated in tournaments. His only flaw—without which there would be no action leading to the internal chastening of the hero—consisted of a lack of etiquette, and he lost the favor of a lady because he had fallen asleep after a tournament while she was awaiting him.

The ethical revaluation that the ideals of a warrior class experienced made the idea of service central to knighthood. Knights understood their lives to be—in harmony with the three types of knights—an ongoing voluntary service rendered to the Church and to Christianity, to a lord, or to a lady (van Winter). Once more the initial lines of *Ruodlieb* will illustrate this quite vividly (ll. 1, 1-12):

> A knight was once born / into a distinguished family; / he embellished his native nobility / with impeccable manners; / as the story goes, he / had taken up service with many a wealthy lord / and he served them according to their wishes. . . . / Whatever any one of these lords told him, / whatever they asked him to do, / be it in the name of revenge, / or otherwise, / he never dallied at all, / but took care of it swiftly. / It was for these lords that he had to / risk his life many times, / be it by hunting or fighting in battle, / or any other time.

However, Ruodlieb received no reward, so he moved on to other countries.

It is generally agreed that knighthood underwent a crisis by the thirteenth century. People had recognized the innate contradiction between ideal and reality (or at least this is what a more realistic literature seems now to indicate). It would, of course, be erroneous to measure this "decline" against the hyperbolic, literary ideal of the flowering age of chivalry. Indeed, there were earlier warnings hinting at the severe discrepancy between the literary ideal and reality. In his treatise *De nugis curialium*, Walter Map compared the English royal court to hell, and Peter of Blois criticized the decline of military discipline in a letter dating from approximately 1170.[49]

> In earlier days, knights had promised under oath not to leave the battlefield and to place public before personal gain; nowadays, they also accept their swords at the altar and promise to honor priests, protect the poor, and punish criminals; however, they do just the opposite: they turn against the anointed of the Lord [the priests] and lay waste the patrimony of the cross [Church properties], despoil the *pauperes Christi* [the monks], oppress the wretched and satisfy their own desires through

the pain of others. Instead of testing their strength in battle against the enemies of Christ's cross, they engage in drinking contests; knights go into battle, not with their swords, but with wine in their hands, not with their lances, but with cheese, and not with their javelins, but with roasting spits. They lead a life of leisure, dishonoring the knightly calling (*officium militiae*); with their golden shields they ridicule their duty to fight, and their desire to fight is replaced by their lust for booty and innocent virgins; they have wars depicted in paintings in order to delight vicariously in something they do not really wish to experience first-hand.

If a monk, who found his ideal of true knighthood in the age of the Roman emperors, had to remind the knights of their calling, one cannot more directly emphasize the existence of a widely accepted ideal. However, we must not confuse with reality criticism rooted in ethical polemics; neither are we to picture knights as a bunch of drunkards. Once again, a negative contrast suggests that the knightly ideal of all three types—the warrior, the Christian soldier, and the virtuous hero— did not represent knighthood in its entirety, but that one must take the Church's demands, as well as the knightly self-image portrayed in literature, with a grain of salt. Particularly the concluding remark, that knights only have wars depicted in paintings in order to delight in them vicariously, sounds a warning against confusing art with reality; it merely serves as a generalizing illustration of how knights wished to live.

　　With these preliminaries in mind, let us now take a look at courtly life.

4. Courtly Life

Everyday Life and Courtly Culture

　　The everyday life of knights[50] is more difficult to describe than the everyday life of peasants, which consisted essentially of labor. Rather, knightly life evokes images of festivities and tournaments, events which were anything but everyday affairs and were merely occasional highlights. If we follow the sources, then the work of a knight consisted of fighting (indeed the Middle High German term *arebeit* ought to be translated as "strenuous struggle"). Epic heroes rode around the countryside, emerging victorious from adventure after adventure in order to please wives or win the favor of some other lady. After Erec set out on his second adventure with Enîte, for example, they were ambushed first by three, then by five more robbers; all this happened during their first night out. Next morning they were received by the lord of a castle; another host wished to have Enîte for himself, whereupon Erec defeated him and six of his men. Soon after, he had to endure a trial by combat against a dwarfish territorial lord. Gawan invited him and Enîte to visit the court of King Arthur, but they managed to stay only one night there. After their departure, they traveled for a mere mile before they came upon a woman whose husband Erec liberated from two violent giants. . . .

No "everyday knight," of course, would ever encounter such adventures. Fights and adventures were exceptions worth describing in literature (and worth being compressed temporally into a single poetic unit). We may assume that lords also spent part of their days performing normal labors, administering their estates and safeguarding their rights. Territorial lords had to take special care of their territories, and the nobility had to discharge services as vassals and warriors, while knights and *ministeriales* had to see to official duties. On the other hand, everyday life undoubtedly afforded knights a great deal more time for leisure and pastimes than it would peasants; one simply must not make the mistake of referring to the everyday life of knights as idleness.

Though knighthood was generally idealized in literature, it was also later satirized, for instance in the "rogue epic" *Helmbreht*, where two knightly images are juxtaposed. Young Helmbreht leaves his father's tenement in order to become a knight. After a year of "courtly" life, father and son exchange their experiences. Inspired by a certain lack of understanding, the father offers a portrayal of an earlier, ideal knightly society (ll. 913-963):

> Many years ago, when I was still a young man / and your grandfather Helmbreht / sent me to court / with cheese and eggs / according to the custom, / I took a good look at the knights / and took note of their behavior. /They were courtly and lovely / . . . and they practiced a custom / that greatly pleased the ladies: / they called it "buhurdieren" / . . . they charged each other as if mad /—and were praised for doing so! /—each group of knights running to and fro / . . . When they were done, / they danced and sang happy songs. / That helped them pass the time. / Soon a minstrel would appear / and play on his fiddle. / Then the ladies got up / . . . and the knights strode toward them / and took them by their hands / . . . Afterwards some man appeared who read / about a certain Ernst [the epic *Herzog Ernst*]. / Each one could find whatever pleased him. / Some were engaged in target practice, shooting arrows. / They never lacked pleasure: / one would find his pleasure giving chase to wild animals, / another tracking them down.

According to this view, knighthood consisted of tournaments, festivities, amusements, and sports, and it distinguished itself through its courtly attitude. (Incidentally, the members of the audience were the very same members of nobility; old Helmbreht alludes therefore to an unmistakable ethical tendency, while attempting at the same time to dissuade his son from his ambitions.) Young Helmbreht contrasts this description with a portrayal of his idea of contemporary knightly life, unwittingly attesting to the decline of knighthood (ll. 986ff.):

> Nowadays, courtly life looks like this: / "drink, my lord, drink and drink!" / . . . In earlier days one could encounter noble lords / in the company of beautiful women; / today you meet them in the pubs. / From morning till night, / their greatest concern / is that the innkeeper / will be able to serve an equally good wine / in the event that he should run out of the one / that had previously put them into such a good mood. / They speak of love as follows: / ". . . a veritable fool is he / who has ever yearned / more for a woman / than for good wine." Falsehood and deceit are signs of courtly manners today. / . . . The old tournaments have long since gone, / now people engage in new games. / In the olden days you would hear them shout: / "Hey, my dear fellow, be cheerful." / Today, you can hear them yell all day: / "Give chase, / stab and attack! / Poke out this fellow's eyes, / chop off that one's foot / and again another's hands! / Hang this one! / Capture that rich man / for he will yield us 100 pounds ransom!"

(Helmbreht unintentionally anticipates his own fate.) This quote recalls the robber-knights of the late Middle Ages; in any case, young Helmbreht confuses genuine knighthood with the life of highway robbers out of his inordinate desire to rise above his station. Still, courtly audiences could easily discern the irony in the story. Both descriptions are purposely exaggerated in an attempt to illustrate the extremes of knightly life. While contemporary knightly culture was already wrestling with the dichotomy of pleasure and character, the two had to be in harmony.

The "culture," the customs and forms of courtly society, were imported from southern France. Literary descriptions and archaeological finds such as decorated nail and ear cleaners give us an idea of a certain degree of hygienic concern. Combs also frequently depicted scenes from courtly literature, and mirrors came into use only a short while later. Enough attention was paid to personal hygiene to make neglecting it exceptional, a product of asceticism. Thus Ruotger reports of Brun, the brother of Otto the Great;[51] "When he took a bath, he hardly ever used any soap or preparations to make his skin shiny, which is even more surprising, since he was familiar with such cleansing methods and royal comforts from early childhood." After a gracious reception by his host, a knight would first take off his armor in preparation for being bathed, combed, and anointed by the daughter (!) of the lord of the castle. The extent to which hygiene may have been practiced remains largely unclear.

We can also speak of a certain degree of cultivation in dining. Meals were served by a great number of servants and often took a very long time, although literary descriptions exaggerate considerably, as usual (Illustration 25). Einhard reports that Charlemagne drank moderately, but he showed less restraint at the dinner table; thus an average meal comprised "merely' four courses (not counting the roast on the spit).[52] We certainly ought to refrain from applying this standard to every castle, but meat (including wild game) undoubtedly appeared on the table here more frequently than in the hovels of peasants. At least during special occasions, meals were accompanied by music and jugglers. (According to Einhard, Charlemagne had a habit of listening to a musician or a reader during his meals, preferring stories and deeds from the past.) Finally, table manners written down during the later Middle Ages also attest to cultivated dining. Exhortations such as to eat with one's own spoon (frequently the only dinnerware was a shared knife) and to refrain from burping or blowing one's nose on the table cloth, from wiping one's mouth or eyes with it, or tossing picked bones into the common bowl, would have been unnecessary if good table manners had already been widely observed.

Illustration 25. *A Medieval Feast with Musicians and Stewards: David's Engagement to the Daughter of King Saul* (Peter Lombard Manuscript, late 12th century; excerpts).

The way people dressed underwent interesting innovation as something akin to fashion began to appear at courts. Previously, the nobility had shown a frequently criticized preference for "exotic" silk attire, patterned for the most part after Byzantine fashion. In the lives of saints, simple attire is extolled as an attribute of the ascetic life. According to Ruotger, Archbishop Brun of Cologne shunned wearing the soft finery he had grown up with; rather, he appeared among his servants, who wore crimson and brocade attire, dressed in simple clothes and a rustic sheepskin.[53] Charlemagne also reputedly preferred Frankish dress to foreign attire[54] and according to an anecdote related by Notker of St. Gall, Charlemagne criticized the silken attire of the high nobility, demonstrating the usefulness of simple sheepskin on the occasion of a hunt.[55] However, Charlemagne did don "brocaded clothes and shoes studded with precious stones at festive occasions, wearing a coat fastened with a golden brooch and on his head a golden crown adorned with precious stones."[56] At the high medieval courts of princes, such fashionable attire was a component of the courtly life. Poets frequently described clothes in minute detail in keeping with the latest fashion (particularly French), apparently entertaining an appreciative audience with such descriptions. There is further evidence of this in the miniatures. However, we must assume that festive clothes were not everyday attire. Amply pleated garments and coats—in the case of women often also a type of outer garment—reached to the floor, elaborated with wide sleeves, and adorned with a train; made of precious fabrics (such as silk), they were colorful, coming in many, ever-different variations. Later the outer garment of both men and women acquired a similar look (see Illustration 7). Clothes came to be tailored more tightly, revealing the shape of the body. Not until then did clothes truly and obviously reflect class distinctions.

The Highlights: Festivals and Tournaments

The sources devoted the most effort to the festive highlights of chivalric life. Einhard, for example, reports that Charlemagne quite rarely hosted banquets, but that he held them on holidays, inviting great numbers of guests.[57] In most cases, people observed such pre-established opportunities with grandiose celebrations, including Church holidays (which were not always celebrated with strictly religious purposes in mind). Festivities always included the celebration of mass followed by "social" time. Princes of the Church also celebrated. According to a ninth-century anecdote by Notker of St. Gall, one bishop who was a poor preacher sought to win over royal messengers, who had come to check on him, by throwing a festive banquet.[58]

> After mass they entered a hall decked out with colorful carpets and wall hangings of all kinds where a meal was intended to stimulate the appetite of those who were suffering from a lack of enthusiasm or from nausea; it was served in grand style in golden, silver, and gem-studded bowls. The bishop himself sat on the softest of down pillows covered with the most splendid silk; he was dressed in imperial crimson, so that all he lacked was a scepter and a royal title. There he sat, surrounded by the wealthiest of his vassals. . . . He had the most skillful master musicians play on every imaginable instrument, their melodies and play melting the hardest of hearts or making the most liquid waves of the river Rhine freeze solid. The greatest variety of beverages was mixed with all sorts of spices and ingredients, topped with herbs and flowers, and adorned with sparkling gold and precious stones which kept reflecting back and forth; still, nobody drank from the cups, since their stomachs were already too full. Meanwhile, bakers, butchers, cooks, and sausage makers demonstrated their rare skills by preparing all sorts of morsels for the full stomachs, a meal so large that none larger had ever been prepared for Charlemagne.

The anecdote's purpose was to deride the arrogant conduct of bishops, so it was exaggerated. The issue was apparently opulence, trimmings, and splendor, and the monk Notker described the most splendid feast he could imagine. Notker was not criticizing the fact a bishop was celebrating, but that his lavish display outdid the emperor. Even Bishop Ulrich of Augsburg (later canonized) regularly finished Lent on Easter Sunday with a sumptuous meal served at three festively decorated tables, although his biographer took great pains to emphasize the religious, decorous aspects of the occasion.[59]

> At the indicated time, such a huge number of minstrels appeared that they filled almost the entire gallery of the hall, lined up according to their rank; they performed three musical cycles. When spirits grew high, the canons received a "love potion" [*Minnetrank*] at the bishop's request while singing alternately about the resurrection of the Lord. [The typical mingling of spiritual and secular affairs is clearly noticeable even on this level]. . . . Toward evening the high-spirited bishop had the cups served for himself and those who sat at his table, inviting all of them to drink to each other the third "sip of love" [*Minneschluck*]. Subsequently, all the

assembled clerics joyfully intoned the third antiphon. While intoning a hymn they rose and went to attend vespers.

We can gather from these examples that we should not imagine such festivities occurred too frequently. Festivities required an occasion during the Middle Ages: a wedding, an enthronement, a return from a journey or a military campaign, or (last but not least) the celebration of a major Church holiday, when young knights might be knighted before the assembled courtly society. Courtly splendor and display have always caught people's fancy. However, at least during the earlier Middle Ages they only conditionally reflected reality, and staging these festivities was possible—if at all—only at the larger courts, not in the cramped castles of most knights. Bishop Liudprand of Cremona, who was sent on a royal mission to tenth-century Byzantium, could only observe with amazement the lavish display there, particularly when he reported gilded trees with artificial birds, a self-elevating throne, and automated lion statues within the palace.[60] Meals were taken in Roman fashion, lying down, accompanied by minstrels and acrobats. The golden bowls were so heavy that they had to be lowered from the ceiling by windlasses.[61]

Music played an important role at the courts (Illustration 26). People were accompanied by musicians not only during meals, but also while taking baths or taking trips. Music was said to stimulate the emotions[62] and, in addition to the banquet, was a natural component of any medieval celebration; there was also an opportunity to listen to various types of poetry, to dance, and to watch actors and acrobats. (*Minnesang*, in effect, was a social game played by the nobility.) Thus, the minstrels[63] played a permanent role in courtly entertainment as buffoons (*scurrae*), mimes (*mimi*), or jugglers and jesters (*ioculatores*), typically performing in strikingly colorful costumes. (Even the terms used hint at the versatility of these artists.) Minstrels were both poets and storytellers who recited their own poetry as well as that of others. They were musicians who mastered several instruments, often home-made; harp, lute, fiddle (a three-stringed violin), and flute were the most popular. All told, twenty-nine instruments are known, among them a glockenspiel made of individual bells, a type of organ, horns, bass drums, zither, and monochord. Minstrels could also be actors, dancers, tightrope walkers, acrobats, animal trainers, and illusionists. Giraud de Calanson relates that he knew how to write poetry, dance, play the drum, throw knives, play a stringed instrument, let marionettes dance, jump through four hoops, imitate birds, and also train dogs and monkeys.[64] Furthermore, minstrels needed to know how to scold and

Illustration 26: *Music at the Royal Court: David as a Secular Musician with Two Warriors and Four Instrumentalists inside a Mandala which Normally Surrounds Christ and the Evangelists; the Four Cardinal Virtues are Portrayed in the Corners* (Vivian Bible, Tours, c. 845/46).

mock. (It is in this capacity that we encounter a *scurra* several times in Notker's *Gesta Karoli Magni*.) Such characters distinguished themselves because of their quick wit and the fact that they were permitted to voice criticism. For instance, a *scurra* scolded Charlemagne for neglecting the relatives of his first wife following her sudden death.[65] In effect, minstrels were the precursors of the later court jesters in evidence since the twelfth century; jesters, however, were not widely accepted until the late Middle Ages, when they donned fool's clothes and wielded a crotchet (*Marotte*, a scepter with a glass bulb that symbolized the world).[66] Minstrels were more versatile; each mime had his own special skills and, displaying them, he wandered from court to court where people were always eager to see and hear new things. At the same time, these traveling minstrels fulfilled an additional, important function as carriers of new information for courtly gossip.

Precursors of the courtly minstrels of the Middle Ages existed as early as classical antiquity[67] and are also seen in the Germanic *skûp*, a singer and harpist. There appeared to be greater demand for them during the eleventh century, especially in France, when the minstrels joined forces to become a professional group. They came in part from the impoverished lower nobility, but also in part from the urban population, the lower clergy, and later the descendants of former minstrels. Relatively speaking, they lacked rights and property, so that they depended on the nobility's protection and patronage. Their reward consisted in payments of money, food, accommodations, clothing, instruments, horses, or letters of recommendation. Sometimes they also enjoyed permanent employment, but the "minstrel's fief" (in the form of landed property) remained more the exception than the rule. Still, minstrels could also be enlisted for other missions at the court. In the *Nibelungenlied*, for example, Etzel sends his minstrels as emissaries to the royal court of the Burgundians. Here the minstrel was integrated into courtly society (although one must not discard the fact that minstrels also composed these epics and knew how to improve their lot by heaping praise upon themselves). We also know that many princes enjoyed acting as minstrels. Volker in the *Nibelungenlied*, for instance, is referred to as a minstrel, since he was an expert on the fiddle, and Duke William IX of Aquitaine is said to have been among one of the first troubadours.

The Church took an ambiguous stand on these persons.[68] In addition to generally rebuffing plays and similar performances, the bad reputation of many a minstrel undoubtedly had an impact. *Ioculatores* were considered servants of the Devil, beyond all hope for salvation in the eyes of the twelfth-century Pope Honorius II;[69] female minstrels and dancers were equated with prostitutes. Even though Abelard considered minstrels dangerous competitors with the Christian mass,[70] many a Christian apparently preferred listening to a minstrel to hearing a priest. There can be little doubt that the Church's admonitions were fruitless, especially since later goings-on at episcopal courts were essentially the same as those at the castles of knights. In addition to speechifiers, dream-readers, and astrologers, Bishop Adalbert of Bremen employed minstrels at his court; he is reputed to have banished only buffoons from his presence because of their indecent gestures.[71] The archbishop himself, in fact, indulged in another courtly pastime, since he loved slandering other people.[72]

Gala dinners, music, dancing, and artistic performances provided the background for the true highlight of a courtly feast, the tournament. This is first attested to in France as a grandiose event as early as the second half of the eleventh century, and in Germany at Würzburg in 1127.[73] Tournaments promoted both weapons practice and athletic activity and were also the most striking form of self-portrayal of knighthood and knightly society.[74] They could take place only at the large courts and not at any of the cramped castles. During the later Middle Ages, cities became favorite sites for tournaments. A tournament was a contest played according to set rules which had developed over time. Its origins can be seen in the old mock battles fought in preparation for actual warfare. Especially in the beginning, these group mock combats may be likened to a real cavalry battle, with victory as their sole goal. (These contrasted with feuds, where the object was to inflict damage on one's opponent.) Frequently knights fought with blunted weapons; nevertheless, many injuries occurred, particularly contusions and fractures, but even fatalities. One of the two most popular forms of combat was the *Buhurt*, a group contest patterned after cavalry battles. It was later joined by the *Tjost*, (jousting), a type of individual combat on horseback with a tilting lance. An opponent was no sooner unhorsed than the fight continued with the sword until one of the combatants surrendered. More peaceful variations on horseback attempted to pick off a ring with a lance, or hit a post whose every turn was counted; these are probably of more recent vintage. Individual combat frequently took place as well as combat by whole units, although the individual combatant's ultimate honor was always at stake. In the epics, heroes rush from one tournament victory to another, consolidating their reputation while winning the favor of their lady, who was among the courtly spectators. By the twelfth century, other prizes are mentioned which enticed impoverished knights to compete. The histories reveal few details, but at least they corroborate the central significance of the tournament in the life of a knight, which is reflected by the frequent portrayal of tournaments in courtly art. Tournaments—which often lasted for days—were highlights of courtly life which did not occur all that often, since they had to be announced well in advance in order to allow for the timely registration of participants. They were combined with celebrations in which minstrels also participated. The tournament itself was a social game played within a courtly society; it was later even referred to as "playing with lances" (*hastiludium*). The Church was quick to forbid tournaments, for the first time at a papal council at Clermont in 1130. They were forbidden not because of the dangers they posed, but because of the display of vanity and the attendant amusements.[75] The tournament is inseparably connected to chivalry, however, and its history mirrors the history of knighthood.

Emperor Frederick I Barbarossa celebrated a particularly impressive court festival on the occasion of the imperial diet at Pentecost, 1184, in a specially erected "festival city" before the gates of the city of Mainz.[76] Princes and their vassals arrived from all four corners of the Empire. The Duke of Bohemia arrived with a retinue supposedly consisting of 2,000 knights, the Count Palatine of the Rhine, Konrad (the emperor's brother), and Landgrave Louis III of Thuringia with over 1,000 each; Duke Bernhard of Saxony with 700; and Duke Leopold of Austria with 500. Similarly, the ecclesiastical princes arrived with their knights, Archbishop Philip of Cologne with 1,700, Archbishop Conrad of Mainz with 1,000, the archbishop of Magdeburg with 600, the abbot of Fulda with 500 knights, etc. A total of over 70,000 knights are said to have participated in the festivities, which commenced with a festive coronation of the emperor, the empress, and her son (Henry), followed by a gala dinner. Pentecost Monday was the day for the knighting of the emperor's sons, Henry and Frederick, the nominal occasion for festivities. Subsequently prisoners, knights, crusaders, and male and female jesters received gifts. Minstrels and poet-knights, among them Heinrich von Veldeke, assumed responsibility for entertainment. Finally, on Monday and Tuesday a tournament was staged (with blunted weapons). Reportedly, "the knights joyfully carried their shields, lances, and banners during the tournament without administering any blows." The festivities ground to a sudden halt, however, when a violent storm arose, toppling houses, destroying tents, and causing some fatalities.

Other Pastimes

Although festivities and tournaments ranked among the highlights of courtly life, remaining leisure time was occupied with other activities.

One such favorite of the nobility was undoubtedly hunting,[77] particularly since the forests (and thus hunting rights) belonged to the lords. Besides, hunting red deer, wild boar, and bear was a privilege belonging to lords alone; "forest" originally designated royal woodlands and had become synonymous with the right to hunt by Carolingian times. Hunting demonstrated social position, manifested authority and physical prowess, and tested courage all at once. Hunting was so popular that the nobility had to be reminded not to neglect its Sunday obligations. A particularly stylish form of hunting was with trained falcons. (Emperor Frederick II even wrote a manual, *De arte venandi cum avibus*, preserved in an illuminated manuscript.) Not surprisingly, in literature the falcon was a symbol of manliness.

Inside a castle—and not merely among women—games such as dice and board games were often played with priceless pieces depicting courtly or literary scenes. These constituted a favorite pastime (Illustration 28). Particular favorites were backgammon, checkerboard, and chess. Chess in particular was documented in castles by the early

Illustration 27: *Knightly Combat with Marionettes* (Herrad von Landsberg, *Hortus deliciarum*, twelfth century; illustration of Ecclesiastes 1:1ff.).

eleventh century, constituting a mirror of courtly activities. However, there were other games as well. A miniature dating from the late twelfth century (Illustration 27) depicts two boys playing marionettes with two battling knights. (Things such as this existed, although the drawing serves to illustrate a biblical quotation condemning vanity.) Later there were other favorites: such parlor games as blindman's buff, the *quintaine*, in which both a lady and a lord tried to knock each other over while keeping one foot off the ground, or *la main chaude* (during the course of which a lord had to rest his head in the lap of a lady while trying to guess who had slapped him). There is naturally considerable doubt if this had anything to do with chivalric "culture."

Chivalric life was expensive. Most of the income was already absorbed by the upkeep of the castle and the care of horses and equipment, while the rest was spent on travel, clothes, and pastimes, although some was also donated to endow religious causes. When income dwindled during the later Middle Ages, many knights became impoverished, and the significance and reputation of knighthood dwindled.[78] Militarily speaking, forces of knights were frequently no longer a match for armies of mercenary infantrymen, while the princes referred an increasing number of administrative tasks to municipal "officials" rather than to knights and vassals, since a new vital sphere had emerged, leaving its mark on the times: the medieval city.

Illustration 28: *Courtly Games: Backgammon Pieces with Literary Scenes from France* (eleventh-twelfth century).

City and Citizenry

Originally an alien element within a largely agrarian society, in the course of the later Middle Ages the medieval city[1] developed into a self-confident and ultimately sovereign sphere of life which was the seed of modern, urban society. (Just how much the modern city was idolized as a model for the entire state is illustrated by the fact that the German word *Bürger*, formerly used to designate city dwellers entitled to certain rights, became the preferred term to describe every citizen.) Even though cities were not fully developed until the later Middle Ages, foundations for the city were laid much earlier. Any attempt to describe the appearance of an early medieval city will encounter almost insurmountable difficulties, since the old cities have generally been built over with the exception of a few preserved church structures, so that even archaeologists are at best able to reconstruct early townscapes only in outline form, particularly since excavations are necessarily restricted to a few fixed sites. At best, the present appearance of preserved centers of "medieval" cities date (with many changes) only from the fifteenth or sixteenth centuries. However, in the face of enormous structural changes in the late Middle Ages, one must be careful not to attribute more recent structures to an earlier time. As a result, there is generally very little information about the appearance of early and high medieval cities.

We know even less about everyday life in the city. So long as cities had not yet risen to be independent political factors, so long as their citizenry had not developed the kind of self-image partly reflected in late medieval city chronicles,[2] we simply do not have sufficient evidence to do justice to the subject. As early as the thirteenth and fourteenth centuries, however, the modest beginnings of a specifically urban literature may be discerned.[3] (In Rudolf of Ems's *Der Gute Gerhard*, written about 1215, we encounter for the first time a merchant in a central literary role.) Still, authors of the early and high Middle Ages mention cities merely in passing, briefly referring to them as centers of trade or as places where people gathered.[4] Cities were apparently not perceived as separate, clearly defined areas of life; rather, city and countryside were still much more closely connected. Although cities had developed since the eleventh century into legal and political institutions and set themselves off more markedly from their environment, reports about people sharing their lives together in one place remained rather sparse. Only in Italy do we encounter an urban population "worthy of a literature" as early as the twelfth century.[5] Today the number of studies dealing with medieval cities has reached enormous proportions—Ennen mentions almost a thousand entries in her selective bibliography. Yet these studies necessarily skirt the question raised here, "Does any meaningful way exist to describe everyday life during the earlier Middle Ages".[6] Therefore, while a study of early and high medieval cities might be able to cover their gradual development into a full sphere of life, that life can barely be described coherently. Even more so than in previous chapters, we can comprehend it only by making deductions based on surrounding conditions, shedding at least indirect light on a number of important elements of everyday life. Before we attempt to clarify anything else, we must scrutinize the nature of the phenomenon called "city," its roots and the forms in which it manifested itself and developed.

1. The Institution:
Origins and Development of the Medieval City

The Concept of a City

It is not entirely clear what constitutes a city; differentiation from a village is often as complicated as the question about the point in time when we may safely speak of cities in the Middle Ages. Earlier research has proceeded by employing legal categories whose characteristics had been summed up by Dilcher:[7] the city was characterized by an urban peace reflected in the legal provisions regulating community life, an urban freedom which allowed residents to shed the signs of serfdom, special municipal laws and a court of law, as well as a municipal constitution. In this sense, cities primarily developed as a result of privileges granted by kings and municipal lords up to the end of the Salian era (that is, the early twelfth century). Prior to this time, legal history speaks of "cities in the process of emerging."[8]

Although the urban situation was slow to evolve, legal and institutional protections are only one element out of many, and it is still possible to speak of cities proper prior to this period. Modern urban research is more inclined to distinguish between a "later city" (in the legal sense just mentioned) and an "earlier city" (using topographical and socio-economic criteria). The phenomenon "city" cannot be defined in simple terms; rather, we need to employ a number of criteria. First, there is its external appearance: cities were distinguished from the countryside by the agglomeration of people in a small space (pictures of late medieval cities emphasize this distinction). To be sure, this concentration of people in one place was not equally intense everywhere. Otto of Freising described the city of Mainz during the earlier twelfth century as follows: "This city, situated along the banks of the Rhine, is big and strong, and the side closest to the river is densely populated, while the other has merely a scant number of inhabitants and is enclosed by a strong wall with many towers. The city extends endlessly in length, although it is not as wide. The necessities of its location characterize it: on the side bordering on Gaul, it is hemmed in by a moderately high mountain, on the other side, bordering on Germany, its frontier is formed by the Rhine; it is splendidly decked out with churches and buildings along the Rhine, while the other side has vineyards and other fertile land."[9] (Typically, Otto mentions the city for strategic reasons alone, since Duke Frederick of Swabia attacked Archbishop Adalbert of Mainz in the city.) On the occasion of a treaty signed between the citizens and Henry IV in 1073, Lampert of Hersfeld describes the city of Worms as follows: "The city was very crowded; it was impossible to capture because of the strength of its walls; the fertility of the surrounding countryside was responsible for its extraordinary wealth, and it was equipped most plentifully with all those provisions necessary for war."[10] Based on the evidence of these descriptions, medieval cities not only varied in density of population, but—although this is not universally true until the high Middle Ages—they were also walled, that is, they were fortified to such a degree that contemporaries referred to them as "fortresses."[11] Indeed, during the high Middle Ages, walls helped constitute a city, since some cities were specifically founded for the purposes of fortification.

An additional, economic criterion was the presence of trade and spectrum of crafts which the city provided. Although both of these did not remain restricted to cities and as Otto's description shows, farm operations were part of them, a concentration of occupations later referred to as "civic" was nevertheless typical. At any rate, a city was primarily a non-agrarian settlement. Against this background, the market also became an important characteristic, although it was not exclusively found in cities.[12] Moreover, in recent times the city's central function in relationship to its hinterland has been emphasized: owing to its administrative, ecclesio-cultic, cultural, or secular institutions, as well as its market, the city formed a center for the surrounding countryside, whence the large majority of the city's population had come.[13] All in all, medieval cities differed significantly from one another so far as their origins and circumstances of founding, lay-out, appearance, laws, and functions were concerned. Whether or not one may refer to a given settlement as a "city" is frequently very hard to answer; however, we need not dwell on this issue any further here, since we intend to illustrate the typical features of cities and to discuss those settlements whose sphere of life clearly distinguished them from its counterpart in the countryside, the rural village.

A medieval city's self-perception can be characterized by contemporary descriptive terminology, the decisive criterion in both Latin terms for city was its fortification: civitas (which often, but not exclusively referred to an episcopal city) and *urbs*.[14] Smaller cities were often described by the term *oppidum*. The corresponding German term for the early medieval city was *burg*, preserved in numerous names of cities[15] (Rome, too, is referred to as *Rumburg* in Old High German poetry); later on, the inhabitants of a city came to be referred to as "burghers" (*burgaere*). Thus no fundamental distinction was drawn at first between *burg* and *stadt*, since both were fortified. It is probably no accident that the term *stat*, which originally merely referred to a site (Modern German: *Stätte*), was not preferred to *burg* until the twelfth century, when *burg* became restricted to its narrower meaning, "castle." Hidden beneath this linguistic development is the transformation of the city to a legal entity which has already been described.[16] Henceforth, its legal nature would be the city's most significant characteristic.

Beginnings and Roots of the Medieval City

The institution of the city was nothing new.[17] There is evidence for urban cultures in the Near East by the seventh millennium B.C., and in the Eastern Mediterranean as early as the second, while in western and south-central Europe we encounter spacious fortifications (*oppida*) during the Celtic Latène period. On the basis of its political and social impact, the culture of classical antiquity is also often summarily characterized as urban, while the Middle Ages are considered rural in nature (with their monasteries, castles, and villages). The two are not mutually exclusive, but during the early Middle Ages cities still gave the impression of "islands surrounded by a rural environment."[18] They were relics left over from classical antiquity, especially since the older cities indeed dated back to antiquity. The city in late Roman antiquity was an administrative center ruling the surrounding countryside. The *civitates* of Gaul, for example, originally developed from the principal centers of conquered tribes, while north of the Loire, the administrative districts were more expansive. The most important settlements, such as Cologne, Xanten, or the imperial residence at Trier, were upgraded to "colonies" in accordance with Roman law, then enlarged into planned communities divided by two axes, patterned as if they were Roman military camps. Many cities along the Rhine and the Danube (such as Mainz, Bonn, Augsburg, and Regensburg) developed from provincial settlements attached to Roman camps. Beginning with late antiquity, a return to an agrarian culture caused cities to shrink and lose their importance, particularly since the upper levels of society had migrated to the countryside. Pressed by the onslaughts of the Germanic tribes, cities were fortified with walls and thus set apart from the surrounding countryside. Many of these settlements outlasted the period of migrations and continued to exist throughout the Middle Ages. However, the question of urban continuity is one of the most hotly disputed issues in urban research. Today we know that careful distinctions must be made, that the intensity of continuity varied by area. The greatest continuity was in Italy, which always retained its urban character despite shifts in the towns' site and shape. Gaul also revealed a certain degree of continuity, although intensity decreased from south to north. On the other hand, there are hardly any traces of Roman continuity east of the Rhine.

Even in places where there is evidence of continuous settlement, shrinking was substantial; only sections of the Roman city whose walls had endured for quite some time remained inhabited. At Trier (Illustration 29) the population decreased from approximately 60,000 during Roman imperial days to a few thousand during the sixth century (although new traces of settlements have recently been discovered near churches built outside city walls). Roman buildings were not always utilized for their original purpose either. A former granary served as a royal palace, while the former imperial palace (today the "basilica") first became the seat of the count and subsequently (during the twelfth century) of the bishop; a section of the *Porta Nigra* (Black Gate) likewise was used as a church. The central buildings of the old city (the thermal baths and the *praetorium*) deteriorated, since the Franks had no use for them. It is difficult to determine whether the network of roads continued, since the layouts of these cities have been barely preserved.[19] The size cities achieved in antiquity was hardly ever reached again

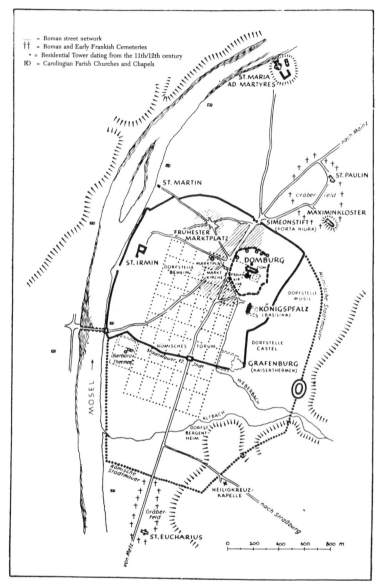

Illustration 29: *From the Antique to the Medieval City: The City of Trier around 1100, with a Superimposition of the 'insulae' of Late Antiquity* (Thomas Hall, *Mittelalterliche Stadtgrundrisse. Versuch einer Übersicht der Entwicklung in Deutschland und Frankreich*, Antikvarist arkiv 66 [Stockholm, 1978], p. 48).

(with the exception of Cologne), even when cities experienced renewed growth during the high Middle Ages. Old settlements were sometimes completely relocated, as was the case of Xanten, where a new settlement was established in the vicinity of the memorial monastery (*Memorien-cella*)—the subsequent collegiate church of St. Victor—using the bricks of the abandoned Roman city. This also occurred at Bonn, where the settlement around the *Canisiusstift* gradually replaced the old Roman camp. In general, continuity had some effect on the remaining or re-established churches within the city, as well as on manorial churches at places where saints had been buried outside city walls, but it must not be overrated, since it affected the settlement and its commerce only conditionally. Where old administrative centers continued to exist during the Middle Ages, it was because they also happened to be episcopal residences.

It was to these bishops that the medieval city owed its immediate origin. During turbulent times, bishops often rose to become protectors of cities, thus also acquiring secular power. The medieval cathedral normally remained where the ancient episcopal church had been situated, generally at the city's periphery. When the cathedral close (*Domburg*) became the center of a new settlement after the dramatic shrinking of ancient cities, most medieval cities moved to the periphery of their Roman predecessors, thus gradually taking on a new shape. At Cologne, for instance, a settlement for artisans and traders emerged between the cathedral, the castle, and the Rhine. The dwindling significance of ancient cities reduced the importance of the urban form of life during the early Middle Ages; nevertheless, it remained the seed for a new beginning during Carolingian and Ottonian times. The medieval city, then, was no longer a direct continuator of the city of antiquity, but was rather erected on the Roman city's foundations.

Since Carolingian days at the latest, partial continuity with Roman cities provided a starting point for the formation of city-like settlements, revealing a renewed need for urban life. Where there were no ancient models, in those parts of Germany which had formerly been spared Roman influence, Frankish settlements often developed into cities. Taken all in all, the medieval city possessed a great variety of roots which supplied it with special features and differentiated it from both the ancient and modern city. The formation of cities was advanced by dependence on existing seignorial institutions which attracted greater numbers of craftsmen and traders because of opportunities for sales, and towns were frequently intentionally founded by lords as marketing centers. Towns might also grow around centers of religion. In addition to developing around episcopal palaces as described, monastery, collegiate, and pilgrimage churches became a location for the establishment of commercial settlements. Frequently additional churches emerged in episcopal cities near the cathedral, attracting settlements which eventually combined to form a city of their own in turn. The layout of the city of Cologne clearly reveals distinct regions around the cathedral itself as well as the monasteries of St. Pantaleon or St. Gereon.[20] In turn, new parish churches were erected in newly established settlements. Larger cities of the high Middle Ages therefore distinguished themselves by the great number of churches which characterized their townscape. (During the early Middle Ages, the municipal area of Metz had approximately forty churches, and Paris had twenty-six.) Particularly important monasteries and collegiate churches (*Stifte*), originally founded in relatively remote locations, gradually had to face the possibility of developing into *bona fide* settlements. Fulda, established by St. Boniface in the mid-eighth century, attracted a settlement on which Henry II conferred the right to hold public markets in 1114. Five years after the founding of the monastery at Siegburg by Archbishop Anno II of Cologne in 1064, a settlement developed with market rights of its own. Attracting pilgrims from afar to the tombs of important saints, the cult of relics often promoted the establishment of settlements. Many a city, such as Le Puy in France, owed its importance to a pilgrimage church.

A further vital element of city development was the castle (or palace) as the lord's residence. (During the early Middle Ages the same name was used for both city and castle.) As mentioned in the previous chapter, castles of the early Middle Ages were still located in the lowlands in close proximity to the manor; cities could emerge from surrounding settlements, whence most of the members of the manorial *familia* originally came, whenever the agrarian way of life gave way to a commercial specialization or when other elements were added. In 831, for example, when an episcopal cathedral was placed inside the "Hammaburg" (the city of Hamburg, a walled castle with its own church) the city's expansion accelerated. However, even at the foot of the hilltop castles which appeared in increasing numbers after the eleventh century, settlements often emerged which were situated below (*sub-*) and protected by the castle (*urbs*), literally "suburbs." In Italy and southern France the term *burgus* was adopted more and more frequently. It is mentioned for the first time in 700 near Chalon-sur-Saône and was in common use since 850. Initially, such *burgi* still lacked fortification, in contrast to the castle itself. Cities such as Frankfurt or Dortmund trace their origins to important manorial estates and royal palaces. Rural beginnings were particularly noticeable in such cases and could be shed gradually only as a result of other elements (such as the location of a trade center at Duisburg on the Rhine).

One element promoting the formation of cities was provided by the market.[21] Large annual fairs attracting merchants from far away were frequently held in accordance with some tradition, especially in cities dating back to antiquity. (When increased commerce made such fairs insufficient, some regions, such as the Champagne, Flanders, or Lombardy, organized cycles of alternating annual fairs.) Local markets (weekly markets), the next development, appear in great numbers in the Carolingian age, and they proved much more instrumental in the formation of cities. In 744 Pepin ordered that every *civitas* organize a weekly market,[22] and in 864 Charles the Bald requested his counts to list the markets in their counties.[23] The market was the manifestation of an emerging "division of labor" within the countryside, even if producers and merchants remained by and large identical and at least some merchants and artisans remained integrated into the manorial system.[24] In order to stage a market, a privilege was needed from a lord,[25] frequently blending the right to hold a market, to collect tolls, and even to mint coins in the case of royal privileges. Not all markets subsequently developed into cities in a legal sense; however, all important cities probably possessed the right to hold markets. Supraregional markets in particular attracted additional traders and settlers. The core of the medieval city took shape out of the market Archbishop Henry of Trier established in 958 at the entrance to the cathedral close, for example.

Finally, bridges spanning rivers were significant, since cities frequently derived their names from them (such as Innsbruck, or Zweibrücken). Together with tolls gathered because of the bridge privilege, bridges at the intersection of waterways and roads symbolized a favorable location for cities. As in the case of Landsberg am Lech, the bridge frequently gave rise to a settlement, especially if the location was associated with a market.[26] Rivers were also important for fishing and water-power, and in contrast to rural settlements, medieval cities were characteristically situated on the banks of a river.

The *Wik*,[27] located primarily along the coast but also on flat land, proved another source of city-building. The term was preserved by numerous locations such as Schleswig, or Braunschweig (Schütte counted 670 place names ending in -*wik* in northern Europe). Originally, *Wik* denoted a village.[28] A *Wik*, therefore, would not necessarily develop into a city, and in fact did so only in a few cases.[29] The early medieval *Wik* was primarily a place of trade catering to long-distance commerce in luxury articles, characterized chiefly by a harbor.[30] It was not merely a shipment point (*emporium*), however, as assumed by earlier studies;

rather, a *Wik* constituted a fixed settlement with a sedentary population largely but not exclusively mercantile, protected by the king and endowed with privileges. In 815, for example, Louis the Pious absolved merchants who had traveled to Dorestad of their duty to entertain and to pay a death tax. (In addition to Dorestad in Frisia and Quentowic in Flanders, Haithabu played an important role in the Baltic trade of the Danish settlement on the Schlei river, near Schleswig.) Many a *Wik* disappeared as a result of Viking raids; however, during the ninth century new trade settlements such as Bruges or Ghent emerged in their place and subsequently blossomed into full-fledged cities.

Many of the most important early cities were characterized by a variety of such roots—for example, when a settlement emerged with a market at a favorable location (on a river, or at the crossing of major trade routes) which already had a church, an endowed chapter, or a castle. The primary element varied from instance to instance, so that medieval cities cannot be traced back to a single root. In Flanders and the Netherlands, for instance, the coexistence of a count's castle, possibly a royal palace, and a port was a characteristic conflux.[31] Just as the cathedral close attracted settlement, and trading posts were common in episcopal cities (such as Cologne, Mainz, or Worms), a bishopric could in turn be established at an already existing market and commercial settlement (as was the case at Bremen in 831, or at Magdeburg during the time of Otto the Great). Later cities not only had several roots encouraging their establishment, but also frequently possessed a layout revealing several core areas,[32] settlements developing around distinct centers: these would not merge into one entity until the high Middle Ages.

The Bavarian center of Regensburg could serve as an example of just such urban development over several centuries.[33] Here the point of departure was a Roman camp whose specific fate is unknown. The foundations of the new development were the palace (with the tomb of a saint) and the two endowed chapters, Niedermünster in the northeastern corner (late seventh century) and Obermünster in the southwestern corner of the camp (mentioned in 833). The third element was provided by the cathedral district of the episcopal community (prior to 778). Outside the gates was the monastic chapter of St. Emmeram. During Ottonian times, the *translatio s. Dionysii Areopagitae* already distinguished between an inner city and a new city, with three districts reserved respectively for the king (to the east around Niedermünster), the clergy (in the center around the cathedral and Obermünster), and merchants (north of St. Emmeram, now enclosed by a wall). Development beyond the Roman walls suggests substantial expansion. Moreover, the city contained several palaces belonging to out-of-town bishops and monasteries. The city experienced its peak period during the twelfth and thirteenth centuries. At this time new monasteries originated, attesting as much as the stone bridge across the Danube to the importance of the city, or the forty-odd residential towers (*Geschlechtertürme*), some still preserved, which belonged to patricians. The city did not attain its ultimate shape until the thirteenth century, when a renewed wave of construction set in; this took place especially near the city hall, as well as to the west and east, where suburbs were annexed. By 1322, the city had already attained its nineteenth-century size.

The development of Regensburg suggests that medieval cities developed only gradually, growing together in stages. Their beginnings can be detected during Frankish and Ottonian times, but actual periods of growth and expansion did not commence until the eleventh century (Illustration 30). During the twelfth century, a city-like character with dense construction had developed in the important cities. This growth was primarily a result of immigration from the countryside, the result of a widespread rural exodus; from a completely economic point of view, it presupposed rural surplus production.[34] The specific cause for the rural exodus stemmed from the desire of serfs to remove themselves from seignorial rule and to enjoy the liberties of the city; at first, only manorial serfs came into the cities, not manse peasants. Before the increase in population, any large-scale professional differentiation or specialization was impossible; such differentiation typified the high medieval, and especially the late medieval city, with its significant number of different crafts. Peasants obligated to pay their levies in money depended increasingly on the city's weekly market in order to be able to sell their farm produce and provide themselves with the city's goods.

For the most part, the origin and expansion of cities did not result from planning; rather, it occurred because the lords of the cities (namely the kings and bishops) promoted it. Later, in the high Middle Ages, emerging territorial states pursued a regular policy of promoting the establishment of cities. The period between the late eleventh and the mid-thirteenth centuries teemed with newly established cities (called "chartered cities" or *Gründungsstädte*). Using measures and stakes, locaters laid out lots and created new municipal areas whose distribution was marked by exact planning. (Earlier views concerning the design of certain types of cities by their founders—for instance, the presumed "Zähringer cities," with their characteristic cross-axis—have been largely abandoned.) Much more common, however, was the partial redesign, relocation, or even enlargement of an earlier settlement into a new

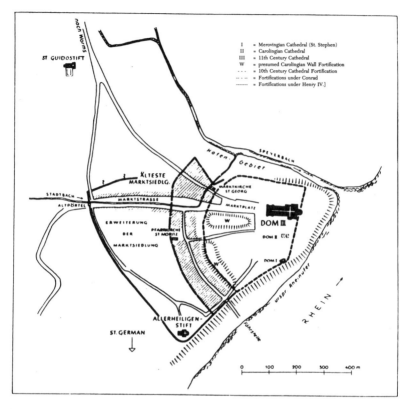

Illustration 30: *Growth of a High Medieval City: Speyer c. 1100, with Expansions.* (from Hall, p. 96.)

planned community. Many cities differentiate between an "old" and a "new" city, a distinction that goes back to this time,[35] while other settlements remained unchanged and were merely proclaimed cities. During this epoch, when legal concepts predominated, the founding of a city essentially amounted to such a proclamation.

The oldest example of a chartered city on German soil is considered to be the city of Freiburg, which was founded by the Zähringer house. According to the charter,[36] which is still disputed, a market originated in 1120, together with a settlement of merchants and other settlers who had entered into a covenant (*Schwurverband*) with the previous residents (*burgenses*).[37] For an annual rent of one shilling, each newcomer received a property measuring 50 by 100 feet to be held in hereditary tenancy (*Erbzinsrecht*). He was allowed to use the commons, take advantage of the marketplace, and enjoy exemption from paying customs. Such incentives were apparently established to attract settlers. The priest along with the magistrate (who administered the city on behalf of the territorial lord) and the advocate (in his role as aide to the court) were elected by the citizenry. Lübeck represents another famous example of a chartered city. In 1143, Count Adolf of Schauenburg founded a port and city close to an abandoned castle. When the market flourished, curtailing trade at Bardowik (a city belonging to Duke Henry the Lion of Saxony), Duke Henry demanded half of Lübeck's receipts. Since Adolf declined, the Duke closed the market in Lübeck, exempting only staples. When Lübeck burned down in 1157—a typical occurrence with the wooden construction in medieval cities which allowed for repeated reconstruction and redistributions—the residents asked Henry for a new place to settle. Thereupon the Duke founded a new settlement in the vicinity, naming it Löwenstadt. The port, however, proved too small. After renewed negotiations with the count, the merchants finally returned to the old place, building new churches, houses, and walls. Henry conferred a number of privileges on Lübeck, and the settlement quickly developed into the most important merchant city on the Baltic.

These examples also illustrate the importance of a city policy as part of territorial expansion. Cities within this scheme became objects of prestige. Not all new foundations were as successful as Freiburg or Lübeck, and some remained mere walled villages. The foundation and the granting of privileges alone did not suffice for the emergence of city life and cities therefore remained legally dependent on previously existing factors of settlement if they wished to survive. Neither could a city allow its competition to become too powerful. In the *Statutum in favorem principum* of 1232, for instance, territorial lords prevailed over the king, who had to promise to refrain from establishing new markets if they infringed on old ones.

Because of the great number of foundations and charters, the number of cities rose enormously. By about 1150, there were perhaps 200 cities within the Empire, whereas fifty years later their number had tripled. The network of cities also became denser, although it remained essentially dependent on existing conditions. In the lower Rhine region, for instance, the "landscape of cities" was sufficiently developed in principle by about 1040, but it was significantly elaborated during the following century.[38] Cities were not evenly distributed over the countryside, and rural regions continued to contrast with true "urban landscapes."[39] Upper Italy, with its maritime cities and the towns of Tuscany, was a prime example, as were the southern regions of France. Furthermore, the Netherlands and Flanders (especially modern-day Belgium with Bruges and Ghent) also belong to this category. Remaining regions displayed a less urban character, although genuine cities could be found in great numbers in the Champagne and the Paris basin; in the Meuse region; along the middle and lower Rhine with its venerable bishoprics; in the Hanseatic cities along the Baltic, in the vicinity of Lake Constance, and in old Bavaria and central Swabia; and in several other regions. Their numbers during the thirteenth century were greater than ever before and greater than they would ever be again.

The influence exerted by territorial lords suggests that cities were by no means free from dominion. Lords in the cities (such as bishops and territorial princes) did not differ in principle from ecclesiastical and manorial lords. On the other hand, cities quickly became characterized by the freedom they provided their inhabitants, since rulership in the city was apparently different from that in the countryside. Both extremes, dominion and freedom, constituted the basis for urban life during the Middle Ages.

Rule and Freedom in the Medieval City

Like any other area of medieval life, the city was characterized by definite power relationships. The city population and urban life were embedded in a city whose rule was rooted in special rights and privileges over against kings, bishops, and secular lords.[40] However, this did not separate the city from the countryside, since municipal and manorial lords were frequently identical. During the early period when episcopal cities predominated, the authority documented best was that exercised by bishops, but even this did not manifest itself everywhere in like fashion.[41] The retreat of secular powers to the countryside during late antiquity and Merovingian times had strengthened the position of the bishops in the cities, and these spiritual "shepherds," who had been members of the ruling Gallo-Roman senatorial aristocracy in the former Roman areas of Gaul, emerged as "counts of the cities."[42] They were responsible for administration, jurisdiction, and warfare. The kings, in their capacity as seldom-present municipal lords proper, were forced to rely on the bishops, granting them additional rights. (These rights were subsequently lost, in part to the newly appointed counts during Carolingian times.) At the same time, as "Frankish imperial bishops," the bishops came to be tied even more closely to the king; they were integrated into the constitution and the administration of the realm. When the cathedral town, with its properties—usually including at least parts of the city—and its serfs, were subsequently placed under public administration and jurisdiction, therefore directly under the king, the resulting immunity became a new source of secular episcopal authority. It was exercised by the bishop himself, or his secular deputy, the advocate. In the course of time, most bishoprics received a grant of immunity. City rule itself did not devolve completely or universally upon the bishops; they had attained it by the early Middle Ages in northern France, while it took until the eleventh or twelfth centuries in southern France, and many cities were under a diarchy shared by bishop and count, resulting in a division of rulership between the two. Both frequently came from the same family, however, since bishoprics were controlled by the local aristocracy. In the German Empire, the so-called Ottonian-Salian imperial church system (which distinguished itself by degree, although not essence, from other countries) integrated bishops into the imperial constitution. In consideration for and as a prerequisite of their services to the Empire (the *servitium regis*, comprising military services, levies, and the accommodation of the king), bishops were vested with a number of regal privileges or royal sovereignty rights such as the right to fortification, jurisdiction, and proscription, as well as mint, toll, and market rights within the city. These were the privileges forming the basis for city rule, leading to an interest on the part of the bishops in the economic growth of a city. In 975 the archbishop of Cologne, for instance, received the right to collect tolls. This was very lucrative, due to Cologne's location on the Rhine. In 988/89 he received the additional right to hold markets. Market rights were especially important for the development of any city and could lead even to the founding of one where previously there had been none, as was the case with Munich. In 1158 Henry the Lion destroyed the bridge crossing the river Isar near Föhring (a market under the jurisdiction of the bishop of Freising). He then established his own market at Munich, soon to develop into one of the most important Bavarian cities. Later, during arbitration proceedings, the bishop of Freising was compensated with one-third of the proceeds from tolls and the mint at Munich. But Munich's rise could not be halted, even after Föhring was rebuilt in 1180.

Thus, the "city rule" of bishops (as well as other municipal lords) encompassed a great number of individual rights which had grown both from granted privileges and the manorial system. In addition to bishops and kings, other officials (dukes, counts) and noblemen, followed particularly by the territorial princes during the chartering period, exercised municipal rights. Frequent divisions of authority were common. A treaty dating from 1205, for example, guaranteed both the Bavarian duke (the Wittelsbach duke Ludwig) and the bishop (Conrad IV) half rule over the city, dividing all rights and levies between them.[43] These privileges both ushered in the development of cities as legal entities and separated them from the surrounding countryside. The code of Bishop Burchard of Worms of 1205, for instance, recognized different types of punishment inside and outside the city,[44] and from that time on, cities developed into separate juridical spheres.

At first only certain office-holders and ministeriales held rule. They were referred to (as was the case at Cologne) as "burgraves" (= city counts) or magistrates (*Schultheiss*). Magistrates and advocates frequently competed against each other while exercising their rights; thus, power was both graduated and divided, similar to the situation in the countryside. (This occasionally led to a peculiar division of labor. According to the code of the city of Strasbourg, an episcopal official was to position the axe over a thief's wrist while the advocate's executioner struck it with a hammer; thus both participated in the administration of justice.[45])

Beginning in the eleventh century, municipal lords sought to promote urban expansion by granting special privileges to certain segments of the municipal population, for example, by releasing merchants from ordeal and trial by combat, or as was the case in Freiburg, by promising them especially favorable trade conditions. The oldest comprehensive example is generally agreed to be a document drawn up in 1066 for Huy on the Meuse, in which the bishop of Liège transferred to the citizens the proceeds from the vacant episcopal see in gratitude for their contribution to constructing a church. During the Investiture Controversy, when the king had to attract followers, some upper Rhenish cities such as Worms (1074) and Speyer (1104) received royal privileges directed against the episcopal lords of the city.[46] The citizenry was thus recognized as a legal body enjoying a certain degree of freedom. Later, the saying "City air liberates within a year and a day" and the many variations thereof were invoked by newcomers. This in effect freed them from manorial bonds (as long as the manorial lord did not seek them within this set period) and placed them under the jurisdiction of the city and municipal courts, as well as the lord of the city. Calling this condition "freedom"—for it was undoubtedly a restricted form of freedom—was justified by the fact that the relative improvement in status did trigger a widespread rural exodus. Privileges granted by municipal lords provided settlers with an incentive and a certain degree of free space which might even be enhanced by personal privileges. However, this freedom was always additionally conditioned by the possession of private property.[47]

Soon the sum total of these special rights and liberties led to the development of special municipal codes regulating life among citizens, their administrative affairs, and their relationship to the lord of the city. Since municipal codes such as these were passed on (in modified form) from city to city, entire "families" of municipal codes emerged. For instance, the code of Cologne became a model for Westphalian cities, the code of Magdeburg for the regions of German colonization in the east, and the code of Lübeck for the Baltic regions.

In connection with the granting of privileges, municipal lords were gradually replaced by an increasingly better-organized citizenry, which was ultimately permitted to share in the discharge of municipal laws. The resulting communities were by and large referred to as a municipality (*Gemeinde*), or even as commune (*Kommune*) and beginning at least in the high Middle Ages municipal constitutional life was characterized by cooperation (or counteraction) between municipal lords and municipalities.[48] The beginnings of this politically conceived community are controversial. Their models and parallels (although hardly their origins) are undoubtedly to be sought in cooperative associations and fraternities such as merchant guilds, at least from the eleventh century on. Guilds were religious congregations obligating their voluntary members to mutual assistance. Guilds were criticized by the Church for their worldliness, but they did not as yet discharge any communal activity. Another possible model for the organization of municipalities may have been the Church's own division into parishes or congregations, reflected in the cities during the eleventh and twelfth centuries and leading to frequent subdivisions into several parishes within the city. Courts are also touted as possible forerunners for communes, since panels of jurors judging city cases were transformed into municipal administrative authorities after having purged themselves of their seignorial origins.

If one presumes that the formation of a commune did not take place on assumption of autonomous rule, but rather at the moment citizens were recognized as legally responsible parties,[49] their origins may be traced to the eleventh century, when segments of the city's population formed conspiracies (*coniurationes, Schwurvereinigungen*) whose purpose was not clearly defined and probably differed within one and the same community. Their purpose, perhaps was safeguarding peace in the city, similar to the Peace of God. Frequently the *coniurationes* also fought for the freedom of their city in conjunction with the *libertas*-ideal of the Church.[50] In any event, we may assume a religious basis[51] which soon, although not from the onset, became linked to political goals. Frequently, *coniurationes* demanded participation in city politics, and in doing so they often turned against their municipal lord. They were therefore a unifying element, and in this fashion the citizenry became a political factor. The first evidence of this was in Cremona, where a conspiracy drove episcopal vassals from the city and destroyed their castle. In 1070, another group representing a commune (*conspiratio quam communionem vocabant*) at Le Mans rebelled against tax burdens imposed on them by their municipal lord, the duke of Normandy. At the turn of the century, several more *coniurationes* followed in northern France (1099 at Beauvais, 1101 at Cambrai). Around this time signs of an impending confrontation increased throughout the Empire. By 1073, the citizens of Worms expelled their bishop and his soldiers, swore loyalty to Henry IV and opened their gates to him.[52] (Henry subsequently issued a privilege granting merchants and Jews exemption from customs.[53])

Scholars believe that the famous 1074 merchants' rebellion against Archbishop Anno II at Cologne was spontaneous, triggered by a specific event (the archbishop's confiscation of a merchant's ship); it did not yet signify a planned and united front against the municipal lord. Still, the rebellion shows that tensions already existed, that the municipal lord's regime was meeting with growing resistance. Once again, the formation of parties played an important role during the Investiture Controversy, since a citizenry loyal to the king opposed pro-papal bishops who were town lords in several cities (though the situation might be reversed). In 1077 there was a rebellion at Mainz in favor of Henry IV against Archbishop Siegfried, who had allied himself with the rival king, Rudolf of Rheinfelden. At another venue there were two bishops (one imperial and one papal), so that the citizens were forced to take sides (as at Constance in 1092, where they opposed the rival bishop, Arnold, who had been appointed by Henry). In the long run, these movements led first to a participation of the citizens in city politics and ultimately to their takeover of city government. To be sure, this required a lengthy process stretching over several centuries, not always unilinear and certainly not at all uniform. At Cologne[54] a whole series of confrontations occurred (for instance, concerning an arbitrary, illegally erected wall) until the archbishop recognized municipal self-government with his Great Proclamation of 1257. Although he remained municipal lord in the original proclamation, he lost more and more of his rights in subsequent armed confrontations. Proceeding from the *coniurationes*, the citizenry developed into a legal body of its own over and above the municipal lord, whose power was absorbed piece by piece; citizens attained at least partial autonomy by imitating the immunity and special status of the nobility and the Church, operating still entirely within the framework of the feudal world.[55] The external symbol of this legal status was the citizenry's own seal, attested for the first time in Germany at Cologne in 1149. Seals programmatically reflect the self-image shared by citizens, without initially registering their rejection of a municipal lord. The seal of the city of Aachen, for example, dating from 1134, still portrayed the emperor. The second seal of the episcopal city of Speyer, dating from 1212/13, hinted at the city wall and pictured the cathedral with its patron saint, the Virgin Mary. The second seal of the city of Lübeck, dating from 1253/56 (Illustration 31), already showed evidence of civic life. Featuring a merchant ship with a helmsman and the ship's owner, it had a cross emblazoned on the mast to emphasize the religious element and a reference to the *coniuratio* by way of the raised right hand of the merchant. An additional sign of civic community-building was the "citizens' house" (*domus civium*), which first appeared in 1149 in Cologne's first seal.

The institutions of the city's communal self-government were at first almost entirely embodied by the panel of jurors and the association of *meliores*, the city's upper stratum, often headed by two mayors (*magistri civium*). Initially, jurors in charge of jurisdiction and administration derived their authority from the municipal lord; however, they managed to acquire more and more rights of their own. In Italy and southern France, a constitution consisting of a senate and consuls prevailed, beginning at the end of the eleventh century (1095 at Asti, 1117 at Milan, 1127 at Cremona). In Germany, many cities also adopted a municipal council (*Ratsverfassung*), in evidence from the beginning of the thirteenth century (1216 in Cologne). The elected

Illustration 31: *The City as Legal Authority: the Second Seal of the City of Lübeck with Details from the Hanseatic City* (middle of the thirteenth century).

council embodied supreme municipal authority and was in charge of the entire administration. Not every resident of the city, however, was eligible to participate in this self-government; only the upper stratum, consisting of patricians, was eligible, so that one may speak of "rule by patrician families." At Andernach, in fact, people complained in 1171 about jurors being selected from the lower strata and the poor (*ex humilioribus et pauperioribus*) rather than the "better ones" (*non ex melioribus*), the richer and the more powerful (*non ex ditioribus et potentioribus*).[56] And in a Hanseatic city, being a patrician was the prerequisite for membership. Not until the later Middle Ages did the more affluent artisans force themselves into city government, leading to the famous struggles of the guilds to win council membership for the middle strata.

While such burgher autonomy was not evident until the end of the period discussed in this book, city life during the early and high Middle Ages was entirely bound up with the rule of the municipal lord, who possessed a series of additional sovereign rights and held sway through his administrator. During the high Middle Age —parallel to the emergence of the "city in a legal sense"—the upper strata of the city progressively increased its share in sovereignty and city government, ultimately gaining complete control. At the least, the city dweller's political life took form in the tension between municipal sovereignty (with a number of "freedoms" or privileges contributing greatly to form a typical urban life) and personal or legal freedom (at first freedom "from" non-municipal institutions); citizens were determined to vindicate these rights over against the municipal lord. Ultimately, the distinctive development of sovereignty and freedom in the city resulted not least from its firm attachment to the urban space.

2. The Space:
Topography and Buildings

Similar to power relationships on which they were partially dependent, spatial conditions increasingly determined the urban character of larger settlements, thus influencing city life.[57] Our modern conception of the "medieval" city is determined by preserved city centers and old engravings, both generally belonging to the early modern period. At best, a few individual buildings have been preserved from earlier times, and the topography of the early medieval city can be reconstructed only in outline (Illustration 32). It was essentially characterized by the "city-forming" core elements already described, such as church, monastery, or

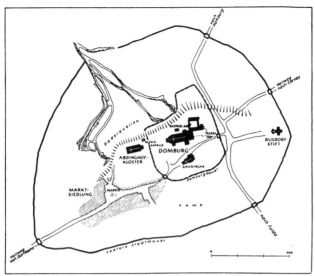

Illustration 32:

above: *The City of Paderborn during the High Middle Ages* (reconstruction; from: Hall, p. 74).

below: *The City of Paderborn during the Late Middle Ages* (from: Hall, p. 75).

castle. As a result of this variety, the early city exhibited a "topographical pluralism" (Hall) which remained visible for a long time to come. For instance, Reims emerged from a merger of its cores, the cathedral town and the monastery of St. Remi, while Halberstadt came into existence as a result of a merger between the cathedral town and the convent of Our Lady. (At first, all monasteries were located outside city walls, being gradually incorporated into the city because of enlargements.) A dualism of power—the co-existence of different municipal lords of equal status, as with the bishop and count, or of different status, as with the king and bishop—is clearly reflected by the topography. Different seignorial buildings, for instance, frequently exist, as in the case of a royal palace or count's palace adjacent to a bishop's castle. Even more decisive was the co-existence of seignorial and cooperative elements: the seignorial residence fortified early on (a castle or palace with a cathedral church or monastery), which served as a starting point for the settlement; and a pre-urban, initially still-unfortified market community. Such were the conditions necessary for the development of a "city with citizens" (*Bürgerstadt*) during the high Middle Ages. Henceforth, these two basic elements shaped the urban space. The self-reliance of cities is frequently illustrated by the existence of a separate market church (citizens' church, or *Bürgerkirche*) located across the market square from the cathedral, such as the Gaukirche at Paderborn, St. Lambert's at Münster, St. Gangolf's at Trier, or St. George's at Speyer (Illustration 30). The market church frequently both connected and separated the lord's realm from that of the citizens.

Districts of Immunity. Here, the original elements are still to be gleaned from later city maps. Immunity districts of various churches and monasteries stand out with particular clarity since, together with the castle, they were among the first to be enclosed by walls. (Hence, "cathedral town.") This "incorporation of the cult into the city" typifies the Middle Ages, whereas temple districts of antiquity were always situated outside the walls.[58] With its cathedral and episcopal palace (or monastery church), the immunity district in a narrower sense was itself distributed into three sections. These consisted of the church, cloisters, and the monastic buildings, the living space of clerics or monks, ordinarily facing south; the transitional buildings (providing contact with the outside world) vestibule, bell tower and paradise ordinarily facing north; and the buildings occupied by artisans and serfs (*Hintersassen*) facing west. When the vita communis, the communal life of clerics inside monastic structures, began to dissolve by the tenth century, the canons lived in places of their own (*curiae*) encircling the church, frequently abutting the immunity wall. These residences formed an external border for the immunity district, a phenomenon which can still be seen in many city plans. Thus the urban living space of the early and high Middle Ages was still far from forming a compact unit, and the immunity district remained strictly separate from the rest of the city.

Markets were frequently located between the immunity district and the settlement, constituting the center of the burgher settlement and of urban life. There existed not only market squares (particularly in southern Germany), but also street markets situated along widened main roads leading right through the heart of a settlement. During Ottonian-Salian times, marketplaces completely enclosed by buildings emerged, characteristic for the period. These later changed little and characterize the townscape of older cities to this very day. The market square was lined with patrician homes and official buildings, such as the city hall and courthouse, the mint, the toll house, and the scales. The city's fountain was also located here, providing all the water, since public water mains did not come into even sporadic use until the twelfth century. Because of the growth of the cities, one market alone soon no longer sufficed; by 1076, for example, there is evidence of a "new market" at Cologne. As crafts became more and more differentiated, individual markets also emerged for such goods as fish, hay, horses, and the like.

Walls and Streets. While immunity districts and castles were early enclosed by walls, burgher settlements initially remained unfortified, located at their feet. (Hence *suburbia.*) It was not until joint efforts were made to build a surrounding wall that the immunity district(s) and the market settlement drew more closely together. In France, the old Roman walls were often deemed sufficient until the twelfth century, but in other areas, in reaction to the Viking raids of the ninth century, large-scale reconstruction or construction of new city walls began. In Germany, for instance, individual merchant settlements such as Cologne, Namur, Verdun, or Regensburg had been fortified beginning in the tenth century, although elsewhere only the more important cities were surrounded by walls prior to the twelfth century. Most ring walls originated during the twelfth and thirteenth centuries, leaving numerous cities still unfortified. An earthen mound with moat and palisades, typical during the early period, was soon replaced by walls built of stone. Surviving fortifications with many towers and double walls date from the late Middle Ages, or even the early modern period. City walls were erected during the high Middle Ages with the design of castles in mind, consisting only of a surrounding wall with towers atop the city gates. Sometimes homesteads and houses abutted directly on the walls, but they were often also separated from them by an alley. While external walls and gates projected a martial image, they were still integrated into the townscape by appropriate design.

At best, only fragments of the old walls have been preserved, and only the pattern of streets or water mains still reveals the course and location of earlier walled enclosures. The reason for this may be found in the fact that many cities grew considerably during the eleventh and twelfth centuries, leading to the emergence of new settlements (suburbs) around the cities, additions to some, and the demolition of others. Sometimes only certain sections of the city were enclosed by a new wall; frequently, however, cities were surrounded by completely new walls. There were, of course, variations. For instance, the upper Rhenish episcopal city of Worms, which had already been relatively large, did not require a new wall until the thirteenth century. Its sister episcopal city, Speyer, on the other hand, received new walls on three different occasions during the eleventh century (Illustration 30), growing from 10 hectares during Ottonian times to approximately 60 hectares by the middle of the twelfth century. Likewise, Strasbourg's Old Town, which had evolved from fourth-century Roman fortifications, covered an area of 19 hectares (including the episcopal palace); the new city with its eleventh-century wall extended over 54 hectares. Cologne, however, was by far the largest German city. It grew as a result of the wall erected against the wishes of the archbishop in 1180 and survived until the end of the nineteenth century, increasing in size from 236 to 400 hectares. Of course, most cities were considerably smaller. The typical built-up area of chartered cities amounted to only 20 hectares, and until the eleventh and twelfth centuries the city was unable to distinguish itself completely from the countryside. Every new suburb, while emerging outside of the walled enclosure and extending beyond the confines of the city, still provided conditions similar to urban life. While it was still possible for many cities to shift their centers (from castle to market, for instance), complete relocations also occasionally occurred. Such was the case of Hildesheim, where the main market changed its location twice, pushing aside the original seignorial elements of city formation.[59] Soon, however, the layout and the existing buildings became permanent and unchangeable, due to an increase in population density and the addition of walls. By the time the great wall projects were complete, generally during the twelfth and thirteenth centuries, the space referred to as "city" had definitely set itself apart from the surrounding countryside. Henceforth, city walls characterized both the external appearance and the urban self-image; in numerous miniatures, for instance, walls appeared as the critical characteristic of a city (Illustration 33). Walls turned cities into "fortresses" (Haase), imbuing them with a compact defensive posture and protecting their residents from external threats and the feuds of lords. In effect, walls were a prerequisite for the development of a separate urban living sphere. However, a strip of urban land serving both protective and food production purposes did remain outside the walls.[60]

To keep the walls as small as possible (at least in the case of new building during the Hohenstaufen period) efforts were undertaken both to round them off on their outer perimeter and to make them controllable and usable inside. Thus, Hohenstaufen-era cities frequently reveal an overall design, although their layouts were rarely strictly geometrical, since they had to take terrain, water supply routes, and historical development into account. To the extent that we can determine this for central European cities, the network of streets inside the walled enclosures was regularly connected at its ends. Streets were built continuously, unlike the cul-de-sacs of southern Europe. The one-street system or, more frequently, the parallel-street system (often shaped like a bobbin, merging at both ends) typically prevailed, arranged in cross-rows, with wide main and narrow side streets. Streets could also form a grid like

Illustration 33: *The Wall as the Landmark of a City: Christ's Entrance into Jerusalem* (Trier Epistolary, late tenth century).

a checkerboard, or even form square blocks.[61] The system of streets in turn determined the construction of buildings. Lots formed the smallest unit of settlement, with a house in front and a garden in the rear, often extending all the way to the next street. Lots had merged early into large, irregular blocks surrounded on all sides by streets. At the beginning of the eleventh century, homesteads at Regensburg measured 40 x 80 feet; by the twelfth century, measurements of 40 x 60, 40 x 80, 50 x 100, or 60 x 100 feet were common. Streets themselves were narrow, angled, dark and dirty, since waste of all kind ended up there. Paved streets such as were common in antiquity no longer existed. The streets of early and high medieval cities were constructed of tamped-down dirt or gravel. Archaeologists have brought to light different layers covered over in gravel or sand, preserving the deep ruts caused by pedestrians, carts, and horses. At the old market in Duisburg, five such layers were unearthed from the period between 900 to 1300, causing the ground level to rise by approximately one meter during that time.[62] It was not until the thirteenth century that pavement reappeared.

The various cores, combined with the enlargements which cities underwent, created individual quarters. Strictly speaking, the term applies only to planned cities divided into four quarters by two main axes, but "quarters" of a neighborhood kind emerged because different crafts were increasingly concentrated in certain districts and streets. This fact is still frequently reflected by the names for streets and various sections of towns. The beginnings of such developments may be detected during the high Middle Ages, although in larger cities the producers of goods needed daily (such as bakers) continued to be scattered over the entire city. By the tenth century, particularly in the old episcopal cities along the Rhine and the Danube, voluntary and imperfectly segregated Jewish settlements with synagogues and ritual bathhouses had also emerged, frequently located near the market. But actual ghettoes confining Jews to these quarters and strictly setting them apart from the rest of the city belong to the late Middle Ages, when social contrasts became aggravated.

Buildings. Cityscapes were dominated from an early time by the steeples of churches, later joined by the tower of a city hall. As already mentioned, medieval cities were characterized by their great number of churches. Sometimes, particularly during Ottonian times, they abandoned their isolated locations and were symmetrically placed or arranged in cruciform patterns, as at Paderborn, Hildesheim, or Bamberg, where original plans called for this arrangement. They were also arranged in circular fashion, surrounding the center of the city.

At Constance, for instance, the bishop's palace, St. Mary's Cathedral and St. Stephen's parish church were grouped around the original core. Judging from their arrangement and their patron saints, these churches and the five additional ones erected during the tenth century strove to imitate the model of Rome, copying the Roman practice of establishing principal churches.[63] St. Mary's Cathedral was conceived as a counterpart to Santa Maria Maggiore in Rome, while St. Mauritius' chapel (founded next) emphasized its connection to the Ottonians, whose principal saint was St. Mauritius. Under Bishop Conrad, St. John's was added in the north (corresponding to San Giovanni in Laterano). St. Paul's in the south was situated outside of the walled enclosure during the twelfth century (corresponding to San Paolo fuori le mura), as was St. Lawrence (patterned after the Roman church of San Lorenzo). Finally, under Gerhard, St. Gregory's monastery church was erected in the west on the opposite side of the Rhine (on the site of today's Petershausen). It was clearly intended to imitate St. Peter's Basilica in the Vatican, located across the river Tiber, and in fact was soon also referred to as St. Peter's. The original relic of the patron saint, St. George, had also been transferred to Constance from Rome. Planning and a definite program apparently lay behind such church structures, reflecting a desire to make Constance into a second Rome. The fact that similar ambitious designs were almost unheard of in the eleventh century illustrates a gradual shift in emphasis from 'church' to 'civil settlement.' The Church, however, lost its influence only with respect to the topography; it remained integrated into the life of the city. The late medieval city churches in particular brimmed with altars donated by wealthy citizens, while merchant churches of early medieval settlements often served a dual purpose, as houses of prayer and as warehouses. Church bells also regulated the passage of time and the course of the urban day. Churches were surrounded by churchyards or *Friedhöfe* (that is, "places of peace") which only gradually became burial places; the term persisted long after graves were transferred to outlying areas of the city.

The second topographical element, the castle, ought to be briefly mentioned here as a symbol of power. While the episcopal palace was frequently located west of the cathedral within the immunity district, the royal palace (if one was present), often erected where the former Roman *praetoria* had once stood, was pushed to the periphery. During the high Middle Ages, it was surrounded by houses owned by the *ministeriales*.

Churches, castles, and palaces were the first structures made of stone. Among the remaining buildings only a few residential towers ("patrician towers") have survived from the eleventh century; these belonged to lords and were particularly common in Italy, although they could also be found north of the Alps, for instance at Regensburg. While a few individual stone structures dating from the twelfth century have been preserved (Illustration 34), the fact that they were exceptional is made

Illustration 34: *An Early Patrician Stone House: The "Romanesque House" at Münstereifel* (twelfth century; photograph in Meckseper, table 44).

clear by specific references to them in the sources as "stone houses." Called "hall-story houses" (*Saalgeschosshäuser*, because of a hall on the upper floor), they were the first multi-story houses. They were scattered but can be found, along with the residential towers, in nearly every region. Their architecture is frequently patterned after monastic and convent structures, and they were probably originally adorned by lords with colorful façades. However, most houses—particularly those belonging to artisans—were simple, wooden, half-timbered structures erected on narrow supports. (Most extant specimens date from the fourteenth and fifteenth centuries.) Essentially two types developed, probably during the twelfth century. The "vestibule house" (*Dielenhaus*) was common in northern Germany, its ground floor frequently consisting of a hall or living room with chambers on each side. In southern Germany, however, the living room was frequently moved to the upper story, while downstairs on one side were an entrance, a staircase, a passageway to the courtyard, while there was a workshop on the other side.[64] Until the thirteenth century, houses only had a few small windows which could be closed with shutters or curtains; more luxurious buildings, such as castles, simply tended to have arched windows. After approximately 1200 there is also evidence of an intimate and heatable *Stube* or family room in patrician family homes, a chamber separate from the main living room.[65] Originally the furnishings did not differ from those used in the countryside. In addition to short beds, chests and benches comprised the most important pieces, and they were frequently the only furnishings in a home. Houses were not numbered; rather, they were marked by names and symbols, such as "The Colorful Ox," "The Blue Sky," "The Hot Stone," or even "The Lecherous Monk."[66]

Some houses were built with their long sides to the street, but most houses in the older towns were built with their short side to the street in order to permit a maximum number of citizens access to the street and the life of the city. (The confining construction still seen today is usually a result of later development.) In order to get the most out of it, the upper level frequently extended beyond the ground floor, making lanes even narrower. Artisan and merchant houses might differ slightly in layout, and development led to the emergence by the early thirteenth century of typically patrician residences, which for the most part lined the market square. From this point on, increased value was placed on façades with windows and bays. Also noteworthy is the fact that not all houses were occupied by their owners; at least since the thirteenth century there is evidence of many rental homes.

Public buildings important for civic life were also located near the market. Following the enforcement of the citizens' right of co-determination, "civic houses" emerged as forerunners to city halls. In 1120 a *domus consulum* is attested for the city of Soest and a *domus civium* for Cologne in 1149. City halls abounded by the early thirteenth century, although as "city houses" they still frequently served different purposes. In the Dortmund city hall (c. 1232), for instance, there was a wine cellar in the basement (the forerunner of the ever-popular *Rathausstuben*), a hall for displaying textiles and a courtroom on the ground floor, and a town hall on the upper floor. The town hall was also the place where official festivities were staged. Sometimes the city council simply took over the office building of the previous lord's administration, as is the case with the city hall at Gelnhausen (c. 1200) which was originally the office of the lord's magistrate. Other times they simply added another level to the "merchants' exchange" (*Kaufhaus*). However, as a symbol of civic freedom, city halls soon shown in splendor, decorated inside and out in keeping with their significance. Here was displayed a city's coat of arms, as well as the standard weights and measures supervised by the council.

Beginning with the high Middle Ages, there is evidence of a merchants' exchange with one or more stories and two or three naves, providing local merchants (as well as those merchants who were merely passing through) with an opportunity to display certain goods for sale. Some of the most common were various types of cloth.[67] In keeping with the right to enforce the sale of staples (*Stapelrecht*) attested by the twelfth century, many cities required merchants who happened to be passing through to offer their goods for sale in order to increase exchange. Other cities took undue advantage of their sources of income by forbidding aliens to trade with one another. Commercial buildings, such as storage facilities, were usually located inside the city, while windmills (which appeared during the twelfth century) were mostly situated outside of the city walls. Naturally there were also pubs, houses belonging to specific artisan associations, and (perhaps as early as the twelfth century) bathhouses. By the end of the twelfth century, especially during the thirteenth century, hospices also emerged for the first time, serving as guesthouses, shelters for pilgrims, poor houses, and hospitals. They were connected to a church and were frequently operated by orders of knights, particularly the Order of the Holy Ghost, founded toward the end of the twelfth century.

There were connections between the location of buildings and their social prominence. The fact that castles were located at the periphery of cities is explained by the fact that a gradual shift took place from a seignorial town to a city run by citizens. As a result, many houses belonging to *ministeriales* also moved to the periphery of the city, where there are still so-called "seignorial streets" (*Herrenstrassen*) or "knight streets" (*Ritterstrassen*), such as at Rothenburg ob der Tauber and Rinteln. Contrary to earlier research, which would like us to believe that locations near the periphery of a city were assigned entirely to the lower strata of the population, peripheries were in part also occupied by distinguished families, depending on the structure of a city's population. The market was dominated by the leading merchants who built their homes there, while artisans preferred their own shop quarters or homes on streets close by. Slums did develop over a period of time as a result of such concentrations, and topographically separate, privileged districts of church immunities also persisted. The spatial design of cities made allowances for a heavily concentrated, differentiated population which needs to be examined more closely.

3. The People: Citizens and City Residents

Cities were characterized by the fact that many people lived together in a narrow space, although exact numbers remain unknown. Reliable criteria (such as lists of houses or tax rolls) permitting at least approximate estimates are not available until the late Middle Ages. As for earlier centuries, there is no basis whatsoever for exact calculations. By modern standards, however, any large medieval city would undoubtedly have amounted to little more than a quaint small town today. Hektor Ammann classifies all cities within the German-speaking area with populations above 10,000 as large,[68] while other researchers consider 25,000 as a lower limit (based on a European scale). The largest cities during the early and high Middle Ages, those with populations of over 50,000, were located outside the confines of Western Civilization, situated as they were in the Byzantine Empire or Muslim Spain. Among the three largest cities in England at the end of the eleventh century, London had only about 10,000, and Winchester and York 8,000 inhabitants each. The great period of expansion and growth did not occur until the twelfth and the beginning of the thirteenth centuries. The largest city in the West was Paris, whose population probably amounted to approximately 80,000 at the beginning of the fourteenth century.[69] Large cities with populations above 25,000 were located in Italy (Florence, Genoa, Milan, Venice, Padua, Bologna, Napels, Palermo), in Spain (Barcelona, Córdoba, Seville, Granada), and also in Flanders (Bruges, Ghent, Brussels, Louvain, Ypres, Tournai, Liège). In fourteenth-century France, the cities of Rouen, Toulouse, Lyon, Bordeaux, and Amiens had over 20,000 residents, and Marseille, Avignon, Montpellier, and Lille all over 10,000 inhabitants. The largest German city was Cologne, with approximately 10,000 inhabitants around 1000 A.D. and approximately 20,000 inhabitants during the twelfth century. Big-city status was still claimed during the later Middle Ages by Nuremberg, Strasbourg, Augsburg, Ulm, Würzburg, Erfurt, Breslau, Brunswick, Lüneburg, Prague, Vienna, and several Hanseatic cities (such as Lübeck, Bremen, Hamburg, Danzig, and Rostock). Since most of these places did not become so large until much later, however, and then did so relatively quickly, there are hardly any cities of such magnitude during the period discussed in this book.

Medium-sized cities were much more numerous (ranging between 5,000 and 25,000 inhabitants on a European scale, but between 2,000 and 10,000 on the more modest German scale). In Germany, there were at best fifty cities with populations larger than 5,000; most small cities had populations of up to 2,000 inhabitants, and there were also minute towns with populations under 200. An average German city thus numbered merely a few thousand inhabitants. From this we may surmise that not every city, *per se*, was in the position to develop a truly "urban" life.

The urban living sphere in the more important and larger cities was not created by mere numbers alone, but also by the sense of community which developed among people who shared their lives in a narrow space. This was originally expressed by a common geographical bond as a result of the orientation toward the seignorial element (such as castles or churches), and later above all because of the construction of walled enclosures. This bond was furthered still more by common tasks (such as defense). Initially, like anywhere else, class distinctions prevailed in the city. The clerics, who formed a substantial contingent among city populations enjoyed special rights. Other groups "without rights," such as the Jews, were excluded from the rights shared by the citizens and had to depend on protection from the king or municipal lord. The remaining population was divided—as in the countryside— into freemen and serfs. As artisans, traders, peasants, or *ministeriales*, many city dwellers descended from the *familia* of the municipal lord or lords. Others had simply immigrated. Serfs from the countryside remained serfs until they gradually obtained freedom on a large scale following the formation of city codes upholding the saying that "City air makes free within a year and a day." Although not universal, such codes ushered in equality before the law, disarming old class distinctions. During the high Middle Ages, this equality before the law was augmented by the *coniuratio* (the corporation formed by the citizens for political purposes), and the prospect of relative freedom contributed to a sense of community. Both equality and freedom prevailed, since wealthy citizens pushed for home rule. Lords showed increased economic interest in the cities, no longer demanding complete control over the population in order to attract more citizens. During the struggle for or against municipal lords, in the struggle for civic as well as personal freedom, the city's population coalesced.

Still, no uniform and equally entitled citizenry had as yet emerged. The feeling of community arose, as in the countryside, not so much from social equality as though sharing a common space; the inhabitants of a city formed a legal and in some respects an economic association but were quite differentiated socially. Beginning in the eleventh century, city dwellers were referred to as *cives* or *burgenses*. This term originally denoted inhabitants of the *burgus*, the suburb, in southern France, and it clung to the city population even after the city no longer conceived of itself as a *burg*. However, the terms *burgensis* and the Middle High German *burgaere* were ambiguous, particularly since their use was restricted to city dwellers who possessed full citizenship following the emergence of the "city in the legal sense," and not all city dwellers were also "citizens" in a legal sense. "Citizenship," the enjoyment of civic freedom by joining the government of the city, ordinarily entailed the ownership of land but hardly ever attached to particular livelihoods. Thus, admission to the citizen body required land acquisition and was frequently quite expensive. Later it took place as a result of formal proceedings, together with the swearing of a civic oath on the city code that had developed from the once-voluntary *coniuratio*.[70] However, exact rules and regulations varied from city to city and changed in the course of time. Among the numerous non-citizens there were clerics, Jews, and immigrants. Women did participate fully in civic freedom, sharing their equality before the law with men; however, they took no part in political life.

Occupation, privilege, financial circumstances, and public recognition gave rise to a social stratification within the city which became significantly defined only in the late Middle Ages. While upper, middle, and lower strata existed, none of these have been sufficiently researched. Any attempt at concrete classification faces significant obstacles, not the least of which is a lack of criteria (particularly where identification with certain occupations is concerned). Social stratification depended, above all, on the social composition of a given city. Generally speaking, only a few basic underlying trends can be pointed out requiring careful scrutiny in each individual case.

Two initially separate groups, incapable of taking on more definite shape prior to the eleventh and twelfth centuries, later belonged to the upper strata in the city: merchants and *ministeriales*. The first group, long-distance traders who had once been constantly on the road and in need of the king's protection, in time rallied together in cooperatives or guilds in order to protect themselves[71] and then became sedentary during the high Middle Ages, conducting their business from their city homes. This was thanks to Mediterranean merchants, who developed a special form of commercial partnership—the *commenda* (for just one journey) or the compagnia (for a number of years)—whereby one associate provided capital, while the other one assumed responsibility for the business trip. It was no accident that the urban upper strata had not pushed for a voice in city government before this change took place, and sedentary merchants turned out to be an important condition for the formation of typical city life, in whose shaping they participated. Long-distance traders found their social niche as the upper stratum within the high-medieval city. Beginning with the thirteenth century, bookkeeping emerged as an important business, and education in schools became a desirable goal in burgher circles.

A second, equally important group of the city's upper strata, and one whose significance in relation to the traders was not recognized until recently, consisted of the *ministeriales*. These individuals originally saw to law and order in the city as functionaries and employees of the municipal lord. They soon also gained a decisive influence in the formation of the community, an influence often directed against the municipal lord. During this transitional period, they occupied a dual role as both citizens and officials of the municipal lord.[72] At the head of the *ministeriales* ranked the burgrave, the magistrate (*Schultheiss*), the toll collectors, the masters of the mint, the usual court officers, and the entire castle garrison. Although the long-distance trade element did not prevail in all cities, *ministeriales* frequently shouldered a dominant role in the struggle for freedom from the municipal lord and for civic home rule, especially during the twelfth century.

In smaller cities in particular, the upper strata were finally joined by a few wealthy artisans, although this was not always the rule. The social position of the individual was ultimately determined by the social composition of the city's total population. Italy was the exception, where the nobility also lived in the city and naturally counted as a part of the upper stratum. The social upper strata—the *meliores* (the better ones), the *optimi* (the best), the *sapientiores* (the wiser ones), or the *pruden-tiores* (the more prudent ones)—simultaneously provided the leading political stratum, the patriciate from the ranks of which the council members were later recruited. They soon attempted to segregate them-selves, although they held on to a degree of social mobility for some time to come.

The city's middle strata[73] were recruited primarily from the ranks of artisans and businessmen, who were regularly both producers and traders. Although the *ministeriales* and merchants accounted for the leading occupational groups, it was not until the arrival of artisans from the countryside that typically urban characteristics evolved. In at least some regions such as Flanders, the lower and central Rhineland, West-phalia, and Bavaria, the *censuales* (those obligated to pay dues to the Church or other manorial lords), belonged to the upper peasant stratum and frequently settled as artisans in the cities, sharing decisively in the growth and progress there.[74] The *censuales* provide us with a good look at the development toward civic freedom as visible in a single group of people. Frequently, they were soon relieved of the encumbrances which characterized serfdom. In 1114 at Worms, for example, and in 1182/84 at Speyer, they were released from the so-called *Buteil*, a tax paid to the lord when somebody married outside of his or her social group or manor, which threatened the lord's control of descendants and property, reducing future inheritance-fees and death taxes. A second step toward civic freedom consisted in the release from the poll tax during the course of the twelfth century. As a result, "censuality"'was effectively removed; the *censuales*, whose traces are lost in the sources, were integrated into the city and, like merchants and *ministeriales*, could concentrate entirely on civic life. This development exemplifies how class distinctions which had originally applied to the city during the course of the high Middle Ages yielded to differentiation based on occupation. This was entirely in accord with the living sphere of the city and gave rise to a typically urban population.

Originally, the life of artisans was determined both by their occu-pations and by local market conditions.[75] In the beginning, specialization was still not very advanced. For instance, butchers also sold the pelts and hides of the animals they had slaughtered. The living quarters, workshop, and possibly small store where artisans offered their products for sale were all under one roof. To be sure, the specialization of crafts advanced rapidly; individual businesses were purposely kept small, and different crafts were stratified horizontally in keeping with their activi-ties. (Examples were bakers, millers, butchers, or brewers as producers of food; glass processors; potters; metal processors; leather processors;

wool processors, etc.) They were also vertically stratified in keeping with the production process, resulting in significant benefits to quality. Wool alone, as an example, required numerous distinct processes, being beaten, washed and sorted, carded or untangled, spun on the spindle, twisted and spooled, woven on the loom (attested since the eleventh century), fulled in vats, and finally dyed.

In larger cities, artisans from the various occupations associated in professional groups from which the guilds emerged. Neither *Gilde* nor *Zunft* originally separated merchants from artisans; rather, the two were synonymous terms, although various regions used still different words to describe these organizations. They were referred to as *Gilde* in northern Germany, *Innung* in central Germany, *Zeche* in Austria and Hungary, and *Zunft* in western upper Germany.[76] The earliest evidence of such fraternities dates from the twelfth century. In 1106, the bishop and the count of Worms established an *Innung* comprising twenty-three fishmongers with the right to membership in perpetuity, or eligibility following a joint decision by the citizenry.[77] These provisions illustrate the interest of lords in such associations, as well as the beginnings of a right to self-rule by members, whose number was apparently already limited (for reasons of income protection). Passing on a business and a craft from father to son was probably the rule, and was definitely desirable. In Würzburg in 1128, shoemakers formed a *consortium*, and the rights and the municipal taxes they were to pay were put in writing.[78] There is also a deed from 1149 recording the founding of the Cologne fraternity of bedsheet weavers, the *fraternitas textorum culcitrarum pulvinarium*,[79] to which all bedsheet weavers of Cologne voluntarily submitted. This voluntary provision led over a period of time to compulsory guild membership, with the purpose of eliminating all non-guild enterprises. At the same time, the fraternity form preserved its religious component, which (in addition to social and economic needs) played a role that must not be underestimated. Thus, guilds developed from religious fraternities and compulsory civic associations of individual occupations into autonomous corporations which participated in the political governing of the city in many places during the late Middle Ages. They functioned as a kind of cartel in cities by controlling the quality of goods, preserving traditions, safeguarding the livelihood of their members, and taking care of the training of apprentices. Often apprenticeship began in childhood and, depending on one's occupation, might last between four and twelve years. The time spent thereafter as a journeyman was predetermined as a minimum number of years. Not all journeymen became masters later on, however, and only masters could become members of the guild. The purpose of obligatory guild membership was to keep out foreign artisans, while membership limitation assured that undesirable competition was eliminated. However, strict segregation did not likely take place until the late Middle Ages; particularly in smaller cities, not all crafts were organized in guilds.

Journeymen (in part), apprentices, shop assistants who had not benefited from any training, day laborers, and domestics in wealthy households, all belonged to the lower civic strata.[80] Lower status was also the lot of those born out of wedlock or who practiced certain occupations considered "dishonorable" (such as executioners, skinners, or undertakers). Members of the lower strata possessed no civic rights and did not regularly own property, although they did not have to be entirely indigent. Their numbers figured prominently among a city's inhabitants, contributing significantly to the typically urban concentration of population as well as to urban life as a whole. Their share in the population is estimated at approximately forty percent, although their actual numbers are incalculable; even during the late Middle Ages they are not recorded in any city residential register, property-list, or house roll. Some may have been renters, but they also frequently resided in the houses of their masters. This domestic arrangement applies to domestics, journeymen and apprentices as well, who really belonged to the family.

There was also a significant segment of "sub-civic" strata and peripheral groups,[81] especially beggars who pursued no occupation or were completely impoverished. While accepted as socially unavoidable, they were still despised. Later, civic authorities attempted, with little success, to restrict begging. Aliens also resided in the cities, as well as the so-called "proxy citizens" (*Pfahlbürger*) of the high Middle Ages who lived in the countryside but had themselves registered as citizens in order to be able to enjoy the benefits derived from the civic liberties. However, territorial princes soon took action against this practice, since it curtailed their own claims. The exact composition of the population varied from city to city, and was augmented by a significant number of animals, especially dogs and pigs.[82]

4. The Beginnings of an Urban Way of Life

Everyday life in the city may be described only on the basis of rudimentary evidence. According to earlier remarks, it should have become clear that urban life unfolded only gradually, that it varied in size and type, and that composition of the population also varied during the period discussed in this book. During the early Middle

Ages, urban life surfaced only to the extent that contemporary society developed an awareness of the city's own life and legal existence. First, it was less of a separate living space than a part of some lordship, since the population was still determined by lordship, and its own social composition—inasmuch as it can be recognized—grew out of the needs of the lord. From the very beginning, everyday life in the city differed from life in a monastery, and in many respects also from life in an early medieval castle; however, an artisan's life in the city did not originally differ significantly from life in the village. Later, special conditions did evolve. The spatial proximity to the seignorial component, the increasing concentration of population, the market-oriented sales possibilities, the specialization of a large segment of inhabitants in commercial and business activities, and the settlement of the most diverse crafts in a single place produced a life-style entirely the city dwellers' own, a life-style of which they would soon become conscious and which awakened the need for a legal differentiation of the city and its citizenry from the countryside. This was externally manifested by the walled enclosure. These conditions began to take shape by the eleventh century, when the populations of cities increased everywhere; when merchants settled permanently in the city and united, like the artisans, in fraternities of their own; and when civic liberties created a special position and a sort of equality before the law for most inhabitants. This was a time when the citizenry participated in self-government and municipal government, acquiring an increased interest in their own metropolis as a political body and sphere of life. Henceforth, the city was no longer a settlement appended to a district ruled by a lord; rather, it fused with the latter and integrated the seignorial district within its walls.

Not until this development could a typical urban life evolve characterized by the experience of neighborhood, with its typically narrow housing lots, and by the concentration of the like crafts in the same street or section of town. Urban life was also typified by the gathering into a confined space of the most diverse occupations and strata, ranging from patricians to dependent domestics. It goes without saying that the specific strata of the city differed in life-style, both in private and public. Wealthy citizens were not striving for a "burghers" life-style, which developed instead necessarily in conjunction with factually different urban conditions; rather, in many matters they sought to imitate the life of the nobility. Such a life-style suggested itself naturally to the *ministeriales* and the members of the castle garrison. With the exception of military obligation and participation in tournaments, it also applied to the private life of merchants, even though they pursued entirely different economic and professional goals. Members of the lowest strata, however, who frequently barely managed to eke out an existence, could not afford such a life-style, and the rising middle strata were specifically forbidden to adopt such a life-style by the thirteenth century, when social barriers were put into legal terms by many cities. Thus "male servants" were not permitted to participate in a round dance (for instance at Augsburg) at which a female burgher was present, they were not allowed to have large weddings, they had to adhere to a certain dress code, and they were prevented by *de facto* means from gaining any form of political influence.[83] Class distinctions developed in the city both in spite and because of the single living space.

The life of artisans was primarily characterized by their work. When compared to journeymen, masters enjoyed far greater opportunities based on their social position and independence. Although the work rhythm, largely independent of season, afforded them greater freedom than was the case for peasants, the combination of workshop and living quarters under one roof prevented them from working limited hours. Still, because the work was performed in the home, the family drew more closely together; journeymen and apprentices also living in the house were integrated into the household community, and the wives of artisans frequently participated in the family business as well as in the commercial life of the city.[84] Many women, particularly those from the lower strata, pursued a wide variety of occupations in the city. However, their share in guild businesses has been overestimated for a long time, and their domestic engagement (in the broadest sense of the term) probably typified them much more.[85]

The concentration of population and bustle of city life also promoted an increase in the number of service-oriented occupations which provided partly "public" services. Bailiffs and executioners, in their capacity as functionaries of the municipal lord and the council, are two examples, although they had private interests as well. Travel promoted the establishment of inns, and in approximately the twelfth century the first civic bathhouses emerged where bath attendants frequently took over the functions of barbers and physicians or non-medical practitioners. At about the same time, prostitution also appeared in the cities, although first reports about organized prostitution and bordello-like houses (with such typical names as "Beautiful Woman") do not show up until the thirteenth century. In compensation for the monotony of everyday life, feast days and holidays were considered both religious celebrations and opportunities for merrymaking; people enjoyed watching minstrels and illusionists, buffoons and jugglers who happened to be passing through, and they also learned about the latest "world" news from such pilgrims and travelers.

City life was probably characterized most deeply by the market activities, although these were restricted to just a few specific days. Annual fairs (*Jahrmärkte*), which were always staged on the feast day of a saint or the day on which a church had been consecrated (*Kirmes*), were the highlight of the year. Not only did they promote business, but they also offered attractions and diversion. Weekly markets were a much more common affair. Goods such as wine, grain, herring, and livestock were brought by barrel to market from the countryside, carried on carts, boats, horses, or donkeys. Consequently, roads were rather busy, and booths bustled with active trading. Various needs and the goods to meet them available at city markets promoted the expansion of the monetary system, even though barter was more common. The Cologne penny became the standard currency in the Empire. Financial and loan transactions, the forerunners of modern banking, also evolved in the cities.

Still, the city did not bustle on market days alone. Lampert of Hersfeld noted that Cologne, the most populous city in the Empire, became deserted for a while following the rebellion of its merchants in 1074, who feared being punished by the archbishop; whereas once there had been great numbers of pedestrians in the streets, now there was scarcely a soul to be seen.[86] Such great numbers of people and the hustle and bustle in a confined space also brought with them many environmental problems, noise probably being the least irksome. Much more critical was the supply of water from the public wells, and cities such as Verdun, praised by Richer of Reims for its great number of wells and fountains, were the exception.[87] The removal of refuse was still strictly the responsibility of the individual and therefore also left much to be desired. Not until the thirteenth century is there evidence of civic rules decreeing that water be kept clean (for instance, away from dumps) and that waste disposal measures be taken (such as the construction of sewers).[88]

The future belonged to the city, with its civic form of life and its burgher ideas. In summary, the beginnings of city life were rather modest. During the early and high Middle Ages, conditions for urban life evolved only gradually, and medieval cities contained many echoes of other spheres of life which still typically distinguish medieval life from everyday life in other ages. In this sense, the fact we are unable to gain more concrete insights into the everyday aspects of urban life during those times is not merely a matter of a lack of proper sources, but a reflection of the age. Nevertheless, this overview of the beginnings clarifies the foundations upon which civic life began to build and develop at this rather early stage.

Conclusion: Everyday Life and the Sphere of Life in the Middle Ages—A Résumé

It was the purpose of this book to present everyday life during the early and high Middle Ages as reflected in the living conditions of medieval people, viewing what sparse evidence we possess of everyday life from the perspective of the sphere of life it created. Readers should not expect a brief summary in view of this generously designed overview, which was intended to describe and gather evidence without advocating any definite theses. Individual chapters will have to speak for themselves. Still, it seems appropriate here to present the reader with a composite view as well as a general characterization of life during the Middle Ages.

"Medieval everyday life" was multi-faceted. Everyday monastic life differed from the everyday life of the nobility in spite of convergences based on the same social background. The everyday life of peasants took a different course from that of city dwellers, although, at least in the beginning, there was no strict separation of the two. There existed various forms of life, the most important of which were discussed in this book. They depended on the pertinent goals and functions and social status of people, and they frequently corresponded to the spatio-social living spheres (monastery, manor house, princely court, city). These spheres effected a certain external similarity in the form of everyday life; however, even within these spheres, life varied depending on social status, position, and property. Even the everyday life of monks varied among different orders and monasteries.

In addition, everyday life depended on an attitude toward life wherein an often uniform tendency within specific living spheres is recognizable. In the cases of monasticism, knighthood, and burghers, this tendency resulted not only from common goals and ideas, but also from a sense of community or (as in the case of the peasantry) from similar activity and experience. These circumstances also led, fairly late, to the formation of a sense of consciousness about their estate in life. Typically, the goals of medieval men and women incorporated their conduct of life: monks wished to lead an apostolic life (*vita apostolica*), while knights sought to emulate courtly ideals. Within thier own circles, and despite real differences, such common interests favored a type of life which appears externally uniform and an accompanying mentality. This life and outlook manifest themselves most clearly in the knightly code of ethics (as an ideal), or in the monks' sense of being among the chosen (although they had to work hard to achieve perfection). They were also reflected in the peasants' own sense of self-awareness, as well as in the low esteem which others held toward peasants. A civic mentality (in the form of an occupation-oriented mentality) developed only gradually, since the urban population was originally quite hetero-geneous; still, it was promoted during the political struggle for com-munal self-administration. Even though a special type of life emerged earlier among the ruling classes, monks, and nobility than among the dependent segments of the population, it is nevertheless striking that this development did not lead to a conscious and mutual separation of knights, citizens, and peasants until the high Middle Ages.

In connection with a mentality oriented toward specific social strata, the different type of life led by individual groups resulted in distinct life-styles. Monks and nobles set themselves off as upper strata when compared to the working population, although life was *Arbeit* (work in the medieval sense) for all levels of society. To peasants and artisans, it suggested a kind of manual work often amounting to heavy labor because of a lack of technical aids; to the knight, fighting became *Arebeit*; to the monk, the simple observance of the Rule amounted to *labor* (effort). Underneath all this lies the conception that life itself, especially proper life, requires effort. Thus, everyday life was also in-fluenced by the religiously oriented worldview of medieval people: life (on earth) is perceived as punishment for original sin and is therefore unavoidably tedious. This belief probably lightened the burden of a hard life. To peasants and knights, everyday life always indicated the struggle for survival, and most parties agreed that there was little purpose in discussing the issue. Only the exceptional experiences, not the common everyday, were to be recorded. Life on earth was perceived quite simply as a test in preparation for the true, future, and eternal life. (This did not preclude that individuals also knew how to fight for their rights here on earth.)

There is therefore very little justification for idealizing medieval life. Life was not free; rather, it was enmeshed in multiple relationships, dependencies, and obligations. Social status and living sphere could not be chosen freely; one was born into them. While there was substantial mobility during the Middle Ages—we may want to recall briefly the rural exodus which was a prerequisite for the growth of cities—it would take a long time for people significantly to improve their social lot. Even the rise of the steward from peasant to lord took several generations, although social ascent did alter life-styles. Medieval people were dependent upon nature as well as norms and modes of conduct which they had created themselves and which could not be easily discarded. Serfs were subject to their lord, but the lords were not free either; rather, they in turn were bound to do what was expected of them as lords (all the way to the lofty, unrealistic ideals advocated by knightly society). Everyday life was characterized by living conditions which were determined, on the one hand, by predisposed nature and, on the other hand, by human interference, the sphere of living people created for themselves. Here, three painstakingly analyzed factors appear to be especially significant: institutional framework, living space, and social relationships. We would get caught in a vicious circle if we were to base everyday life entirely on these three determinants, which underlay this study from the beginning. However, their influence on the everyday life of people in various living spheres proved so obvious that we cannot deny their decisive significance.

Frequently, a particular institution formed the political and spatial framework for individual spheres of life, making conditions that differed from other spheres and resulted in a specific orientation to everyday human life. We cannot understand monastic life, for example, without knowing the goal of monasticism, which was isolation from the world for the sake of faith, nor will we come to understand a monastery without seeing the social function which forced monasteries into serving society and the world. Within the lay world, courtly life required powerful sponsors in the person of princes and territorial lords, but also a sense of personal worth on the part of the knights, as representatives of a ruling class and as proponents of a new lay culture. The rural life of the bond peasant received its special characterization from the widespread manorial system, since peasants were not merely dependent economically, but entirely tied to their lords as persons. In exchange for their labor peasants obtained protection, not wages. Furthermore, this need for protection led many free peasants into a dependency which could easily turn into oppression. Nevertheless, a manse of one's own left room for independence. Finally, an urban life characterized by specialized occupations developed in the high Middle Ages, threatening gradually to bring down traditional institutions. Life during the Middle Ages depended on institutions, their representatives, and their functions and self-image; it was characterized by a typically medieval (feudal) social form and was determined by existing relationships of authority. Monastery, village, castle, and city were always in the hands of one lord or several lords; demands were placed upon citizens and peasants by manorial lords, on monks by the abbot and the monastic lord, and on the knight by the liege lord and the territorial lord. All were obligated to serve and obey, although these conditions relaxed over the centuries in favor of increased self-government.

Living space was in many respects predetermined by the institution and political conditions, although it did not always coincide with authority. Frequently, several lords of the manor resided in one village, or a division of authority existed within the city (whose separate development led to forming an exclusive living sphere of its own). Without anticipating a more precise analysis, we may speak here of a mutual effect. Individuals were tied to their living spaces: a monk to his monastery by virtue of the monastic rule, a knight to the castle by virtue of his sense of status and prestige. By necessity, peasants rarely left the familiar surroundings of their village. However, as far as its design was concerned, the living space was also adapted very functionally to the existing interests, goals, needs, as well as the life-style of its inhabitants. This was illustrated by the design of the monastery, with its various wings, and by the knightly castle, which architecturally represented the military and social sovereignty of the nobility and fulfilled a great many functions within a narrow space. This was as clear in the case of the early city, housing several facilities within its walled enclosure, as it was in the case of a village, which was entirely made to suit agriculture. Individual spaces were clearly set off from one another, made externally visible by fortification in the case of a monastery, castle, or city. Inside the city the immunity districts were emphasized, while inside a monastery the cloisters served a similar purpose. Even monasteries had constant contact with the outside world, architecturally provided for by the abbot's house or the guesthouse. While individual knights still sought to symbolize their distance from the village by locating their castles on isolated hills, the large princely courts opened their doors to an active courtly life. Villages and cities were already linked by markets, and the city became a gathering place for great numbers of people. Finally, it is striking that many cities also formed around a castle or a monastic complex, showing that no matter how much these separate living spaces contributed to the formation of specific forms of life, they still provided the necessary elements of a whole in which each individual space took on specific functions while remaining dependent on the others. Castles or monasteries would be unthinkable without the manorial system, and city life impossible without the constant market-oriented supply of agricultural goods. The city, therefore, must not be viewed as simply an alien element within an essentially feudal society. Neither was life during the Middle Ages imaginable without monasteries and castles as symbols of religion and sovereignty. Although everyday life as a whole was "typically medieval," it was not invariable, but was itself subject to constant change. This, too, should have become clear in spite of the generalizing, structural approach of this overview.

Individual living spaces were characterized in large part by the group of people who were its representatives: the monastery by the monks, the castle by the knights, the village (despite proximity to the lord) by the peasants, and the city by its citizens. Social groups thus became segregated into various areas of life, a tendency corroborated by the exclusivity of monastic life and the increasingly exclusive status of the nobility. On the other hand, living spaces also steadily united people and groups who espoused various functions and positions while representing different levels of society. The monastery complex, for example, did not house only monks and lay brothers, but also artisans and serfs belonging to the monastic *familia*. The manorial system, likewise, linked a lord to his serfs by way of various property and financial arrangements, while peasant administrators grew more and more into seignorial roles of their own. In the village, small manorial lords and free peasants lived next door to serfs, day laborers, and farm hands. The manorial association was occasionally even broken up. In a castle, knights lived in close proximity to their dependents, just as the urban *ministeriales* and merchants lived next door to artisans, journeymen, and domestics. Thus, the spheres of life we have discussed provide us with glimpses of a life which was decisively characterized by the meshing of social relationships. The spheres and the goals of life united people into communities. As a rule, life during the Middle Ages was tantamount to a communal form of living determined by cooperative elements in keeping with the example provided by the family. This was true in the monastic community; in the peasant villages, with their associations of neighbors; in the manorial *familia*; and in the comparatively densely populated city. Knights, on the other hand, whose families led a rather isolated life in a castle, sought contact with people of equal status at the larger courts. Class distinctions were always maintained, and it was no accident that, according to the sources, the life of peasants is characterized by labor, while the life of knights was characterized more as one filled with leisure and amusements. Still, the sphere of life and the affiliation with a certain manor or a specific city could at times loom greater than one's class origin. The community created a sphere

of life all its own for the first time by building a sense of belonging
(whenever there were overlaps of affiliations and competencies). Where
communal life demanded order, spheres of life developed rules and
regulations, such as the *consuetudines* of the monasteries, manorial
rules, or civic laws.

Even though, based on the state of available sources, everyday life
during the earlier Middle Ages can be illustrated at best in sketchy form,
it nevertheless was embedded into a framework provided by existing
conditions and relationships. Medieval everyday life unfolded within
definite bonded relationships. These relationships created a "norm"
which characterized that life; yet the norm was far from being universally met. Norm (ideal) and reality frequently went their separate
ways, and recognizing how reality departed from the given guidelines
ranks among one of the most difficult tasks for historians who deal with
the history of everyday life. Life during the Middle Ages possessed an
orderliness constantly in danger of being broken; that, too, constitutes
a significant aspect of everyday life.

Everyday life during the Middle Ages may be explained by such indicated conditions. They provide reasons why everyday life followed one
specific course and not another. Everyday life must not be equated with
the demands and ideas advocated by clerics; neither does it correspond
to political history (with the exception of wars and feuds, the feuds
having the fewer repercussions on individual human beings). Likewise
it is not a simple mirror of socio-economic factors, although various
convergences made everyday life dependent on such vital conditions
when they came to the fore in compelling numbers. Rather, one has
to assume the existence of mutual interaction between all these factors,
even if the sources remain silent on this issue. To be sure, so far as
individual lives were concerned, only a rather limited free space was
likely to remain within the reciprocal relationships of institution, space,
and society, partly because the material basis was highly unfavorable
for individual self-realization, partly because class affiliation locked individuals into a specific life-style, and partly because individuality was
possible during the Middle Ages only within the framework of a group.
This free space was restricted even further because of pre-established
forms of conduct and norms. Family life was hardly private, constantly
invaded and scrutinized as it was by one's neighbor (due to cramped living conditions), the state (represented by the authority of the lord), and
the Church (through canon law and ecclesiastical fines). Individual ways
of life supported substantially different economic conditions, resulting in
a rich or a poor life-style as reflected in meals, attire, furniture, utensils,
houses, and dwellings. One gets the impression that showing off one's

circumstances tended to serve the purpose of overcoming class barriers; wealthy peasants not only wished to lead a rich life, but also a seignorial one, while the wealthy citizen wished to imitate the nobility. External appearances which seem trivial today frequently conveyed a symbolic message (thus rendering them no longer *simply* "everyday"). If we are no longer capable of drawing an accurate picture of early medieval everyday life corresponding to our own notions of everyday life, then the reasons lie also in the Middle Ages' fundamentally different ideas and values, evidenced in this everyday life.

It is difficult to determine whether or not people during the Middle Ages were satisfied with their lives. Many things which strike us as unusual today were accepted then as perfectly normal. Not the least of these conditions was the compulsory labor performed by peasants, as well as authority-based relations as a whole. People bemoaned natural disasters (and did penance for them), and they fought encroachments by the nobility which they perceived as unjust. For the most part, however—probably out of a sense of helplessness—they resigned themselves to their fates. Rebellions as such assumed the form of conspiracies (*coniurationes*) and were led not by the oppressed, but by the rising strata of the population; these individuals had (as was the case in the cities) political goals which directly affected in turn everyday political life.

Many details of medieval everyday life should have become clear in the course of this study, but other questions doubtless remain, and many aspects will need to be investigated further. This book makes no claim to completeness; rather, certain aspects were purposely selected and highlighted in an effort to begin the task at hand. Much remains to be done. What is still necessary is a systematic collection and interdisciplinary evaluation of all textual sources, with an eye to regional as well as individual differences and developments. This book may encourage further interest in the subject, and perhaps its treatment of some issues will generate constructive contradiction and further clarification. The discipline of everyday life during the Middle Ages is a historical perspective shedding new light on already familiar issues; it will also make accessible to us a world which may initially strike us as passing strange.

ABBREVIATIONS

Abhh.	Abhandlungen (der Akademie der Wissenschaften, philosophisch- historische Klasse)
AKG	Archiv für Kulturgeschichte
Bll. dt. LG	Blätter für deutsche Literaturgeschichte
DA	Deutsches Archiv für Erforschung des Mittelalters
FMSt	Frühmittelalterliche Studien
FS	Freiherr-vom-Stein-Gedächtnisausgabe (Ausgewählte Quellen zur Geschichte des Mittelalters, Darmstadt)
GWU	Geschichte in Wissenschaft und Unterricht
HDWSG	Handbuch der deutschen Wirtschafts- und Sozialgeschichte
HEWSG	Handbuch der europäischen Wirtschafts- und Sozialgeschichte
HJb	Historisches Jahrbuch der Görres-Gesellschaft
HRG	Handbuch zur deutschen Rechtsgeschichte
HZ	Historische Zeitschrift
JGF	Jahrbuch für die Geschichte des Feudalismus
JWG	Jahrbuch für Wirtschaftsgeschichte
MA	Moyen Age
MG	Monumenta Germaniae Historica
Capit.	Capitularia
Conc.	Concilia
DD	Diplomata
DH IV	Diplom Heinrichs IV.
DK I	Diplom Konrads I.
DLD	Diplom Ludwigs des Deutschen
Dt. MA	Deutsches Mittelalter
Epp.	Epistolae
SS	Scriptores
SSrG	Scriptores rerum Germanicarum
SSrerMerov	Scriptores rerum Merovingicarum
MIÖG	Mitteilungen des Instituts für österreichischen Geschichtsforschung
MPI	Max Planck-Institut für Geschichte (Göttingen)
QFIAB	Quellen und Forschungen aus italienischen Archiven und Bibliotheken

RB	Regula Benedicti
RH	Revue historique
Sbb.	Siztungsberichte (der Akademie der Wissenschaften, philoso- phisch- historische Klasse)
SMGBO	Studien und Mitteilungen zur Geschichte des Benediktineror- dens und seiner Zweige
SSCI	Settimane di studi del centro italiano sull' alto medioevo
VSWG	Vierteljahresschrift für Sozial- und Wirtschaftsgeschichte
VuF	Vorträge und Forschungen
WdF	Wege der Forschung
ZBLG	Zeitschrift für bayerische Landesgeschichte
ZfG	Zeitschrift für Geschichtswissenschaft
ZGO	Zeitschrift für die Geschichte des Oberrheins
ZKG	Zeitschrift für Kirchengeschichte
ZRG	Zeitschrift der Savigny-Stiftung für Rechtsgeschichte
Germ. Abt.	Germanistische Abteilung
Kan. Abt.	Kanonistische Abteilung

NOTES

Introduction

1. Concerning the theoretical foundations cf. Hans-Ulrich Wehler, *Geschichte als Historische Sozialwissenschaft* (Frankfurt, 1973); Karl-Georg Faber and Christian Meier, eds., "Historische Prozesse," in *Theorie der Geschichte*, Beiträge zur Historik 2 (München, 1978); Jürgen Kocka and Thomas Nipperdey, eds., *Theorie und Erzählung in der Geschichte*, Theorie der Geschichte. Beiträge zur Historik 3 (München, 1979); Jörn Rüsen and Hans Süssmuth, eds., *Theorien in der Geschichtswissenschaft, Geschichte und Sozialwissenschaften*. Studientexte zur Lehrerbildung 2 (Düsseldorf, 1980).

2. See the pioneering collective volumes: Jürgen Reulecke and Wolfhard Weber, eds., *Fabrik, Familie, Feierabend. Beiträge zur Sozialgeschichte des Alltags im Industriezeitalter* (Wuppertal, 1978); Lutz Niethammer, ed., *Wohnen im Wandel. Beiträge zur Geschichte des Alltags in der bürgerlichen Gesellschaft* (Wuppertal, 1979).

3. Cf. Henri Lefevre, *Das Alltagsleben in der modernen Welt* (Frankfurt, 1972); Agnes Heller, *Das Alltagsleben. Versuch einer Erklärung der individuellen Reproduktion* (Frankfurt, 1978).

4. Kurt Hammerich and Michael Klein, eds., *Materialien zur Soziologie des Alltags*, Kölner Zeitschrift für Soziologie und Sozialpsychologie, Sonderheft 20 (Opladen, 1978); Hans Gerd Prodoehl, *Theorie des Alltags*, Soziologische Schriften 39 (Berlin, 1983). It may serve as an (ideologically tainted) explanation, but hardly further understanding, if Prodoehl defines everyday life as the socio-individual medium of conflict reduction which is necessary for the reproduction of the total social system and for the purpose of securing the ability to reproduce the individuals.

5. See Klaus Bergmann and Rolf Schörken, eds., *Geschichte im Alltag—Alltag in der Geschichte*, Geschichtsdidaktik 7 (Düsseldorf, 1982); Lutz Niethammer, "Anmerkungen zur Alltagsgeschichte," *Geschichtsdidaktik 3* (1980): 231–242; Hubert Ch. Ehalt, ed., *Geschichte von unten. Fragestellungen, Methoden und Projekte einer Geschichte des Alltags*, Kulturstudien 1 (Vienna-Cologne-Graz, 1984).

6. Cf. Peter Schöttler, "Eine 'grüne' Geschichtsschreibung?—Von der Alltagsgeschichte zur 'Geschichtswerkstatt'," *Moderne Zeiten* (1983/9): 47–49.

7. Cf. Hammerich and Klein, *Materialien zur Soziologie des Alltags*, 7ff; Norbert Elias, *Zum Begriff des Alltags*, 22–29; Bergmann and Schörken, *Geschichte im Alltag—Alltag in der Geschichte*, 7ff; Ehalt, *Geschichte von unten*, 24ff.

8. I do not wish to follow Prodoehl and equate everyday life with a time without conflict and contrast it with times of conflict; the conflicts merely take place on a different plane.

9. Cf. Niethammer, "Anmerkungen zur Alltagsgeschichte," 12ff. Concerning an introduction, cf. Jean-Marie Pesez, "Histoire de la culture matérielle," in Jacques Le Goff, Roger Chartier and Jacques Revel, eds., *La nouvelle histoire* (Paris, 1978), 98ff., as well as the research published by the Institut für mittelalterliche Realienkunde Österreichs.

10. See Ehalt, *Geschichte von unten*, 22.

11. Cf. Anneliese Mannzmann, ed., *Geschichte der Familie oder Familiengeschichten? Zur Bedeutung von Alltags- und Jedermanns-geschichte*, Historie heute 3 (Königstein, 1981). 'Man' as used by Heidegger is an indefinite pronoun similar to the French 'on.'

12. Cf. Theodor Schieder, "Der Typus in der Geschichtswissenschaft," *Studium Generale* 5 (1952): 228–234.

13. Therefore, the meaning of the concept of history of everyday life does not necessarily constitute a departure from structural history; see also the controversy between Jürgen Kocka, "Klassen oder Kultur? Durchbrüche und Sackgassen in der Arbeitergeschichte," *Merkur* 36 (1982): 955–965, and Martin Broszat, "Plädoyer für eine Alltagsgeschichte. Eine Replik auf Jürgen Kocka," loc. cit., 1244–1248.

14. Cf. Günter Wiegelmann, *Geschichte der Alltagskultur. Aufgaben und neue Ansätze, Beiträge zur Volkskultur in Nordwestdeutschland* 21 (Münster, 1980); concerning the relationship between mentality and behavior/conduct, see the recent study by Volker Sellin, "Mentalität und Mentalitätsgeschichte," *HZ* 241 (1985): 555–598.

15. Cf. Hans-Werner Goetz, "Alltag im Mittelalter. Methodische Überlegungen anläßlich einer Neuerscheinung," *AKG* 67 (1985): 215ff.

16. E.g. Günther Schweikle, "Mittelalterliche Realität in deutscher höfischer Lyrik und Epik um 1200," *Germanisch-romanische Monatschrift*, new series, 32 (1982): 265–285, esp. 279ff.

17. In addition to Schweikle, see also Hugo Kuhn, "Soziale Realität und dichterische Fiktion am Beispiel der höfischen Ritterdichtung Deutschlands (1952)," in Arno Borst, ed., *Das Rittertum im Mittelalter*, WdF 349 (Darmstadt, 1976), 172–197, and Wilhelm Störmer "'Spielmannsdichtung' und Geschichte. Die Beispiele 'Herzog Ernst' und 'König Rother,'" *ZBLG* 43 (1980): 551–574.

18. Helga Schüppert, "Spätmittelalterliche Didaktik als Quelle für adeliges Alltagsleben?" in *Adelige Sachkultur des Spätmittelalters* (Vienna, 1982), 214–257, demands a fleshing out of rhetorics, topicality, typology, and literary convention. Cf. in a general way, Gerhard Jaritz, "Mittelalterliche Realienkunde. Quellenbefund und Quelleninterpretation," in *Die Erforschung von Alltag und Sachkultur* (Vienna, 1984), 33–44.

19. Theoretical reflection is demanded by Detlev Peukert, "Neuere Alltagsgeschichte und Historische Anthropologie," in Hans Süssmuth, ed., *Historische Anthropologie* (Göttingen, 1984), 57–72, and "Arbeiteralltag—Mode oder Methode?" in Heiko Haumann, ed., *Arbeiteralltag in Stadt und Land. Neue Wege der Geschichtsschreibung*, Argument Sonderband 94 (Berlin, 1982), 8–39.

20. See now for the correct view, Klaus Tenfelde, "Schwierigkeiten mit dem Alltag," *Geschichte und Gesellschaft* 10 (1984): 376–394. It seems to me that Jürgen Kocka is pointing in the right direction in his essay "Historisch-anthropologische Fragestellungen—ein Defizit der Historischen Sozialwissenschaft?" in *Historische Anthropologie*, 73–83; Detlev Peukert, "Ist die Neuere Alltagsgeschichte theoriefeindlich?" in Herta Nagl-Docekal and Franz Wimmer, eds., *Neue Ansätze in der Geschichtswissenschaft*, Conceptus-Studien 1 (Vienna, 1984), 7–17.

21. One ought to especially mention here the publications of the Institut für Realienkunde Österreichs: 1. *Die Funktion der schriftlichen Quelle in der Sachkulturforschung*, Sbb 304 (Vienna, 1976); 2. *Das Leben in der Stadt des Spätmittelalters* 325 (Vienna, 1977); 3. *Klösterliche Sachkultur des Spätmittelalters* 367 (Vienna, 1980); 4. *Europäische Sachkultur des Mittelalters. Gedenkschrift aus Anlaß des zehnjährigen Bestehens des Instituts für mittelalterliche Realienkunde Österreichs* 374 (Vienna, 1980); 5. *Adelige Sachkultur des Mittelalters* 400 (Vienna, 1982); 6. *Die Erforschung von Alltag und Sachkultur des Mittelalters* 433 (Vienna, 1984), which contains contributions concerning the individual disciplines; 7. *Bäuerliche Sachkultur des Spätmittelalters* 439 (Vienna, 1984); 8. *Frau und spätmittelalterlicher Alltag* (1986). Summarizing surveys may be found in: Otto Borst, *Alltagsleben im Mittelalter*, Insel Taschenbuch 513 (Frankfurt, 1983) (see Goetz' commentary in *AKG* 67 [1987]: 205–223); especially Harry Kühnel, ed., *Alltag im Spätmittelalter* (Graz-Vienna-Cologne, 1984). English structural histories which frequently include everyday life have always shown preference for the late Middle Ages.

22. Individual aspects are discussed now by Harry Kühnel, "Das Alltagsleben zur Babenbergerzeit," in Erich Zöllner, ed., *Das babenbergische Österreich* (976–1246), Schriften des Instituts für Österreichkunde 33 (Vienna, 1978), 98–118; Margarete Weidemann, *Kulturgeschichte der Merowingerzeit nach den Werken Gregors von Tours*, Römisch-Germanisches Zentralmuseum. Monographien 3 (Bonn, 1982), esp. vol. 2, 359ff.; *Alltag in der Stauferzeit. Vorträge der 9. Göppinger Staufertage*, Schriften zur staufischen Geschichte und Kunst 8 (Göppingen, 1984); Norbert Ohler, "Zuflucht der Armen. Zu den Mirakeln des hl. Anno," *Rheinische Vierteljahresblätter* 48 (1984): 1–33; Norbert Ohler, "Alltag im Marburger Raum zur Zeit der hl. Elisabeth," *AKG* 67 (1985): 1–40. Concerning the tenth century, see now Heinrich Fichtenau, *Lebensordnungen des 10. Jh. Studien über Denkart und Existenz im einstigen Karolingerreich*, Monographien zur Geschichte des Mittelalters 30, 2 vols., (Stuttgart, 1984). Cord Meckseper and Elisabeth Schraut, eds., *Mentalität und Alltag im Spätmittelalter* (Göttingen, 1985).

23. *La vie quotidienne dans l'Empire carolingienne* (Paris, 1973); Edmond Pognon, *La vie quotidienne en l'an mille* (Paris, 1981); Leo Moulin, *La vie quotidienne des religieux du moyen âge. X^e–XVe siècle* (Paris, 1978); Michel Pastoureau,

La vie quotidienne en France et en Angleterre au temps des chevaliers de la table ronde (XIIe–XIIIe siècles) (Paris, 1976).

24. Arno Borst, *Lebensformen im Mittelalter* (Frankfurt-Berlin, 1973), esp. 9ff. Just how much material can be assembled about the mode of life even during as sparsely a documented epoch as the tenth century is demonstrated by the excellent survey in Fichtenau's *Lebensordnungen.*

25. Concerning this problem, see Michael Mitterauer, "Probleme der Stratifikation in mittelalterlichen Gesellschaftssystemen," in Jürgen Kocka, ed., *Theorien in der Praxis des Historikers,* Geschichte und Gesellschaft, Sonderheft 3 (Göttingen, 1977), 13–43; Karl Bosl, "Kasten, Stände, Klassen im mittelalterlichen Deutschland. Zur Problematik soziologischer Begriffe und ihrer Anwendung auf die mittelalterliche Gesellschaft," *ZBLG* 32 (1969): 477–494.

26. See Karl Schmid, "Über das Verhältnis von Person und Gemeinschaft im früheren Mittelalter," *FMSt* 1 (1967): 225–249; Walter Ullmann, *Individuum und Gesellschaft im Mittelalter* (Göttingen 1974).

27. Cf. Otto Gerhard Oexle, "Die mittelalterlichen Gilden. Ihre Selbstdeutung und ihr Beitrag zur Formung sozialer Strukturen," in Albert Zimmermann, ed., *Soziale Ordnungen im Selbstverständnis des Mittelalters 1,* Miscellanea Mediaevalia 12 (Berlin-New York, 1979), 203–226; Oexle, "Gilden als soziale Gruppen in der Karolingerzeit," in Herbert Jankuhn, Walter Janssen, Ruth Schmidt-Wiegand and Heinrich Tiefenbach, eds., *Das Handwerk in vor- und frühgeschichtlicher Zeit 1,* 2 vols., Abhh. (Göttingen, 1981–83), 284–354; Oexle, in Berent Schwineköper, ed., *Gilden und Zünfte. Kaufmännische und gewerbliche Genossenschaften im frühen und hohen Mittelalter,* VuF 29 (Sigmaringen, 1985), 151–214.

28. The concept originated with the philosopher Edmund Husserl who had used it in order to characterize a pre-scientific sensorial perception of everyday life; concerning this, cf. Paul Janssen, *Geschichte und Lebenswelt. Ein Beitrag zur Diskussion von Husserls Spätwerk,* Phänomenologica 35 (Den Haag, 1970). This concerns space as an area of activity (*Bewegungsfeld*), cf. August Nitschke, *Revolutionen in Naturwissenschaft und Gesellschaft* Problemata 83 (Stuttgart-Bad Cannstatt, 1979).

29. Cf. Otto Brunner, "'Bürgertum' und 'Feudalwelt' in der europäischen Sozialgeschichte (1956)," in Carl Haase, *Die Stadt des Mittelalters,* 3 vols., WdF 243–245 (Darmstadt, 3d ed., 1978), 480–501.

Chapter I

1. *MG, Capit.* 2, no. 186, cap. 7, of 829 (p. 7); no. 193, cap. 7, of 829 (pp. 19f.).

2. Concerning Saint-Germain, see Henri Sée, "Peut-on evaluer la population de l'ancienne France?" *Revue d'Economie politique* 38 (1924): 647ff., and Charles-Edmond Perrin, "Note sur la population de Villeneuve-Saint-Georges au IXe siècle," *MA* 69 (1963): 75–86, who oppose Ferdinand Lot, "Conjectures démographiques sur la France au IXe siècle," *MA* 22 (1921): 1–27, 109–137.

3. Cf. Jan van Houtte, *HEWSG* 2, 14ff.; J. C. Russell, *Lexikon des Mittelalters* 2 (1983), col. 11ff.; Wilhelm Abel, *HEWSG* 1, 83ff.; J. C. Russell, Carlo

M. Cipolla and Knut Borchardt, eds., *Bevölkerungsgeschichte Europas* (München, 1971), 21. For the sake of comparison, the estimates of Russell are reproduced here (populations in millions):

Year	500	650	1000	1340
Balkans/Greece	5	3	5	6
Italy	4	2.5	5	10
Iberian Peninsula	4	3.5	7	9
Mediterranean Lands	13	9	17	25
France/LC	5	3	6	19
British Isles	0.5	0.5	2	5
Germany/Scand.	3.5	2	4	11.5
Western//Northern Europe	9	5.5	12	35.5
Slavic Areas	5	3	8	11
Hungary	0.5	0.5	1.5	2
SW/SE Europe	5.5	3.5	9.5	13
Europe Total	27.5	18	38.5	73.5

4. Cf. Charles Higounet, "Les forêts de l'Europe occidentale du Ve au XIe siècle," *Agricoltura e mondo rurale in Occidente nell'alto medioevo*, SSCI 13 (Spoleto 1966), 343–398 (with map).

5. Lampert of Hersfeld, *Annalen anno 1073*, ed. Adolf Schmidt and Wolfgang Dietrich Fritz, FS 13 (Darmstadt, 1957]), 188–189.

6. See Abel's example in *HDWSG* 1 (1971): 173–174. for the areas between the rivers Weser and Diemel. There were only isolated settlements especially along rivers around 500; by 1300, the forest had been dramatically pushed back to the benefit of villages and arable land.

7. Walter Janssen, *Methodische Probleme archäologischer Wüstungsforschung*, Nachrichten der Akademie Göttingen, philosophisch-historische Klasse 2 (1986), 27–56; Janssen, "Dorf- und Dorfformen des 7. bis 12. Jahrhunderts im Lichte neuer Ausgrabungen in Mittel- und Nordeuropa," in Herbert Jankuhn, Rudolf Schützeichel and Fred Schwind, eds., *Das Dorf der Eisenzeit und des frühen Mittelalters. Siedlungsform–wirtschaftliche Funktion–soziale Struktur*, Abhandlungen der Akademie der Wissenschaften Göttingen, philosophisch-historische Klasse 3, 101 (Göttingen, 1977), 338ff.

8. See examples from the sources, Herbert Helbig and Lorenz Weinrich, eds., *Urkunden und erzählende Quellen zur deutschen Ostsiedlung im Mittelalter*, FS 26a/b (Darmstadt, 3rd ed. 1985]; Walter Schlesinger, ed., *Die deutsche Ostsiedlung des Mittelalters als Problem der europäischen Geschichte*, VuF 18 (Sigmaringen, 1975).

9. The most recent research on this subject, Margaret Wade Labarge's *Mediaeval Travellers: The Rich and Restless* (London, 1982), deals not accidentally

with the upper levels of society despite the fact that she restricts herself to the late Middle Ages. Concerning urban streets, see Jean-Pierre Leguay's recent *La rue au moyen âge* (Rennes, 1984).

10. Richer, *Historiae* 4, 50, ed. Robert Latouche, Les classiques de l'histoire de France au moyen âge 17 (Paris, 1937, reprinted, 1964), 224ff.

11. Epistola Einhardi nr. 52 (*MG, Epp.* 5, p. 135).

12. See Anna-Dorothee von den Brincken, "Mappa mundi und chronographia. Studien zur *imago mundi* des abendländischen Mittelalters," *DA* 24 (1968): 118–186; Günther Hamann, "Das Weltbild im 11. Jahrhundert im Rahmen der Kartographie des Mittelalters," *JGF* (1982): 53–86; Patrick Gautier Dalche, "Tradition et renouvellement dans la répresentation de l'espace géographique au IXe siécle," *Studi mediaevali 3*, 24 (1983): 121–165.

13. Concerning the broadening of one's horizons by way of penitential pilgrimages, see Heinrich Fichtenau, "Gentiler und europäischer Horizont an der Schwelle des ersten Jahrtausends," *Römische Historische Mitteilungen* 23 (1981): 227–243. Concerning hostels, see Hans Conrad Peyer "Gastfreundschaft und kommerzielle Gastlichkeit im Mittelalter," *HZ* 235 (1982): 265–288; Hans Conrad Peyer in collaboration with Elisabeth Müller-Luckner, eds., *Gastfreundschaft, Taverne und Gasthaus im Mittelalter*, Schriften des Historischen Kollegs. Kolloquien 3 (München-Wien, 1983). Concerning pilgrimages, see Ludwig Schmugge, *Gastfreundschaft, Taverne und Gasthaus im Mittelalter*, 37–60; Schmugge, "Die Anfänge des organisierten Pilgerverkehrs im Mittelalter," *QFIAB* 64 (1984): 1–83.

14. See Norbert Elias, *Über die Zeit*, Arbeiten zur Wissenssoziologie 2 (Frankfurt, 1984); Ferdinand Seibt, "Die Zeit als Kategorie der Geschichte und als Kondition des historischen Sinns," *Die Zeit Schriften der Karl-Friedrich von Siemens-Stiftung* 6 (Munich-Vienna, 1983), 145–188; Jean Leclercq, "Zeiterfahrung und Zeitbegriff im Spätmittelalter," in Albert Zimmermann, ed., Antiqui und Moderni. *Traditionsbewusstsein und Fortschrittsbewusstsein im späten Mittelalter*, Miscellanea Mediaevalia 9 (Berlin-New York, 1979), 1–20, esp. 2ff. (concerning the early Middle Ages); Arnold Esch, "Zeitalter und Menschenalter. Die Perspektiven historischer Periodisierung," *HZ* 239 (1984): 309–351; Hans-Ulrich Grimm, " 'Zeit' als 'Beziehungssymbol': Die soziale Genese des bürgerlichen Zeitbewusstseins im Mittelalter," *GWU* 37 (1986): 199–221.

15. For a description of such a clepsydra from the thirteenth century, cf. Albert d'Haenens, "La Clepsydre de Villers," in *Klösterliche Sachkultur* (Vienna, 1980), 321–342

16. Annales Regni Francorum anno 807, ed. Reinhold Rau, FS 5 (Darmstadt, 1955), 84ff.

17. Thus, for instance Honorius Augustudunensis, Imago mundi 2, 4–10, ed. V. I. J. Flint, *Archives d'histoire doctrinale et littéraire du Moyen Age* 57 (1983): 93f.

18. For a number of years, French research has devoted an entire branch of research to this topic. See Emmanuel Le Roy Ladurie, *Histoire du climat depuis l'an mil* (1967) (*Times of Feast, Times of Famine. A History of Climate since the year 1000* (London, 1972); P. Alexandre, "Histoire du climat et sources narratives

du Moyen Age," *MA* 80 (1974): 101–116, demands a collection of textual refer-
ences based on a critique of the sources. Finally, Ulrich Willerding, "Über Klima-
Entwicklung und Vegetationsverhältnisse im Zeitraum Eisenzeit bis Mittelalter," in
Das Dorf der Eisenzeit, 357–405, and H. H. Lamb, "Climate in the Last Thousand
Years: Natural Climatic Fluctuations and Change," in Hermann Flohn and Roberto
Fantechi, eds., *The Climate of Europe: Past, Present, and Future. Natural and Man-
induced Climatic Changes. An European Perspective* (Dordrecht-Boston-Lancaster,
1984), 25ff., especially, 35.

    19. Annales regni Francorum anno 820 (pp. 124f.).

    20. See the summary in Fritz Curschmann, *Hungersnöte im Mittelalter. Ein
Beitrag zur deutschen Wirtschaftsgeschichte des 8. bis 13. Jahrhunderts*, Leipziger
Studien aus dem Gebiet der Geschichte 6, 1 (Leipzig, 1900; reprinted, Aalen, 1970).
Based on an examination of rationing in monasteries for monks and lay people, and
a calculation of the corresponding caloric intake, Michel Rouche, in "La faim à
l'epoque carolingienne: essai sur quelques types de rations alimentaires," *RH* 250
(1973): 295–320, disputes the existence of a genuine widespread famine and is
thinking more of a psychologically induced fear of hunger; still, numerous reports
state the facts rather clearly. A critical position was taken by Jean-Claude Hocquet,
"Le pain, le vin et la juste mésure à la table des moines carolingiens," *Annales ESC*
40 (1985): 661–686.

    21. Cf. Annales Fuldenses anno 881, ed. Reinhold Rau, FS 7 (Darmstadt,
2nd. ed., 1960), 114f.

    22. Notker, *Gesta Karoli* 1, 23, ed. Reinhold Rau, FS 7 (Darmstadt, 2nd.
ed., 1960), 354ff.

    23. Annales Fuldenses anno 850, ed. Reinhold Rau, FS 7 (Darmstadt, 2nd.
ed., 1960), 40ff.

    24. *MG, Capit.* 1, nr. 44, chap. 4 (pp. 122f.) from the beginning of the ninth
century.

    25. *MG, Capit.* 1, nr. 124, anno 807 (pp. 245f.).

    26. Annales Xantenses anno 873, ed. Reinhold Rau, FS 6 (Darmstadt, 1958),
pp. 370f.

    27. Cf. Michel Mollat, *Die Armen im Mittelalter* (München, 1984) (French
1st edition, Paris, 1978); Egon Boshof, "Untersuchungen zur Armenfürsorge im
fränkischen Reich des 9. Jahrhunderts," *AKG* 58 (1976): 265–339; Boshof, "Armenfürsorge im Frühmittelalter: Xenodochium, matricula, hospitale pauperum,"
VSWG 71 (1984): 153–174; Uta Lindgren, "Europas Armut. Probleme, Methoden,
Ergebnisse einer Untersuchungsserie," *Saeculum* 28 (1977): 396–418; Hans-Werner
Goetz, "'Unterschichten' im Gesellschaftsbild karolingischer Geschichtsschreiber
und Hagiographen," in Hans Mommsen and Winfried Schulze, eds., *Vom Elend
der Handarbeit. Probleme historischer Unterschichtenforschung*, Geschichte und
Gesellschaft. Bochumer Historische Studien 24 (Stuttgart, 1981), 108–130.

    28. Cf. *Skelette erzählen . . . Menschen des frühen Mittelalters im Spiegel der
Anthropologie und Medizin*, Ausstellung des Württembergischen Landesmuseums
(Stuttgart, 2nd ed., 1983), where the results obtained from Alemannic cemeteries for
the sixth-eighth centuries are presented. Concerning miraculous cures, see Norbert

Ohler, "Zuflucht der Armen. Zu den Mirakeln des heiligen Anno," *Rheinische Vierteljahresblätter* 48 (1984): 98–118; for the most recent research concerning illnesses and medical care, cf. Anette Niederhellmann, *Arzt und Heilkunde in den frühmittelalterlichen Leges. Eine Wort- und sachkundliche Untersuchun*, Arbeiten zur Frühmittelalterforschung 12 (Berlin-New York, 1983).

29. Gerhard, *Vita Oudalrici* 4, ed. Hatto Kallfelz, *Lebensbeschreibungen einiger Bischöfe des 10.-12. Jahrhunderts*, FS (1973), 74f.

30. To be sure, skeletal analyses vary greatly from village to village, so that averages such as these must be viewed with caution. Concerning infant mortality, more precise research is still to be done.

31. See Rolf Sprandel, *Altersschicksal und Altersmoral. Die Geschichte der Einstellungen zum Altern nach der Pariser Bibelexegese des 12.-16. Jahrhunderts*, Monographien zur Geschichte des Mittelalters 22 (Stuttgart, 1981).

32. *Ruodlieb* 15, verse 1ff., ed. Karl Langosch, *Waltharius, Ruodlieb, Märchenepen. Lateinische Epik des Mittelalters mit deutschen Versen* (Darmstadt, 1956), 198ff.

33. Today's highly contested culture concept is taken in a rather broad sense here, including everything people create while shaping their environment. Because of the scope of this study, the "culture of everyday life" will be all which is of interest here; the spiritual-educated-artistic sphere, commonly classified as "culture," must be set aside.

34. Concerning music (as a science, in church, in everyday life), which will not be discussed here in any great detail, see Peter Gülke, *Mönche, Bürger, Minnesänger. Musik in der Gesellschaft des europäischen Mittelalters* (Vienna-Cologne-Graz, 1975). Concerning the courts, see Sabine Zak, *Musik als 'Ehr und Ziehr' im mittelalterlichen Reich. Studien zur Musik im höfischen Leben, Recht und Zeremoniell* (Neuss, 1979).

35. See Walter Janssen, "Essen und Trinken im frühen und hohen Mittelalter aus archäologischer Sicht," in T. J. Hoekstra, ed., *Liber Castellorum. 40 Variaties op het thema kasteel* (Zutphen, 1981), 324–337; Paul Rachbauer, "Essen und Trinken um 1200," *Nibelungenlied*, Ausstellung Hohenems 1979, Ausstellungskatalog des Vorarlberger Landesmuseums 86 (Bregenz, 1979), 135–147; *Manger et boire au moyen âge. Actes du Colloque de Nice* (1982), 2 vols. (Nice, 1984) (I had no access to this work).

36. See for example, though only for the fifteenth and sixteenth century, Karl-Heinz Knörzer and Gustav Müller, "Mittelalterliche Fäkalien-Fassgrube mit Pflanzenresten aus Neuss," in *Beiträge zur Archäologie des Mittelalters*, Beihefte der Bonner Jahrbücher 28 (Cologne-Graz, 1968), 131–169.

37. Concerning the technology employed in brewing beer, see R. van Uytven, *Lexikon des Mittelalters* 2, columns 135ff.

38. See Ulrich Willerding, "Anbaufrüchte der Eisenzeit und des frühen Mittelalters, ihre Anbauformen, Standortverhältnisse und Erntemethoden," in *Das Dorf der Eisenzeit*, 126–196.

39. *Formul* Sangallenses no. 15 (*MG, Formulae*, 405f.).

40. *Capitularia Ansegisi* 1, 138 (*MG, Capit.* 1, 412).

41. See Hermann Hinz, "Die karolingische Keramik in Mittelalter," in *Karl der Grosse. Lebenswerk und Nachleben*, 3 vols. (Düsseldorf, 1965), 262–287; Uwe Lobbedy, *Untersuchungen mittelalterlicher Keramik vornehmlich aus Südwestdeutschland, Arbeiten zur Frühmittelalter-Forschung* 3 (Berlin, 1968).

42. See Max Hasse, "Neues Hausgerät, neue Häuser, neue Kleider—Eine Betrachtung der städtischen Kultur im 13. und 14. Jahrhundert sowie ein Katalog der metallenen Hausgeräte," *Zeitschrift für Archäologie des Mittelalters* 7 (1979): 7–83 (contains retrospectives of earlier times).

43. See Michèle Beaulieu, *Le costume antique et médiéval*, Que sais-je 501 (Paris, 3rd ed., 1961); François Boucher, *A History of Costume in the West* (London, 1967).

44. Notker, *Gesta Karoli* 1, 34 (pp. 372ff.). As to the actual clothes Charlemagne wore, see Einhard, *Vita Karoli* 23, ed. Reinhold Rau, FS 5 (Darmstadt, 1955), 194–195.

45. Cf. Heinrich Fichtenau, *Lebensordnungen des 10. Jahrhunderts. Studien über Denkart und Existenz im einstigen Karolingerreich*, Monographien zur Geschichte des Mittelalters 30, 2 vols. (Stuttgart, 1984), 11–12.

46. See K.-S. Kramer, "Brauchtum," *Lexikon des Mittelalters* 2 (1983), columns 580ff.

Chapter II

1. See Karl Bosl, "Die 'familia' als Grundstruktur der mittelalterlichen Gesellschaft," *ZBLG* 38 (1975), 403–424; concerning the disintegration of the gentility of antiquity and its organizations as the basis for the medieval family, see Adel' L'vovna Jastrebickaja, "Die Familie als soziale Gruppe der mittelalterlichen Gesellschaft," *JGF* 6 (1982): 185–193. Concerning the family as a sociological model, see Heinrich Fichtenau, *Lebensordnungen des 10. Jahrhunderts. Studien über Denkart und Existenz im einstigen Karolingerreich*, Monographien zur Geschichte des Mittelalters 30 (Stuttgart, 1984), 165ff. Cf. Hans K. Schulze, *Grundstrukturen der Verfassung im Mittelalter*, 2 vols. (Stuttgart, 1985–86), 9ff.

2. Cf. Bernhard Schimmelpfennig, "Zölibat und Lage der 'Priestersöhne' vom 11. bis 14. Jahrhundert," *HZ* 227 (1978): 1–44; Ann Llewellyn Barstow, *Married Priests and the Reforming Papacy: The Eleventh Century Debates*, Texts and Studies in Religion 12 (New York-Toronto, 1982); concerning reform legislation and its effects, see Jan Gaudemet, "Le célibat ecclésiastique. Le droit et la pratique du XIᵉ au XIIIᵉ siècle," *ZRG, Kan. Abt.* 99 (1982): 1–31.

3. Cf. Réginald Grégoire, "Il matrimonio mistico," in *Il matrimonio nella società altomedievale*, vol. 2 , *SSCI* 24 (Spoleto, 1977), 701–817.

4. Concerning this section, cf. Georges Duby and Jacques Le Goff, eds., *Famille et parenté dans l'occident médiéval. Actes du Colloque de Paris [1974] organisé par l'École pratique des hautes études (VIᵉ section) en collaboration avec le Collège de France et l'École Française de Rome*, Collection de l'École Française de Rome 30 (Rome, 1977); Thomas Schuler, "Familien im Mittelalter," in Heinz Reif, ed., *Die Familie in der Geschichte*, Kleine Vandenhoeck-Reihe 1474 (Göttingen,

1982), 28–60; David Herlihy, *Medieval Households*, Studies in Cultural History (Cambridge, Mass.-London, 1985); Fichtenau, *Lebensordnungen*, 113ff.; Alexander Callender Murray, *Germanic Kinship Structure: Studies in Law and Society in Antiquity and Early Middle Ages*, Studies and Texts 65 (Toronto, 1983); for general information on pre-industrial society, see Michael Mitterauer, "Zur Struktur alteuropäischer Gesellschaftssysteme am Beispiel des mittelalterlichen Österreich," in *Grundtypen alteuropäischer Sozialformen. Haus und Gemeinde in vorindustriellen Gesellschaften*, Kultur und Gesellschaft. Neue Historische Forschungen 5 (Stuttgart-Bad Cannstatt, 1979), 13–34. Mitterauer argues against Bosl's concept of *familia* though both views seem compatible.

5. See Ruotger, *Vita Brunonis* 42, ed. Hatto Kallfelz, *Lebensbeschreibungen einiger Bischöfe des 10.-12. Jahrhunderts*, FS 22 (Darmstadt, 1973), 242ff., on the occasion of Pentecost Sunday 965, when Otto the Great met with his brother, the archbishop of Cologne, his mother Mathilde, his sister Gerberga, the queen of France, and his sons and nephews.

6. See Otto Gerhard Oexle, "Die Gegenwart der Toten," in Herman Braet and Werner Verbeke, eds., *Death in the Middle Ages*, Mediaevalia Lovaniensia 1, 9 (Louvain, 1983), 19–77.

7. Because of varying forms within the different spheres of life, the house as a dwelling shall be discussed in subsequent chapters.

8. Cf. Otto Brunner, *Land und Herrschaft. Grundfragen der territorialen Verfassungsgeschichte Österreichs im Mittelalter* (Wien-Wiesbaden, 4th ed., 1959), esp. 240ff (an English translation by Howard Kaminsky and James Melton is coming from the University of Pennsylvania Press); Walter Schlesinger, "Herrschaft und Gefolgschaft in der germanisch-deutschen Verfassungsgeschichte (1953)," in Hellmut Kämpf, ed., *Herrschaft und Staat im Mittelalter*, WdF 2 (Darmstadt, 1955), 135–190. For a critical response to Brunner and Schlesinger, see Karl Kroeschell, *Haus und Herrschaft im frühen deutschen Recht. Ein methodischer Versuch*, Göttinger rechtswissenschaftliche Studien 70 (Göttingen, 1968), who points out the independent quality of royal rule.

9. Concerning fiefs, a capitulary dating from 821 awarded her one third of the *conlaboratus*, that is, the proceeds (*MG, Capit.* 1, no. 148, cap. 9, p. 301).

10. Cf. Kroeschell, "Söhne und Töchter im germanischen Erbrecht," in Götz Landwehr, ed., *Studien zu den germanischen Volksrechten. Gedächtnisschrift für Wilhelm Ebel*, Rechtshistorische Reihe 1 (Frankfurt-Bern, 1982), 87–116.

11. See the restrictive treatment in Felix Genzmer, "Die germanische Sippe als Rechtsgebilde," ZRG, Germ. Abt. 67 (1950): 34–49; also Karl Kroeschel, "Die Sippe im germanischen Recht," *ZRG, Germ. Abt.* 77 (1960): 1–25; against Walter Schlesinger, "Randbemerkungen zu drei Aufsätzen über Sippe, Gefolgschaft und Treue," in *Alteuropa und die moderne Gesellschaft*. Festschrift Otto Brunner (Göttingen, 1963), 11–59. Concerning a critique of a Germanic "clan"-based society, see now Murray, *Germanic Kinship*, 33ff; on the other hand, David Herlihy, in his *Medieval Households*, 44ff., attributes yet more functions to the Germanic clan.

12. Gregor von Tours, *Historien* 6, 36, ed. Rudolf Buchner, FS 3 (Darmstadt, 1955), 62f.

13. Even among the Romance peoples, clan or tribal names disappeared beginning with the fourth century. Family names are not used until the twelfth/thirteenth centuries, first in the southern and western German regions in the form of names which were derived from everyday life (references to occupation or the homestead, nicknames); see Hugo Stever, "Zur Motivik mittelalterlicher und neuzeitlicher Namengebung," in Bruno Boesch, ed., *Alemannica. Landeskundliche Beiträge*, FS 3 (= Alemannisches Jahrbuch 1973/75) (Bühl, Baden 1976), 143–156.

14. For basic information on the following subject, see Karl Schmid, "Zur Problematik von Familie, Sippe und Geschlecht, Haus und Dynastie beim mittelalterlichen Adel," *ZGO* 105 (1957): 1–62; Karl Schmid, "Über das Verhältnis von Person und Gemeinschaft im früheren Mittelalter," *FMSt* 1 (1967): 225–249. Concerning the cognatic character of the family during the early Middle Ages, cf. Murray, *Germanic Kinship*, 113ff.

15. For example, Chlothar = *kluto-hari*, had the meaning of 'famous warrior', Nithard that of 'severe hatred'.

16. In his "Untersuchungen zur Namensgebung im frühen Mittelalter nach den bayerischen Quellen des 8. und 9. Jahrhunderts," *ZBLG* 45 (1982): 3–21, Ludwig Holzfurtner argued against the handing down of names by citing the relationships among relatives attested by the Bavarian inheritance records; in fact, the handing down of names ought to be considered even more significant, since in each instance we are only familiar with a few relatives. In Swabia, entries concerning groupings of relatives in the memorial books (*Gedenkbücher*) speak for themselves. Concerning the Alamannic upper classes, cf. Hans-Werner Goetz, "Zur Namengebung in der alamannischen Grundbesitzerschicht der Karolingerzeit. Ein Beitrag zur Familienforschung," *ZGO* 133 (1985): 1–41.

17. Gerhard, *Vita Bennonis* 1, ed. Hatto Kallfelz, *Lebensbeschreibungen einiger Bischöfe des 10.-12. Jahrhunderts*, FS 29 (Darmstadt, 1973), 376–377.

18. Entries into the Book of Fraternization of Reichenau, which were intended to be classified in accordance with the respective spiritual communities, were soon broken up by family entries. Cf. in chapter 3, the section on the relationship of monasteries among themselves and with the outside world.

19. See Joachim Wollasch, "Eine adlige Familie des frühen Mittelalters. Ihr Selbstverständnis und ihre Wirklichkeit," *AKG* 39 (1957): 150–188. Edition Pierre Riché, *Sources chrétiennes* 225 (Paris, 1975).

20. See Lutz von Padberg, "Heilige und Familie. Studien zur Bedeutung familiengebundener Aspekte in den Viten des Verwandten- und Schülerkreises von Willibrord, Bonifatius und Liudger," Dissertation Münster, 1981.

21. Cf. Wilhelm Störmer, *Früher Adel. Studien zur politischen Führungsschicht im fränkisch-deutschen Reich vom 8. bis zum 11. Jahrhundert*, Monographien zur Geschichte des Mittelalters 6 (Stuttgart, 1973), especially 55; Herlihy, *Medieval Households*, 79ff.

22. The trend can be well observed in the case of the Guelfs: The "Genealogia Welforum" of 1130 was followed by the "Historia Welforum" in 1170, Erich König, ed., *Schwäbische Chroniken der Stauferzeit* 1 (Sigmaringen, 1978).

23. Cf. Martin Heinzelmann, "Beobachtungen zur Bevölkerungsstruktur einiger grundherrschaftlicher Siedlungen im karolingischen Bayern," *FMSt* 11 (1977): 202–217; 12 (1978): 433–437; Carl I. Hammer, "Family and familia in early-medieval Bavaria," in Richard Wall et al., *Family Forms in Historic Europe* (Cambridge, 1983), 217–248.

24. See Charles Verlinden, "Le 'mariage' des esclaves," in *Il matrimonio nella società altomedievale*, 569–601.

25. See Council of Orléans 541, can. 24 (*MG, Conc.* 1, 92); Verberie 753, can. 8 (*MG, Capit.* 1, no. 16, pp. 40f.).

26. *Epistola Einhardi* no. 37 (*MG, Epp.* 5, 128). This privilege of a lord even extended to vassals: Einhard himself intervened on behalf of a vassal who had planned to marry the daughter of one of his followers (*Epistola Einhardi* no. 62, p. 140).

27. Typical examples from the *Polyptychon* of Saint-Germain-des-Prés, ed. Auguste Longnon (Paris, 1895) are:

Arnulfus ∞*Farberta*: son *Farbert*us (Celle-les-Bordes 2); *Sointhad*us ∞Teutberga: daughter *Sointhada* (Celle-les-Bordes 21); *Adal*marus ∞Winegildis: sons *Adal*bertus, *Adal*modus, *Adal*ongus, *Adal*gis (Celle-les-Bordes 56); *Anse*garius ∞ INGalteus: daughters *Anse*gildis, *ING*risma (Gagny 2); *Hilde*gaudus ∞Agen-TRUDIS: daughter *Hil*TRUDIS (Gagny 17).

28. *MG, Formulae, Collectio Sangallensis* 18 (p. 406); concerning marriage, see also W. Knoch et al., the article on marriage ("Ehe") in *Lexikon des Mittelalters* 3 (1986), cols. 1616ff.

29. Cf. Michael M. Sheehan, "Choice of Marriage Partners in the Middle Ages: Development and Mode of Application of a Theory of Marriage," *Studies in Medieval and Renaissance History*, n.s. (1978): 3–33.

30. According to Herlihy, *Medieval Households*, 73ff., marriage partners during the early Middle Ages were supposed to be preferably the same age; it was not until approximately 1200 that the differences increased, husbands often approaching the late twenties at the time of the marriage.

31. See Silvia Konecny, "Eherecht und Ehepolitik unter Ludwig dem Frommen," *MIÖG* 85 (1977): 1–21.

32. By overemphasizing the importance of the dower, earlier scholarship referred to the practice as "marriage by purchase" (Kaufehe).

33. *MG, DLD* 108, dating from 862.

34. Cf. the manor house code of Burchard of Worms of 1023/25, chap. 1, ed. Lorenz Weinreich, *Quellen zur deutschen Verfassungs, Wirtschafts- und Sozialgeschichte bis 1250*, FS 32 (Darmstadt, 1977), no. 23, pp. 90f.

35. The Synod of Ver under Pepin (*MG, Capit.* 1, no. 14, cap. 15, p. 36) prescribed *publicae nuptiae*. A favorite example is the wedding of Lemberslint to Gotelint in *Helmbreht* which is performed by an eloquent old man (v. 1503ff.), yet one must not overlook the fact that we are dealing here with a satire whose intention was to point out the uncourtly aspects of the ceremony.

36. Tit. 99, ed. Karl August Eckhardt, *Gesetze des Merowingerreiches* [= Germanenrechte] (Göttingen, 1956), 414–415.

37. Thietmar von Merseburg, *Chronik* 4, 39–42; 6, 86, ed. Werner Trillmilch, FS 9 (Darmstadt, 1957), 154ff., 334–335.

38. See Silvia Konecny, *Die Frauen des karolingischen Königshauses. Die politische Bedeutung der Ehe und die Stellung der Frau in der fränkischen Herrscherfamilie vom 7. bis zum 10. Jahrhundert*, Dissertations of the University of Vienna 132 (Vienna, 1976).

39. Regino von Prüm, *De synodalibus causis* 2, 134, ed. F. G. A. Wasserschleben (Leipzig, 1840, reprinted Graz, 1964), 266.

40. Regino, *De synodalibus* 2, 146, pp. 269f. It is true that Regino quotes from an old, late Roman law from the Codex Theodosianus.

41. In addition to Korbinian Ritzer's *Formen, Riten und religiöses Brauchtum der Eheschliessung in den christlichen Kirchen des ersten Jahrtausends*, Liturgiewissenschaftliche Quellen und Forschungen 38 (Münster 1962), cf. Cyrille Vogel, "Les rites de la célébration du mariage; leur signification dans la formation du lien durant le haut moyen âge," in *Il matrimonio* 1, 397–472.

42. Gerhard, *Vita Oudalrici* 9, ed. Hatto Kallfelz, *Lebensbeschreibungen einiger Bischöfe des 10.–12. Jahrhunderts*, FS 22 (Darmstadt, 1973), 92–93.

43. Cf. Marc Glasser, *Marriage in Medieval Hagiography*, Studies in Medieval and Renaissance History, n.s. 4 (1981): 1–34.

44. Gregor von Tours, *Historien* I, 47 (pp. 46ff.).

45. See Heinrich J. F. Reinhardt, *Die Ehelehre der Schule des Anselm von Laon. Eine theologie- und kirchenrechtgeschichtliche Untersuchung zu den Ehetexten der frühen Pariser Schule des 12. Jahrhunderts*, Beiträge zur Geschichte und Thelogie des Mittelalters, neue Folge 14 (Münster, 1974).

46. During marriage trials in the late Middle Ages, wives attempted time and again to prove that they were the legitimate spouses by insisting that they had been the first ones to sleep with a certain man (a fact which did not necessarily enhance their good reputation).

47. See Rudolf Weigand, "Liebe und Ehe bei den Dekretisten des 12. Jahrhunderts," in Willy van Hoecke und Andries Welkenhuysen, eds., *Love and Marriage in the Twelfth Century*, Mediaevalia Lovaniensia 1, 8 (Leuven, 1981), 41–58.

48. Concerning the contribution made by the penitentials, cf. Raoul Manselli, "Il matrimonio nei penitenziali," *Il matrimonio* 1, 287–319; Raymond Kottje, "Ehe und Eheverständnis in den vorgratianischen Bußbüchern," in *Love and Marriage*, 18–40.

49. See Council of Tribur of 895 (*MG, Capit.* 2, no. 252, cap. 40, pp. 236f.)

50. Chap. 45a, p. 239.

51. See *Vita Norberti* 14, ed. Hatto Kallfelz, *Lebensbeschreibungen einiger Bischöfe des 10.–12. Jahrhunderts*, FS 22 (Darmstadt, 1973), 504ff.

52. *MG, Capit.* 1, no. 7, cap. 2 (p. 15).

53. During the twelfth century, Hugh of St. Victor distinguished in his "De sacramentis christianae fidei," 2, 11, 17 (Migne, *Patrologia Latina* 176, col. 518ff.) between *consanguinitas* (blood relationship), *affinitas* (relationship by marriage), and *spiritualis germanitas* (sponsorship) with respectively varying degrees.

54. *MG, Conc.* 1, chap. 22 (p. 92).

55. Cf. Constance B. Bouchard, "Consanguinity and noble marriages in the 10th and 11th centuries," *Speculum* 56 (1981): 268–287.

56. Decree of Verberie of 753 (*MG, Capit.* 1, nr. 16, chap. 6, p. 40); decree of Compiègne of 757 (*Monumenta*, nr. 15, cap. 7, p. 38)

57. *Monumenta*, cap. 16 (p. 38).

58. De institutione laicali 2, 12 (Migne, *Patrologia Latina* 106, cols. 188ff.) (written prior to 828).

59. *MG, Capit.* 2, no. 252, cap. 38 (p. 235).

60. *Pactus legis Salicae* tit. 100f., ed. Karl August Eckhardt, *Gesetze des Merowingerreiches* [= Germanenrechte] (Göttingen, 1956), 414ff.

61. See *Collectio capitularium Ansegisi* 1, 42 (*MG, Capit.* 1, p. 400); Capitulary of Worms of 829 (*MG, Capit.* 2, no. 193, cap. 3, pp. 18f.); concerning the penance books, see Kottje, "Ehe und Eheverständnis," 26ff.

62. Gregor von Tours, *Historien* 4, 26 (pp. 226ff.).

63. The episode is amply documented by Regino of Prüm in his *Chronik* *anno 864–869*, ed. Reinhold S. Rau, FS 7 (Darmstadt, 2nd ed. 1960), 192ff./218ff.), by the Acts of the Synods (*MG, Capit.* 2, no. 305ff., pp. 463ff.) and papal letters (cf. *MG, Epp.* 6, 207ff.).

64. Concerning her relationship, cf. Karl Schmid, "Ein karolingischer König-seintrag im Gedenkbuch von Remiremont," *FMSt* 2 (1968): 128ff.

65. The sources are summarized in Karl Kroeschell, *Deutsche Rechtsge-schichte* 1 (Reinbek, 1972), no. 37, pp. 144ff.

66. Lampert von Hersfeld, *Annalen anno 1069*, ed. Adolf Schmidt and Wolfgang Dietrich Fritz, FS 13 (Darmstadt, 1957), 114ff.

67. The literature concerning women in the Middle Ages can hardly be surveyed at a glance any longer. Therefore, the bibliography lists only the most important works. Concerning the late Middle Ages, see now Claudia Opitz, *Frauenalltag im Mittelalter. Biographien des 13. und 14. Jahrhunderts*, Ergebnisse der Frauenforschung 5 (Weinheim-Basel, 1985).

68. See Suzanne Fonay Wemple, *Women in Frankish Society: Marriage and the Cloister 500 to 900* (Philadelphia, 1981).

69. *Vita Liutbirgae* 5, ed. Ottokar Menzel, *MG, Dt. MA* 3 (Leipzig, 1937), 13.

70. By way of exception, Bonizo of Sutri does list "ruling women" (*mulieres imperantes*) in his handbook for princes (*Fürstenspiegel*); cf. Walter Berschin, "Herrscher, ⟨Richter⟩, Ritter, Frauen . . . Die Laienstände nach Bonizo," in *Love and Marriage*, 116–129.

71. *Pactus legis Salicae* 20 (pp. 182ff.).

72. The manuscripts list different rates here.

73. *Lex Alamannorum* 56, ed. Karl August Eckhardt, *Germanenrechte* (Witzenhausen, 1962), 47.

74. See *MG, Capit.* 1, no. 138 of 818/819, cap. 21 (p. 278).

75. See the laws of the city of Freiburg dating from the end of the twelfth century: *omnis mulier est genoz viri sui in hac civitate et vir mulieris similiter, Elenchus fontium Historiae Urbanae* 1, no. 55 (Leiden, 1967), 98.

76. Cf. Robert Fossier, "La femme dans les sociétés occidentales," in *La femme dans les civilisations du Xᵉ au XIIᵉ siècle,* Cahiers de civilisation médiévale 20 (1977): 93–104; Marie-Thérèse d'Alverny, "Comment les théologiens et les philosophes voient la femme," in *La femme,* 105–129.

77. Hugh of St. Victor, *De sacramentis christianae fidei* 1, 6, 35 (Migne, *Patrologia Latina* 176, col. 284); Petrus Lombardus, *Sententiae* 2, dist. 18, c. 2, *Spicilegium Bonaventurianum* 4 (Rome, 3rd ed. 1971), 416f..

78. Cf. Jane Tibbets Schulenburg, "Sexism and the celestial gynaeceum from 500 to 1200," *Journal of Medieval History* 4 (1978): 117–133.

79. There were approximately seventy convents in the German-speaking area c. 900.

80. Wemple, *Women in Frankish Society,* 190–191.

81. See Herbert Grundmann, *Religiöse Bewegungen im Mittelalter. Untersuchungen über die geschichtlichen Zusammenhänge zwischen Ketzerei, den Bettelorden und der religiösen Frauenbewegung im 12. und 13. Jahrhundert und über die geschichtlichen Grundlagen der deutschen Mystik* (Berlin, 1935; reprinted Darmstadt, 2nd ed., 1961), 170ff. An English translation by Steven Rowan, *Religious Movements in the Middle Ages,* is pending from Notre Dame University Press.

82. Chap. 1, 23f., ed. Bruno Krusch, *MG, SSrerMerov.* 2 (1888), 372.

83. See Hinkmar of Reims, *De ordine palatii* 5 (22), ed. Thomas Gross and Rudolf Schieffer, *MG, Fontes iuris Germanici antiqui* 3, (2nd. ed. 1980), 72ff.; *Capitulare de villis* 16, ed. Günther Franz, *Quellen zur Geschichte des deutschen Bauernstandes im Mittelalter,* FS 31 (Darmstadt, 2nd ed. 1974), 42–43.

84. Cf. Thilo Vogelsang, *Die Frau als Herrscherin im hohen Mittelalter. Studien zur «consors regni»-Formel,* Göttinger Bausteine zur Geschichtswissenschaft 7 (Göttingen, 1954).

85. Not until Agnes were objections launched culminating in the famous abduction of Henry IV at Kaiserswerth; according to Lampert of Hersfeld, *Annalen anno* 1062 (p. 72ff.), only her moral conduct and the manner in which she ruled were criticized; however, according to Adam of Bremen 3, 34, ed. Werner Trillmich, FS 11 (Darmstadt, 1961), 368ff., female rule itself was the issue.

86. See especially David Herlihy's fundamental study, "Land, Family and Women in Continental Europe, 701–1200," *Traditio* 18 (1962): 89–120, which offers a count of the donations made by women (an average of twelve percent), mentioning by name the mother of the donor (up to more than seven percent); however, his conclusions are controversial.

87. See Wemple, *Women in Frankish Society,* 106ff., concerning the transfer of ownership.

88. *De gloria et honore filii hominis super Matthaeum* 12 (Migne, *Patrologia Latina* 168, col. 1601); cf. Peter Dinzelbacher, "Über die Entdeckung der Liebe im Hochmittelalter," *Saeculum* 32 (1981): 197.

89. See Franco Munari, *Ovid im Mittelalter* (Zürich-Stuttgart, 1960), where the twelfth century is referred to as the *aetas Ovidiana* (p. 5).

90. See Wolfgang Haubrichs, "Deutsche Lyrik," in Henning Krauss, ed., *Europäisches Hochmittelalter, Neues Handbuch der Literaturwissenschaft* 7 (Wiesbaden, 1981), 61ff.

91. William of Malmesbury, *De gestis regum Anglorum* 5, 439, ed. William Stubbs, Rolls Series 90 (1889, reprinted 1964), 510–511.

92. Thus, Joachim Bumke, "Liebe und Ehebruch in der höfischen Gesellschaft," in Rüdiger Krohn, ed., *Liebe als Literatur. Aufsätze zur erotischen Dichtung in Deutschland* (München, 1983), 25–45; Bumke, *Höfische Kultur. Literatur und Gesellschaft im hohen Mittelalter* 2 (München, 1986), 529ff; cf. Sylvette Rouillan-Castex, "L'amour et la société féodale," *RH* 552 (1984): 295–329.

93. See Ulrich Mölk, "Die französische Lyrik," in *Europäisches Hochmittelalter*, 44.

94. Gilbert of Hoyland, *Sermones in Canticum* 31 (Migne, *Patrologia Latina* 184, col. 163). A more restrictive view of the ideal of beauty is presented by Rüdiger Schnell, *Causa Amoris. Liebeskonzeption und Liebesdarstellung in der mittelalterlichen Literatur*, Bibliotheca Germanica 27 (Bern-München, 1985), 185ff.

95. See Alfred Karnein, *Europäisches Hochmittelalter*, 125.

96. 1, 1, ed. E. Trojel (1892, reprinted München, 1964), p. 3. English translation ed. P. G. Walsh (London, 1982).

97. Cf. Bruno Roy, ed., *L'eroticisme au moyen âge. Etudes présentées au Troisième Colloque de l'Institute d'etudes mediévales* (Montréal-Québec, 1977); John T. Noonan, *Empfängnisverhütung. Geschichte ihrer Beurteilung in der katholischen Theologie und im kanonischen Recht*, Walberburger Studien der Albertus-Magnus-Akademie. Theologische Reihe 6 (Mainz, 1969, Engl. 2nd ed. 1967); Pierre J. Payer, "Early Medieval Regulations Concerning Marital Sexual Relations," *Journal of Medieval History* 6 (1980): 353–376; Payer, *Sex and the Penitentials. The Development of a Sexual Code 550–1150* (Toronto-Buffalo-London, 1984).

98. v. 1613ff., ed. Ulrich Pretzel (Tübingen, 4th ed. 1973), 102.

99. v. 7, 118f., ed. Karl Langosch, *Waltharius, Ruodlieb, Märchenepen. Lateinische Epik des Mittelalters mit deutschen Versen* (Darmstadt, 1956), 198ff.

100. Can. 45 (*MG, Capit.* 2, no. 252, p. 239).

101. Concerning the penitentials, cf. Manselli, "Il Matrimonio nei penitenziali," and Kottje, "Ehe und Eheverständis," as well as Payer, *Sex and the Penitentials*.

102. See Jonas of Orléans, *De institutione laicali* 2, 6 (Migne, *Patrologia Latina* 106, cols. 179ff.).

103. Regino, *De synodalibus causis* 2, 250f. (p. 312).

104. Thus, John Boswell, *Christianity, Social Tolerance and Homosexuality. Gay People in Western Europe from the Beginning of the Christian Era to the Fourteenth Century* (Chicago-London, 1980). Also, Albert Gauthier's more discriminating "La sodomie dans le droit canonique médiévale," *L'eroticisme*, 111f. Boswell's thesis of tolerance is criticized by Payer, *Sex and the Pentitentials*, 135ff., and Harry J. Kuster and Raymond J. Cormier, *Studi medievali* III, 25 (1984): 587–610.

105. See Regino, *De synodalibus causis* 2, 369; Hrabanus Maurus, *Poenitentiale* 30 (Migne, *Patrologia Latina* 110, col. 491); Burchard of Worms, *Decretum* 19, 152 (Migne, *Patrologia Latina* 140, cols. 1012–13).

106. See Regino, *De synodalibus causis* 2, 62ff.; Burchard von Worms, *Decretum* 17, 52 (Migne, *Patrologia Latina* 140, col. 931).

107. Burchard of Worms, *Decretum* 19, 156 (140, cols. 1013–14).

108. Liudprand of Cremona, *Antapodosis* 4, 10, ed. Albert Bauer and Reinhold Rau, FS 8 (Darmstadt, 1971), 410ff. William of Conches, *De philosophia mundi* 4, 14 (Migne, *Patrologia Latina* 172, col. 89) held women to be more lascivious than men because their bodies were colder.

109. Liudprand, *Antapodosis* 4, 14 (pp. 416f.).

110. Liudprand, *Antapodosis* 2, 48ff. (pp. 332ff.)

111. *De philosophia mundi* 4, 14 (Migne, *Patrologia Latina* 172, col. 89).

112. *De philosophia mundi* 4, 15 (172, col. 90).

113. *Heilkunde*, Hildegard von Bingen, *Werke* 2, ed. Heinrich Schipperges (Salzburg, 2nd ed. 1957), 208f.

114. Hansueli F. Etter and Jörg E. Schneider, "Zur Stellung von Kind und Frau im Frühmittelalter. Eine archäologisch-anthropologische Synthese," *Zeitschroft für schweizerische Archäologie und Kunstgeschichte* 39 (1982): 48–57.

115. According to archeological evidence from early medieval burial grounds in Swabia, the infant mortality was significantly lower, nine percent lower for children up to the age of six; cf. *Skelette erzählen*, 10f. This issue has not been definitively decided yet.

116. The absolute number of children possibly ranged somewhat higher because we may presume that older (adult) children had already left the home, entered other people's services, or established a family of their own. (The polyptych says nothing about age differences.)

117. Thus, Emily R. Coleman, "L'infanticide dans le Haut Moyen Age," *Annales ESC* 29 (1974): 315–335.

118. See most recently, Herlihy, *Medieval Households*, 63ff.

119. *Vita Liudgeri* 1, 6, ed. Wilhelm Diekamp, *Die Vitae sancti Liudgeri, Die Geschichtsquellen des Bistums Münster* 4 (Münster, 1881), 10–11.

120. See Hansueli F. Etter and Jörg E. Schneider, "Zur Stellung von Kind und Frau im Frühmittelalter. Eine archäologisch-anthropologische Synthese," *Zeitschrift für schweizerische Archäologie und Kunstgeschichte* 39 (1982): 48–57.

121. Cf. Gerhard Schmitz, "Schuld und Strafe. Eine unbekannte Stellungnahme des Rathramnus von Corbie zur Kindestötung," *DA* 38 (1982): 363–387.

122. See, for instance, Petrus Damiani, epistola 8, 4 (Migne, *Patrologia Latina* 144, cols. 468ff.).

123. See Jacques Le Goff, *Kultur des europäischen Mittelalters* (München-Zürich, 1970), 478f.

124. *Vita Karoli* 19, ed. Reinhold Rau, FS 5 (Darmstadt,1955), 190–191.

125. Georges Duby, "Dans la France du Nord-Ouest au XIIᵉ siécle: Les 'Jeunes' dans la société aristocratique," *Annales ESC* 19 (1964): 835–846.

Chapter III

1. Cf. here and everywhere else the maps in the appendix of Friedrich Prinz, *Frühes Mönchtum im Frankenreich. Kultur und Gesellschaft in Gallien,*

den Rheinlanden und Bayern am Beispiel der monastischen Entwicklung (4. - 8. Jahrhundert), 2 vols. (Halle/S., 1892–94; reprinted Darmstadt, 1965).

2. Thus, Arnold Angenendt, *Monachi Peregrini. Studien zu Pirmin und den monastischen Vorstellungen des frühen Mittelalters*, Münstersche Mittelalter Schriften 6 (Münster, 1972), 124ff.

3. Concerning Pirmin, who founded such important monasteries as Hornbach and Reichenau, see Angenendt, *Monachi Peregrini*.

4. See Rudolf Schieffer, *Die Entstehung von Domkapiteln in Deutschland*, Bonner Historische Forschungen 43 (Bonn, 1976), 171ff.

5. See Prinz, *Frühes Mönchtum*, 263ff. Friedrich Prinz, "Monastische Zentren im Frankenreich," *Studi medievali* 19 (1978): 571–590, mentions several other possibilities (including Constantius of Albi). At any rate, the Benedictine rule entered the West via Rome.

6. See Josef Semmler, "Benedictus II: Una regula—una consuetudo," in W. Loudaux and D. Verhelst, eds., *Benedictine Culture 750–1050*, Mediaevalia Lovaniensia II, 11 (Louvain, 1983), 1–49.

7. Cf. Klaus Schreiner, "Mönchtum zwischen asketischem Anspruch und gesellschaftlicher Wirklichkeit. Spiritualität, Sozialverhalten und Sozialverfassung schwäbischer Reformmönche im Spiegel ihrer Geschichtsschreibung," *Zeitschrift für württembergische Landesgeschichte* 41 (1982); 250–307.

8. See Ernst Sackur, *Die Cluniacenser in ihrer kirchlichen und allgemeingeschichtlichen Wirksamkeit bis zur Mitte des 11. Jahrhunderts*, 2 vols. (Halle/S., 1892–94; reprinted Darmstadt, 1965).

9. Cf. Franz J. Felten, *Äbte und Laienäbte im Frankenreich. Studie zum Verhältnis von Staat und Kirche im früheren Mittelalter*, Monographien zur Geschichte des Mittelalters 20 (Stuttgart, 1980).

10. Concerning Cluny, see Joachim Wollasch, "Parenté noble et monachisme réformateur. Observations sur les 'conversions' à la vie monastique aux XIᶜ et XIIᶜ siècles," *RH* 264 (1980): 3–24, section on Cluny.

11. See Karl Schmid, "Adel und Reform in Schwaben," in *Investiturstreit und Reichsverfassung*, VuF 17 (Sigmaringen, 1973), 295–319.

12. See Ruotger, *Vita Brunonis* 10, ed. Hatto Kallfelz, *Lebensbeschreibungen einiger Bischöfe des 10.–12. Jahrhunderts*, FS 22 (Darmstadt, 1973), 192f..

13. Thietmar, *Chronik* 6, 21, ed. Werner Trillmilch, FS 9 (Darmstadt, 1957), 264–265.

14. Concerning Cluny, see Helmut Richter, ed., *Cluny. Beiträge zu Gestalt und Wirkung der cluniazensischen Reform*, WdF 241 (Darmstadt, 1975); Guy de Valous, *Le monachisme clunisien des origines au XVᵉ siécle* (Paris, 2nd ed. 1970); Gerd Tellenbach, ed., *Neue Forschungen über Cluny und die Cluniazenser* (Freiburg i. B., 1959); Johannes Fechter, "Cluny, Adel und Volk. Studien über das Verhältnis des Klosters zu den Ständen (910–1156)," Dissertation, Tübingen, 1966; H. E. J. Cowdrey, *The Cluniacs and the Gregorian Reform* (Oxford, 1970); Neithard Bulst, *Untersuchungen zu den Klosterreformen Wilhelms von Dijon (962–1031)*, Pariser Historische Studien 11 (Bonn, 1973).

15. Cf. Hermann Jakobs, *Die Hirsauer. Ihre Ausbreitung und Rechtsstellung im Zeitalter des Investiturstreites*, Kölner Historische Abhandlungen 4 (Graz-Cologne, 1961).

16. See Hermann Jakobs, *Der Adel in der Klosterreform von St. Blasien*, Kölner Historische Abhandlungen 16 (Graz-Cologne, 1968).

17. Cf. Josef Semmler, *Die Klosterreform von Siegburg. Ihre Ausbreitung und ihr Reformprogramm im 11. und 12. Jahrhundert*, Rheinisches Archiv 53 (Bonn, 1959).

18. Lampert of Hersfeld, *Annalen a. 1075*, ed. Adolf Schmidt and Wolfgang Dietrich Fritz, FS 13 (Darmstadt, 1957), 332f.

19. Lampert, *Annalen a. 1071* (150ff.).

20. Cf. the catalog of the exhibit at Aachen, *Die Zisterzienser*. Cistercian research was the focus at the Berlin seminar on the history of religious orders, discussed: *Zisterzienserstudien*, vols. 1–4 (Berlin, 1975–79); supplement ed. Kaspar Elm (1982). Concerning the hermits in their role as predecessors of this order, see now Henrietta Leyser, *Hermits and the New Monasticism: A Study of Religious Communities in Western Europe, 1000–1150* (London, 1984).

21. See Michael Töpfer, *Die Konversen der Zisterzienser. Untersuchungen über ihren Beitrag zur mittelalterlichen Blüte des Ordens*, Berliner Historische Studien 10 (= Ordensstudien 4) (Berlin, 1983).

22. See Wolfgang Ribbe, "Die Wirtschaftstätigkeit der Zisterzienser im Mittelalter: Agrarwirtschaft," in *Die Zisterzienser*, 203.

23. An assessment of their performance is found in a recent article by Werner Rösener, "Zur Wirtschaftstätigkeit der Zisterzienser im Hochmittelalter," *Zeitschrift für Agrargeschichte und Agrarsoziologie* 30 (1982): 117–148. Accordingly, the clearing activities of the Cistercians must not be overestimated; more often than not, they drained and colonized marshland rather than forests.

24. See Jürgen Miethke, "Bernhard von Clairvaux," in *Die Zisterzienser*, 50–51.

25. *Chronik* 7, 35, ed. Walther Lammers, FS 16 (Darmstadt, 1960), 564f.

26. Jonas, *Vita Columbani* 1, 10, ed. Herbert Haupt, FS 4a (Darmstadt, 1982), 428ff.

27. Wetti, *Vita s. Galli* 10ff., ed. Bruno Krusch, MG, SSrerMerov 4, 262ff.

28. See Prinz, *Frühes Mönchtum*, 544.

29. Altfrid, *Vita Liudgeri* I, 21, ed. Wilhelm Diekamp, *Die Vitae sancti Liudgeri*, Die Geschichtsquellen des Bistums Münster 4 (Münster, 1881), 24–25; *Vita* II, 1, 29, pp. 75ff.; cf. Wilhelm Stüwer, *Die Reichsabtei Werden an der Ruhr*, Germania Sacra, 2d series 12: Das Erzbistum Köln 3 (Berlin-New York, 1980), 88ff.

30. See Wilhelm Kohl, "Bemerkungen zur Typologie sächsischer Frauenklöster in karolingerischer Zeit," in *Untersuchungen zu Kloster und Stift*, Veröffentlichungen des MPI 68 (= Studien zur Germania sacra 14) (Göttingen, 1980), 112–139.

31. See Wilhelm Störmer, "Beobachtungen zur historisch-geographischen Lage der ältesten bayerischen Klöster und ihres Besitzes," *Frühes Mönchtum in Salzburg*, Salzburg-Diskussionen 4 (Salzburg, 1983), 109–123.

32. See Prinz, *Frühes Mönchtum*, map VI.

33. Cf. Josef Semmler, "Traditio und Königsschutz. Studien zur Geschichte der königlichen monasteria," *ZRG, Kan. Abt.*, 76 (1959): 1–33.

34. Concerning the following discussion, see Karl Suso Frank, "Vom Kloster als *scola dominici servitii* zum Kloster *ad servicium imperii*," *SMGBO* 91 (1980): 80–97.

35. See the essays by Karl Schmid, most of which have been collected in his book *Gebetsgedenken und adliges Selbstverständnis im Mittelalter. Ausgewählte Beiträge*. Festgabe zu seinem 60. Geburtstag (Sigmaringen, 1983); also, Franz-Josef Jakobi, "Früh- und hochmittelalterliche Sozialstrukturen im Spiegel liturgischer Quellen," *GWU* 31 (1980): 1–20. Cf. also Karl Schmid and Joachim Wollasch, eds., *Memoria. Der geschichtliche Zeugniswert des liturgischen Gedenkens im Mittelalter*, Münstersche Mittelalter-Schriften 48 (Münster, 1984). The oldest memorial book of St. Peter in Salzburg dates from the eighth century.

36. Hermann Wartmann, ed., *UB der Abtei St. Gallen* 2 (Zürich, 1866), no. 691.

37. See Arnold Angenendt, "Pirmin und Bonifatius. Ihr Verhältnis zu Mönchtum, Bischofsamt und Adel," in Arno Borst, ed., *Mönchtum, Episkopat und Adel zur Gründungszeit des Klosters Reichenau*, VuF 20 (Sigmaringen, 1974), 251–304.

38. See Otto Gerhard Oexle, *Forschungen zu monastischen und geistlichen Gemeinschaften im westfränkischen Bereich*, Münstersche Mittelalter-Schriften 31 (München, 1978), 101–111.

39. *Urkundenbuch der Abtei St. Gallen* 2, no. 697.

40. *MG, Capit.* 1, nr. 22, cap. 72 (p. 60).

41. Concerning teachers' manuals, see Paul Abelson, *The Seven Liberal Arts. A Study in Mediaeval Culture* (New York, 1965); Günter Glauche, *Schullektüre im Mittelalter. Entstehung und Wandlungen des Lektürekanons bis 1200 nach den Quellen dargestellt*, Münchener Beiträge zur Mediävistik und Renaissanceforschung 5 (Munich, 1970).

42. Concerning the period of reforms, see Raymund Kottje, "Klosterbibliotheken und monastische Kultur in der 2. Hälfte des 11. Jahrhunderts," *ZKG* 80 (1969): 145–162.

43. Ordericus Vitalis, *Historia ecclesiastica* 3 (2, 49f.), ed. Marjorie Chibnall, 2 vols. (Oxford, 1980), 50; the quotations are found in Wilhelm Wattenbach, *Das Schriftwesen im Mittelalter* (Leipzig, 3rd. ed. 1896), 431ff.

44. Concerning typical monastic culture, cf. Jean Leclercq, *Wissenschaft und Gottverlangen. Zur Mönchstheologie des Mittelalters* (Düsseldorf, 1963; French, 1957).

45. Cf. Hans Patze, "Klostergründung und Klosterchronik," *Bll. dt. LG* 113 (1977): 89–121; Ludwig Holzfurtner, *Gründung und Gründungsüberlieferung. Quellenkritische Studien zur Gründungsgeschichte der bayerischen Klöster der Agilolfingerzeit und ihrer hochmittelalterlichen Überlieferung*, Münchener Historische Studien, Abt. Bayerische Geschichte 11 (Kallmünz, 1984).

46. *Chronik* 7, 35 (pp. 562–563).

47. See chapter I, n. 27.

48. Cf. Siegfried Epperlein, "Zur weltlichen und kirchlichen Armenfürsorge im karolingischen Imperium. Ein Beitrag zur Wirtschaftspolitik im Frankenreich," *JWG* (1963): 41–50.

49. Georges Duby, Krieger und Bauern. *Die Entwicklung von Wirtschaft und Gesellschaft im frühen Mittelalter* (Frankfurt, 1977; French, 1973), esp. 52ff.

50. See Joachim Wollasch, "Gemeinschaftsbewusstsein und soziale Leistung im Mittelalter," *FMSt* 9 (1975): 268–286.

51. See chapter I, n. 13.

52. *La Regle de Saint Benoît*, ed. Adalbert Vogüé and Jean Naufville, *Sources chrétiennes* 181–186 (Paris, 1971–72), (with commentary), cap. 53, 1f. (vol. 182, p. 610). This and all subsequent translations of the Rule are taken from David Parry, *The Rule of St. Benedict* (London, 1984).

53. Wartmann, *UB der Abtei St. Gallen* 2, no. 572.

54. See Hans Goetting, *Das reichsunmittelbare Kanonissenstift Gandersheim*, Germania sacra, new series 7, Das Bistum Hildesheim 1 (Berlin-New York, 1973), 81ff.

55. Regino of Prüm, *Chronik*, ed. F. Kurze, *MG, SSrG* (1890), 41f.

56. Cf. Karl Schmid, "Religiöses und sippengebundenes Gemeinschaftsbewusstsein in frühmittelalterlichen Gedenkbucheinträgen," *DA* 21 (1965): 18–81. Concerning entries in the memorials, see chapter II.

57. Wartmann, *UB der Abtei St. Gallen* 2, no. 697.

58. Concerning the military service of bishops and abbots, see Friedrich Prinz, *Klerus und Krieg im früheren Mittelalter: Untersuchungen zur Rolle der Kirche beim Aufbau der Königsherrschaft*, Monographien zur Geschichte des Mittelalters 2 (Stuttgart, 1971).

59. See Theo Kölzer "Mönchtum und Kirchenrecht. Bemerkungen zu monastischen Kanonessammlungen der vorgratianischen Zeit," *ZRG, Kan. Abt.* 100 (1983): 121–142.

60. Cf. Hans-Peter Wehlt, *Reichsabtei und König, dargestellt am Beispiel der Abtei Lorsch mit Ausblicken auf Hersfeld, Stablo und Fulda*, Veröffentlichungen des MPI 28 (Göttingen, 1970).

61. See Josef Semmler, "Karl der Grosse und das fränkische Mönchtum [1965]," in Friedrich Prinz, ed., *Mönchtum und Gesellschaft im Frühmittelalter*, WdF 312 (Darmstadt, 1976), 204–264; Felten, *Äbte und Laienäbte im Frankenreich*.

62. See Felten, *Äbte und Laienäbte im Frankenreich*, 248–249.

63. *Gesta abbatum Fontanellensium* 10, ed. S. Loewenfeld, *MG, SSrG* (1886), 29ff.

64. Lampert, *Annalen a. 1063* (80–81).

65. *MG, DK I.*, 19.

66. *MG, DLD*, 70.

67. Hans-Peter Wehlt, *Reichsabtei und König, dargestellt am Beispiel der Abtei Lorsch mit Ausblicken auf Hersfeld, Stablo und Fulda*, Veröffentlichungen des MPI 28 (Göttingen, 1970), 75–76. Concerning the *servitium*, see Carlrichard Brühl, *Fodrum, Gistum, Servitium Regis. Studien zu den wirtschaftlichen Grundlagen des Königtums im Frankenreich und in den fränkischen Nachfolgestaaten Deutschland,*

Frankreich und Italien vom 6. bis zur Mitte des 14. Jahrhunderts, Kölner Historische Abhandlungen 14 (Cologne-Graz, 1968).

68. Cf. Joachim Wollasch, "Kaiser und Könige als Brüder der Mönche. Zum Herrscherbild in liturgischen Handschriften des 9. bis 11. Jahrhunderts," *DA* 40 (1984): 1–20.

69. See Peter Willmes, *Der Herrscher-'Adventus' im Kloster des Frühmittelalters,* Münstersche Mittelalter-Schriften 22 (Munich, 1976).

70. Ekkehard IV, *Casus s. Galli,* 14/16, ed. Hans F. Haefele, FS 10 (Darmstadt, 1980), 40ff.

71. A list dating from 817 (*MG, Capit.* I, no. 171, 349ff.) stipulates which monasteries were obligated to contribute both *dona* and military service, which monasteries gave merely *dona,* and which were to pray. However, during the course of time, military service increased substantially.

72. See Walther Laske, "Zwangsaufenthalt im frühmittelalterlichen Kloster," *ZRG, Kan. Abt.* 95 (1978): 321–330.

73. *MG, Epp.* 4 (Epistolae Variorum no. 33, caps. 2 and 17, 548ff.).

74. *Casus s. Galli,* 5f., pp. 24ff.

75. *Regula Benedicti* 67, 3ff.

76. Richer, *Historiae* 3, 36, ed. Robert Latouche, *Les classiques de l'histoire de France au moyen âge* 17 (Paris, 1937; reprinted, 1964), 44.

77. *Regula Benedicti* 66, 6ff.

78. This copy merely represents a simplified drawing; the original is in the form of a large parchment leaf with explanations in red ink. Cf. Johannes Duft. ed., *Studien zum St. Galler Klosterbau,* Mitteilungen zur vaterländischen Geschichte (St. Gallen, 1962); Walter Horn and Ernest Born, *The Plan of St. Gall: A Study of the Architecture and Economy of, and Life in a Paradigmatic Carolingian Monastery,* 3 vols., University of California Studies in the History of Art 19 (Berkeley-Los Angeles-London, 1979). Cf. the recent, rather balanced approach by Konrad Hecht, *Der St. Galler Klosterplan* (Sigmaringen, 1984).

79. On the other hand, Günter Noll in "The origin of the so-called plan of St. Gall," *Journal of Medieval History* 8 (1982): 191–240, underscores the Anglo-Saxon influence and considers it the original for a plan for the cathedral monastery of Canterbury from the end of the seventh century.

80. Cf. Fred Schwind, "Zu karolingerzeitlichen Klöstern als Wirtschaftsorganismen und Stätten handwerklicher Tätigkeit," in *Institutionen, Kultur und Gesellschaft im Mittelalter.* Festschrift Josef Fleckenstein (Sigmaringen, 1984), 101–123.

81. Johannes Duft, "Regula Benedicti und abendländisches Leistungsprinzip," *SMGBO* 91 (1980): 61–79.

82. Gesta Aldrici, c. 26, ed. G. Waitz, *MG, SS* 15/1, 319f.

83. Cf. Jacques Hourlier, "Das Kloster des hl. Odilo (1962)," in *Cluny. Beiträge zu Gestalt und Wirkung der cluniazensischen Reform,* 1–21 (with drawing).

84. Listed in this order in the translation by Ernst Müller-Holm (Berlin, 1910), 11ff.

85. Lampert, *Annalen a. 1063* (74ff.).

86. Karl Schmid, Gerd Althoff, "Die Klostergemeinschaft von Fulda im früheren Mittelalter. Nachträge," *FMSt* 14 (1980): 188–218. Cf. Joachim Wollasch, *Mönchtum des Mittelalters zwischen Kirche und Welt*, Münstersche Mittelalter-Schriften 7 (Munich, 1973).

87. Cf. Franz Neiske, "Konvents- und Totenlisten von Montier-en-Der," *FMSt* 14 (1980): 243-273.

88. See Eduard Hlawitschka, "Beobachtungen und Überlegungen zur Konventsstärke im Nonnenkloster Remiremont während des 7.-9. Jahrhunderts," *Secundum regulam vivere*. Festschrift Norbert Backmund (Windberg, 1978), 31–39.

89. Concerning St. Gall, see the soon-to-be-published research of Alfons Zettler, *Klosterbau und Mönchskonvent. Untersuchungen zum frühmittelalterlichen Mönchtum in den Bodenseeklöstern, vornehmlich nach der Memorialüberlieferung, archäologischen Zeugnissen und dem St. Galler Klosterplan.*

90. Concerning the West Frankish monasteries, see Oexle, *Forschungen zu monastischen und geistlichen Gemeinschaften im westfränkischen Bereich*, 96ff.

91. See Karl Schmid, "Mönchslisten und Klosterkonvent von Fulda zur Zeit der Karolinger," in *Die Klostergemeinschaft von Fulda* 2.2, 571–639; Otto Gerhard Oexle, "Mönchslisten und Konvent von Fulda im 10. Jahrhundert," in *Die Klostergemeinschaft von Fulda*, 2.2, 640–691.

92. Eckhard Freise, "Studien zum Einzugsbereich der Klostergemeinschadt von Fulda," in *Die Klostergemeinschaft von Fulda*, 2/3, 1003–1269.

93. This had nothing to do with a shortage of names, since it merely applied to 58 percent of the witnesses and 50 percent of the serfs.

94. Concerning the abbot, see Benno Hegglin, *Der benediktinische Abt in rechtsgeschichtlicher Entwicklung und geltendem Kirchenrecht*, Kirchenrechtliche Quellen und Studien 5 (St. Ottilien, 1961); Albert de Vogüe, *La communauté et l'abbé dans la règle de saint Benoît*, Textes et Études des Théologiques (Bruges, 1961); Pierre Salmon, *L'abbé dans la tradition monastique, contribution à l'histoire du caractère perpétuel des superieurs religieux en Occident*, Histoire et sociologie de l'Église 2 (Paris, 1962).

95. Cf. Robert Sommerville, "'Ordinatio abbatis' in the Rule of St. Benedict," *Revue bénédictine* 77 (1967): 246-263; Herbert Grundmann, "Zur Abt-Wahl nach Benedikts Regel," *ZKG* 77 (1966): 217–223.

96. *Casus s. Galli*, 128ff. (pp. 248ff.).

97. Bruun Candidus, *Vita Eigilis* 5, ed. Georg Waitz, *MG, SS* 15/1, 224f.

98. Lampert, *Annalen a. 1075*, 324f.

99. *Gesta abbatum Fontanellensium* 17, ed. S. Loewenfeld, *MG, SSrerG* (1886), 49–50.

100. See Mechthild Sandmann, "Wirkungsbereiche fuldischer Mönche," *Die Klostergemeinschaft von Fulda*, 2/2, 692–791.

101. *MG, Capit.* 1, no. 106 (pp. 221f.).

102. See the facsimile edition by Johanne Authenrieht, Dieter Geuenich, and Karl Schmid, *MG, Libri memoriales et necrologi*, n.s. 1 (1979).

103. See Karl Schmid, "Probleme der Erforschung frühmittelalterlicher Gedenkbücher," *FMSt* 1 (1967), 366–389. A survey may be found in Karl Schmid

and Joachim Wollasch, "Societas et Fraternitas. Begründung eines kommentierten Quellenwerks zur Erforschung der Personen und Personengruppen des Mittelalters," *FMSt* 9 (1975): 1–48.

104. See Franz-Josef Jakobi, "Früh- und hochmittelalterliche Sozialstrukturen im Spiegel liturgischer Quellen," *GWU* 31 (1980): 1–20.

105. Franz-Josef Jakobi, "Die geistlichen und weltlichen Magnaten in den Fuldaer Totenannalen," in *Die Klostergemeinschaft von Fulda*, 2/2, 792–887.

106. Concerning monastic life, see Leo Moulin, *La vie quotidienne des religieux du moyen âge. X^e–XVe* (Paris, 1978); Heinrich Fichtenau, *Lebensordnungen des 10. Jahrhunderts. Studien über Denkart und Existenz im einstigen Karolingerreich*, Monographien zur Geschichte des Mittelalters 30, 2 vols. (Stuttgart, 1984), 347ff. Concerning monastic hygiene, see Gerd Zimmermann, *Ordensleben und Lebensstandard. Die cura corporis in den Ordensvorschriften des abendländischen Hochmittelalters*, 2 vols., Beiträge zur Geschichte des alten Mönchtums und des Benediktinerordens 32 (Münster, 1973).

107. Klaus Schreiner, "Mönchtum zwischen asketischem Anspruch und gesellschaftlicher Wirklichkeit. Spiritualität, Sozialverhalten und Sozialverfassung schwäbischer Reformmönche im Spiegel ihrer Geschichtsschreibung," *Zeitschrift für württembergische Landesgeschichte* 41 (1982), 258.

108. Cf. Kassius Hallinger, "Zur geistigen Welt der Anfänge Clunys," in *Cluny. Beiträge zu Gestalt und Wirkung der cluniazensischen Reform*, 96ff.

109. Schreiner, "Mönchtum zwischen asketischem Anspruch und gesellschaftlicher Wirklichkeit," 260ff.

110. *Chronik* 7, 35 (pp. 560ff.).

111. Hermann Greeven, "Die Wirksamkeit der Cluniacenser auf kirchlichem und politischem Gebiete im 11. Jahrhundert," Dissertation, Jena, 1870, 12–13, 25.

112. *Gesta Frederici* I, 14, ed. Franz-Josef Schmale, FS 17 (Darmstadt, 1965), 154ff.

113. *Gesta Karoli* I, 31, ed. Reinhold Rau, FS 7 (Darmstadt, 2nd. ed. 1960), 368ff.

114. Lampert, *Annalen a. 1064* (92f.).

115. See Zimmermann, *Ordensleben und Lebensstandard*, 140.

116. *Dialogus Miraculorum* 4, 38, tr. Ernst Müller-Holm (Berlin, 1910), 81–82.

117. *Historica ecclesiastica*, 3, 8, 26, ed. Marjorie Chibnall, 2 vols. (Oxford, 1980), 320f.

118. *Gesta Karoli* 2, 12 (pp. 402ff.).

119. Cf. Jean Leclercq, "Zur Geschichte des Lebens in Cluny," in *Cluny. Beiträge zu Gestalt und Wirkung der cluniazensischen Reform*, 254–318, esp. 297ff.

120. *Chronik* 7, 35 (pp. 562f.).

121. *Casus s. Galli*, 105 (pp. 212–213).

122. Cf. Semmler, "Benedictus II: Una regula—una consuetudo," 45–46.

123. Cf. Alfred Wendehorst, "Die geistliche Grundherrschaft im mittelalterlichen Franken. Beobachtungen und Probleme," in Hans Patze, ed., *Die Grundherrschaft im späten Mittelalter* 2, 2 vols., VuF 27 (Sigmaringen, 1983), 9–10.

Concerning the controversy surrounding the amount of food consumed by a monk, cf. chapter I, n. 20.

124. *Casus s. Galli*, 137–143 (pp. 266–267).

125. Cf. Semmler, "Benedictus II,"44–45.

126. Cf. Gerd Zimmermann, *Ordensleben und Lebensstandard. Die cura corporis in den Ordensvorschriften des abendländischen Hochmittelalters*, 2 vols., Beiträge zur Geschichte des alten Mönchtums und des Benediktinerordens 32 (Münster, 1973), 238.

127. Cf. Paul Gerhard Schmidt, *Ars loquendi et ars tacendi. Zur monastischen Zeichensprache des Mittelalters*, Berichte zur Wissenschaftsgeschichte 4 (1981), 13–19; Walter Jarecki, ed., *Signa loquendi. Die cluniazensischen Signa-Listen*, Saecula Spiritualia 4 (Baden-Baden, 1981).

128. Cf. Zimmermann, *Ordensleben und Lebensstandard*, 120–121.

129. *Casus s. Galli*, 14 (pp. 40–41).

130. Cf. Zimmermann, *Ordensleben und Lebensstandard*, 88.

131. *Dialogus miraculorum*, tr. Ernst Müller-Holm (Berlin, 1910), 236–237.

132. Richer von Reims, *Historiae* 3, 37, ed. Robert Latouche, *Les classiques de l'histoire de France au moyen âge* 17 (Paris, 1937, reprinted 1964), 44ff.

133. *Casus s. Galli*, 52/62 (pp. 116–117, 134–135).

134. Zimmermann, *Ordensleben und Lebensstandard*, 211.

Chapter IV

1. In addition to the general literature see the collection of sources, Günther Franz, ed., *Quellen zur Geschichte des deutschen Bauernstandes im Mittelalter*, FS 31 (Darmstadt, 2nd ed. 1974), 192–193.

2. See Kurt Ranke, "Agrarische und bäuerliche Denk- und Verhaltensweisen im Mittelalter," in Reinhard Wenskus, Herbert Jankuhn, and Klaus Grinda, eds., *Wort und Begriff 'Bauer'*, Abhh 3, 89 (Göttingen, 1975), 207–221.

3. See Siegfried Epperlein, *Der Bauer im Bild des Mittelalters* (Leipzig-Berlin-Jena, 1975); Siegfried Epperlein, "Bäuerliche Arbeitsdarstellungen auf mittelalterlichen Bildzeugnissen. Zur geschichtlichen Motivation von Miniaturen und Graphiken vom 9. bis 15. Jahrhundert," *JWG* 1 (1976): 181–208.

4. Einhard, *Vita Karoli* 29, ed. Reinhold Rau, FS 5 (Darmstadt,1955), 200–201.

5. Concerning the manorial system, also consult (in addition to the literature listed in the bibliography), Otto Brunner, *Land und Herrschaft. Grundfragen der territorialen Verfassungsgeschichte Österreichs im Mittelalter* (Vienna-Wiesbaden, 4th ed. 1959); Friedrich Lütge, *Geschichte der deutschen Agrarverfassung vom frühen Mittelalter bis zum 19. Jahrhundert*, Deutsche Agrargeschichte 3 (Stuttgart, 2nd ed. 1967); Friedrich Lütge, *Die Agrarverfassung des frühen Mittelalters im mitteldeutschen Raum vornehmlich in der Karolingerzeit*, Quellen und Forschungen zur Agrargeschichte 17 (1937; reprinted Stuttgart, 1966); Alfons Dopsch, *Die Wirtschaftsentwicklung der Karolingerzeit vornehmlich in Deutschland*, 2 vols. (Weimar 1921/22; reprinted Darmstadt, 1962); Alfons Dopsch, *Herrschaft und*

Bauer in der deutschen Kaiserzeit. Untersuchungen zur Agrar- und Sozialgeschichte des hohen Mittelalters mit besonderer Berücksichtigung des südostdeutschen Raumes, Quellen und Forschungen zur Agrargeschichte 10 (Stuttgart, 2nd ed. 1964); Ludolf Kuchenbuch, *Bäuerliche Gesellschaft und Klosterherrschaft im 9. Jahrhundert. Studien zur Sozialstruktur der familia der Abtei Prüm*, VSWG, supplement 66 (Wiesbaden, 1978).

6. Cf. Klaus Schreiner, "'Grundherrschaft'. Entstehung und Bedeutungswandel eines geschichtswissenschaftlichen Ordnungs- und Erklärungsbegriffs," in Hans Patze, ed., *Die Grundherrschaft im späten Mittelalter* 1, 2 vols, VuF 27 (Sigmaringen, 1983), 11–74.

7. Thus, Adriaan Verhulst, "La genèse du régime domanial classique en France au haut moyen âge," in *Agricoltura e mondo rurale in Occidente nell' alto medioevo*, SSCI 13 (Spoleto, 1966), 135–160.

8. See Dieter Hägermann, "Einige Aspekte der Grundherschaft in den fränkischen Formulae und in den Leges des Frühmittelalters," in Adriaan Verhulst, ed., *Le grand domaine aux époches mérovingienne et carolingienne. Die Grundherrschaft im frühen Mittelalter* (Ghent, 1985), 51–77.

9. Concerning clerical manorial authority, see Wolfgang Metz, "Zu Wesen und Struktur der geistlichen Grundherrschaft," in *Nascità dell'Europa ed Europa carolingia: un' equazione da verificare*, SSCI 27 (Spoleto, 1981), 147–169.

10. Concerning the specifics of these theories, see Hans K. Schulze, article on 'Grundherrschaft,' *HRG* 1 (1971): cols. 824ff.

11. See Lütge, *Geschichte der deutschen Agrarverfassung*, 31ff.

12. Ibid., 38ff.

13. Thus, Werner Rösener, *Bauern im Mittelalter* (Munich, 1985), 24.

14. Concerning the system of these relationships, see Ludolf Kuchenbuch, "Probleme der Rentenentwicklung in den klösterlichen Grundherrschaften des frühen Mittelalters," in W. Lourdaux and D. Verhelst, eds., *Benedictine Culture 750–1050*, Mediaevalia Lovaniensia I, 11 (Louvain, 1983), 132–172.

15. *MG*, Capit. 1, no. 128, cap. 25ff. (pp. 254ff.).

16. For a rather similar inventory, cf. the record at the manor at Staffelsee in Upper Bavaria, *MG*, pp. 251–252 in *Quellen zur Geschichte des deutschen Bauernstandes im Mittelalter*, no. 22, pp. 78ff.

17. *MG*, Concilia 2, 1, nr. 39, c. 122 (p. 401) in *Quellen zur Geschichte des deutschen Bauernstandes im Mittelalter*, no. 33, pp. 78ff.

18. *MG*, Capit. 1, no. 32 (pp. 254ff.), in *Quellen zur Geschichte des deutschen Bauernstandes im Mittelalter*, no. 22, pp. 38ff.

19. Concerning the late Middle Ages, see Werner Rösener, "Grundherrschaften des Hochadels in Südwestdeutschland im Spätmittelalter," in *Die Grundherrschaft im späten Mittelalter* 2, 87–176.

20. Cf. Franz Irsigler, "Die Auflösung der Villikationsverfassung und der Übergang zum Zeitpachtsystem im Nahbereich niederrheinischer Städte während des 13./14. Jahrhunderts," in *Die Grundherrschaft im späten Mittelalter* 1, 295–311. The development portrayed in this article cannot be simply applied to other regions and certainly did not always follow such a systematic course.

21. Dopsch already doubts any sweeping changes in *Herrschaft und Bauer in der deutschen Kaiserzeit*, 129ff.

22. Again, in specific situations we must consider regional differences and the various systems represented by individual representatives of the manorial system.

23. According to Otto Brunner, "Europäisches Bauerntum," in Günther Franz, ed., *Deutsches Bauerntum im Mittelalter*, WdF 416 (Darmstadt, 1976), 12.

24. Norbert, *Vita Bennonis* 8, ed. Hatto Kallfelz, *Lebensbeschreibungen einiger Bischöfe des 10.–12. Jahrhunderts*, FS 22 (Darmstadt, 1973), 386f.

25. Cf. Karl Bosl, "Die 'familia' als Grundstruktur der mittelalterlichen Gesellschaft," ZBLG 38 (1975): 403–424.

26. Franz, *Quellen zur Geschichte des deutschen Bauernstandes im Mittelalter*, no. 54, 134ff.

27. *MG*, Capit. 1, no. 128, cap. 62. (pp. 54ff.).

28. According to Erich Wisplinghoff, "Bäuerliches Leben am Niederrhein im Rahmen der benediktinischen Grundherrschaft," in Walter Janssen and Dietrich Lohrmann, eds., *Villa–curtis–grangia. Landwirtschaft zwischen Loire und Rhein von der Römerzeit zum Hochmittelalter*, Beihefte der Francia 11 (Munich-Zürich, 1983), 149–163, esp. 154f.

29. See Waltraut Bleiber, "Grundherrschaft und Markt zwischen Loire und Rhein während des 9. Jahrhunderts. Untersuchungen zu ihrem wechselseitigen Verhältnis," *JWG* (1982/3): 105–135.

30. See *MG*, Capit. 1, no. 41, cap. 5 (pp. 117ff.); no. 56, cap. 1 (p. 143).

31. *MG*, Capit. Ansegisi IV, 1 (p. 436).

32. Cf. Hanna Vollrath, "Herrschaft und Genossenschaft im Kontext frühmittelalterlicher Rechtsbeziehungen," *HJb* 102 (1982): 33–71. To be sure, common law did not supersede manorial authority; cf. Hans-Werner Goetz, "Herrschaft und Recht in der frühmittelalterlichen Grundherrschaft," *HJb* 104 (1984): 392–410.

33. Cf. Dopsch, *Die Wirtschaftsentwicklung der Karolingerzeit vornehmlich in Deutschland* 2, 51; Bosl, "Die 'familia' als Grundstruktur der mittelalterlichen Gesellschaft," 413.

34. Lorenz Weinreich, ed., *Quellen zur deutschen Verfassungs-, Wirtschafts- und Sozialgeschichte bis 1250*, FS 32 (Darmstadt, 1977), no. 23, 88ff.

35. For a basic analysis, see Siegfried Epperlein, *Herrschaft und Volk im karolingischen Imperium. Studien über soziale Konflikte und dogmatisch-politische Kontroversen im fränkischen Reich*, Forschungen zur mittelalterlichen Geschichte 14 (Berlin 1969); Siegfried Epperlein, *Bauernbedrückung und Bauernwiderstand im hohen Mittelalter. Zur Erforschung der Ursachen bäuerlicher Abwanderung nach Osten im 12. und 13. Jahrhundert, vornehmlich nach den Urkunden geistlicher Grundherrschaften*, Forschungen zur mittelalterlichen Geschichte 6 (Berlin, 1960).

36. *MG*, Capit. 2, no 273, cap. 29 (p. 323).

37. See Wolfgang Eggert, "Formen der sozialen Auseinandersetzung im frühmittelalterlichen Frankreich," *JWG* (1971/4): 273–285; older essays may be found in Eckhard Müller-Mertens, ed., *Feudalismus. Entstehung und Wesen*, (Berlin, 1985). Marxist scholarship, which underscores the class struggle in this uprising, is in disagreement over whether it already represented a rebellion of the serfs against

their lords, or whether it constituted an uprising among free peasants against the introduction of feudal order and the manorial system.

38. See Wolfgang Eggert, "Rebelliones servorum. Bewaffnete Klassenkämpfe im Früh- und frühen Hochmittelalter und ihre Darstellung in zeitgenössischen erzählenden Quellen," *ZfG* 23 (1975): 1147–1164.

39. *Landrecht* I, 54, sect. 2 f., ed. Karl August Eckhardt, *Germanenrechte* (Göttingen, 1955), 54.

40. *Epistola*. 30, c. 5 (*MG, Epp.* 5, p. 452). Cf. Epperlein, *Herrschaft und Volk im karolingischen Imperium*, 37–38.

41. Ekkehard IV, *Casus s. Galli* 48, ed. Hans F. Haefele, FS 10 (Darmstadt, 1980), 108ff.

42. See Eberhard Linck, *Sozialer Wandel in klösterlichen Grundherrschaften des 11.–13. Jahrhunderts. Studien zu den familiae von Gembloux, Stablo-Malmedy und St. Trond*, Veröffentlichungen des MPI 57 (Göttingen, 1979), 51ff.

43. Franz, *Quellen zur Geschichte des deutschen Bauernstandes im Mittelalter*, no. 149, 384ff.

44. Concerning peasant houses, see Hermann Hinz, Konrad Bedal, 'Bauernhaus,' *Lexikon des Mittelalters* I1 (1980): cols. 1606–1619; Konrad Bedal, *Historische Hausforschung. Eine Einführung in Arbeitsweise, Begriffe und Literatur* (Münster, 1978); Hildegard Dölling, *Haus und Hof in westgermanischen Volksrechten*, Veröffentlichungen der Altertumskommission im Provinzialinstitut für westfälische Landes- und Volkskunde 2 (Münster, 1958); Günter P. Fehring, "Zur archäologischen Erforschung mittelalterlicher Dorfsiedlungen in Südwestdeutschland," *Zeitschrift für Agrargeschichte und Agrarsoziologie* 21 (1973): 1–35; Peter Donat, *Haus, Hof und Dorf in Mitteleuropa vom 7. bis 12. Jahrhundert: Archäologische Beiträge zur Entwicklung und Struktur der bäuerlichen Siedlung* Schriften zur Ur- und Frühgeschichte 33 (Berlin 1980); Jean Chapelot, Robert Fossier, *Le village et la maison au moyen âge* (Paris, 1980).

45. Cf. Walter Schlesinger, "Die Hufe im Frankenreich," in Heinrich Beck, Dietrich Denecke and Herbert Jankuhn, eds., *Untersuchungen zur eisenzeitlichen und frühmittelalterlichen Flur in Mitteleuropa und ihre Nutzung*, vol. 1, Abhh. 3, 115/116 (Göttingen, 1979), 47–70. Originally, *mansus* and *hoba* were probably two different entities; ever since the eighth century, *mansus* is attested to in the West Frankish area, and *hoba* in the East Rhenish areas since the eighth century. According to Lütge, *mansus* was characterized by a small degree of dependency; according to Perrin, it signified the agricultural area used; according to Schlesinger, it was primarily the farm itself and became only later known as a manse as a result of Charlemagne's legislation. During the time that followed, both concepts became identical.

46. Dopsch, *Die Wirtschaftsentwicklung der Karolingerzeit vornehmlich in Deutschland* 1, 329ff.

47. Cf. Kuchenbuch, *Bäuerliche Gesellschaft und Klosterherrschaf*, 68–69.

48. A *bunuarium* corresponded to approximately 130 ares (= 3.13 acres, or 13,000m2). Cf. also Charles-Edmond Perrin, "Observations sur le manse dans la région parisienne au début du IXe siècle," *Annales d'histoire sociale* 8 (1945): 39–52.

49. Entirely similar proportions were ascertained for Farfa by Thomas Schuler, "Familien im Mittelalter," in Heinz Reif, ed., *Die Familie in der Geschichte*, Kleine Vandenhoeck-Reihe 1474 (Göttingen, 1982]) 28–60.

50. See Kuchenbuch, *Bäuerliche Gesellschaft und Klosterherrschaft*, 86–87.

51. *MG*, Capit. 2, no. 275, cap. 12 (p. 337).

52. Incidentally, at Lauterbach, I encountered the only example familiar to me where a married couple had both parents living with them, meaning that the father was still alive: Josef Widemann, ed., *Die Traditionen des Hochstifts Regensburg und des Klosters St. Emmeram*, Quellen und Erörterungen zur bayerischen Geschichte, n.s. 8 (Munich, 1943; reprinted Aalen, 1969), no. 17, p. 21; see also Martin Heinzelmann, "Beobachtungen zur Bevölkerungsstruktur einiger grundherrschaftlicher Siedlungen im karolingischen Bayern," *FMSt* 11 (1977): 202–217; 12 (1978): 433–437.

53. See J. Bessmerny, "Les structures de la famille paysanne dans les villages de la Francia au IXe siècle," *MA* 90 (1984): 165–193, who arrives at the incorrect conclusion that a return to the expanded family had occurred.

54. Concerning Southern France, see Stephen Weinberger, "Peasant House-holds in Provence, c. 800–1100," *Speculum* 48 (1973): 247–257, who determines in this article that eleventh-century society underwent a complete change in the direction of expansion and flexibility. Concerning the problematic nature of this term, see Jean-Pierre Devroey, "*Mansi absi*: indices de crise ou de croissance de l'économie rurale au haut moyen âge?" *MA* 82 (1976): 421–451.

55. At Lauterbach II, which belonged to a monastery (see this chapter, n. 52) only three of the twenty manses list a *mancipium*, or a *puella*; on the other hand, the estate of Abbot Siegfried records a total of ten *mancipia* on four out of ten manses. At the Prüm manor, we encounter *mancipia* on one-fourth (440) of the approximately 1700 manses (Kuchenbuch, p. 79).

56. The numbers at Saint-Germain varied between none and nine, averaging two to three children per family. At Gagny, one family had six, two families five, five families four, eight families three, four families two children, five one, and four families had none.

57. At Lauterbach a distinction is made between *infantes* and *filii*; only the latter were mentioned by name.

58. Concerning the village, see Herbert Jankuhn, Rudolf Schützeichel, and Fred Schwind, eds., *Das Dorf der Eisenzeit und des frühen Mittelalters. Siedlungsform–wirtschaftliche Funktion–soziale Struktur*, Abhh. 3, 101 (Göttingen, 1977); Donat, *Haus, Hof und Dorf*; Chapelot and Fossier, *Le village et la maison au moyen âge*; W. Rösener, W. Janssen, H. Jäger, J.-M.Pesez, K.S. Bader, L. Genicot, et al., 'Dorf,' *Lexikon des Mittelalters* 3 (1985): cols. 1266ff.; Hans K. Schulze, *Grundstrukturen der Verfassung im Mittelalter* 2, Urban 371/372 (Stuttgart, 1985–86), 59ff.

59. See Rudolf Schützeichel, "'Dorf.' Wort und Begriff," in *Das Dorf der Eisenzeit*, 9–36; Helmut Jäger, "Das Dorf als Siedlungsform und seine wirtschaftliche Funktion," in *Das Dorf der Eisenzeit*, 62–80.

60. See Harald von Petrikovits, "Kleinstädte und nichtstädtische Siedlungen im Nordwesten des römischen Reiches," in *Das Dorf der Eisenzeit*, 86–135.

61. See Michael Müller-Wille, "Bäuerliche Siedlungen der Bronze- und Eisenzeit in den Nordseegebieten," in *Das Dorf der Eisenzeit*, 153–218; Herbert Jankuhn, "Typen und Funktionen eisenzeitlicher Siedlungen im Ostseegebiet," in *Das Dorf der Eisenzeit*, 219–252. Concerning the village as a new form of organizing land, see Phillippe Leveau, "La ville antique et l'organisation de l'espace rurale: villa, ville, village," *Annales ESC* 38 (1983), 920–942.

62. See Ernst Schubert, "Entwicklungsstufen der Grundherrschaft im Lichte der Namenforschung," in Walter Janssen and Dietrich Lohrmann, eds., *Die Grundherrschaft im späten Mittelalter* 1, Francia Beiheft 11 (Munich-Zürich, 1983), 75–95.

63. See Fred Schwind, "Beobachtungen zur inneren Struktur des Dorfes in karolingischer Zeit," in *Das Dorf der Eisenzeit*, 444–493; Dopsch, *Die Wirtschaftsentwicklung der Karolingerzeit vornehmlich in Deutschland* 1, 130–131.

64. See Walter Janssen, "Dorf und Dorfformen des 7. bis 12. Jahrhunderts im Lichte neuer Ausgrabungen in Mittel- und Nordeuropa," in *Das Dorf der Eisenzeit*, 285–356, esp. 313ff.

65. Concerning this, see Beck, Denecke, and Jankuhn, *Untersuchungen zur eisenzeitlichen und frühmittelalterlichen Flur in Mitteleuropa und ihrer Nutzung*.

66. See Ulrich Scheuermann, "Die sprachliche Erschliessung der Dorfflur mit Hilfe von Flurnamen," in *Untersuchungen zur eisenzeitlichen und frühmittelalterlichen Flur in Mitteleuropa und ihrer Nutzung* 2, 323–353.

67. See Ulrich Willderding, "Anbaufrüchte der Eisenzeit und des frühen Mittelalters, ihre Anbauformen, Standortverhältnisse und Erntemethoden," in *Untersuchungen zur eisenzeitlichen und frühmittelalterlichen Flur in Mitteleuropa und ihrer Nutzung* 2, 126–196.

68. Janssen, "Dorf und Dorfformen des 7. bis 12. Jahrhunderts im Lichte neuer Ausgrabungen in Mittel- und Nordeuropa," in *Das Dorf der Eisenzeit*, 338ff.; Walter Janssen, "Mittelalterliche Dorfsiedlungen als archäologisches Problem," *FMSt* 2 (1968): 305–367.

69. See Lynn White, Jr., "The Life of the Silent Majority," in Robert S. Hoyt, ed., *Life and Thought in the Early Middle Ages* (Minneapolis, 1967), 85–100, in reference to *Ruodlieb*.

70. See Ruth Schmidt-Wiegand, "Das Dorf nach den Stammesrechten des Kontinents," in *Das Dorf der Eisenzeit*, 408–443.

71. Tit. 45 (De migrantibus) in *Quellen zur Geschichte des deutschen Bauernstandes im Mittelalter*, no. 6, pp. 10ff.

72. See Walter Jannsen, "Gewerbliche Produktion des Mittelalters als Wirtschaftsfaktor im ländlichen Raum," in Herbert Jankuhn, Walter Jannsen, Ruth Schmidt-Wiegand und Heinrich Tiefenbach, eds., *Das Handwerk in vor- und frühgeschichtlicher Zeit* 2, Abhh. 3, 122 (Göttingen, 1981–83), 317–394.

73. Cf. *Die Anfänge der Landgemeinde und ihr Wesen*, 2 vols., VuF 7/8 (Constance-Stuttgart, 1964) (Summary by Theodor Mayer, 2, 465–495); Karl

Siegfried Bader, *Studien zur Rechtsgeschichte des mittelalterlichen Dorfes*. 1: *Das mittelalterliche Dorf als Friedens- und Rechtsbezirk* (Cologne-Graz-Weimar, 1957), 2: *Dorfgenossenschaft und Dorfgemeinde* (Cologne-Graz, 1962), 3: *Rechtsformen und Schichten der Liegenschaftsnutzung im mittelalterlichen Dorf* (Vienna-Cologne-Graz, 1973); Marlene Nikolay-Panter, *Entstehung und Entwicklung der Landgemeinde im Trierer Raum*, Rheinisches Archiv 97 (Bonn, 1976).

74. *MG, DLD*, 145.

75. Concerning this section, see Reinhard Wenskus, Herbert Jankuhn and Klaus Grinda, eds., *Wort und Begriff 'Bauer,'* Abhh. 3, 89 (Göttingen, 1975); Fritz Martini, *Das Bauerntum im deutschen Schrifttum von den Anfängen bis zum 16. Jahrhundert*, Deutsche Vierteljahresschrift für Literaturwissenschaft und Geistesgeschichte 27 (Halle/S., 1944); Rösener, *Bauern im Mittelalter*; Epperlein, *Der Bauer im Bild des Mittelalters*; Guy Fourquin, *Le Paysan d'Occidente au moyen âge* (Paris, 1972). Furthermore, see Kuchenbuch, *Bäuerliche Gesellschaft und Klosterherrschaft*; Günther Franz, *Geschichte des deutschen Bauernstandes vom frühen Mittelalter bis zum 19. Jahrhundert*, Deutsche Agrargeschichte 4 (Stuttgart, 1970); Franz, *Deutsches Bauerntum im Mittelalter*; Philippe Dollinger, *Der bayerische Bauernstand vom 9. bis 13. Jahrhundert* (Munich, 1982; French, 1949). Concerning the problematic nature of the concept, see Reinhard Wenskus, " 'Bauer'—Begriff und historische Wirklichkeit," in *Wort und Begriff 'Bauer'*, 11–28; Werner Rösener, *Lexikon des Mittelalters* 1 (1980): cols. 1563ff.

76. "Peasant" is a person who cultivates the land; cf. Latin *agricola* derives from *agrum colere*.

77. See Ruth Schmidt-Wiegand, "Der 'Bauer' in der Lex Salica," in *Wort und Begriff 'Bauer,'* 128–152.

78. See Wenskus, " 'Bauer'—Begriff und historische Wirklichkeit," 25; Rolf Bergmann, "Althochdeutsche Glossen zu 'Bauer'," in *Wort und Begriff 'Bauer'*, 89–127; Karl Stackmann, "Bezeichnungen für 'Bauer' in frühmittelhochdeutschen Quellen," in *Wort und Begriff 'Bauer'*, 153–180; Gerhard Köbler, " 'Bauer' (agricola, colonus, rusticus) im Frühmittelalter," in *Wort und Begriff 'Bauer'*, 230–245.

79. See the list in Bergmann, "Althochdeutsche Glossen zu 'Bauer'," 103ff. and 122ff.

80. Franz, *Geschichte des deutschen Bauernstandes vom frühen Mittelalter bis zum 19. Jahrhundert*, 13.

81. See Georges Duby, *Die drei Ordnungen. Das Weltbild des Feudalismus* (Frankfurt, 1981; French, 1978); Otto Gerhard Oexle, "Die funktionale Dreiteilung der 'Gesellschaft' bei Adalbero von Laon. Deutungsschemata und soziale Wirklichkeit im früheren Mittelalter," *FMSt* 12 (1978): 1–54; Josef Fleckenstein, "Zur Frage der Abgrenzung von Bauer und Ritter," in *Wort und Begriff 'Bauer'*, 246–253; Josef Fleckenstein, "Zum Problem der Abschliessung des Ritterstandes," in *Historische Forschungen für Walter Schlesinger* (Cologne-Vienna, 1974), 252–271.

82. Cf. Werner Rösener, "Bauer und Ritter im Hochmittelalter. Aspekte ihrer Lebensform, Standesbildung und sozialen Differenzierung im 12. und 13. Jahrhundert," in *Institutionen, Kultur und Gesellschaft im Mittelalter. Festschrift Josef Fleckenstein* (Sigmaringen, 1984), 665–692.

83. Weinreich, *Quellen zur deutschen Verfassungs-, Wirtschafts- und Sozial-geschichte bis 1250,* no. 57, #12, 220–221.

84. Ibid., no. 73, #14, 294–295.

85. Franz, *Quellen zur Geschichte des deutschen Bauernstandes im Mittelal-ter,* no. 122, #71, 326ff.

86. Ibid., no. 82, 220ff.

87. Ibid., no. 122, #71, 328–329.

88. See Jacques Le Goff, "Les paysans et le monde rural dans la littérature du haut moyen âge (V^e–VIe siècles)," in *Agricoltura e mondo rurale in Occidente nell' alto medioevo,* 723–741

89. Epperlein, *Der Bauer im Bild des Mittelalters*; Epperlein, "Bäuerliche Arbeitsdarstellungen auf mittelalterlichen Bildzeugnissen."

90. Cf. Franz, *Geschichte des deutschen Bauernstandes vom frühen Mittelal-ter bis zum 19. Jahrhundert,* 38.

91. *Speculum ecclesiae. Sermo generalis* (Migne, *Patrologia Latina* 172, col. 866).

92. Franz, *Quellen zur Geschichte des deutschen Bauernstandes im Mittelal-ter,* no. 56, 144–145.

93. See Kurt Ranke, "Agrarische und bäuerliche Denk- und Verhaltensweisen im Mittelalter," in *Wort und Begriff 'Bauer',* 211.

94. Ultimately, *villanus* (peasant), became "villain" in English and a term to describe a boorish person in French (*vilain*).

95. Wenskus, "'Bauer'—Begriff und historische Wirklichkeit," 16ff.

96. Kuchenbuch, *Bäuerliche Gesellschaft und Klosterherrschaft,* 318–319; Fichtenau, *Lebensordnungen des 10. Jahrhunderts. Studien über Denkart und Ex-istenz im einstigen Karolingerreich,* Monographien zur Geschichte des Mittelalters 30 (Stuttgart, 1984), 399ff.; Regino of Prüm, *De synodalibus causis* 2, 5, 42ff., ed. F. G. A. Wasserschleben (Leipzig, 1840, reprinted Graz, 1964), 212ff.

97. See Kurt Ranke, "Germanische Flurumgänge," in *Untersuchungen zur eisenzeitlichen und frühmittelalterlichen Flur in Mitteleuropa und ihrer Nutzung* 2, 361–369; Holger Homann, "Der Indiculus superstitionum et paganiarum ·und verwandte Denkmäler," Dissertation Göttingen, 1965, p. 133.

98. Quoted from Le Goff, *Kultur des europäischen Mittelalters* (Munich-Zürich, 1970), 495.

99. *Die Lieder Neidharts,* L 10, 6f., ed. Siegfried Beyschlag (Darmstadt, 1975), 48ff.

100. *Helmbreht,* ll. 1106f.: "I'd rather be a peasant than a poor courtier."

101. Cf. Dollinger, *Der bayerische Bauernstand vom 9. bis 13. Jahrhun-dert,* 196ff. Concerning the early period, see Hermann Nehlsen, *Sklavenrecht zwischen Antike und Mittelalter. Germanisches und römisches Recht in den german-ischen Rechtsaufzeichnungen,* Göttinger Studien zur Rechtsgeschichte 7 (Göttingen-Frankfurt-Zürich, 1972).

102. *Coloni* were absent from the manor of Saint-Remi near Reims; the land register differentiated solely between *ingenuii, epistolarii,* and *servi.* Here, the proportion of free persons was relatively higher.

103. See Kuchenbuch, *Bäuerliche Gesellschaft und Klosterherrschaft*, 356ff.

104. Concerning the Swabian region, see Karl Hans Ganahl, *Studien zur Verfassungsgeschichte der Klosterherrschaft St. Gallen von den Anfängen bis ins hohe Mittelalter*, Forschungen zur Geschichte Vorarlbergs und Liechtensteins 6 (Innsbruck, 1931), 94ff.

105. Soon, however, *mancipia* could also refer to all serfs.

106. Weinreich, *Quellen zur deutschen Verfassungs, Wirtschafts- und Sozialgeschichte bis 1250*, no. 25, 108–109.

107. Heinrich Beyer, ed., *Urkundenbuch zur Geschichte der mittelrheinischen Territorien* I, 1, no. 119f. of 881/82 (Coblenz, 1860); cf. Kuchenbuch, *Bäuerliche Gesellschaft und Klosterherrschaft*, 249ff.

108. Cf. n. 52 above.

109. See chapter 3 above.

110. Concerning Prüm, see Kuchenbuch, *Bäuerliche Gesellschaft und Klosterherrschaft*, 314ff.: Sunday services had to be performed soberly and in proper attire, care of the poor and the sick, communion, baptisms, burials, etc.

111. See Knut Schulz, "Zum Problem der Zensualität im Hochmittelalter," in *Beiträge zur Wirtschafts- und Sozialgeschichte des Mittelalters. Festschrift Herbert Helbig* (Cologne-Vienna, 1976), 86–127.

112. *Chronicon Ebersheimense* 3 (*MG, SS* 23 [1874], 433)

113. Cf. George Duby, *L'économie rurale et la vie des campagnes dans l'occident médiéval (France, Angleterre, Empire). IXe–XVe-siècles* 1 (Paris, 1962), 91.

114. Otto Brunner, "Europäisches Bauerntum," in *Deutsches Bauerntum im Mittelalter*, 9.

115. Concerning the work of peasants, see Wilhelm Abel, *Geschichte der deutschen Landwirtschaft vom frühen Mittelalter bis zum 19. Jahrhundert*, Deutsche Agrargeschichte 2 (Stuttgart, 2nd ed., 1967); Duby, *L'économie rurale et la vie des campagnes dans l'occident médiéval*; Kuchenbuch, *Bäuerliche Gesellschaft und Klosterherrschaft*; Rösener, *Bauern im Mittelalter*. Furthermore, see François-Louis Ganshof, *HEWSG* 2, 157ff.; Wilhelm Abel, *HEWSG* 1, 83ff. and 169ff; Fichtenau, *Lebensordnungen des 10. Jahrhunderts*, 437ff.

116. See Epperlein, *Der Bauer im Bild des Mittelalters*, 207ff.; G. Wirth, A. Hertz, J. Le Goff, Ch. Verlinden, 'Arbeit,' *Lexikon des Mittelalters* 1, cols. 869ff.; G. Binding, article on 'Arbeitsbilder' (images of work), *Lexikon des Mittelalters* 1, cols. 883ff.; Jacques Le Goff, 'Arbeit,' *Theologische Realenzyklopädie* 3 (1978), 626ff.

117. Franz, *Quellen zur Geschichte des deutschen Bauernstandes im Mittelalter*, no. 43, 110ff.

118. Concerning the types of farm implements used, see Ulrich Bentzien, *Bauernarbeit im Feudalismus. Landwirtschaftliche Arbeitsgeräte und -verfahren in Deutschland von der Mitte des 1. Jahrtausends unserer Zeitrechnung bis um 1800*, Akademie der Wissenschaften der DDR. Zentralinstitut für Geschichte. Veröffentlichungen für Volkskunde und Kulturgeschichte 67 (Berlin, 1980); cf. Axel Steensberg, "Agrartechnik der Eisenzeit und des frühen Mittelalters," in

Untersuchungen zur eisenzeitlichen und frühmittelalterlichen Flur in Mitteleuropa und ihrer Nutzung 2, 55–76.

119. *Die mittelalterliche Technik und der Wandel der Gesellschaft* (Munich, 1968; English, 1963), 42ff.

120. *L'économie rurale et la vie des campagnes dans l'occident médiéval* 1, 74ff.

121. See Marc Bloch, "Avènement et conquête du moulin d'eau (1935)," in Marc Bloch, *Mélanges historiques* 2 (Paris, 1963), 800–821; and Dietrich Lohrmann, "Le moulin à eau dans l'expansion de l'économie neustrienne," in *La Neustrie. Les pays au nord de la Loire entre 650 et 850*, Francia Beiheft (Sigmaringen, 1987).

122. Concerning the distribution, see illustration 4 in Ulrich Willerding, "Anbaufrüchte der Eisenzeit und des frühen Mittelalters, ihre Anbauformen, Standortverhältnisse und Erntemethoden," in *Untersuchungen zur eisenzeitlichen und frühmittelalterlichen Flur in Mitteleuropa und ihrer Nutzung* 2, 143.

123. Hermann Wartmann, ed., *Urkundenbuch der Abtei St. Gallen* 1 (Zürich, 1866), no. 39.

124. Bernard Guérard, ed., *Polyptyche de l'abbé Irminon* 1 (Paris, 1848), 925.

125. See Wolfgang Metz, "Die Agrarwirtschaft im karolingischen Reiche," in *Karl der Große. Lebenswerk und Nachleben* 1 (Düsseldorf, 3rd ed., 1967), 489–500.

126. See Abel, *Geschichte der deutschen Landwirtschaft vom frühen Mittelalter bis zum 19. Jahrhundert*, 23ff.

127. *HDWSG* 1, 88.

128. A. Déléage, *La vie rurale en Bourgogne jusqu' au début du onzième siècle* 2 (Macon, 1941), 1096 (quoted by Kuchenbuch, *Bäuerliche Gesellschaft und Klosterherrschaft*, p. 73, n. 66).

129. Franz, *Quellen zur Geschichte des deutschen Bauernstandes im Mittelalter*, no. 22, cap. 69, 58f.

130. See Harald Siems, "Flurgrenzen und Grenzmarkierungen in den Stammesrechten," in *Untersuchungen zur eisenzeitlichen und frühmittelalterlichen Flur in Mitteleuropa und ihrer Nutzung* 1, 267–309.

131. *De mensium duodecim nominibus signis culturis aerisque qualitatibus*, ed. Ernst Dümmler, *MG, Poetae latini* 2, 604ff.

132. See Perrine Mane, "L'apport de l'iconographie des calendriers pour l'étude de la vie rurale en France et en Italie aux XIIᵉ et XIIIᵉ siècles (exemple: la taille de la vigne)," in *Bäuerliche Sachkultur des Spätmittelalters*, Sbb 439 (Vienna, 1984), 265–275.

133. See especially Peter Ketsch, *Frauen im Mittelalter*, 2 vols., Geschichtsdidaktik: Studien, Materialien 8 (Düsseldorf, 1983/84), 79ff.

134. Kuchenbuch, *Bäuerliche Gesellschaft und Klosterherrschaft*, 109.

135. Odo of Cluny, *Vita Geraldi* 1, 21 (Migne, *Patrologia Latina* 133, cols. 655–656.)

136. *MG, Capit.* 1, no. 22, cap. 81 (p. 61).

137. See Kuchenbuch, *Bäuerliche Gesellschaft und Klosterherrschaft*, 108ff.

138. The prohibition just quoted and expressed in the *Admonitio generalis* was repeated at one of the councils at Mainz in 852 (*MG, Capit.* 2, no. 249, cap. 14, p. 190). At the beginning of the tenth century, Regino of Prüm included it in his visitation handbook (Regino of Prüm, *De synodalibus causis*, cap. 1, 383/85 [pp 175f.]).

139. *Vita Liudgeri III*, 2, 10, ed. Wilhelm Diekamp, *Die Vitae sancti Liudgeri*, Die Geschichtsquellen des Bistums Münster 4 (Münster, 1881), 118f.

140. *MG, Capit.* 1, no. 31 of 800 (pp. 81f.).

141. See Erich Wisplinghoff, "Bäuerliches Leben am Niederrhein im Rahmen der benediktinischen Grundherrschaft," in *Villa–curtis–grangia. Landwirtschaft zwischen Loire und Rhein von der Römerzeit zum Hochmittelalter*, 153.

142. *Codex Laureshamensis*, no. 3571, ed. Karl Glöckner, vol. 3 (Darmstadt, 1936), 173.

143. *Das Prümer Urbar*, ed.Ingo Schwab, *Rheinische Urbare* 5 (Düsseldorf, 1983), cap. 6, pp. 171f.

144. *Die Urbare der Abtei Werden an der Ruhr*, ed. Rudolf Kötzschke, *Rheinische Urbare* 2 (Bonn, 1906).

145. Kuchenbuch, *Bäuerliche Gesellschaft und Klosterherrschaft*, 233ff. Cf. Kuchenbuch, "Probleme der Rentenentwicklung in den klösterlichen Grundherrschaften des frühen Mittelalters," 32–172.

146. According to one tradition, St. Bartholomew was martyred by flaying.

147. *MG, Capit.* 1, no. 128, 3, cap. 25 (p. 254).

148. Cf. Raymond Delatouche, "Regards sur l'agriculture aux temps carolingiens," *Journal des Savants* (1977): 73–100; Joachim Herrmann, "Probleme der Fruchtwechselwirtschaft im Ackerbau des 8. und 9. Jahrhunderts am Beispiel ausgewählter schriftlicher und archäologischer Quellen," *Zs. für Archäologie* 15 (1981): 1–9. Jean Durliat, "De conlaboratu: faux rendements et vrai comptabilité publique à l'époche carolingienne," *Revue historique de droit français et étranger* 56 (1978): 445–457, however, interprets the amounts as the share remaining to the king after all levies had been paid.

149. "Bäuerliches Leben am Niederrhein im Rahmen der benediktinischen Grundherrschaft," in *Villa–curtis–grangia. Landwirtschaft zwischen Loire und Rhein von der Römerzeit zum Hochmittelalter*, 157f.

Chapter V

1. Concerning palaces, see *Deutsche Königspfalzen. Beiträge zu ihrer historischen und archäologischen Erforschung*, 3 vols., Veröffentlichungen des MPI 11 (Göttingen, 1963, 1965, 1979); Adolf Gauert, "Königspfalzen," *HRG* 2 (1978): cols. 1044–1055; Jacques Gardelle, "Les palais dans l'Europe occidentale chrétienne du X^c au XIII^c siècle," *Cahiers de civilisation médiévale* 19 (1976): 115–134; Thomas Zotz, ed., *Die deutschen Königspfalzen. Repertorium der Pfalzen, Königshöfe und übrigen Aufenthaltsorte der Könige im deutschen Reich des Mittelalters* (appears in installments).

2. See Carlrichard Brühl, *Fodrum, Gistum, Servitium Regis. Studien zu den wirtschaftlichen Grundlagen des Königtums im Frankenreich und in den fränkischen Nachfolgestaaten Deutschland, Frankreich und Italien vom 6. bis zur Mitte des 14. Jahrhunderts,* Kölner Historische Abhandlungen 14 (Cologne-Graz, 1968), 168ff.

3. During the late Middle Ages, they often relocated at a small site nearby, away from the cathedral chapter and the community of burghers.

4. See Josef Fleckenstein, ed., *Investiturstreit und Reichsverfassung,* VuF 17 (Sigmaringen, 1973).

5. Cf. Theodor Mayer, *Fürsten und Staat. Studien zur Verfassungsgeschichte des deutschen Mittelalters* (Weimar, 1950; reprinted Cologne-Graz, 1969).

6. Cf. Theodor Mayer, "Die Ausbildung der Grundlagen des modernen deutschen Staates im hohen Mittelalter [1939]," in *Herrschaft und Staat im Mittelaltes,* WdF 2 (Darmstadt, 1956), 284–331.

7. See, for example, Ursula Peters, *Fürstenhof und höfische Dichtung. Der Hof Hermanns von Thüringen als literarisches Zentrum,* Konstanzer Universitätsreden 113 (Constance, 1981).

8. Cf. Joachim Bumke, ed., *Literarisches Mäzenatentum. Ausgewählte Forschungen zur Rolle des Gönners und Auftraggebers in der mittelalterlichen Literatur,* WdF 598 (Darmstadt, 1982); Joachim Bumke, *Mäzene im Mittelalter. Die Gönner und Auftraggeber der höfischen Literatur in Deutschland 1150–1300* (München, 1979), 455ff.

9. *Vita Brunonis* 5, ed. Hatto Kallfelz, *Lebensbeschreibungen einiger Bischöfe des 10.–12. Jahrhunderts* FS 22 (Darmstadt, 1973), 186ff.

10. Bumke, ed., *Literarisches Mäzenatentum,* 1. Concerning the social background see Bumke's recent study *Höfische Kultur. Literatur und Gesellschaft im hohen Mittelalter* 2, dtv 4442 (München, 1986), 595ff.

11. Cf. Hans Patze, "Adel und Stifterchronik. Frühformen territorialer Geschichtsschreibung im hochmittelalterlichen Reich," *Bll. dt. LG.* 100 (1964): 8–81; 101 (1965): 67–128.

12. Louis Halphen and René Poupardin, eds., *Chronica de gestis consulum Andegavensium* (Paris, 1913), 162–163.

13. See Henning Krauss, ed., *Europäisches Hochmittelalter,* Neues Handbuch der Literaturwissenschaft 7 (Wiesbaden, 1981); Hans Eggers, "Deutsche Dichtung in der Stauferzeit," *Die Zeit der Staufer* 3 (exhibit catalog) (Stuttgart, 1977), 187–199.

14. Not until the thirteenth century does a certain realism emerge in literature; even idealized heroes, such as Gawain, occasionally reveal their weaknesses.

15. Concerning Hartmann von Aue's *Erec,* see above. Concerning courtly love, see Bumke, *Höfische Kultur,* 2, 503ff.

16. Halphen and Poupardin, *Chronica de gestis consulum Andegavensium,* 140.

17. Restrictively, Michael Curschmann, *Hören-Lesen-Sehen. Buch und Schriftlichkeit im Selbstverständnis der volkssprachlichen literarischen Kultur Deutschlands um 1200,* Beiträge zur Geschichte der deutschen Sprache und Literatur 106 (1984), 218–257.

18. Concerning this chapter, see H. Hinz, M. Petry "Befestigung," *Lexikon des Mittelalters* 1 (1980), cols. 1785–1793; G. Binding, H. Ebner et al., "Burg," *Lexikon des Mittelalters* 2 (1983), cols. 957–1003; Herwig Ebner, "Die Burg als Forschungsproblem mittelalterlicher Verfassungsgeschichte," in Hans Patze, ed., *Die Burgen im deutschen Sprachraum. Ihre rechts- und verfassungsgeschichtliche Bedeutung* 1, VuF 19 (Sigmaringen, 1976), 11–82; Fred Schwind, "Zur Verfassung und Bedeutung der Reichsburgen, vornehmlich im 12. und 13. Jahrhundert," in *Die Burgen im deutschen Sprachraum* 1, 85–122; Hans Patze, "Die Burgen in Verfassung und Recht des deutschen Sprachraumes," in *Die Burgen im deutschen Sprachraum* 2, 421–441; Kurt-Ulrich Jäschke, *Burgenbau und Landesverteidigung um 900. Überlegungen zu Beispielen aus Deutschland, Frankreich und England,* VuF, Sonderband 16 (Sigmaringen, 1975); Walter Hotz, *Pfalzen und Burgen der Stauferzeit. Geschichte und Gestalt (Darmstadt, 1981); Hans-Martin Maurer, "Burgen," in Die Zeit der Staufer* 3 (Stuttgart, 1977), 119–1⁀ Hermann Hinz, *Motte und Donjon. Zur Frühgeschichte der mittelalterlichen Adelsburg,* Zeitschrift für Archäologie des Mittelalters, supplement 1 (Cologne-Bonn, 1981); Elsbet Orth, "Ritter und Burg," in *Das ritterliche Turnier im Mittelalter. Beiträge zu einer vergleichenden Formen- und Verhaltensgeschichte des Rittertums,* Veröffentlichungen des MPI 80 (Göttingen, 1985), 19–4; Hans K. Schulze, *Grundstrukturen der Verfassung im Mittelalter* 2, Urban 371/372 (Stuttgart, 1985–86]) 83ff.; Bumke, *Höfische Kultur* 1, 137ff.

19. See Ebner, "Die Burg als Forschungsproblem," 35.

20. See Jäschke, *Burgenbau und Landesverteidigung um 900,* 7–8, 115.

21. Otto von Freising, *Gesta Frederici* I, 12, ed. Franz- Josef Schmale, FS 17 (Darmstadt, 1965), 152f

22. Cf. Walter Janssen, "Die Bedeutung der mitterlalterlichen Burg für die Wirtschafts- und Sozialgeschichte des Mittelalters," in Herbert Jankuhn, Walter Janssen, Ruth Schmidt-Wiegand and Heinrich Tiefenbach, eds., *Das Handwerk in vor- und frühgeschichtlicher Zeit,* 2 vols., Abhh. 3, 122 (Göttingen, 1981–1983), 261–316.

23. Cf. Ursula Lewald, "Burg, Kloster, Stift," in *Die Burgen im deutschen Sprachraum* 1, 155–180; especially also the recent study by Gerhard Streich, *Burg und Kirche während des deutschen Mittelalters. Untersuchungen zur Sakraltopographie von Pfalzen, Burgen und Herrensitzen,* 2 vols. VuF, Sonderband 29 (Sigmaringen, 1984).

24. For instance Altenberg in 1133, when the counts of Berg moved to "Castle" Burg.

25. Concerning the actual construction, see Alexander Antonow, "Planung und Bau von Burgen im süd- und südwestdeutschen Raum im 12. und 13. Jahrhundert," in *Das Handwerk* 2, 535–594. A detailed study of the construction and the occupants of a castle, although covering almost exclusively the late Middle Ages, may be found in Hellmut Kunstmann, *Mensch und Burg. Burgenkundliche Betrachtungen an ostfränkischen Wehranlagen,* Veröffentlichungen der Gesellschaft für fränkische Geschichte. Reihe IX. Darstellungen aus der fränkischen Geschichte 25 (Würzburg, 1967).

26. See Jürgen Tauber, *Herd und Ofen im Mittelalter. Untersuchungen zur Kulturgeschichte an archäologischem Material vornehmlich der Nordwestschweiz*, Schweizer Beiträge zur Kulturgeschichte und Archäologie des Mittelalters 7 (1980).

27. *Gesta Frederici* 4, 86 (pp. 712–713).

28. Hans-Martin Maurer, "Rechtsverhältnisse der hochmittelalterlichen Adelsburgen, vornehmlich in Südwestdeutschland," in *Die Burgen im deutschen Sprachraum* 2, 183f.

29. General literature about knighthood: Johanna Maria van Winter, *Rittertum. Ideal und Wirklichkeit* (Munich, 1969); Arno Borst, ed., *Das Rittertum im Mittelalter*, WdF 394 (Darmstadt, 1976), with a substantial bibliography; Karl Brunner, Falko Daim, *Ritter, Knappen, Edelfrauen. Ideologie und Realität des Rittertums im Mittelalter* (Vienna-Cologne-Graz, 1981); Josef Fleckenstein, "Das Rittertum der Stauferzeit," in *Die Zeit der Staufer* 3, 103–118; Benjamin Arnold, *German Knighthood* 1050–1300 (Oxford, 1985). Concerning early history, see Jean Flori, *L'idéologie du glaive. Préhistoire de la chevalerie*, Travaux d'histoire éthico-politique 43 (Geneva, 1984); Bumke, *Höfische Kultur*, 2, 381ff.

30. Forty-five shillings according to the *Lex Ribuaria*. See Fleckenstein, "Das Rittertum der Stauferzeit," 104; Werner Rösener, "Ritterliche Wirtschaftsverhältnisse und Turnier im sozialen Wandel des Hochmittelalters," in *Das ritterliche Turnier im Mittelalter*, 296–338.

31. See P. van Luyn, "Les milites dans la France du XIᵉ siècle. Examen des sources narratives," *MA* 77 (1971): table 3, 46ff.

32. Concerning the term "knight," see Hans-Georg Reuter, *Die Lehre vom Ritterstand. Zum Ritterbegriff in Historiographie und Dichtung vom 11. bis zum 13. Jahrhundert*, Neue Wirtschaftsgeschichte 4 (Cologne-Vienna, 2nd ed., 1975); Joachim Bumke, *Studien zum Ritterbegriff im 12. und 13. Jahrhundert*, Euphorion supplement 1 (Heidelberg, 1964); Johann Johrendt, "'Milites' et 'Militia' im 11. Jahrhundert. Untersuchung zur Frühgeschichte des Rittertums in Frankreich und Deutschland," Dissertation, Erlangen-Nürnberg, 1971; van Luyn, "Les milites dans la France du XIᵉ siècle. Examen des sources narratives," 5–51, 193–238.

33. Georges Duby, *La société aux XIᵉ et XIIᵉ siècles dans la région mâconnaise*, Bibliothèque Générale de l' École Pratique des Hautes Études. VIᵉ section (Paris, 1971), esp. 191ff.

34. See Arno Borst, "Das Rittertum im Hochmittelalter. Idee und Wirklichkeit [1959]," in *Das Rittertum im Mittelalter*, 212–246; John B. Freed, "The Origins of the European Nobility: The Problem of the Ministerials," *Viator* 7 (1979): 211–241.

35. See Josef Fleckenstein, "Zum Problem der Abschließung des Ritterstandes," in *Historische Forschungen für Walter Schlesinger* (Cologne-Vienna, 1974), 252–271; Josef Fleckenstein, "Die Entstehung des niederen Adels und das Rittertum," in Josef Fleckenstein, ed., *Herrschaft und Stand. Untersuchungen zur Sozialgeschichte im 13. Jahrhundert*, Veröffentlichungen des MPI 51 (Göttingen, 1977), 17–39.

36. It had already occurred *c.* 1100 in Italy; cf. Hagen Keller, "Adel, Rittertum und Ritterstand nach italienischen Zeugnissen des 11.–14. Jahrhunderts," in

Institutionen, Kultur und Gesellschaft im Mittelalter. Festschrift für Josef Flecken-stein (Sigmaringen, 1984), 581–608.

37. Concerning the training of knights in England, see now Nicholas Orme, *From Childhood to Chivalry. The Education of the English Kings and Aristocracy 1066–1530* (London-New York, 1984), whose examples, to be sure, are all taken from the late Middle Ages. Concerning the knighting ceremony, see Jean Flori, "Chevalerie et liturgie. Remise des armes et vocabulaire 'chevaleresque' dans les sources liturgiques du IXᵉ au XIVᵉ siècle," *MA* 84 (1978): 247–278 and 409–442; Jean Flori, "Les origines de l'adoubement chevaleresque. Étude des remises d'armes et du vocabulaire qui les exprime dans les sources historiques latines jusqu'au début du XIIIᵉ siècle," *Traditio* 35 (1979): 209–272; Jean Flori, "Du nouveau sur l'adoubement des chevaliers (XIᵉ–XIIIᵉ siècle)," *MA* 91 (1985): 201–226.

38. Louis Halphen and René Poupardin, eds., *Historia Gaufredi ducis Nor-mannorum* 1 (Paris, 1913), 162–163.

39. John of Salisbury, *Policraticus* 6, 10, ed. C. C. J. Webb, ed., vol. 2 (Oxford, 1909; reprinted 1965), 25.

40. They must also be viewed in connection with the emergence of the nobil-ity's power. Cf. Lutz Fenske, "Adel und Rittertum im Spiegel früher heraldischer Formen und deren Entwicklung," in *Das ritterliche Turnier im Mittelalter*, 75–160.

41. Ll. 1, 18–47, *Waltharius, Ruodlieb, Märchenepen. Lateinische Epik des Mittelalters mit deutschen Versen*, ed. Karl Langosch (Darmstadt, 1956), 86ff.

42. Concerning the origins of this development, see Gerd Althoff, "Nunc fiant Christi milites, qui dudum extiterunt raptores. Zur Entstehung von Rittertum und Ritterethos," *Saeculum* 32 (1981): 317–333.

43. See Paul Rousset, "La description du monde chevaleresque chez Orderic Vital," *MA* 75 (1969) 427–444.

44. Fulcher von Chartres, *Historia Hierosolymitana* 1, 3, 7, ed. Heinrich Hagenmeyer (Heidelberg, 1913), 136. The word *Christi* was expunged in most manuscripts.

45. *Policraticus* 6, 8 (pp. 23).

46. Thus Althoff, "Nunc fiant Christi milites, qui dudum extiterunt raptores. Zur Entstehung von Rittertum und Ritterethos," *Saeculum* 32 (1981): 333.

47. See Günter Eifler, ed., *Ritterliches Tugendsystem*, WdF 56 (Darmstadt, 1970).

48. Ll. 1–262, ed Ulrich Pretzel (Tübingen, 4th ed. 1973).

49. *Epistola* 94 (Migne, *Patrologia Latina* 207, cols, 293ff.).

50. The few studies dealing with courtly life—especially Alwyn Schultz, *Das höfische Leben zur Zeit der Minnesänger*, 2 vols. (Leipzig, 1879; reprinted 1965) and Michel Pastoureau, *La vie quotidienne en France et en Angleterre au temps des chevaliers de la table ronde* (XIIᶜ–XIIIᵉ siècles) (Paris, 1976)—are all based on literary sources. For a more recent study, see Bumke, *Höfische Kultur*.

51. *Vita Brunonis* 30 (pp. 222–223).

52. *Vita Karoli* 24 , ed. Reinhold Rau, FS 5 (Darmstadt, 1955), 194f.

53. *Vita Brunonis* 30 (pp. 222–223).

54. *Vita Karoli* 24 (pp. 194f.); see *Vita Hludowici* 19 (p. 228) about Louis the Pious.

55. *Gesta Karoli Magni* 2, 17, ed. Reinhold Rau, FS 7 (Darmstadt, 2nd. ed., 1960), 416ff.

56. *Vita Karoli* 23 (pp. 194–195). Concerning attire in literature, see Bumke, *Höfische Kultur* 1, 172ff.

57. *Vita Karoli* 24 (pp. 194f.).

58. *Gesta Karoli Magni* 1, 18 (pp. 346ff.).

59. Gerhard, *Vita Oudalrici* 4, ed. Hatto Kallfelz, *Lebensbeschreibungen einiger Bischöfe des 10.–12. Jahrhunderts*, FS 22 (Darmstadt, 1973), 74f.

60. Liudprand of Cremona, *Antapodosis* 6, 5, ed. Albert Bauer and Reinhold Rau, FS 8 (Darmstadt, 1971), 488f.

61. *Antapodosis* 6, 8f. (pp. 490ff.). Concerning festivals in courtly literature, see Bumke, *Höfische Kultur* 1, 276ff.

62. See Walter Salmen, *Der Spielmann im Mittelalter*, Innsbrucker Beiträge zur Musikwissenschaft 8 (Innsbruck, 1983), 67ff. Concerning the music enjoyed at the courts, see Sabine Zak, *Musik als 'Ehr und Zier' im mittelalterlichen Reich. Studien zur Musik im höfischen Leben, Recht und Zeremoniell* (Neuss, 1979).

63. Cf. Wolfgang Hartung, *Die Spielleute. Eine Randgruppe in der Gesellschaft des Mittelalters*, VSWG, supplement 72 (Wiesbaden, 1982); Salmen, *Der Spielmann im Mittelalter*.

64. Hartung, *Die Spielleute*, 9f.

65. *Gesta Karoli Magni* 1, 13 (pp. 338f.).

66. Cf. Werner Mezger, *Hofnarren im Mittelalter. Vom tieferen Sinn eines seltsamen Amtes* (Konstanz, 1981).

67. See Philippe Corbett, "The scurra," in *Hommages à André Boutemy* Collection Latomus 145 (Brussels, 1976), 23–31.

68. See, in addition to Hartung and Salmen, Carla Casagrande and Silvana Vecchio, "Clercs et Jongleurs dans la société médiévale (XIIᵉ–XIIIᵉ siècles)," *Annales ESC* 34 (1979): 913–928.

69. *Elucidarium* 2, 18 (Migne, *Patrologia Latina* 172, cols. 1148).

70. *Theologia christiana* 2, 129, ed. E. M. Buytaert, Corpus Christianorum. Cont. med. 12 (Turnhout, 1969), 192f. See also Hartung, *Die Spielleute*, 41–42.

71. Adam of Bremen, *Gesta Hammaburgensis ecclesiae pontificum* 3, 39, ed. Werner Trillmich, FS 11 (Darmstadt, 1961), 376ff.

72. *Gesta Hammaburgensis ecclesiae pontificum* 3, 40 (pp. 378f.).

73. Cf. regarding tournaments, see *Das ritterliche Turnier im Mittelalter*. This study has made earlier research such as R. Coltman Clephan, *The Tournament: Its Periods and Phases* (London, 1919) obsolete, since it is based entirely on late medieval practices. Concerning French origins, see Michel Parisse, "Le tournoi en France, des origines à la fin du XIIIᵉ siècle," in *Das ritterliche Turnier im Mittelalter*, 175–211. Concerning the treatment of the tournament in poetry, see Bumke, *Höfische Kultur* 1, 342ff.

74. Josef Fleckenstein, "Das Turnier als höfisches Fest im hochmittelalterlichen Deutschland," in *Das ritterliche Turnier im Mittelalter*, 229–256, specifically 256.

75. See Sabine Krüger, "Das kirchliche Turnierverbot im Mittelalter," in *Das ritterliche Turnier im Mittelalter*, 401–422.

76. Cf. Josef Fleckenstein, "Friedrich Barbarossa und das Rittertum. Zur Bedeutung der großen Mainzer Hoftage 1184 und 1188 (1971)," in *Das Rittertum im Mittelalter*, 392–418. The most important source is found in the *Chronicon Hanoniense* of Giselbert of Mons 108, ed. Léon Vanderkindere, Commission royale d'histoire 3, 1 (Brussels, 1904), 156ff.

77. Concerning the early Middle Ages, see now Jörg Jarnut, "Die frühmittelalterliche Jagd unter rechts- und sozialgeschichtlichen Aspekten," in *L'uomo di fronte al mondo animale nell'alto medioevo*, SSCI 31 (Spoleto, 1985), 765–808.

78. See Werner Goez, "Das Leben auf der Ritterburg," in Cord Meckseper and Elisabeth Schraut, eds., *Mentalität und Alltag im Spätmittelalter* (Göttingen, 1985), 9–33.

Chapter VI

1. Concerning the history of urban constitutions, a collection of source material is offered by B. Diestelkamp, M. Martens, C. van den Kieft, B. Fritz, eds., *Elenchus fontium historiae urbanae*, part 1 (Leiden, 1967). Concerning the general literature, see the bibliography and Hans K. Schulze, *Grundstrukturen der Verfassung im Mittelalter* 1, Urban 371/72 (Stuttgart, 1985–86), 127ff.

2. See Heinrich Schmidt, *Die deutschen Städtechroniken als Spiegel des bürgerlichen Selbstverständnisses im Spätmittelalter*, Schriftenreihe der Historischen Kommission bei der Bayerischen Akademie der Wissenschaften 3 (Göttingen, 1958).

3. See Ursula Peters, *Literatur in der Stadt. Studien zu den sozialen Voraussetzungen und kulturellen Organisationsformen städtischer Literatur im 13. und 14. Jahrhundert*, Studien und Texte zur Sozialgeschichte der Literatur 7 (Tübingen, 1983).

4. See Gerhard Theuerkauf, "Accipe Germanam pingentia carmina terram. Stadt- und Landesbeschreibungen des Mittelalters und der Renaissance als Quellen der Sozialgeschichte," *AKG* 65 (1983): 89–116; Carl Joachim Classen, *Die Stadt im Spiegel der Descriptiones und Laudes urbium in der antiken und mittelalterlichen Literatur bis zum Ende des 12. Jahrhunderts*, Beiträge zur Altertumswissenschaft 2 (Hildesheim-New York, 1980).

5. See Franz-Josef Schmale, "Das Bürgertum in der Literatur des 12. Jahrhunderts," *Probleme des 12. Jahrhunderts*, VuF 12 (Constance-Stuttgart, 1969), 409–424.

6. In addition to the general studies indicated, Introduction, n. 21, see Joseph and Frances Gies, *Life in a Medieval City* (London, 1969); *Aus dem Alltag der mittelalterlichen Stadt*, Handbuch zur Sonderausstellung im Bremer Landesmuseum für Kunst- und Kulturgeschichte; Hefte des Focke-Museums 62 (Bremen, 1983). Also: "Die Stadt um 1200," *Zeitschrift für Archäologie des Mittelalters* (1986).

7. Gerhard Dilcher, "Rechtshistorische Aspekte des Stadtbegriffs," in Herbert Jankuhn, Walter Schlesinger, and Heiko Steuer, eds., *Vor- und Frühformen der europäischen Stadt im Mittelalter*, Abhh. 3, 83/84 (Göttingen, 1973–74), 12–32.

8. See the most recent study by Gerhard Köbler, "Mitteleuropäisches Städtewesen in salischer Zeit. Die Ausgliederung exemter Rechtsbezirke in mittel- und niederrheinischen Städten," in Bernhard Diestelkamp, ed., *Beiträge zum hochmittelalterlichen Städtewesen*, Städteforschung A: Darstellungen 11(Cologne-Vienna, 1982), 1–13.

9. *Gesta Frederici* 1, 13, ed. Franz-Josef Schmale, FS 17 (Darmstadt, 1965), 152f.

10. *Annalen anno 1073*, ed. Adolf Schmidt, Wolfgang Dietrich Fritz, FS 13 (Darmstadt, 1957), 208f.

11. See Carl Haase, "Die mittelalterliche Stadt als Festung (1936)," in Carl Haase, ed., *Die Stadt des Mittelalters* 1, WdF, 243–245 (Darmstadt, 3rd. ed. 1978), 384–414; Manfred Petry, "Die niederrheinische Stadt als Festung im Mittelalter," *Rheinische Vierteljahresblätter* 45 (1981): 44–74.

12. Markets were also held in the countryside; especially in Bavaria, a distinction was made in the classification between "city" and "market" as a form of suburban settlement.

13. See Emil Meynen, ed., *Zentralität als Problem der mittelalterlichen Stadtgeschichtsforschung*, Städteforschung A: Darstellungen 8 (Cologne-Vienna, 1979).

14. See, for instance, Walter Schlesinger's basic studies: "Burg und Stadt," in Walter Schlesinger, *Beiträge zur deutschen Verfassungsgeschichte des Mittelalters* 2 (Göttingen, 1963), 92–147; "Stadt und Burg im Lichte der Wortgeschichte (1963)," in *Die Stadt des Mittelalters* 1, 102–128. See also Gerhard Köbler, "Civitas und vicus, burg, stat, dorf und wik," in *Vor- und Frühformen der europäischen Stadt im Mittelalter*, 61–76, and " 'burg' und 'stat'—Burg und Stadt?" *HJb* 87 (1967): 305–325.

15. The Slavic *-gorod /-grad* has the same meaning.

16. Köbler, "Mitteleuropäisches Städtewesen in salischer Zeit. Die Ausgliederung exemter Rechtsbezirke in mittel- und niederrheinischen Städten," 13.

17. For this section, see especially Edith Ennen, *Die europäische Stadt des Mittelalters* (Göttingen, 3rd, ed. 1979), 14ff.; Ennen, *Frühgeschichte der europäischen Stadt*, Veröffentlichungen des Instituts für geschichtliche Landeskunde der Rheinlande an der Universität Bonn (Bonn, 3rd ed. 1981); *Studien zu den Anfängen des europäischen Städtewesens* VuF 4 (Konstanz-Lindau, 1958); Jankuhn, Schlesinger, and Steuer, *Vor- und Frühformen der europäischen Stadt im Mittelalter*; Fernand Vercauteren, "Die europäischen Städte bis zum 11. Jahrhundert," in Wilhelm Rausch, ed., *Die Städte Mitteleuropas im 12. und 13. Jahrhundert*, Beiträge zur Geschichte der Städte Mitteleuropas 1 (Linz, 1963), 13–26.

18. Ennen, *Europäische Stadt*, 46–47.

19. See Thomas Hall, *Mittelalterliche Stadtgrundrisse. Versuch einer Übersicht der Entwicklung in Deutschland und Frankreich*, Antikvarist arkiv 66 (Stockholm, 1978), 35ff.

20. Concerning the Roman and medieval roots of today's townscapes, see Emil Meynen, "Der Grundriss der Stadt Köln als geschichtliches Erbe," in *Civitatum Communitas. Studien zum europäischen Städtewesen. Festschrift Heinz Stoob*, vol. 1, Städteforschung A: Darstellungen 21 1 (Cologne-Vienna, 1984), 281–294.

21. See *Das Marktproblem im Mittelalter*, Referate und Aussprachen auf der 3. Arbeitstagung des Kreises für Stadtgeschichte, Westfälische Forschungen 15 (1962), 43–95; Walter Schlesinger, "Der Markt als Frühform der deutschen Stadt," in *Vor- und Frühformen der europäischen Stadt im Mittelalter*, 262–293; Michael Mitterauer, *Markt und Stadt im Mittelalter. Beiträge zur historischen Zentralitätsforschung*, Monographien zur Geschichte des Mittelalters 21 (Stuttgart, 1980).

22. *MG*, Capit. 1, no. 12, cap. 6 (p. 30).

23. *MG*, Capit. 2, no. 273, cap. 19 (pp. 317–318).

24. See Waltraut Bleiber, *Naturalwirtschaft und Ware-Geld-Beziehungen zwischen Somme und Loire während des 7. Jahrhunderts*, Forschungen zur mittelalterlichen Geschichte 27 (Berlin, 1981); Bleiber, "Grundherrschaft und Markt zwischen Loire und Rhein während des 9. Jahrhunderts. Untersuchungen zu ihrem wechselseitigen Verhältnis," *JWG* (1982–93): 105–135.

25. See Traute Endemann, *Markturkunde und Markt in Frankreich und Burgund vom 9. -11. Jahrhundert* (Constance-Stuttgart, 1964).

26. See Erich Maschke, "Die Brücke im Mittelalter," in Erich Maschke and Jürgen Sydow, eds., *Die Stadt am Fluss*, Stadt in der Geschichte 4 (Sigmaringen, 1978), 9–39.

27. See Leopold Schütte, *Wik. Eine Siedlungsbezeichnung in historischen und sprachlichen Bezügen*, Städteforschung A: Darstellungen 2 (Cologne-Vienna, 1976); this was criticized by Ruth Schmidt-Wiegand in "Wik und Weichbild. Möglichkeiten und Grenzen der Rechtssprachgeographie," *ZRG* Germ. Abt. 95 (1987): 121–157.

28. See Köbler, "Civitas und vicus, burg, stat, dorf und wik," 66ff.

29. Ennen (*Die europäische Stadt des Mittelalters*, 51) would prefer to avoid the term entirely.

30. Many sources merely mention *portus*.

31. See Co van de Kieft, "Das Reich und die Städte im niederländischen Raum zur Zeit des Investiturstreits," in *Beiträge zum hochmittelalterlichen Städtewesen*, 149–169

32. Thomas Hall, *Mittelalterliche Stadtgrundrisse. Versuch einer Übersicht der Entwicklung in Deutschland*, Frankfurter Forschungen zur Architekturgeschichte 2 (Berlin, 1964), 62ff.

33. Cf. Richard Strobel "Regensburg als Bischofsstadt in bauhistorischer und topographischer Sicht," in Franz Petri, ed., *Bischofs- und Kathedralstädte des Mittelalters und der frühen Neuzeit*, Städteforschungen A: Darstellungen 1 (Cologne-Vienna, 1976), 60–83; Karl Bosl, *Die Sozialstruktur der mittelalterlichen Residenz- und Fernhandelsstadt Regensburg. Die Entwicklung ihres Bürgertums vom 9. - 14. Jahrhundert*, Abhh. neue Folge 63 (Munich, 1966).

34. See Karl-Heinz Spiess, "Zur Landflucht im Mittelalter," in Hans Patze, ed., *Die Grundherrschaft im späten Mittelalter*, 1, VuF 27 (Sigmaringen, 1983) 157–204.

35. See Karl Bosl's recent study, "Alt(en)stadt und Neustadt als Typen in Bayern," *Civitatum Communitas*, 158–180.

36. See Hagen Keller's recent study, "Über den Charakter Freiburgs in der Frühzeit der Stadt," in Berent Schwineköper, ed., *Ausgewählte Quellen zur Geschichte des Mittelalters*, FS (Sigmaringen, 1982), 249–282.

37. Keller assumes the existence of a settlement beginning in 1091, founded by the Zähringer, Konrad.

38. Klaus Flink, "Stand und Ansätze städtischer Entwicklung zwischen Rhein und Maas in salischer Zeit," in *Beiträge zum hochmittelalterlichen Städtewesen*, 170–195, esp. 188.

39. See Walter Schlesinger, "Über mitteleuropäische Städtelandschaften der Frühzeit (1957)," in Haase, *Die Stadt des Mittelalters* 1, 246–280.

40. See Berent Schwineköper, *Königtum und Städte bis zum Ende des Investiturstreits. Die Politik der Ottonen und Salier gegenüber den werdenden Städten im östlichen Sachsen und in Nordthüringen*, VuF, Sonderband 11 (Sigmaringen, 1977).

41. See Friedrich Prinz, "Die bischöfliche Stadtherrschaft im Frankenreich vom 5. bis zum 7. Jahrhundert," in *Bischofs- und Kathedralstädte des Mittelalters und der frühen Neuzeit*, 1–26; Reinhold Kaiser, *Bischofsherrschaft zwischen Königtum und Fürstenmacht. Studien zur bischöflichen Stadtherrschaft im westfränkisch-französischen Reich im frühen und hohen Mittelalter*, Pariser Historische Studien 17 (Bonn, 1981).

42. Prinz, "Die bischöfliche Stadtherrschaft im Frankenreich vom 5. bis zum 7. Jahrhundert," 19. Cf. Georg Scheibelreiter, *Der Bischof in merowingischer Zeit*, Veröffentlichungen des Instituts für Österreichische Geschichtsforschung 27 (Vienna-Cologne-Graz, 1983), 177ff.

43. See Richard Strobel, "Regensburg als Bischofsstadt in bauhistorischer und topographischer Sicht," in *Bischofs- und Kathedralstädte des Mittelalters und der frühen Neuzeit*, 79.

44. Lorenz Weinreich, ed., *Quellen zur deutschen Verfassungs-, Wirtschafts- und Sozialgeschichte bis 1250*, FS 23 (Darmstadt, 1977), no. 23, c. 20 and 27f., 96ff.

45. See Philippe Dollinger, "Der Aufschwung der oberrheinischen Bischofsstädte in salischer Zeit (1025–1125)," in Diestelkamp, *Beiträge zum hochmittelalterlichen Städtewesen*, 138.

46. In Saxony and Thuringia, citizens did not noticeably resist their lords. On this, see Schwineköper, *Königtum und Städte bis zum Ende des Investiturstreits*, 156ff.

47. Cf. Georg Droege, "Der Einfluss der mittelalterlichen Freiheitsbewegung auf die frühe Stadt," in *Civitatum Communitas*, 56–70.

48. See especially Hermann Jakobs, "Stadtgemeinde und Bürgertum um 1100," in *Beiträge zum hochmittelalterlichen Städtewesen*, 14–54 (including a list of records documenting the founding of cities). Concerning Mainz, see Dieter Demandt, *Stadtherrschaft und Stadtfreiheit im Spannungsfeld von Geistlichkeit und Bürgerschaft in Mainz (11.–15. Jahrhundert)*, Geschichtliche Landeskunde 15 (Wiesbaden, 1977). Concerning guilds, see now Berent Schwineköper, ed., *Gilden und Zünfte. Kaufmännische und gewerbliche Genossenschaften im frühen und hohen*

Mittelalter, VuF 29 (Sigmaringen, 1985). Their influence on the emerging cities is again given more credit; however, merchant guilds are often not documented until after the city was formed.

49. See Jakobs, "Stadtgemeinde und Bürgertumum 1100," 16ff.

50. Ibid., 29.

51. Hagen Keller emphasizes this in "Der Übergang zur Kommune: Zur Entwicklung der italienischen Stadtverfassung im 11. Jahrhundert," in *Beiträge zum hochmittelalterlichen Städtewesen*, 55–72, especially 62ff. with respect to Italy.

52. Lampert of Hersfeld, *Annalen anno 1073*, ed. Adolf Schmidt and Wolfgang Dietrich Fritz, FS 13 (Darmstadt, 1957), 208–209.

53. *MG*, DH IV., 267.

54. See Edith Ennen, "Erzbischof und Stadtgemeinde in Köln bis zur Schlacht von Worringen (1288)," in *Bischofs- und Kathedralstädte des Mittelalters und der frühen Neuzeit*, 27–46.

55. This is emphasized by Eckhard Müller-Mertens in "Bürgerlich-Städtische Autonomie in der Feudalgesellschaft. Begriff und geschichtliche Entwicklung," *ZfG* 29 (1981): 205–225.

56. Diestelkamp, et al., *Elenchus fontium historiae urbanae*, no. 80, 137–138.

57. Concerning the topography of the city, see also Cord Meckseper, "Städtebau," in *Die Zeit der Staufer* 3 (Stuttgart, 1977), 75–86. In addition, see Erich Herzog, *Die ottonische Stadt. Die Anfänge der mittelalerlichen Stadtbaukunst in Deutschland*, Frankfurter Forschungen zur Architekturgeschichte 2 (Berlin, 1964); Hall, *Mittelalterliche Stadtgrundrisse. Versuch einer Übersicht der Entwicklung in Deutschland und Frankreich*; Enrico Guidoni. *Die europäische Stadt. Eine baugeschichtliche Studie über ihre Entstehung im Mittelalter* (Stuttgart, 1980; Italian ed., 1978); Norbert Leudemann, *Deutsche Bischofsstädte im Mittelalter. Zur topographischen Entwicklung der deutschen Bischofsstadt im Heiligen Römischen Reich* (Munich, 1980); Cord Meckseper, *Kleine Kunstgeschichte der deutschen Stadt im Mittelalter* (Darmstadt, 1982). Also, see Hans Koepf, "Das Stadtbild als Ausdruck der geschichtlichen Entwicklung," in Hans Eugen Specker, ed., *Stadt und Kultur*, Stadt in der Geschichte 11 (Sigmaringen, 1983), 9–28.

58. See Meckseper, *Kleine Kunstgeschichte der deutschen Stadt im Mittelalter*, 263.

59. See Leudemann, *Deutsche Bischofsstädte im Mittelalter*, 57ff.

60. See Anne Lombard-Jourdan, "Oppidum et banlieu. Sur l'origine et les dimensions du territoire urbain," *Annales ESC* 27 (1972): 373–395. (The French term *banlieu* actually means "neutral zone" [*Bannmeile*].)

61. See Meckseper, *Kleine Kunstgeschichte der deutschen Stadt im Mittelalter*, 71f. Concerning streets in late medieval cities, cf. the recent study by Jean-Pierre Leguay, *La rue au moyen-âge* (Rennes, 1984).

62. See *Duisburg im Mittelalter* (Duisburg, 1983), 29ff.

63. Cf. Helmut Maurer, *Konstanz als ottonischer Bischofssitz. Zum Selbstverständnis geistlichen Fürstentums im 10. Jahrhundert*, Veröffentlichungen des MPI 39 = Studien zur Germania sacra 12 (Göttingen, 1973); Helmut Maurer, "Kirchengründung und Romgedanke am Beispiel des ottonischen Bischofssitzes

Konstanz," in *Bischofs- und Kathedralstädte des Mittelalters und der frühen Neuzeit*, 47–59.

64. See Meckseper, *Kleine Kunstgeschichte der deutschen Stadt im Mittelalter*, 108ff. Concerning the patrician houses in the Rhineland, see Anita Wiedenau, *Romanischer Wohnbau im Rheinland*, 16. Veröffentlichung der Abteilung Architektur des Kunsthistorischen Instituts der Universität Köln (Cologne, 1979).

65. See Oskar Moser, "Zum Aufkommen der «Stube» im Bürgerhaus des Spätmittelalters," in *Das Leben in der Stadt des Spätmittelalters*, Veröffentlichungen des Instituts für Realienkunde Österreichs; Sitzungsberichte der Akademie der Wissenschaften, philosophisch-historische Klasse 325 (Vienna, 1977), 207–228.

66. See Meckseper, *Kleine Kunstgeschichte der deutschen Stadt im Mittelalter*, 149.

67. See Gerhard Nagel, *Das mittelalterliche Kaufhaus und seine Stellung in der Stadt. Eine baugeschichtliche Untersuchung an südwestdeutschen Beispielen* (Berlin, 1971).

68. Hektor Ammann, "Wie gross war die mittelalterliche Stadt? (1956)," in *Die Stadt des Mittelalters* 1, 415–422.

69. Estimates vary, however, between 80,000 and 275,000; The "Etat général des feux" of 1328 counts more than 61,000 hearths.

70. See Wilhelm Ebel, *Der Bürgereid als Geltungsgrund und Gestaltungsprinzip des deutschen mittelalterlichen Stadtrechts* (Weimar, 1958).

71. Cf. Schwineköper, *Gilden und Zünfte*.

72. See Knut Schulz, *Ministerialität und Bürgertum in Trier. Untersuchungen zur rechtlichen und sozialen Gliederung der Trierer Bürgerschaft vom ausgehenden 11. bis zum Ende des 14. Jahrhunderts*, Rheinisches Archiv 66 (Bonn, 1968); Bosl, *Die Sozialstruktur der mittelalterlichen Residenz- und Fernhandelsstadt Regensburg*.

73. Erich Maschke and Jürgen Sydow, eds., *Städtische Mittelschichten*, Veröffentlichungen der Kommission für geschichtliche Landeskunde in Baden-Württemberg, Series B, 69 (Stuttgart, 1972).

74. See Knut Schulz, "Zensualität und Stadtentwicklung im 11./12. Jahrhundert," in *Beiträge zum hochmittelalterlichen Städtewesen*, 73–93; Renate Brandl-Ziegert, "Die Sozialstruktur der bayerischen Bischofs- und Residenzstädte Passau, Freising, Landshut und Ingolstadt. Die Entwicklung des Bürgertums vom 9. bis zum 13. Jahrhundert," in Karl Bosl, ed., *Die mittelalterliche Stadt in Bayern*, ZBLG, supplement 6 (München, 1974), 18–127.

75. See Herbert Jankuhn, Walter Janssen, Ruth Schmidt-Wiegand, and Heinrich Tiefenbach, eds., *Das Handwerk in vor- und frühgeschichtlicher Zeit*, 2 vols., Abhh. 3, 122 (Göttingen, 1981–83).

76. See Ruth Schmidt-Wiegand, "Gilde und Zunft. Die Bezeichnungen für Handwerksgenossenschaften im Mittelalter," in *Das Handwerk in vor- und frühgeschichtlicher Zeit* 1, 355–369, esp. 361–362.

77. Diestelkamp et al., *Elenchus fontium historiae urbanae*, part 1, no. 50, 78f.

78. Ibid., no. 56, 102.

79. Ibid., no. 61, 107f.

80. Erich Maschke leads the way here with his article on "Die Unterschichten der mittelalterlichen Städte Deutschlands (1967)," in *Die Stadt des Mittelalters* 3, 345–454.

81. Concerning the late Middle Ages, see now Franz Irsigler, Arnold Lasotta, *Bettler und Gaukler, Dirnen und Henker. Randgruppen und Außenseiter in Köln 1300–1600*, Aus der Kölner Stadtgeschichte (Cologne, 1984).

82. See Georg Wacha, "Tiere und Tierhaltung in der Stadt sowie im Wohnbereich der spätmittelalterlichen Menschen und ihre Darstellung in der bildenden Kuns," in *Das Leben in der Stadt des Spätmittelalters*, 229–260.

83. See Maschke, "Die Unterschichten der mittelalterlichen Städte Deutschlands (1967)," in *Die Stadt des Mittelalters* 3, 361.

84. Concerning the late Middle Ages, see now Alfred Haverkamp, ed., *Haus und Familie in der spätmittelalterlichen Stadt*, Städteforschung Reihe A: Darstellungen 18 (Cologne-Vienna, 1984).

85. See Peter Ketsch, *Frauen im Mittelalter* 1, Geschichtsdidaktik: Studien, Materialien 14/19 (Düsseldorf, 1983/84), 141ff. (concerning the late Middle Ages).

86. *Annalen anno 1074*, ed. Adolf Schmidt and Wolfgang Dietrich Fritz, FS 13 (Darmstadt, 1957), 248f.

87. *Historiae* 3, 101, ed. Robert Latouche, *Les classiques de l'histoire de France au moyen âge* 17 (Paris, 1937, reprinted 1964), 128–129.

88. See Jürgen Sydow, ed., *Städtische Versorgung und Entsorgung im Wandel der Geschichte*, Stadt in der Geschichte 8 (Sigmaringen, 1981).

BIBLIOGRAPHY

General and Related Works

Bishop, Morris. *The Penguin Book of the Middle Ages*. Harmondsworth, 1971.

Boockmann, Hartmut. *Einführung in die Geschichte des Mittelalters*. Beck'sche Elementarbücher. Munich, 1981.

Borst, Arno. *Lebensformen im Mittelalter*. Frankfurt and Berlin, 1973.

Delort, Robert. *La vie au moyen âge*. Lausanne and Paris, 1982.

Fichtenau, Heinrich. *Lebensordnungen des 10. Jh.: Studien über Denkart und Existenz im einstigen Karolingerreich*. 2 vols. Monographien zur Geschichte des Mittelalters 30. Stuttgart, 1984.

Fossier, Robert. *Enfance de l'Europe, X^e-XIIe siècle: Aspects économiques et sociaux*. Vol. 1: *L'homme et son espace*. Vol. 2: *Structures et problèmes*. Nouvelle Clio 17/17. Paris, 1982.

Handbuch der deutschen Wirtschafts- und Sozialgeschichte. Vol. 1. Ed. Hermann Aubin and Wolfgang Zorn. Stuttgart, 1971.

Handbuch der europäischen Wirtschafts- und Sozialgeschichte. Vol. 2: *Europäische Wirtschafts- und Sozialgeschichte im Mittelalter*. Ed. Jan van Houtte. Stuttgart, 1980.

Le Goff, Jacques. *Kultur des europäischen Mittelalters*. Munich and Zurich, 1970.

Meyer, Werner. *Hirsebrei und Hellebarde: Auf den Spuren des mittelalterlichen Lebens in der Schweiz*. Olten-Freiburg/B., 1985.

Pognon, Edmond. *La vie quotidienne en l'an mille*. Paris, 1981.

Riché, Pierre. *La vie quotidienne dans l'Empire carolingienne*. Paris, 1973. German trans.: *Die Welt der Karolinger*. Stuttgart, 1981.

Schulze, Hans K. *Grundstrukturen der Verfassung im Mittelalter*. 2 vols. Urban 371 and 372. Stuttgart, 1985, 1986.

I. People, Nature, Culture

Bevölkerungsgeschichte Europas. Ed. Carlo M. Cipolla and Knut Borchardt. Munich, 1971.

293

The Climate of Europe: Past, Present, and Future. Natural and Man-Induced Climatic Changes, an European Perspective. Ed. Hermann Flohn and Roberto Fantechi. Dordrecht, Boston, and Lancaster, 1984.

Curschmann, Fritz. *Hungersnöte im Mittelalter: Ein Beitrag zur deutschen Wirtschaftsgeschichte des 8. bis 13. Jh.* Leipziger Studien aus dem Gebiet der Geschichte 6, 1. Leipzig, 1900. Reprint: Aalen, 1970.

Gastfreundschaft, Taverne und Gasthaus im Mittelalter. Ed. Hans Conrad Peyer, with Elisabeth Müller-Luckner. Schriften des Historischen Kollegs, Kolloquien 3. Munich and Vienna, 1983.

Janssen, Walter. "Essen und Trinken im frühen und hohen Mittelalter aus archäologischer Sicht." In *Liber Castellorum: 40 Variaties op het thema kasteel.* Ed. T. J. Hoekstra. Zutphen, 1981.

Leguay, Jean-Pierre. *La rue au moyen-âge.* Rennes, 1984.

Ladurie, Emmanuel Le Roy. *Histoire du climat depuis l'an mil.* 1967. English trans.: *Times of Feast, Times of Famine: A History of Climate since the Year 1000.* London, 1972.

Skelette erzählen . . . Menschen des frühen Mittelalters in Spiegel der Anthropologie und Medizin. Exhibit of the Württembergischen Landesmuseums. Stuttgart, 1983.

II. The Family

General

Herlihy, David. *Medieval Households.* Studies in Cultural History. Cambridge, Mass., and London, 1985.

Famille et parenté dans l'occident médiéval: Actes du Colloque de Paris (1974) organisé par l'Ecole pratique des hautes études (VIᵉ section) en collaboration avec le Collège de France et l'Ecole Française de Rome. Ed. Georges Duby and Jacques Le Goff. Collection de l'Ecole Française de Rome 30. Rome, 1977

Schuler, Thomas. "Familien im Mittelalter." In *Die Familie in der Geschichte.* Ed. Heinz Reif. Kleine Vandenhoeck series, 1474. Göttingen, 1982.

1. House and Clan

Brunner, Otto. *Land und Herrschaft: Grundfragen der territorialen Verfassungsgeschichte Österreichs im Mittelalter.* Vienna and Wiesbaden, 1959.

Genzmer, Felix. "Die germanische Sippe als Rechtsgebilde." ZRG, Germ. Abt. 67 (1950): 34-49.

Kroeschell, Karl. *Haus und Herrschaft im frühen deutschen Recht: Ein methodischer Versuch.* Göttinger rechtswissenschaftliche Studien 70. Göttingen, 1968.

———. "Die Sippe im germanischen Recht." ZRG, Germ. Abt. 77 (1960): 1-25.

Murray, Alexander Callender. *Germanic Kinship Structure: Studies in Law and Society in Antiquity and Early Middle Ages.* Studies and Texts 65. Toronto, 1983.

Schlesinger, Walter. "Herrschaft und Gefolgschaft in der germanisch-deutschen Verfassungsgeschichte." 1953. In *Herrschaft und Staat im Mittelalter.* Ed. Hellmut Kämpf. WdF 2. Darmstadt, 1955.

————. "Randbemerkungen zu drei Aufsätzen über Sippe, Gefolgschaft und Treue." In *Alteuropa und die moderne Gesellschaft: Festschrift Otto Brunner.* Göttingen, 1963.

Schmid, Karl. "Über die Struktur des Adels im früheren Mittelalter." *Jahrbuch für fränkische Landesforschung* 19 (1959): 1-23.

————. "Zur Problematik von Familie, Sippe und Geschlecht, Haus und Dynastie beim mittelalterlichen Adel." ZGO 105 (1957): 1-62.

2. Marriage

Duby, Georges. *Ritter, Frau und Priester: Die Ehe im feudalen Frankreich.* Frankfurt, 1985. Original in French, 1981.

Glasser, Marc. "Marriage in Medieval Hagiography." *Studies in Medieval and Renaissance History,* new series 4 (1981): 1-34.

Konecny, Silvia. "Die Frauen des karolingischen Königshauses: Die politische Bedeutung der Ehe und die Stellung der Frau in der fränkischen Herrscherfamilie vom 7. bis zum 10. Jh." Dissertation, University of Vienna, 1976.

Love and Marriage in the Twelfth Century. Ed. Willy van Hoecke and Andries Welkenhuysen. Mediaevalia Lovaniensia 1, 8. Louvain, 1981.

Il matrimonio nella società altomedievale. 2 vols. SSCI 24. Spoleto, 1977.

Mikat, Paul. *Dotierte Ehe–rechte Ehe: Zur Entwicklung des Eheschließungsrechts in fränkischer Zeit.* Rheinisch- Westfälische Akademie der Wissenschaften, Geisteswissenschaftliche Vorträge G 277. Opladen, 1978.

————. "Ehe." In HRG, vol. 1 (1971), cols. 809-832.

Ritzer, Korbinian. *Formen, Riten und religiöses Brauchtum der Eheschließung in den christlichen Kirchen des ersten Jahrtausends.* Liturgiewissenschaftliche Quellen und Forschungen 38. Münster, 1962.

Sheehan, Michael M. "Choice of Marriage Partner in the Middle Ages: Development and Mode of Application of a Theory of Marriage." *Studies in Medieval and Renaissance History,* new series, 1 (1978): 3-33.

3. The Wife

Ennen, Edith. *Frauen im Mittelalter.* Munich, 1984.

————. "Die Frau in der mittelalterlichen Stadtgesellschaft Mitteleuropas." *Hansische Geschichtsblätter* 98 (1980): 1-22.

"La femme dans les civilisations du Xᵉ au XIIᵉ siècle." *Cahiers de civilisation médiévale* 20 (1977): 93-260.

Histoire mondiale de la femme. Ed. Pierre Grimal. Vol. 1. Paris, 1965.

Ketsch, Peter. "Aspekte der rechtlichen und politisch-gesellschaftlichen Situation von Frauen im frühen Mittelalter (500-1150)." In *Frauen in der Geschichte*, vol. 2. Geschichtsdidaktik: Studien, Materialien 8. Düsseldorf, 1982.

――――. *Frauen im Mittelalter*. 2 vols. Geschichtsdidaktik: Studien, Materialien 14, 19. Düsseldorf, 1983, 1984.

Lucas, Angela M. *Women in the Middle Ages: Religion, Marriage, and Letters*. New York, 1983.

Portmann, Marie-Louise. *Die Darstellung der Frau in der Geschichtsschreibung des früheren Mittelalters*. Basler Beiträge zur Geschichtswissenschaft 69. Basel and Stuttgart, 1958.

Shulamith, Shahar. *Die Frau im Mittelalter*. Königstein/Taunus, 1981.

Wemple, Suzanne Fonay. *Women in Frankish Society: Marriage and the Cloister 500 to 900*. Philadelphia, 1981.

4. Love and Sexuality

Dinzelbacher, Peter. "Über die Entdeckung der Liebe im Hochmittelalter." *Saeculum* 32 (1981): 185-208.

L'érotisme au moyen âge: Etudes présentées au Troisième Colloque de l'Institut d'etudes médiévales. Ed. Bruno Roy. Montréal and Quebec, 1977.

Europäisches Hochmittelalter. Ed. Henning Krauß. Neues Handbuch der Literaturwissenschaft 7. Wiesbaden, 1981.

Leclercq, Jean. *Monks and Love in Twelfth-Century France*. Oxford, 1979.

Liebe als Literatur: Aufsätze zur erotischen Dichtung in Deutschland. Ed. Rüdiger Krohn. Munich, 1983.

Noonan, John T. *Empfängnisverhütung: Geschichte ihrer Beurteilung in der katholischen Theologie und im kanonischen Recht*. Walberburger Studien der Albertus Magnus Akademie, theological series, 6. Mainz, 1969. Original in English, 1967.

Payer, Pierre J. "Early Medieval Regulations Concerning Marital Sexual Relations." *Journal of Medieval History* 6 (1980): 353-376.

――――. *Sex and the Penitentials: The Development of a Sexual Code, 550-1150*. Toronto, Buffalo, and London, 1984.

Schnell, Rüdiger. *Causa Amoris: Liebeskonzeption und Liebesdarstellung in der mittelalterlichen Literatur*. Bibliotheca Germanica 27. Bern and Munich, 1985.

5. The Children

Arnold, Klaus. *Kind und Gesellschaft in Mittelalter und Renaissance*. Sammlung Zebra B 2. Paderborn and Munich, 1980.

Winter, Matthias. *Kindheit und Jugend im Mittelalter*. Hochschul-Sammlung Philosophie Geschichte 6. Freiburg, 1984.

III. Monasteries and Monastic Life

1. The Institution: Benedictine Monasticism in the West

Benedictine Culture 750-1050. Ed. W. Lourdaux and D. Verhelst. Mediaevalia Lovaniensia 1, 11. Louvain, 1983.

Bulst, Neithard. *Untersuchungen zu den Klosterreformen Wilhelms von Dijon (962-1031).* Pariser Historische Studien 11. Bonn, 1973.

Cluny: Beiträge zu Gestalt und Wirkung der cluniazensischen Reform. Ed. Helmut Richter. WdF 241. Darmstadt, 1975.

Cowdrey, H. E. J. *The Cluniacs and the Gregorian Reform.* Oxford, 1970.

Fechter, Johannes. "Cluny, Adel und Volk: Studien über das Verhältnis des Klosters zu den Ständen (910-1156)." Dissertation, University of Tübingen, 1966.

Felten, Franz J. *Äbte und Laienäbte im Frankenreich: Studie zum Verhältnis von Staat und Kirche im früheren Mittelalter.* Monographien zur Geschichte des Mittelalters 20. Stuttgart, 1980.

Frank, Karl Suso. *Grundzüge der Geschichte des christlichen Mönchtums.* Grundzüge 25. Darmstadt, 1975.

Grégoire, Réginald, Léo Moulin, and Raymond Oursel. *Die Kultur der Klöster.* Stuttgart and Zurich, 1985.

Jakobs, Hermann. *Der Adel in der Klosterreform von St. Blasien.* Kölner Historische Abhandlungen 16. Cologne and Graz, 1968.

——. *Die Hirsauer: Ihre Ausbreitung und Rechtsstellung im Zeitalter des Investiturstreites.* Kölner Historische Abhandlungen 4. Cologne and Graz, 1961.

Lawrence, Clifford Hugh. *Medieval Monasticism: Forms of Religious Life in Western Europe in the Middle Ages.* London and New York, 1984.

Leyser, Henrietta. *Hermits and the New Monasticism: A Study of Religious Communities in Western Europe 1000-1150.* London, 1984.

Mönchtum und Gesellschaft im Frühmittelalter. Ed. Friedrich Prinz. WdF 312. Darmstadt, 1976.

Il monachesimo dell'alto medioevo e la formazione della civiltà occidentale. SSCI 4. Spoleto, 1957.

Neue Forschungen über Cluny und die Cluniacenser. Ed. Gerd Tellenbach. Freiburg/B., 1959.

Prinz, Friedrich. *Askese und Kultur: Vor- und frühbenediktinisches Mönchtum an der Wiege Europas.* Munich, 1980.

——. *Frühes Mönchtum im Frankenreich: Kultur und Gesellschaft in Galien, den Rheinlanden und Bayern am Beispiel der monastischen Entwicklung (4.-8. Jh.).* Munich and Vienna, 1965.

Sackur, Ernst. *Die Cluniacenser in ihrer kirchlichen und allgemeingeschichtlichen Wirksamkeit bis zur Mitte des 11. Jh.* 2 vols. Halle/S., 1892, 1894. Reprint: Darmstadt, 1965.

Schreiner, Klaus. "Mönchtum zwischen asketischem Anspruch und gesellschaftlicher Wirklichkeit: Spiritualität, Sozialverhalten und Sozialverfassung schwäbischer Reformmönche im Spiegel ihrer Geschichtsschreibung." *Zeitschrift für württembergische Landesgeschichte* 41 (1982): 250-307.

Semmler, Josef. *Die Klosterreform von Siegburg: Ihre Ausbreitung und ihr Reform-programm im 11. und 12. Jh.* Rheinisches Archiv 53. Bonn, 1959.

Untersuchungen zu Kloster und Stift. Veröffentlichungen. des MPI für Geschichte 68 = Studien zur Germania Sacra 14. Göttingen, 1980.

Valous, Guy de. *Le monachisme clunisien des origines au XVᵉ siècle.* Paris, 1970.

Wehlt, Hans-Peter. *Reichsabtei und König, dargestellt am Beispiel der Abtei Lorsch mit Ausblicken auf Hersfeld, Stablo und Fulda.* Veröffentlichungen des MPI für Geschichte 28. Göttingen, 1970.

Wollasch, Joachim. *Mönchtum des Mittelalters zwischen Kirche und Welt.* Münstersche Mittelalter-Schriften 7. Munich, 1973.

Die Zisterzienser: Ordensleben zwischen Ideal und Wirklichkeit. Schriften des Rheinischen Museumsamtes 10. Bonn, 1980.

2. The Space: The Monastery as Residence for Monks

Hecht, Konrad. *Der St. Galler Klosterplan.* Sigmaringen, 1984.

Horn, Walter, and Ernest Born. *The Plan of St. Gall: A Study of the Architecture and Economy of, and Life in a Paradigmatic Carolingian Monastery.* 3 vols. University of California Studies in the History of Art 19. Berkeley, Los Angeles, and London, 1979.

Studien zur St. Galler Klosterplan. Ed. Johannes Duft. Mitteilungen zur vaterländischen Geschichte 42. St. Gall, 1962.

3. The Inhabitants: The Monastic Community

Hegglin, Benno. *Der benediktinische Abt in rechtsgeschichtlicher Entwicklung und geltendem Kirchenrecht.* Kirchenrechtliche Quellen und Studien 5. St. Ottilien, 1961.

Die Klostergemeinschaft von Fulda im früheren Mittelalter. Ed. Karl Schmid. 3 vols. in 5 parts. Münstersche Mittelalter-Schriften 8. Munich, 1978.

Oexle, Otto Gerhard. *Forschungen zu monastischen und geistlichen Gemeinschaften im westfränkischen Bereich.* Münstersche Mittelalter-Schriften 31. Munich, 1978.

Salmon, Pierre. *L'abbé dans la tradition monastique, contribution à l'histoire du caractère perpétuel des superieurs religieux en Occident.* Histoire et sociologie de l'Église 2. Paris, 1962.

Vogüé, Albert de. *La communauté et l'abbé dans la règle de saint Benoit.* Textes et Études Théologique. Bruges, 1961.

4. Monastic Life

Bosl, Karl. "Des Mönches Leben am Rande der Gesellschaft und sein Wirken in ihr: Der konstitutive Beitrag des Benediktinerordens zu Europas Christlichkeit und Geistigkeit, Gesellschaft und Kultur." In *Regulae Benedicti Studi* 10-11 (1981-1982): 91-107.

Moulin, Leo. *La vie quotidienne des religieux du moyen âge, Xᵉ-XVᵉ siècle.* Paris, 1978.

Parisse, Michel. *Les nonnes au moyen âge.* Le Puy, 1983.

Zimmermann, Gerd. *Ordensleben und Lebensstandard: Die 'cura corporis' in den Ordensvorschriften des abendländischen Hochmittelalters.* 2 vols. Beiträge zur Geschichte des alten Mönchtums und des Benediktinerordens 32. Münster, 1973.

IV. Peasant Life and the Manorial System

General

Abel, Wilhelm. *Geschichte der deutschen Landwirtschaft vom frühen Mittelalter bis zum 19. Jh.* Deutsche Agrargeschichte 2. Stuttgart, 1967.

Deutsches Bauerntum im Mittelalter. Ed. Günther Franz. WdF 416. Darmstadt, 1976.

Dollinger, Philipp. *Der bayerische Bauernstand vom 9. bis 13. Jh.* Munich, 1982. Original in French, 1949.

Dopsch, Alfons. *Herrschaft und Bauer in der deutschen Kaiserzeit: Untersuchungen zur Agrar- und Sozialgeschichte des hohen Mittelalters mit besonderer Berücksichtigung des südostdeutschen Raumes.* Quellen und Forschungen zur Agrargeschichte 10. Stuttgart, 1964.

———. *Die Wirtschaftsentwicklung der Karolingerzeit vornehmlich in Deutschland.* 2 vols. Weimar, 1921, 1922. Reprint: Darmstadt, 1962.

Duby, Georges. *L'économie rurale et la vie des campagnes dans l'occident médiéval (France, Angleterre, Empire), IXᵉ-XVᵉ siècles.* 2 vols. Paris, 1962.

———. *Krieger und Bauern: Die Entwicklung von Wirtschaft und Gesellschaft im frühen Mittelalter.* Frankfurt, 1977. Original in French, 1973.

Franz, Günther. *Geschichte des deutschen Bauernstandes vom frühen Mittelalter bis zum 19. Jh.* Deutsche Agrargeschichte 4. Stuttgart, 1970.

Kuchenbuch, Ludolf. *Bäuerliche Gesellschaft und Klosterherrschaft im 9. Jh. Studien zur Sozialstruktur der 'familia' der Abtei Prüm.* VSWG Beihefte 66. Wiesbaden, 1978.

Lütge, Friedrich. *Die Agrarverfassung des frühen Mittelalters im mitteldeutschen Raum vornehmlich in der Karolingerzeit.* Quellen und Forschungen zur Agrargeschichte 17. 1937. Reprint: Stuttgart, 1966.

———. *Geschichte der deutschen Agrarverfassung vom frühen Mittelalter bis zum 19. Jh.* Deutsche Agrargeschichte 3. Stuttgart, 1967.

Villa–curtis–grangia: Landwirtschaft zwischen Loire und Rhein von der Römerzeit zum Hochmittelalter. Ed. Walter Janssen and Dietrich Lohrmann. Beihefte der Francia 11. Munich and Zurich, 1983.

1. The Institution: The Medieval Manorial System

Bleiber, Waltraut. *Naturalwirtschaft und Ware-Geld-Beziehungen zwischen Somme und Loire während des 7. Jh.* Forschungen zur mittelalterlichen Geschichte 27. Berlin, 1981.

Epperlein, Siegfried. *Bauernbedrückung und Bauernwiderstand im hohen Mittelalter: Zur Erforschung der Ursachen bäuerlicher Abwanderung nach Osten im 12. und 13. Jh., vornehmlich nach den Urkunden geistlicher Grundherrschaften.* Forschungen zur mittelalterlichen Geschichte 6. Berlin, 1960.

————. *Herrschaft und Volk im karolingischen Imperium: Studien über soziale Konflikte und dogmatisch-politische Kontroversen im fränkischen Reich.* Forschungen zur mittelalterlichen Geschichte 14. Berlin, 1969.

Le grand domaine aux époques mérovingienne et carolingienne / Die Grundherrschaft im frühen Mittelalter. Ed. Adriaan Verhulst. Ghent, 1985.

Die Grundherrschaft im späten Mittelalter. Ed. Hans Patze. 2 vols. VuF 27. Sigmaringen, 1983.

Linck, Eberhard. *Sozialer Wandel in klösterlichen Grundherrschaften des 11.-13. Jh.: Studien zu den 'familiae' von Gembloux, Stablo-Malmedy und St. Trond.* Veröffentlichungen des MPI für Geschichte 57. Göttingen, 1979.

Schulze, Hans K. "Grundherrschaft." In HRG, vol. 1 (1971), col. 1824-1842.

2. The Space: Peasant's House, Manse, Manor, and Village

Die Anfänge der Landgemeinde und ihr Wesen. 2 vols. VuF 7/8. Constance and Stuttgart, 1964.

Bader, Karl Siegfried. *Studien zur Rechtsgeschichte des mittelalterlichen Dorfes:* Vol. 1: *Das mittelalterliche Dorf als Friedens- und Rechtsbezirk.* Cologne, Graz, and Weimar, 1957. Vol. 2: *Dorfgenossenschaft und Dorfgemeinde.* Cologne and Graz, 1962. Vol. 3: *Rechtsformen und Schichten der Liegenschaftsnutzung im mittelalterlichen Dorf.* Vienna, Cologne, and Graz, 1973.

Baumgarten, Karl. *Das deutsche Bauernhaus: Eine Einführung in seine Geschichte vom 9. bis zum 19. Jh.* Berlin and Neumünster, 1980.

Chapelot, Jean, and Robert Fossier. *Le village et la maison au moyen âge.* Paris, 1980.

Dölling, Hildegard. *Haus und Hof in westgermanischen Volksrechten.* Veröffentlichungen der Altertumskommission im Provinzialinstitut für westfälische Landes- und Volskunde 2. Münster, 1958.

Donat, Peter. *Haus, Hof und Dorf in Mitteleuropa vom 7. bis 12. Jh.: Archäologische Beiträge zur Entwicklung und Struktur der bäuerlichen Siedlung.* Schriften zur Ur- und Frühgeschichte 33. Berlin, 1980.

Das Dorf der Eisenheit und des frühen Mittelalters: Siedlungsform–wirtschaftliche Funktion–soziale Struktur. Ed. Herbert Jankuhn, Rudolf Schützeichel, and Fred Schwind. Abhandlungen. Göttingen, phil.-hist. Kl. 3, 101. Göttingen, 1977.

Fehring, Günter P. "Zur archäologischen Erforschung mittelalterlicher Dorfsiedlungen in Südwestdeutschland." *Zeitschrift für Agrargeschichte und Agrarsoziologie* 21 (1973):1-35.

Nikolay-Panter, Marlene. *Entstehung und Entwicklung der Landgemeinde im Trierer Raum.* Rheinisches Archiv 97. Bonn, 1976.

Untersuchungen zur eisenzeitlichen und frühmittelalterlichen Flur in Mitteleuropa und ihrer Nutzung. Ed. Heinrich Beck, Dietrich Denecke, and Herbert Jankuhn. 2 vols. Abhandlungen. Göttingen, phil.-hist. Kl. 3, 115/116. Göttingen, 1979.

3. The People: Peasantry and Serfdom

Brunner, Karl, and Gerhard Jaritz. *Landherr, Bauer, Ackerknecht: Der Bauer im Mittelalter: Klischee und Wirklichkeit.* Vienna, Cologne, and Graz, 1985.

Epperlein, Siegfried. "Bäuerliche Arbeitsdarstellungen auf mittelalterlichen Bildzeugnissen: Zur geschichtlichen Motivation von Miniaturen und Graphiken von 9. bis 15. Jh. JWG 1 (1976): 181-208.

————. *Der Bauer im Bild des Mittelalters.* Leipzig, Berlin, and Jena, 1975.

Fourquin, Guy. *Le paysan d'Occident au moyen âge.* Paris, 1972.

Martini, Fritz. *Das Bauerntum im deutschen Schrifttum von den Anfängen bis zum 16. Jh.* Deutsche Vierteljahresschrift für Literaturwissenschaft und Geistesgeschichte 27. Halle/S., 1944.

Rösener, Werner. *Bauern im Mittelalter.* Munich, 1985.

Wort und Begriff "Bauer." Ed. Reinhard Wenskus, Herbert Jankuhn, and Klaus Grinda. Abhandlungen. Göttingen, phil.-hist. Kl. 3, 89. Göttingen, 1975.

4. The Life of Manse Peasants

Bentzien, Ulrich. *Bauernarbeit im Feudalismus: Landwirtschaftliche Arbeitsgeräte und -verfahren in Deutschland von der Mitte des 1. Jahrtausends u. Z. bis um 1800.* Akademie der Wissenschaften der DDR, Zentralinstitut für Geschichte, Veröffentlichungen für Volkskunde und Kulturgeschichte 67. Berlin, 1980.

White, Lynn. *Die mittelalterliche Technik und der Wandel der Gesellschaft.* Munich, 1968. Original in English.

V. Knighthood and Courtly Life

1. The Institution: Principality, Princely Courts, and Courtly Culture

Bloch, Marc. *Die Feudalgesellschaft.* Frankfurt, Vienna, and Berlin, 1982. Original in French, 1939-1940.

Bumke, Joachim. *Höfische Kultur: Literatur und Gesellschaft im hohen Mittelalter.* 2 vols. dtv 4442. Munich, 1986.

————. *Mäzene im Mittelalter: Die Gönner und Auftraggeber der höfischen Literatur in Deutschland 1150-1300.* Munich, 1979.

Literarisches Mäzenatentum: Ausgewählte Forschungen zur Rolle des Gönners und Auftraggebers in der mittelalterlichen Literatur. Ed. Joachim Bumke. WdF 598. Darmstadt, 1982.

Mayer, Theodor. *Fürsten und Staat: Studien zur Verfassungsgeschichte des deutschen Mittelalters.* Weimar, 1950. Reprint: Cologne and Graz, 1969.

Peters, Ursula. *Fürstenhof und höfische Dichtung: Der Hof Hermanns von Thüringen als literarisches Zentrum.* Konstanzer Universitätsreden 113. Constance, 1981.

2. The Space: The Medieval Castle

Die Burgen im deutschen Sprachraum: Ihre rechts- und verfassungsgeschichtliche Bedeutung. Ed. Hans Patze. 2 vols. VuF 19. Sigmaringen, 1976.

Hinz, Hermann. *Motte und Donjon: Zur Frühgeschichte der mittelalterlichen Adelsburg.* Zeitschrift für Archäologie des Mittelalters, Beihefte 1. Cologne and Bonn, 1981.

Hotz, Walter. *Pfalzen und Burgen der Stauferzeit: Geschichte und Gestalt.* Darmstadt, 1981.

Jäschke, Kurt-Ulrich. *Burgenbau und Landesverteidigung um 900: Überlegungen zu Beispielen aus Deutschland, Frankreich und England.* VuF Sonderband 16. Sigmaringen, 1975.

Streich, Gerhard. *Burg und Kirche während des deutschen Mittelalters: Untersuchungen zur Sakraltopographie von Pfalzen, Burgen und Herrensitzen.* 2 vols. VuF Sonderband 29. Sigmaringen, 1984.

3. The People: Knighthood during the High Middle Ages

Arnold, Benjamin. *German Knighthood 1050-1300.* Oxford, 1985.

Brunner, Karl, and Falko Daim. *Ritter, Knappen, Edelfrauen: Ideologie und Realität des Rittertums im Mittelalter.* Vienna, Cologne, and Graz, 1981.

Bumke, Joachim. *Studien zum Ritterbegriff im 12. und 13. Jh.* Beihefte zum Euphorion H. 1. Heidelberg, 1964.

Duby, Georges. *La société aux XIe et XIIe siècles dans la région mâconnaise.* Bibliothèque Générale de l'Ecole Pratique des Hautes Etudes, VIe section. Paris, 1971.

Flori, Jean. *L'idéologie du glaive. Préhistoire de la chevalerie.* Travaux d'histoire éthico-politique 43. Genf, 1984.

Herrschaft und Stand: Untersuchungen zur Sozialgeschichte im 13. Jh. Ed. Josef Fleckenstein. Veröffentlichungen des MPI für Geschichte 51. Göttingen, 1977.

Johrendt, Johann. "*Milites* und *Militia* im 11. Jh.: Untersuchung zur Frühgeschichte des Rittertums in Frankreich und Deutschland." Dissertation, University of Erlangen, Erlangen and Nuremberg, 1971.

Reuter, Hans Georg. *Die Lehre vom Ritterstand: Zum Ritterbegriff in Historiographie und Dichtung vom 11. bis zum 13. Jh.* Neue Wirtschaftsgeschichte 4. Cologne and Vienna, 1975.

Das Ritterbild in Mittelalter und Renaissance. Edited by the Forschungsinstitut für Mittelalter und Renaissance. Studia Humaniora: Düsseldorfer Studien zu Mittelalter und Renaissance 1. Düsseldorf, 1985.

Das Rittertum im Mittelalter. Ed. Arno Borst. WdF 349. Darmstadt, 1976.

van Luyn, P. "Les milites dans la France du XIe siècle: Examen des sources narratives." MA 77 (1971): 5-51, 193-238.

van Winter, Johanna Maria. *Rittertum: Ideal und Wirklichkeit.* Munich, 1969.

4. Courtly Life

Hartung, Wolfgang. *Das Spielleute: Eine Randgruppe in der Gesellschaft des Mittelalters.* VSWG, Beihefte 72. Wiesbaden, 1982.

Pastoureau, Michel. *La vie quotidienne en France et en Angleterre au temps des chevaliers de la table ronde (XIIe-XIIIe siècles).* Paris, 1976.

Das ritterliche Turnier im Mittelalter: Beiträge zu einer vergleichenden Formen- und Verhaltensgeschichte des Rittertums. Veröffentlichungen des MPI für Geschichte 80. Göttingen, 1985.

Salmen, Walter. *Der Spielmann im Mittelalter.* Innsbrucker Beiträge zur Musikwissenschaft 8. Innsbruck, 1983.

Schultz, Alwin. *Das höfische Leben zur Zeit der Minnesänger.* 2 vols. Leipzig, 1879. Reprint: 1965.

VI. City and Citizenry

1. The Institution: Origins and Development of the Medieval City

Altständisches Bürgertum. Ed. Heinz Stoob. 2 vols. WdF 352/417. Darmstadt, 1978.

Beiträge zum hochmittelalterlichen Städtewesen. Ed. Bernhard Diestelkamp. Städteforschung A, Darstellung 11. Cologne and Vienna, 1982.

Bischofs- und Kathedralstädte des Mittelalters und der frühen Neuzeit. Ed. Franz Petri. Städteforschung A, Darstellung 1. Cologne and Vienna, 1976.

La città nell'alto medioevo. SSCI 6. Spoleto, 1959.

Civitatum Communitas: Studien zum europäischen Städtewesen. Festschrift Heinz Stoob. Vol 1. Städteforschung A, Darstellung 21, 1. Cologne and Vienna, 1984.

Classen, Carl Joachim. *Die Stadt im Spiegel der "Descriptiones" und "Laudes Urbium" in der antiken und mittelalterlichen Literatur bis zum Ende des 12. Jh.* Beiträge zur Altertumswissenschaft 2. Hildesheim and New York, 1980.

Ennen, Edith. *Die europäische Stadt des Mittelalters.* Göttingen, 1979.

———. *Frühgeschichte der europäischen Stadt.* Veröffentlichungen des Instituts für geschichtliche Landeskunde der Rheinlande an der Universität Bonn. Bonn, 1981.

Kaiser, Reinhold. *Bischofsherrschaft zwischen Königtum und Fürstenmacht: Studien zur bischöflichen Stadtherrschaft im westfränkisch-französischen Reich im frühen und hohen Mittelalter.* Pariser Historische Studien 17. Bonn, 1981.

Mitterauer, Michael. *Markt und Stadt im Mittelalter: Beiträge zur historischen Zentralitätsforschung.* Monographien zur Geschichte des Mittelalters 21. Stuttgart, 1980.

Schwineköper, Berent. *Königtum und Städte bis zum Ende des Investiturstreits: Die Politik der Ottonen und Salier gegenüber den werdenen Städten im östlichen Sachsen und in Nordthüringen.* VuF Sonderband 11. Sigmaringen, 1977.

Die Stadt des Mittelalters. Ed. Carl Haase. 3 vols. WdF 243-245. Darmstadt, 1978.

Die Stadt–Gestalt und Wandel bis zum industriellen Zeitalter. Ed. Heinz Stoob. Städtewesen 1. Cologne and Vienna, 1979.

Die Stadt in der europäischen Geschichte: Festschrift Edith Ennen. Bonn, 1972.

Stadt und Städtebürgertum in der deutschen Geschichte des 13. Jh. Ed. Bernhard Töpfer. Forschungen zur mittelalterlichen Geschichte 24. Berlin, 1976.

Die Städte Mitteleuropas im 12. und 13. Jh. Ed. Wilhelm Rausch. Beiträge zur Geschichte der Städte Mitteleuropas 1. Linz, 1963.

Stoob, Heinz. *Forschungen zum Städtewesen in Europa.* Vol. 1: *Räume, Formen und Schichten der mitteleuropäischen Städte.* Cologne and Vienna, 1970.

Studien zu den Anfängen des europäischen Städtewesens. VuF 4. Constance and Lindau, 1958.

Theuerkauf, Gerhard. "*Accipe Germanam pingentia carmina terram:* Stadt- und Landesbeschreibungen des Mittelalters und der Renaissance als Quellen der Sozialgeschichte." AKG 65 (1983): 89-116.

Vor- und Frühformen der europäischen Stadt im Mittelalter. Ed. Herbert Jankuhn, Walter Schlesinger, and Heiko Steurer. 2 vols. Abhandlungen. Göttingen, phil.-hist. Kl. 3, 83 and 84. Göttingen, 1973, 1974.

2. The Space: Topography and Buildings

Guidoni, Enrico. *Die europäische Stadt: Eine baugeschichtliche Studie über ihre Entstehung im Mittelalter.* Stuttgart, 1980. Original in Italian, 1978.

Hall, Thomas. *Mittelalterliche Stadtgrundrisse: Versuch einer Übersicht der Entwicklung in Deutschland und Frankreich.* Antikvarist arkiv 66. Stockholm, 1978.

Herzog, Erich. *Die ottonische Stadt: Die Anfänge der mittelalterlichen Stadtbaukunst in Deutschland.* Frankfurter Forschungen zur Architekturgeschichte 2. Berlin, 1964.

Leudemann, Norbert. *Deutsche Bischofsstädte im Mittelalter. Zur topographischen Entwicklung der deutschen Bischofsstädt im Heiligen Römischen Reich.* Munich, 1980.

Meckseper, Cord. *Kleine Kunstgeschichte der deutschen Stadt im Mittelalter.* Darmstadt, 1982.

3. The People: Citizens and City Residents

Bosl, Karl. *Die Sozialstruktur der mittelalterlichen Residenz- und Fernhandelsstadt Regensburg: Die Entwicklung ihres Bürgertums vom 9.-14. Jh.* Abhandlungen. München, phil.-hist. Kl., new series, 63. Munich 1966.

Gilden und Zünfte: Kaufmännische und gewerbliche Genossenschaften im frühen und hohen Mittelalter. Ed. Berent Schwineköper. VuF 29. Sigmaringen, 1985.

Das Handwerk in vor- und frühgeschichtlicher Zeit. Ed. Herbert Jankuhn, Walter Janssen, Ruth Schmidt-Wiegand, and Heinrich Tiefenbach. 2 vols. Abhandlungen. Göttingen, phil.-hist. Kl. 3, 122. Göttingen, 1981, 1983.

Schulz, Knut. *Ministerialität und Bürgertum in Trier: Untersuchungen zur rechtlichen und sozialen Gliederung der Trierer Bürgerschaft vom ausgehenden 11. bis zum Ende des 14. Jh.* Rheinisches Archiv 66. Bonn, 1968.

Städtische Mittelschichten. Ed. Erich Maschke and Jürgen Sydow. Veröffentlichungen der Kommission für geschichtliche Landeskunde in Baden-Württemberg, series B, 69. Stuttgart, 1972.

ILLUSTRATION SOURCES

1. Herrad von Landsberg, Hortus deliciarum (12th century). Original lost. After the edition by A. Straub and G. Keller (Strasburg 1879-99), ed. Aristide D. Caratzas, New York 1977. Fol. XXXbis (detail).
2. Detail from the Bayeaux Tapestry (late 11th century). Musée de la tapisserie de Bayeux–Bibliothèque, Bayeaux.
3. Vivianbibel (Tours 845/46). Paris, Bibl. Nat. Lat. I, fol. 423r (detail).
4. Herrad von Landsberg, Hortus deliciarum (12th century). Straub and Keller (see 1), fol. XXXbis.
5. Sachsenspiegel, Heidelberger Bilderhandschrift (c. 1330). Universitätsbibliothek Heidelberg, Cod. Palatinus Germanicus 164 (Ldr. III, 27).
6. Grandvalbibel (Tours c. 840) London, British Museum Add. Ms. 10546, fol. 5b (detail).
7. Heidelberger Liederhandschrift. Universitätsbibliothek Heidelberg, Codex Palatinus Germanicus 848, fol. LIII.
8. Augustin, Moralia in Iob (Cîteaux, early 12th century). Dijon, Bibliothèque municipale ms. 170, fol. 75v.
9. Notker, Hymnenbuch, title page (early 11th century). Formerly Berlin, Staatsbibliothek theol. lat. 4°11, fol. 144r. Photo of the manuscript: Wolfram von den Steinen, Homo Caelestrus. dDas Wort der Kunst im Mittelalter, vol. 2, Bern-Munich, 1965, Plate 87a.
10. St. Galler Kosterplan (early 9th century). Drawing from HDWSG 1 (LV 0), p. 100.
11. Codex aureus of Canterbury (after 750). Stockholm, Königliche bibliothek Cod. A 135, fol. 9v.
12. Drogo-Sakramentar (10th century). Paris, Bibl. Nat. Ms. lat. 9428, fol. 87v.
13. Schematic representation of the two-part Grundherrschaft. Sketch by H.-W. Goetz.
14. Stuttgarter Bilderpsalter (Saint-Germain-des-Prés c. 820/30). Stuttgart, Württenbergische Landesbibliothek Bibl. fol. 23, fol. 96.
15. Herrad von Landsberg, Hortus deliciarum (12th century). Straub and Keller (see 1), fol. XXX.
16. Stuttgarter Bilderpsalter (see 14), fol. 146.
17. Hrabanus Maurus, De universo (Montecassino, c. 1023). Photo: Epperlein, Der Bauer im Bild (LV IV.3), plate 4.

18. Astronomische Sammelhandschrift (Salzburg, early 9th century). Viena, Österreichische Nationalbibliothek Cod. 387, fol. 90v.
19. Sachsenspiegel, Heidelberger Bilderhandschrift (see 5), Ldr.II 58 §2.
20. Evangeliar Heinrichs des Löwen (c. 1188). Wolfenbüttel, Herzog August Bibliothek Cod. Guelf. 105 Noviss. 2, fol. 171v.
21. Wartburg, plan. Drawing from Hotz, Pfalzen (LVV.2) Z 131 p. 240.
22. Wartburg, palace wall. Photo: Hotz, Pfalzen, T 141.
23. Otto von Freising, Chronicle (12th century), Codex Jenesis Bose q. 6, fol. 91b. Photo: FS 16 (vgl. Anm. III/25) Taf. 14.
24. Hrabanus Maurus Ms. (Montecassino, 11th century). Florenz, Scala. Photo: Martin Erbstösser, Die Kreuzzüge, Eine Kulturgeschichte, Leipzig 1976, plate 40.
25. Peter Lombard, Commentary on the Psalms (late 12th century). Bamberg, Staatliche Bibliothek Cod. Bibl. 59, fol. 2 (detail).
26. Vivianbibel (see 3) fol. 215.
27. Herrad von Landsberg, Hortus deliciarum (12th century) Straub and Keller (see 1) fol. LV (detail).
28. Tricktracksteine (11th/12th century). Paris, Louvre. Photo: Le Goff, Kultur (LV0) plate 167.
29. Trier c. 1100. From Hall (LV VI.2) plate 7b, p. 48.
30. Speyer c. 1100. From Hall (LV VI.2) plate 29a, p. 96.
31. City seal of Lübeck (13th century). Lübeck, Archive der Hansestadt, Inv.-Nr.A I, 1.
32. Paderborn in the high and late Middle Ages. From Hall (LV VI.2) plate 16A/B, pp. 74/75.
33. Epsitolar (Trier, late 10th centruy), Berlin, Staatsbibliothek Ms. theol. lat fol. 34, fol. 15v.
34. Münster eifel, romanesque house (12th century). Photo: Meckseper (LV VI.2) T44.

INDEX

ABOUT THE AUTHOR, TRANSLATOR, AND EDITOR

Hans-Werner Goetz received his Ph.D. from Ruhr-University at Bochum, where he is currently Professor of Late Ancient and Medieval History. In addition to *Life in the Middle Ages* he has published four books as well as articles on conceptual history and peasant history, among other subjects. Goetz's most recent work is *Das Geschichtsbild Ottos von Freising*.

The translator of *Life in the Middle Ages* is Albert Wimmer. Wimmer is currently Associate Professor of German/Russian Language and Literature at the University of Notre Dame.

Editor Steven Rowan is presently Professor of History at the University of Missouri in St. Louis.